Religions in Practice

An Approach to the Anthropology of Religion

John R. Bowen

Washington University
St. Louis, Missouri

Allyn and Bacon

Boston • London • Toronto • Sydney • Tokyo • Singapore

Series Editor: Jennifer Jacobson
Editor-in-Chief, Social Science: Karen Hanson
Editorial Assistant: Tom Jefferies
Marketing Manager: Jude Hall
Composition and Prepress Buyer: Linda Cox
Manufacturing Buyer: Joanne Sweeney
Cover Administrator: Kristina Mose-Libon
Editorial Production Administrator: Deborah Brown
Editorial–Production Service: P. M. Gordon Associates

Copyright © 2002, 1998 by Allyn & Bacon
A Pearson Education Company
75 Arlington Street
Boston, Massachusetts 02116

Internet: www.ablongman.com

Library of Congress Cataloging-in-Publication Data

Bowen, John Richard, 1951–
    Religions in practice : an approach to the anthropology of religion / John R. Bowen.—
2nd ed.
        p. cm.
    Includes bibliographical references and index.
    ISBN 0–205–33632–9
    1. Religion.   2. Religions.   3. Ethnology—Religious aspects.   I. Title.
BL48.B625 2001
200—dc21

                                                                                        2001045062

Printed in the United States of America.
10 9 8 7 6 5 4 3 2 1   04 03 02 01

To Vicki,
for love and support

Contents

Preface

I have written this book for anyone—from the student of religion to the general reader—who wishes to learn more about the rituals and rules, symbols and laws that shape religious lives in different societies. I am an anthropologist by trade, engaged in a lifetime of ethnographic research on many topics, and I bring to the present work my own perspective and experience. This book grew out of years of teaching an undergraduate course on religion and ritual, for which I found no satisfactory textbook. In that course, and for this book, I presume little previous knowledge about religion or about anthropology, but build toward that knowledge by alternately discussing case studies and general findings.

Taking an ethnographic perspective means starting from what people say and do as they engage in religious activities. I take a broad view of "religion," including in its domain those activities that, in one way or another, invoke realities and powers beyond the reach of ordinary senses. (I discuss the problem of definition in Chapter 1.) Religion thus includes healing through spirit possession and obeying religious taboos, sacrificing to appease the gods and quietly speaking to God, uttering harmful spells and reciting scripture.

In each chapter, I consider a specific practice or aspect of religion, and use examples from both small-scale and large-scale religions. In my discussions of large-scale religious traditions, such as Islam, Hinduism, and Catholicism, I focus on one or more emphases within that tradition rather than attempting to survey all its dimensions and branches. For example, I examine the importance of sacred speech in Navajo, Islamic, and Protestant traditions, with extended examples drawn from Baptist churches as well as from Luther's writings. A study devoted to Protestantism per se would have encompassed Lutheran, Presbyterian, Methodist, and other denominations. This book, concerned with comparisons across religions, must be more selective.

The book is intended to be read on its own by any interested reader. As a course textbook it can be supplemented in various ways. In an anthropology course it might be combined with ethnographic case studies, either those referred to in the chapters or others. In a course on comparative religions it could be used together with some of the many excellent introductions to Islam, Hinduism, religions of China, and other large-scale religions. The companion reader—*Religion in Culture and Society*—contains articles arranged parallel to the chapters in this book. Also very effective are video clips and films on pilgrimage, church singing, sacrifice, and other practices.

In preparing this edition of *Religions in Practice* I benefited from the comments of many readers and users of the first edition, among them Robert Hefner, Jon Anderson, James Boon, Pascal Boyer, Diane Mines, Beiel Dor Cernes, the many students who sent comments and questions by e-mail, and the anonymous readers for this press. From my friends and teachers in the Gayo highlands of Sumatra I have learned much about religion, devotion, and humility. Most of all, my wife, Vicki Carlson, not only taught me much and helped me through months of writing, but also is the coauthor of the opening section of Chapter 1.

I would also like to thank the reviewers for their comments: Joseph Rubenstein, Richard Stockton College; Robert Hefner, Boston University; and Katherine Donahue, Plymouth State University.

I would appreciate your critical comments and suggestions for additional materials; as an inveterate user of e-mail I am best reached at <jbowen@artsci.wustl.edu>.

Studying Religion through Practice

Many friends and relatives attended my mother-in-law's memorial service at the First Presbyterian Church in Colorado Springs. Mary Anne, Annie to her friends, had been reared in this church community. Her father had been an elder in the church and her mother a deaconess, visiting the shut-ins, the hospitalized, and the recently bereaved. Like many women of her time, she helped others through illnesses, tragedy, and heartbreak. Perhaps her most important, yet often invisible, work was to assist elderly relatives as they faced failing health, the diminishing circle of friends and loved ones, and ultimately their deaths.

Mary Anne lived out those traditions of service just as her parents had. They had sat in the same pews to celebrate or grieve the rites of passage of loved ones—baptisms, weddings, and funerals. They listened to sermons, readings, and hymns meant to capture the meaning of this earthly life and that of the spirit. What they heard was a simple story of comfort and direction, that God, through Jesus, gives life, an abundant life here on earth and a never-ending spiritual life—a gift offered for nothing more than faith by the believer. For them, Jesus offered the gift of eternal life and a model of human earthly life centered on love, simplicity, forgiveness, and generosity.

At Mary Anne's memorial service, the minister (who had been her mainstay during her husband's last illness and death years earlier) spoke about her life of service within the community and her faith in her personal relationship with God. He shared with those assembled her one last regret—that she would not be able to see her grandsons grow up as her own mother had shared in her children's upbringing. Only when she had come to accept this loss was she able to let go and die peacefully.

The minister ended his message with a discussion of sainthood, by which he meant service, a life on the path, and the promise of reunion with other saints in the life hereafter. For most in attendance, the image of Mary Anne reunited with her beloved parents and husband and her cherished friends who had gone before, all free from illness and earthly strife, was a source of comfort as they dealt with their own sadness at losing her and with the renewed realization of their own inescapable deaths.

As I listened, I was struck by the disparity of the minister's idea of sainthood and that found in original Presbyterian teachings. Sitting in a church whose official history traced back to the teachings of the sixteenth-century theologian John Calvin, I recalled that "saint" referred to the Elect, those people predestined to salvation, an idea powerful in the early churches of New England. I also thought about how hard to live by were these ideas of an unknowable Election—you might be saved, you might be damned, but you could not change it and you could not know which you were. No wonder the idea of Election was largely supplanted by the idea that we might just save ourselves through good works.

My wife, my main informant on life in this community and church, recalls that the dominant teaching her family heard in this church was that individuals were saved by grace, by simply accepting the gift of God's love. Good works rather than causing salvation follow naturally from it. Many theological realities were represented that day: some Calvinist, some based on faith by works, some agnostic, and perhaps some atheist. Individuals' theological journeys vary even as people come together in community and provide each other comfort and hope.

In St. Louis, our religious community is the First Unitarian Universalist Church. We do not share such a long history with this community but we help each other in similar ways. We hear sermons, readings, hymns, and discussions on spiritual and earthly concerns. In this church there is no set of shared beliefs; in fact the church stands for the liberty to pursue one's own creed. Sainthood is mentioned here, too, as in a sermon preached on the 152nd anniversary of the church's founding by William Greenleaf Eliot in 1835. He was a man of many accomplishments, including the founding of his church, Washington University, the St. Louis public schools, and other civic institutions. In 1852, Ralph Waldo Emerson toured what was then the West and visited Eliot's by then well-established church. In a letter sent back East, Emerson called Eliot the "saint of the West." He could only have been referring to Eliot's earthly accomplishments, for Eliot's still Calvinist Christianity was totally at odds with the nature-oriented transcendentalism Emerson espoused.

My own upbringing was in the framework of the Episcopal Church. I recall attending some Sunday school sessions but little intense church involvement or private religious devotion. I grew closer to the comfort and purposiveness of religion during my fieldwork in Sumatra with the Gayo people, all of whom are Muslims. Living in village and town with them for several years, I helped heal the sick and bury the dead, and I learned about prayer, spells, and collective worship. I fasted during the month of Ramadan and participated in many collective religious activities.

It was during the times leading up to and following the death of a friend or neighbor that I was most drawn into religious life. Deeply saddened by their loss at such times, my Gayo friends focused not on recalling the deceased's life, but on helping the deceased's soul to weather the transition between life and death. Relatives prepared the corpse in a certain way, bathing and wrapping it before burial and, afterward, spoke to the deceased's soul, prayed for its welfare, and engaged in rituals of chanting to God on the soul's behalf.

I remember one such Sumatran funeral, for an older man with whom I had spent many hours over a period of 10 years. On the evening of his death, dozens of men and women gathered at the house of his family to chant Arabic prayers of praise to God. Most believed that their actions helped the soul of the deceased person in its transition from this world to the next. During a rest in the evening's work, a religious teacher explained that we were generating blessings not just for the departed soul of this man, but for the souls of Muslims everywhere. The religious ideas he conveyed satisfied us that our work was for a purpose and that the deceased could be comforted. Our coming together to do this religious work underscored the intense ties of shared responsibility among us. We would gather again on three other occasions to repeat the chanting for this man's soul.

These two events—a funeral carried out by Muslim villagers and a memorial service in a Presbyterian church—were part of very different social and religious contexts but both were religious events. In the Gayo village and the Presbyterian church, someone made a speech that set the death in a religious context by speaking of a soul and of a transition to another life. In both, people participated in a highly scripted event, parts of which took place in a religious building and which included prayers for the spirit's well-being. Both sets of practices attended to the emotional needs of the living and stressed the shared responsibility of friends, relatives, and neighbors.

The practices thus invoked religious ideas, shaped emotions, and created social contexts that performed social functions. In the chapters that follow these same elements will appear recurrently woven together. Ideas, emotions, social contexts shape each other over time to produce complex and differentiated sets of practices and ideas that we call "religions."

Defining Religion

*I*n the 1950s and 1960s, many social scientists and historians in the United States argued that Western societies were becoming secularized and that religion was fading out as an important part of public and even private life. But they were wrong. Religion has not only retained its importance for most people in the United States, it has become the subject of current public debate about national culture and political practice. In the United States and in Europe these discussions have concerned the proper place of religious symbols and practices in public settings, from prayer in the schools to public display of crèches. As Islam becomes increasingly prominent in these countries, notions that national culture is based on a Christian or Judeo-Christian heritage are challenged. Some people welcome this increasing pluralism of religious life. In December 2000, some U.S. high schools announced the beginning and end of the Islamic month of fasting, Ramadan, and excused Muslim students from school to observe these occasions. But others see the future of world politics as a polarization around two or three religion-based civilizations: Christian, Islamic, and Confucian.

Discussions of religion are often based on knowledge of only a few familiar religions. Many U.S. politicians and school officials who support a moment of silence for prayer in schools, for example, assume that all religions include the practice of silent individual prayer to a god; and some people find the Islamic practice of five daily prostrations before God disruptive. German officials have declared that Scientology is not a religion. Indonesian officials exclude animist beliefs and practices from the category of religion.

What then is "religion"? I view religious traditions as ever-changing complexes of beliefs (including those authoritative beliefs called "doctrine"), practices (including formalized rituals), and social institutions. But how do we decide which beliefs, practices, and institutions are to be called "religious"?

In most Western traditions one finds two very common definitions. One emphasizes an individual's beliefs; the other, his or her emotions. The first defines religion as a set of shared beliefs in spirits or gods. The second identifies religion in terms of a sentiment of awe and wonder toward the unknown. For me there is no hard and fast definition of religion. This book examines a wide variety of ways in which people in different societies and times have thought about the world beyond the immediate sense-world. Some posit a set of deities; others do not. Some have a distinct sphere of life called "religion"; others do not distinguish religion from the rest of life.

Sufficient for our purposes is that the collection of phenomena we will study—prayer to God, uses of magic, death rituals—all involve the idea that there is something more to the world than meets the eye. This definition is much broader than standard Western usage. What if we said that religion was whatever involves a stated belief in spirits or gods? In those cultures strongly shaped by modern Christianity, people do indeed tend to think of religion in these terms. The idea of a separate religious sphere is recent, even in Western history. In other societies people define the world in different ways, treating as a natural part of everyday life actions and ideas that we would want to include in a cross-cultural category of religion.

Consider the practices of the Azande people of the southern Sudan that ethnographers have labeled "witchcraft." According to the Azande, some people carry in their bodies a substance called *mangu*. This substance is inherited, and it sends out emanations when the person feels jealousy, anger, or other negative emotions toward another person. The substance causes things to happen, and it fits into everyday ways of explaining misfortune. "I tripped at a place where I never trip; it must be witchcraft that caused me to trip."

When the person causing a particular misfortune is discovered (by using oracles) the person is asked to blow water from his or her mouth and to say: "If I was doing harm, I certainly did not mean to, let it be gone." And that is the end of the matter. The Azande do not concentrate on blame or intentions, but on the particular problem at hand and how to solve it. Indeed, they believe the substance sometimes acts on its own without the person's knowledge.

What do we make of these practices? From a Western point of view they refer to a reality beyond the immediately verifiable, and thus we legitimately may include them in a comparative study of religions. The Azande, on the other hand, see mangu and oracles as everyday, ordinary aspects of reality. Some of the Azande who have converted to Christianity continue their use of oracles and accusations of mangu precisely because they do not see those activities as part of a separate religion, but more as an American Baptist or Catholic might regard the use of an astrological chart.

The diversity of ideas about what constitutes a particular religion places any student of religion in a difficult position. If I write about a particular religion as the symbols, statements, and practices of a particular group of people, I will almost inevitably differ with some of them as to what their religion is. The perspective of an outside observer, who wishes to include a wide array of opinions and activities, may be much broader than that of a practitioner, who may insist on his or her own view of what properly lies within the boundaries of the religion in question.

I have frequently met with objections to the way I define "Islam" when describing certain Sumatran village practices to students in Indonesian Islamic colleges. For example, many villagers gather at ritual meals to ask ancestral spirits for help in healing the sick or in ensuring a good rice crop. These practices may have their origins in pre-Islamic times, but villagers view them as consistent with their understandings of Islam, and they explain them in terms of prophets and angels. For this reason I include them in my own writings about Sumatran Islam. But for the Islamic college students these practices conflict with proper understandings of Islam. "Those practices are what we try to teach them to throw aside," the students say. For some of them, my own writing could become part of the very problem they are trying to solve, that is, an overly broad idea of Islam.

How do we respond to these challenges? My own response has been to realize that definitions of religion are not just academic matters, but part of the very social reality we are studying. I thus refrain from giving too precise a definition for religion or Islam, and instead look at issues and debates among practitioners over the boundaries of religion, recording what they say and what is at stake for them.

People in the United States have not worked out definitive answers to these questions either. Some people would consider modern forms of witchcraft practiced in the United States to be a religion; indeed, the Rhode Island state legislature passed a law making it so in 1989. What limits the state should place on religious freedom is also a matter of continued debate, no more so than in cases of Christian Scientists denying medical treatment to their children. (Until August 1996, treatment given by Christian Science practitioners was considered "medical" for purposes of Medicare and Medicaid reimbursements, on grounds that to deny them that category would be to violate their religious freedom.)

I propose to define religion in two stages. First, we can use an extremely broad definition, such as "ideas and practices that postulate reality beyond that which is immediately available to the senses." This broad definition allows us to look at a very wide range of things. Second, for each society we study, we ask how *these* people construct their world. They may have a shared set of beliefs in spirits and deities and thus fit squarely into Western definitions of religion. Or they may speak about impersonal forces, such as the East Asian idea of a life force or *chi* that permeates the natural and social world. Or, they may not focus on describing beliefs at all, but rather, concentrate on carrying out rituals correctly, with a general understanding that the rituals are important. (This description fits the practitioners of Jain religion in India [Humphrey and Laidlaw 1994].)

What we call *religion* may look quite different from one society to another—in the relative importance of a shared belief system, in the degree to which religious practice involves strong emotions, and in the social functions and contexts associated with religious practices.

An Anthropological Approach to Studying Religion

What distinguishes an anthropological approach to the study of religion from other approaches? Three closely connected features guide an anthropologist's study of any topic.

First, anthropology is based on a *long-term relationship with people* through field-work. We live for a fairly long time, more than one year and sometimes many years, in a particular place. During that time we develop close friendships with some people and gain, we hope, the trust and respect of many more. I spent about six years in Indonesia, about four of them with Gayo people in Sumatra. My experience is not unusual. I developed a very close and continuing friendship with a Gayo family. The eldest daughter now lives in the United States. She began a career with Procter & Gamble in Jakarta, moved to Cincinnati, and then changed her career to pursue interests in consulting and Islamic fashion design. My children call her "Cousin Evi."

Close relationships help us to interpret social life. We trust certain people to report what they think truthfully, and we know enough such people to be able to check our interpretations with people who might be expected to disagree in their views on things. For example, I know people who have very different perspectives on religious rituals, and I can depend on them to disagree with whatever I see. One can compare this source of reliability to that which psychologists obtain by repeating experiments.

Second, anthropologists pursue their study initially through the *local perspectives.* Rather than studying the economy by creating a model of what people might do and then seeing whether they do it, or studying religion by reading scripture and then seeing what they believe, we begin with the ideas and practices we learn about in the field. Then we follow the connections to larger institutions like government agencies, religious schools, or national banks—but we always start from local views of those institutions.

When I studied Islamic law in Indonesia, for example, I began with how Gayo village and townspeople talk about law, how and whether they refer to it when resolving conflicts, and to what extent they make use of courts or religious authorities. Then I study the courts, the universities that educate the authorities, and the national institutions that seek to shape what happens locally, including the Supreme Court and the National Council of Islamic scholars. I learn about colonial law, contemporary civil law, and Islamic codes, but only after studying everyday social life, in order to anchor these codes and institutions in local practices. This feature distinguishes anthropology from disciplines that usually begin with historical, religious, or legal texts, or with national political instituions.

Finally, anthropologists study *connections across social domains.* Rarely do we look only at the economy, or at literature, or at religion. We might wish to focus on one of these domains (indeed it is required when writing a doctoral dissertation), but when we do, we usually discover that our chosen domain is connected to other domains. Suppose I want to learn about rice cultivation and discover that the planting and harvesting is tied to the performance of elaborate religious rituals and that work on the irrigation system depends on local political structures. I have to investigate religion and politics, then, in order to understand how rice is cultivated.

Conversely, my study of Islam in Gayo society involved learning about how rice is grown, how the major rice growing regions were allocated among villages, how healing takes place, the origins of political parties, and the short history of a poetic genre written in Arabic script—all because they were part of local practices that people explained by referring to Islam. Indeed, I focused on Islam only as a third project; I was brought to it because the topics I came to study—social structure and oral literature—were interwoven with Islamic ideas about society and history.

Practices, Contexts, Diversity

The following chapters examine religious life from different perspectives: the relations of doctrines to rituals; the role of religions in explaining misfortune, overcoming grief, and extending human powers; the ways that rituals of pilgrimage, preaching, and sacrificing shape religious belief and experience; the ways that images and taboos can be used to organize religious life or change it; and the role of religions in public life. I consider cases from small-scale and larger-scale societies.

The focus is on religious practices: ways of making offerings, speaking to deities, observing taboos, or reading and hearing about religious ideas. An emphasis on practice includes the study of doctrines, but focuses on how doctrines are embodied in texts or other forms and how they are understood; this relation of doctrine to practice is examined in greater detail in Chapter 2. Religious practices often invoke texts: someone reads, chants, recites, or sings a text. These textual practices are critical in linking local practices to the broader religious traditions, such as Islam, Christianity, and Buddhism.

Religious practices offer material signs of a pathway to spiritual powers. They require work, and work engages a person in a way of being and thinking, and they often involve objects: images, carved or painted; buildings and sacred centers; sense impressions in the form of speech, song, movement. These images, structures, and impressions present and represent the truth of the religion to the individual, providing cognitive and emotional confirmation of the ideas of a religion.

Certain practices especially characteristic of one or more religions are analyzed at length later in the book. For example, images are particularly central to Catholicism, and that religion provides the main example for the discussion of imagery and worship in Chapter 9 (but images in Africa, Buddhist Sri Lanka, and Brazil are also discussed).

These practices occur in the social contexts of specific societies and cultures and in particular historical moments. Analyses of religions in practice must be attentive to the differences such contexts make.

The particular contribution of ethnographic and social historical studies to knowledge of religion lies in the attention to interconnections among domains of social life, among religion, economy, marriage, politics, and so forth, and to the ways that cultural ideas and social institutions shape activities in many of these domains. A specific religious practice such as worship may structure communities in particular ways or lend a religious interpretation to existing social divisions, as when a Hindu priest distributes consecrated foods according to caste standing, or when men and women worship separately in a Muslim mosque, or when church pews are reserved for those who have contributed to the church.

The interpretation of texts and doctrines is strongly shaped by local factors, as Clifford Geertz (1968) showed in contrasting Islam in Morocco with Islam in Java, a contrast I revisit in Chapter 10. Comparing two or more cases of a practice can help to highlight these shaping processes, and in each of the following chapters I engage in such comparisons. In Chapter 4, for example, I contrast treatments of death in Japan, New Guinea, and Sumatra; in Chapter 7, patterns of witchcraft accusation in Africa, New England, and Asia; in Chapter 13, pilgrimage in Mecca and around the Japanese island of Shikoku; in Chapter 15, the relationship of religion and state in Germany, France, Britain, and the United States. Attending to changes over time are another kind of comparison used here. For example, in Chapter 9, I look at the change from a focus on relics to a focus on images in the Roman Catholic Church. Chapters 14 and 15 are strongly historical. Chapter 14 analyzes the ways that the words of prophets give rise to religious movements, drawing on examples of Oceanic "cargo cults," Mormons, and Muslims. Chapter 15 looks at the role of religions in modern nation–states, considering the challenges posed to religious diversity by religious nationalism and state-enforced religious law.

Finally, I consider the diversity of religious understandings and practices even in small-scale societies. Diversity includes questions about how knowledge and ideas are distributed in the society—between men and women, or adults and children, or across other social groupings—and also the debates about how best to understand the norms and forms of religious culture. Anthropology has often been insufficiently attentive to diversity, partly because of the idea inherited from nineteenth-century cultural studies that a "culture" is an integrated whole, and partly because research methods concentrate on a small number of "key informants."

We know that the same practice may be interpreted in myriad and diverse ways. As we saw earlier, the people assembled for the funeral services in Sumatra and in the United States had very different ideas about what was happening to the spirit of the deceased. These differences are explored for Sumatra in Chapter 4. Beginning from particular religious practices and then examining diverse interpretations allows us to capture these diversities, and in some cases explain them in terms of accompanying social differences and changes. Certain religious traditions allow a particularly broad diversity of practices to flourish—the case of Japan is explored in Chapter 2, and India in Chapter 9; China exhibits similar diversity. Other traditions contain a stronger idea of a single best interpretation, which heightens religious debates in those cases. Debates within Islam are explored at several points in this book. I draw on my own fieldwork with the Muslim Gayo of Sumatra in some of these chapters (the reader interested in Islamic debates may wish to compare the study of Iranian Islam in Fischer and Abedi [1990]). I also examine debates within Christianity concerning the role of the Virgin Mary (in Chapter 9) and the nature of Election in Protestant denominations (Chapter 11).

The final chapter concerns a wider set of societal debates about the proper place of religion in public life, and it is with an eye to these debates that I write this book. A great deal of misunderstanding and, to my mind, wrong-headed public policy in many countries, most certainly in the United States, has been based on ideas about religion that ignore diversities, debates, and possibilities. Particular features of certain strata of Middle Eastern societies—the role of women, views on Islamic law, for example—are frequently confused with Islam in general. Religious beliefs are all open to debate and transformation and attending to those debates gives us a sense of religion's open-ended possibilities.

For Further Consideration

*I*s a politician's Fourth of July speech a religious event? What about Thanksgiving? For the idea of a "civil religion" in the United States see Robert Bellah's "Civil Religion in America"(in his *Beyond Belief,* Harper & Row 1970).

For further reading in the anthropology of religion, an excellent text with an emphasis on theory is Brian Morris' *Anthropological Studies of Religion* (Cambridge University Press 1987).

2 Ideas and Practices of "Religion" in Europe and Elsewhere

*M*ost people living in Europe or North America are used to thinking about religions as sets of formal beliefs or doctrines. Christian denominational differences, for example, have developed largely from debates about doctrine. A Christian may ask someone who practices another religion: What do you believe?, and not mean, What particular things do you as an individual believe? but, What are the shared beliefs sanctified in your religion? (Many from Muslim and Jewish backgrounds would ask the same question.)

And yet, the relationship between doctrines and religious lives is quite complex in Western as well as in other societies. This chapter considers the genealogy of Western ideas about the nature of religion. Only relatively recently have people in Western societies seen the world as composed of distinct religions, each with its own set of beliefs. The rise of this idea has colored the way Europeans have understood other religions.

We also explore how Japan illustrates very different ideas about religions in practice. People in Japan freely combine elements of more than one religion to resolve problems of everyday life. However, the issue of religion's definition recently has become highly politicized, as people fiercely debate whether Shinto practices form a religion or a state ideology.

Western Ideas of Religion

*F*or most of Western history, religion was regarded as an individual's personal piety or faith. People did not write books about religion, but about faith, on the one hand, and the institutions of the church, on the other.

The word *religion* comes from the Latin word *religio,* whose early meaning appears to have been a power outside the individual, or a feeling relative to such a power.

Religiosus meant a powerful place and conveyed a sense of mystery. The term also came to refer to the particular pattern of worship, the *religiones,* that was due a certain god (W. C. Smith 1978, 19–31).

The early leaders of the Christian Church adopted these usages from the Romans. Roman authorities forced the early Christians to participate in the traditional Roman cultic ceremonies. If they refused they often were put to death. So, the key issue about religion was how to worship: the Roman way or exclusively the Christian way. This focus on one's own religious rituals as opposed to those of other people gave rise to a new sense of the plural: our way of worship (*nostra religio*) as opposed to the *religiones* of outsiders. In this context the phrase "the Christian religion" was often used to mean the Eucharist, the central ritual performed by people considering themselves Christians.

The concept of religion might then have developed into its current meaning, as a term used to refer to the system of beliefs and practices of each of a number of societies. But it did not develop in this way, and the word religion itself virtually passed out of existence for a thousand years. (An exception is St. Augustine, whose *De Vera Religione* we might translate as "On Proper Piety"; it concerned the bond between an individual and God and not a system of beliefs and practices.)

Despite the general impression, true in many ways, that the European Middle Ages were an age of religion, it appears that no one ever wrote a book using "religion" in the title or as a concept during this period. Not until the fifteenth century, during the Renaissance, was the term was taken up again, and then with the sense of a universal capacity for piety and worship common to all human beings. There was to be only one kind of *religio,* but it would exist in different degrees in different people.

The Reformation continued this line of thought; both Martin Luther and John Calvin stressed the importance of individual piety and faith over and against any external religious system, by which they meant the Catholic Church. Luther inveighed against any "false religion," or putting faith in religion rather than in God. Indeed, Luther inaugurated a tradition in the German language of avoiding the term "religion" altogether in favor of *Gottesdienst,* "service to God" (W. C. Smith 1978, 35).

Religion as a Belief System

The idea of religion as a system of beliefs, as opposed to personal piety, did not take hold until the seventeenth century. The change was partly the result of efforts during the Enlightenment to classify and understand the world as a schema, accessible by the intellect. It was also because of a growing diversity of religious claims within Europe and the increased awareness, because of trade and travel, of religious traditions beyond Europe. By the eighteenth century, treatises on religions of the world (introducing religious pluralism) began to appear. The plural "religions" is possible only when we think of religion as a cultural system rather than a person one. There are no plural forms for piety, reverence, or obedience.

As Europeans began to study other religions, they tended to use the religions most familiar to them, namely Judaism and Christianity, as a general model. They assumed all religions would have three central elements: a central text, exclusivity, and separation.

The central text was assumed to be a collection of doctrines or beliefs that all adherents shared, ideally, written in a sacred book that had been inspired by a god or gods. Exclusivity meant that a person was a member of one and only one religion, at least at any one time. Separation indicated that religion constituted an area of social life distinct from politics or economics. The idea of separation developed in modern Western Europe, partly in response to the destructive religious wars of the seventeenth century. John Locke, writing in the late seventeenth century, advocated the separation of state and religion as a way of ensuring toleration and religious freedom. His argument became the basis for the principle of separation of church and state in the United States; nowhere else was it so fully realized.

While this model of religion worked well to describe European practices, it fit poorly with religions of India, China, and Japan. No one book provides a shared creed for practitioners of religion in these societies; instead, each contains a large number of books written on diverse aspects of life and on teachers and organizations of followers. Today we know these collections of texts and teachers under the general rubrics of *Hinduism, Buddhism, Taoism,* or *Shinto,* but these labels are modern inventions.

Nor does the idea of exclusivity fit with norms in these societies. In Japan, for example, people routinely bring offerings to shrines dedicated to local gods (practices associated with the label *Shinto*) and, in the same temple complex, venerate Buddha. The same people may marry in a Christian church. The idea of a separate religious sphere is also alien to many other religious traditions. Muslims, for example, argue that all of life should be conducted in accord with God's commands. Hinduism involves ideas of purity and pollution that permeate all social life.

Other Religions, Other Models

Modern attempts to understand these other religions have been based on the European model. By the nineteenth century, books appeared about other religions, introducing for the first time the names that we use today. *Buddhism* was first used in 1801, *Hinduism* in 1829. (Before then writers referred, more accurately, to "the wisdom of the Japanese" or "Hindu teachings.") The term *Islam* also began to be used; previously, Europeans referred to *Muhammadism,* treating Islam not as a religion, but as allegiance to a false prophet (W. C. Smith 1978, 51–79).

The nineteenth-century European notions of what counted as a religion have powerfully shaped how other religions and other countries have viewed religion. For, with few exceptions, the creation of terms for *religion* and for particular religions have been the result of Western, Christian influence.

Take what we often refer to as Hinduism. In India today, religious practice and the precise formulations of doctrine vary from place to place. Indeed, it is a central tenet of religious teaching in India that one should follow the inspiration derived from one's teacher in pursuit of enlightenment. Thus, there is not, nor is there supposed to be, one single formulation of Hindu Religion.

The word *Hindu* itself was not used by ancient Indians to refer to their religion. It is a word meaning "river," and in particular is used as the proper name for the Indus

River. Foreigners—Greeks, then Muslim conquerors—came to designate the people living near that river as "Indian" or "Hindu." Under Muslim rule, the term came to be used to refer to all non-Muslims in the country and included Buddhists and Jains. Only recently has *Hindu* been used as a residual term to designate those people, and their beliefs, who are residents of India but who are not Jains, not Sikhs, not Christians, not Muslims, and not animists. But in the 1980s and 1990s some politicians made the creation of a "Hindu India" their party platform, and they succeeded in rallying large numbers of supporters to their cause. Whatever was once the case, today "Hindu" is experienced by many Indians as a unitary social as well as religious category (see Chapter 15).

Consider the Chinese who have traditionally had no word corresponding to the Western idea of religion. They borrowed a word from the Japanese, *Tsung-Chiao,* which the Japanese themselves had created to accommodate the Western concept. Nor did they have words meaning Confucianism, Buddhism, or Taoism in the sense of religions that one joined or left. Instead, people were aware of collections of teachings that could be followed in trying to find a path toward truth; these teachings included the sayings of Confucius, Buddha, and Lao Tse (a possibly mythic figure who urged followers to find the true path, or Tao).

In a rather neat exchange of terms, the Japanese borrowed the word used to refer to indigenous traditions, *shinto,* from the Chinese. In fact the term was first used by foreigners to refer to local practices. The Japanese today use a translation of this term—*kami no michi,* or "the way of the spirits or gods"—to refer to these practices (Reader 1991, 23). The definitions of what is included in "religion" are of much public interest in Japan today. At the end of the nineteenth century, the Japanese government declared that the indigenous, or Shinto, worship at shrines was not a religion. But what came to be called State Shinto, to which the cult of the emperor was central, became an ideological pillar of twentieth-century Japanese efforts to modernize society, and for that reason the cult was abolished under the post–World War II Occupation.

The boundaries of religion were again debated when the new emperor, Akihito, succeeded his father, Hirohito, in January 1989. According to Shinto creed, the emperor is the descendant of the Sun Goddess, and he performs certain rituals at the goddess' shrine when he takes office. Are these rituals to be taken as religious? If so, they imply his claim to be the chief priest of Shinto and the intermediary to the Sun Goddess. But this status was abolished under the occupation, in the Constitution. Are they perhaps just political ritual? There was a fierce debate in Japan over this question, and the matter (which we consider in the next section) remains unsettled.

The names for religions were often provided by outsiders—one can add to the preceding examples that the term *Judaism* is Greek, not Hebrew. The name *Islam,* used from the beginning by the religion's adherents, is the major exception. However, the term means "submission to God," not the set of beliefs and practices themselves. Indeed, the religious scholar Wilfred Cantwell Smith (1978, 114) has argued that if one believes in God as a Jew or Christian, and realizes that from an Islamic perspective Muslims, Christians, and Jews worship the same God, then one cannot truthfully say in Arabic, "I am not a Muslim." One submits to God, after all, in whatever language.

Imposed Definitions of Religion

Even as religions differ in what they include in the definition of "religion," many modern states in Asia, Africa, and Latin America have drawn their ideas of religion from Western, Christian, and, to some extent, Islamic, models. They adhere to a model of religion that does not fit with local beliefs and practices of some peoples within their borders, and may place pressure on them to conform to this model.

Let us turn to Indonesia to consider these problems of state-imposed definitions of religion. Indonesia, the world's fourth largest country, has about 200 million people living on thousands of islands and speaking more than 300 distinct languages. About 85 percent of the people call themselves Muslim, and the remaining 15 percent includes important Christian and Buddhist minorities as well as practitioners of indigenous religions.

The Indonesian government has "belief in one God" as one of the planks of its ideology. The state defines religion as having a sacred book, a monotheistic foundation, exclusive boundaries (such that one person cannot belong to two religions at the same time), and as transcending ethnic boundaries (rather than being essentially an aspect of a hereditary culture).

This model came by way of several large-scale religions. In the early centuries of the present era, rulers adopted the symbols and ideas of Hinduism and Buddhism, sometimes both together. The Indonesian word for religion, *agama,* comes from the Sanskrit, and means "text." The agama of a person was the set of texts from which he or she derived teaching and religious direction: the books of Hinduism, Buddhism, Islam, or others. The idea of a central text does not require that the religion have exclusive boundaries; that idea came later, in the fourteenth through sixteenth centuries, when many rulers began converting to Islam. Islam does insist on absolute exclusivity and on the idea of one and only one true foundational text, the Qur'ân. Christianity, brought to Indonesia at about the same time, shares these ideas.

By the time of Indonesian independence, then, the major religions supported this model of religion. The state decreed that everyone should belong to one of five religions: Catholicism, Protestantism, Islam, Hinduism, and Buddhism. (Confucianism has enjoyed an ambiguous status in these decrees.) One might be surprised to hear that Hinduism, with its many, vividly represented deities, stood for monotheism; the Indonesian resolution of this problem—supported by some Hindus—was to declare that the various Hindu gods were all manifestations of a single absolute deity.

Today, any Indonesians who practice local religions that do not conform to the official model are pressured to join one of the state-recognized religions, although this pressure has begun to ease since the fall of President Suharto in 1998. Those who do not convert may be accused of being atheists and therefore communists, a dangerous label in this strongly anti-communist state. So defining one's religion is a matter of great concern, and for some a matter of sheer survival (Kipp and Rodgers 1987).

What do people who practice other religions do? Some nominally convert but retain some older practices, such as ways of healing that involve calling on spirits to possess a healer and speak through him or her. Other people work to have their indigenous practices counted as a world religion, usually as Hindu. In one such case, a group of people on the island of Sulawesi did manage to become recognized as Hindus, despite the fact that there were few resemblances, other than a few words of Sanskrit, between their religion and anything practiced in India. A problem arose when one member of this group was elected to the local parliament. Members of parliament need to be sworn in on "their book." So what was this fellow's scripture? Well, because the book had to be Hindu, as the group's practices were called that, the parliament wrote to a Hindu association in Jakarta asking for their book. The association sent along a book in Sanskrit (I could not determine what book it was), and the new member was duly sworn in using it. Appearances were saved, and the religion's credentials established: they had a Book.

Wana Practices and Indonesian Definitions

Some people reshape their indigenous ideas in response to state pressures to convert. The 5,000 Wana people of Sulawesi, described by the anthropologist Jane Monnig Atkinson (1987, 1989), practice forms of divination and shamanism, and their ideas about spirits and possession surface in many domains of everyday life. They do not have a distinct domain called "religion."

Central to Wana efforts at dealing with the spiritual domain are the performances called *mabolong*. These rituals of possession and healing are performed by shamans, ritual experts who are possessed by spirits. Shamans are called on to perform mabolong when someone is ill and requires supernatural assistance. Often many people attend these performances. The shaman is invited to feast from a tray of food, and he in turn invites his "spirit familiars" to join him in enjoying the food. He then asks these spirits to discover what is ailing a patient, to rid the patient of foreign objects, and to go with him on a spirit voyage to recover souls or dream spirits that the patient has lost.

Shamans have greater inner powers, and they draw on these powers to keep people healthy and to increase their own social standing. They are heroes in their community. Indeed, they often create new social communities as people seek to live near them. It is in these rituals performed by shamans that ordinary humans engage the spirit world. The Wana have no written texts that prescribe doctrines or beliefs, and their narratives concerning the spirit world are many and varied. What brings their diverse ideas and stories together is collective attendance at shamanic rituals.

But Wana also face intense pressure from Muslim officials and from Christian missionaries to convert to a state-recognized religion, an agama. Wana come into contact with Muslim peoples living on the coast and serving as local state officials, and, more recently, Christian converts living in other upland regions.

As they have come to understand what is meant by agama, some Wana have constructed their own ideas of what their religion must be. These constructions are not about healing and possession, but about what distinguishes Wana from Muslims and Christians: diet, burial practices, and ties to government among them. Most saliently, Wana are people who, unlike Muslims, do eat pig, and, also unlike Muslims, kill chickens by wringing their necks rather than slaughtering them by knife.

Wana have also constructed a set of beliefs along the lines of Muslim and Christian beliefs, but distinct from them. They claim, for example, that they have a single God and that this God is the same as the Muslim and Christian creator. They recently invented a

Wana shaman during possession at a healing session, Indonesia. (COURTESY OF JANE ATKINSON.)

heaven that corresponds to the images of heaven taught them by Muslims and Christians but reverses those groups' teachings about the destiny of the Wana. In the Wana notions, Wana lead poor lives on earth and therefore they will have the best places in heaven. Muslims, by contrast, they believe, will live in pig excrement because they avoid it here. Christians will have only scraps of clouds to eat (an idea probably derived from pictures of Jesus in the clouds in bible schools).

Most Wana have so far resisted conversion, but even in resisting they have transformed their religion in accord with the dominant, ultimately Western, model of proper religion.

Combining Religious Practices in Japan

*J*apan illustrates an orientation toward religion that contrasts with that which developed in the West. Japanese freely blend elements from indigenous practices, state-inspired Shinto, and the traditions of Buddhism, Confucianism, and Taoism. There has been little or no religious inspiration for "purism." One common saying sums up the division of labor as "born Shinto, die Buddhist," referring to the daily appeals to Shinto spirits during one's lifetime, and the Buddhist priest's responsibility for carrying out funeral rites (Reader 1991). Marriages are increasingly conducted in

Christian style, and many Japanese consult practitioners of the New Religions for solutions to recurring illnesses. These sects themselves combine ideas and practices from many sources, including Hinduism, Japanese nativist writings about racial superiority, and indigenous healing practices. To take an extreme example: it seemed not at all unusual or striking to Japanese that the Aum Shinrikyo sect responsible for the 1995 nerve gas attack in Tokyo combined Buddhist and Hindu texts.

Practice and Belief

About 65 percent of Japanese people have told survey-takers in repeated surveys that they have no religious beliefs (compared to fewer than 10 percent in the United States). Only 20 percent to 30 percent say they believe in the existence of spirits (*kami*) or in souls of the dead. But 76 percent of these respondents have in their homes either a Shinto altar devoted to kami, or a Buddhist one devoted to the souls of the dead; 45 percent have both. Eighty-nine percent say they visit the graves of their ancestors to pray for them (Reader 1991, 5–12).

These results are very puzzling to Western readers if we assume that people think of their beliefs as governing their practices. One problem is with the word *religion*, which in Japanese is *shukyo*, a word originally devised to answer pesky missionaries who asked Japanese to state what their religion was. It was taken to refer to a separate set of beliefs, removed from everyday life, and not to some everyday activity like stopping for a moment at a shrine to make an offering. Thus, asking someone in Japan if he or she has a religion or religious beliefs is something like asking a person in the United States if he or she is a member of a religious movement, a question that would elicit denials from many churchgoers.

Many students of Japanese culture have also emphasized that ideas about beliefs and morality are more focused on specific events and situations than is true for European cultures. Anecdotes from World War II relate how Japanese prisoners of war, having just been bent on killing Allied troops, suddenly became model prisoners of war. In their eyes, the situation had changed and so had their responsibilities.

Finally, a pragmatic try-it-and-see attitude underlies the approach taken by many Japanese toward religious ritual. This approach emphasizes the importance of sincerity for the ritual to work, but not a general "belief," and certainly not an exclusive commitment to that religion and no other. It is thus relatively easy, within the Japanese religious world view, to try a new healing religion without abandoning offerings to household spirits and Buddhist deities. This willingness to participate in more than one religion lies behind the common practice of declaring oneself to census takers as both Buddhist and Shinto, marrying in a Protestant church, and attending sessions of a healing sect to seek a cure for an illness. And it is evident in figures about religious membership: about 75 percent of the population are classified as Buddhist by the government, 95 percent as Shinto, and over 10 percent as members of new religious movements (Reader 1991, 6). Japanese do affiliate with religious organizations, and usually more than one.

Perhaps, then, answers to surveys underplay the extent to which Japanese assume that there are spirits at work in the world. It would appear that the practices of keeping an altar at home and reciting prayers for one's ancestors at graveside imply such a set of beliefs. And yet haven't we all engaged in practices for which we are unsure of whether we agree with the associated doctrines? Modern Western religious culture emphasizes the importance of believing in the doctrines behind practices, in the paramount importance of creeds of faith, and this emphasis may make it quite difficult for some people in the United States, for example, to deny belief in God to a survey-taker, whatever his or her doubts might be. Japanese religious culture does not make this same emphasis; consequently, denying the belief while going along with the practice may be easier for the Japanese person than for the American.

This religious–cultural emphasis on practices over doctrines makes it easier for Japanese to combine elements from different religious traditions, as we see in later chapters. First we can explore the roles played by two major traditions—Shintoism and Buddhism—and how people's actions may imply their belief in a proposition about the spiritual world without them directly expressing that belief.

Shinto and Spirits

Basic to the Japanese Shinto tradition are spirits, or *kami* (Earhart 1982), which are located in specific places in the empirical world: in a boulder, or a house, or a shrine. One Japanese estimate is that there are "eight million spirits"—meaning they are innumerable. When foreigners asked Japanese to name their religion, in order to distinguish it from Buddhism, they called it "the way of the *kami*," although it came to be called Shinto in the West (Reader 1991).

The term kami refers both to the sense of power felt in things of the world, and to particular spirits. A waterfall is a powerful kami; calling it a kami communicates the sense an observer has of its immense power. Space may also contain kami and may be demarcated by rocks, or by a shrine with boundaries and a gateway. One sees these *torii*, Shinto gateways, with two pillars and one or two crossbeams, throughout Japan and in many U.S. cities. A Japanese rock garden works similarly, demarcating a sparsely filled space rather than, as in European-style ornamental gardens, featuring a dense collection of plants. Although kami can be anywhere, they are not everywhere; these boundaries serve to separate the sacred from the profane.

Perhaps the most important spirits are those in the house. They occupy particular places and protect the members of the household when in those places: the god of the kitchen lives in the kitchen, the latrine god in the latrine, and so forth. There is also a guardian deity of the household as a whole; this spirit is made up of many ancestors who have merged to guard the household as a corporate unit that exists over time. The village has a guardian deity, often a fox god or an ancestor of a founding member. The village, like the household, is a corporate group, with control over irrigation, cooperative use of some land, and religious festivals. Villagers will ask the village god for help in their rice harvest or for success in schooling. Village elites once controlled the shrine festivals for the village gods, but today, with many villagers engaged in urban pursuits, their importance has diminished.

Also important to everyday life is the spirit of a rice field. This spirit lives a dual existence, as the figure of Inari, the rice deity, and also as the spirit guarding each particular field. Spirits of the fields and of rice live in the mountains and come down in the spring when the soil is tilled. They guard over the rice, and return to the mountains in the fall after the harvest. They are sometimes represented as fox spirits, probably

Temple complex near Narita, Japan, with Shinto and Buddhist shrines, and shops selling amulets, books, and other items. (COURTESY OF J. BOWEN.)

because foxes, also associated with rice, sexuality, and fertility, were thought to come down from the mountains in spring.

People create new spirits as needed. When the Tennis Players' Association was created in Japan before World War II, someone suggested the creation of a new god, to be named "Heavenly God of Speedy Ball." And in a less individuated way, all equipment, from computer chips to cameras to automobile production machinery, are thought to have a spiritual side. The machines are blessed by a Shinto priest before they are used, and in 1990 engineers met at Tokyo's Chomeiji temple to thank their used-up equipment for the service it had given them. Photographs of the cameras and video recorders were burned as a Buddhist priest chanted verses. Even in the electronics industry Shinto and Buddhism are mixed (Sanger 1990).

Kami can also be the spirits of deceased persons. Sometime famous people will become deified as kami and have shrines built to them, but for a mixture of reasons. One ninth-century court official, for example, had died at the hands of his rivals for power. As a spirit he wreaked havoc with their lives until they built a shrine to him.

Spirits and Social Change

Japanese relationships to spirits developed in a civilization centered on enduring social units: the household, the village, and the Imperial house. Household spirits stood for the continuity of the household over generations. Households in a village were protected by

Worship at a shrine, Narita temple complex, Japan. (COURTESY OF J. BOWEN.)

community spirits. And everyone was under the protection of the unbroken imperial line, itself said to come from the Sun Goddess and dating at least back to the seventh century C.E. Although these continuities have been disrupted by massive migrations to cities, older orientations toward spirits of the collectivity—including the emperor and his temples—continue in Japan.

Many kami are venerated in shrines, and some shrines, such as the great shrine at Ise to the Sun Goddess, are the focus of national veneration. The Ise shrine is rebuilt every 20 years as part of a cycle of national renewal of life and fertility; the last rebuilding, in 1993, was widely publicized by banners erected throughout Japan.

Parents routinely take their newborn babies to the local shrine to be placed under the care of the spirit guarding the local community. An offering is placed on the altar, and the shrine priest says prayers requesting these blessings. In the older, agrarian world in which Japanese religions developed, they also would have carried out rites at this shrine to ensure the fertility of the crops. The shrine also served as the place for community meetings and recreational activities; it was thus the center of social life. Often the community shrine was said to be a branch shrine of a famous national shrine, such as that at Ise. Performing rituals at the shrine thus linked the individual to the community and the nation–state.

Since World War II, Japanese have flooded from country to city and from farming to other occupations. In 1950, 62 percent of all Japanese families lived in rural areas, and fully 50 percent of those rural families were full-time farmers. Just 30 years later, in 1980, only 24 percent of families lived in rural areas, and only 10 percent of these families still engaged in full-time farming. This rapid shift in population has meant that a civilization and a set of religious practices that had developed around stable rural households now had to be modified for urban living. But Shinto shrines have been part of this transformation. People who commute to the city from suburbs or rural areas still visit the shrines to seek blessings for their babies and seek further spirit protection for young children, though now they may dress in Western-style clothes and record the occasions with expensive video cameras.

People living in the cities may return to their ancestral villages for harvest festivals and for the New Year's festival, when they acquire new amulets from the shrines to protect their homes during the coming year. For two years Ian Reader (1991, 61–64) watched proceedings at the Katano shrine midway between the cities of Osaka and Kyoto in what has become a commuter village. He records that on festival days, hundreds of people took trains from both cities to the shrine to seek blessings and purchase amulets. A shrine priest could call on office girls to work as temporary "shrine maidens" on these occasions; at one festival, Reader found himself being blessed by one of his own students who had been engaged to work as such a shrine maiden during the holidays. Businesses sent rice, or sake, to be placed on the altar for blessings (and afterward quickly consumed by visitors). The same priest was called upon to bless a new university building nearby. He had a temporary altar to the shrine spirit constructed inside the new building for the occasion.

Increased ease of transport has meant that Japanese increasingly visit the more famous shrines in larger cities. Several million people visit these shrines each year, while some rural shrines, those not on commuter lines and unable to afford priests, have closed. The social ties affirmed by attending a shrine are less and less local and increasingly national in scope.

Buddhism and Souls

Most of the people frequenting these shrines with their newborns, or at festivals, also participate in rituals drawn from Buddhism (Saunders 1964). The Buddhist religion began in the sixth century B.C.E. in South Asia, when the historical Buddha, Siddhartha of the clan Gautama, found enlightenment after long meditation. The followers of Buddha also seek enlightenment; his teachings provide examples and practices to follow rather than creeds to which followers must adhere.

In South Asia, Buddhism diverged into two major streams. One, called "Theravada" ("the elders") emphasizes the role of the monastic community in mediating between laypersons and Buddha. This stream spread from Sri Lanka to mainland Southeast Asia. The second stream was called "Mahayana," or "Greater Vehicle," for its universalistic approach to salvation. In this stream, individuals are encouraged to engage in practices that lead to their salvation and to enter directly into contact with Buddhas and other deities.

The Mahayana stream of Buddhism spread northward from India through Tibet and China. Japanese scholars learned about Buddhism in China, and for that reason Japanese Buddhism adopts the Mahayana orientation. Mahayana Buddhism emphasizes the illusory character of the world and orients the individual toward a transcendent reality in which he or she might achieve salvation. One sees this emphasis in paintings, where individual Buddhas are depicted floating above the world we live in, transcendent of its specific concreteness. These diverse Buddhas—Fudo, Amida, Maitreya—provide multiple sources of divine aid and multiple paths for individuals to seek salvation.

Each of the several major schools of Buddhism in Japan—Zen, Shingon, Nichiren, and others—combines a set of spiritual disciplines that lead to salvation (Reader 1991). They all evince a special concern for death and treatment of ancestors. Zen Buddhism, the best known in the West of these schools, emphasizes meditation. Indeed, the word *Zen* itself means "meditation." Zen teachers point to the example set by the historical Buddha, Gautama, who achieved enlightenment in this world by sitting and meditating. Zen practitioners may use *koan,* problems that appear unsolvable, as a way of breaking down the barriers that everyday linear thinking places in the path to enlightenment. They practice together in communities of meditators, engaging in strenuous physical labor—scrubbing floors, chopping wood—as additional aids to enlightenment. Laypeople may participate in retreats at Zen temples, and businesses routinely send their employees on special retreats that incorporate some of the austerities of temple life.

Japanese Buddhism's emphasis on individual meditation and enlightenment provides a counterpoint in religious practice to the overall Japanese cultural emphasis on the value and continuity of the group. But Buddhism also adapted itself to those values by assuming responsibility for the care of family ancestors. Even if they have no other contact with Buddhism, and would not state that they believe in Buddha, most Japanese "die Buddhist," that is, their children or other relatives seek out the service of a Buddhist priest to perform a funeral service. The main activity at most temples is in fact not meditation but performing memorial services for the dead. Most Japanese households are affiliated with a particular temple for this purpose.

Before Buddhism, Japanese people considered that each person's soul traveled to a world of the dead, where it continued to watch and intervene in the lives of its relatives. People carried out rituals designed to ease the transition to the other world and to keep the spirits happy. When Buddhism came to Japan, people saw the priests as possessing spiritual powers due to their activities of meditation. They began to call on those priests to perform the funeral ceremonies. Priests added new practices to the rituals, practices designed to guide the spirit toward enlightenment after death. The priest and his associates cremate the body to rid the soul of its impurities, and chant Buddhist texts and prayers to lead the soul toward the state of enlightenment. The word for dead soul, *hotoke,* also means a Buddha.

These ancestors continue to affect the lives of their kin, and both Buddhist priests and practitioners of New Religions are concerned with keeping the ancestors happy and resolving problems that occur when they are not. (See Chapter 6 for an example.)

Buddhism coexists with Shinto in Japan. The temple complex at Nara, which I visited in 1994, contains both Buddhist temples and Shinto shrines, and visitors stop at both. Temples may include images of kami alongside those of a Buddha, although the former are said to no longer contain spirits but only to represent them. The two kinds of entities are represented in clearly contrasting ways. In paintings, for example, kami are depicted in a realistic manner as specific, human-looking personages, sometimes identifiable as historical figures, and always standing near or on the place with which they are associated. Buddhas and bodhisattvas, by contrast, are abstract in their appearance, and not confined to specific spaces. Often they are painted as floating above the ground or on clouds.

Two other religious traditions have also influenced Japanese ideas and practices. Taoism (from *tao*, the "way" in Chinese) developed in China as an approach to understanding the way of the universe. Taoism includes methods of divining good or bad days by consulting calendars. Japanese adopted some of these practices—there was even a bureau of divination in early Japan—but no Japanese would identify himself or herself as a Taoist.

Confucianism, based on the teachings of the Chinese philosopher Confucius (551–479 B.C.E.), has played an important role in shaping Japanese social and moral values (Smith 1983, 37–67). Confucius taught that social order and welfare depended on maintaining the proper hierarchical relationships between persons, particularly those of father to son and ruler to subject. In Japan, these ideas strengthened the notion of the family as a corporate entity, with succession passing from father to eldest son, and that of the nation as a family-like entity headed by the hereditary emperor.

The State and Religion

Japan's rulers have added to their legitimacy by drawing on Shinto and Buddhism. The state has variously promoted one or the other of these two complexes of religious ideas and practices. In its encounter with outside cultures and in particular with Christianity, the Japanese state has created indigenous alternatives—systems of ideas and practices that looked like religion as defined in the West.

State promotion of religions began between the sixth and ninth centuries with the adoption of Chinese ideas that the emperor is both divine and the active ruler of society. Just as village guardians often were thought to be the ancestors of the village elite, the emperor declared himself (or herself) the descendant of the Sun Goddess. (These borrowings were a major source of Confucian influence in Japan.)

Scholars began to teach Buddhism in Japan during the Nara period (710–784 C.E.), named after the capital city of Nara. Emperor Shomu (reigned 724–749) quickly made Buddhism the state religion. Buddhism appealed to the emperor and his advisers because it came from China, along with the writing system and ideas of the divinity of the emperor, and also because it could be made the basis of a state-centered system of religious temples, with scriptures and priests. The preexisting religious practices were decentralized, with local spirits and shrines. Buddhism offered the possibility of constructing a religious hierarchy under imperial control.

In 728, the emperor built the Todai temple in Nara (just south of present-day Kyoto) as the first national temple. The statue of Buddha inside the temple, called "Lochana," still stands as the largest Buddhist statue in the world. Lochana, or Dainichi, is the Sun Buddha. When he was building the statue, the emperor had to seek approval from his ancestress, the Sun Goddess Amaterasu, at her temple in Ise. Reportedly the goddess told

Todai temple, Japan, with statue of the Buddha Nyiori. (COURTESY OF JOHN RENARD.)

the emperor that the Sun Buddha was the same as the Sun Goddess, and approved building the statue.

The emperor then ordered two temples built in each province, one as a monastery and one as a nunnery. Monks and nuns were recruited to these temples to recite Buddhist scriptures and accumulate merit, and then to pass on the merit to the nation as a whole. This form of mediated merit was not part of the Mahayana tradition imported by the state; it was created by the emperor for his own project of state building. By venerating the Sun Buddha, the emperor managed to link Buddha to his own Sun Goddess ancestor.

By constructing a national temple system, he linked acts of individual merit-making to the welfare of the nation as a whole, and forged a religious connection between the people and the state. But the temples and their priests, particularly at Todai temple, grew more and more powerful, and the decision to move the Imperial capital to Kyoto in 784 was in part to establish a separate power base away from the temple.

In succeeding centuries the influence of state-sponsored Buddhism waned along with the power of the emperor. But in 1600 the warlord (*shogun*) Tokugawa Ieyasu consolidated power throughout Japan, ending the many centuries of political disorder, and reduced the emperor to a figurehead. Ieyasu once again promoted Buddhism as the state religion, building a new hierarchy of temples. All Japanese were required to register at a temple, proclaim their religion, and use the services of Buddhist priests for funeral services. These state actions were not motivated by religious piety but intended to tighten state control and exclude Christianity, as a disruptive, foreign ideology. Thus, Buddhism was promoted as the best alternative to Christianity, as "not-Christianity."

In 1868 a coalition of warlords and a rising economic elite took power in the name of the Emperor Meiji, and sought to reduce the influence of Buddhism because of its association with the old regime. The Meiji Restoration combined economic restructuring with the creation of a cult of the emperor. A hierarchy of Shinto priests was created, and the result has come to be called State Shinto. Shrines were created to appeal to popular opinion. Foremost among these new shrines were Yasukuni, founded in 1869, where those soldiers who have died for the honor of the state are enshrined and deified, and the Meiji shrine, built in 1920 to honor the deceased emperor. Both produced talismans for people to take home with them, and people were also required to have talismans from Ise in their homes (Hardacre 1989, 79–99).

These efforts were meant to create a religious plane on which individual households would be merged into the state. The Confucian values of filial piety were emphasized as well as the common descent of all Japanese, as in the following section from a teacher's manual used in the 1930s:

The connection between the Imperial House and its subjects is thus: one forms the main house and the others form the branch house, so that from ancient times we have worshiped the founder of the Imperial House and the heavenly gods. Our relationship to this house is sincerely founded on repaying our debt of gratitude to our ancestors (quoted in Smith 1983, 32).

After World War II, the American forces that occupied Japan insisted that the new Constitution remove the aura of divinity from the emperor. The Constitution states that the emperor is not divine, but only "the symbol of the state and of the unity of the people." The Nobel Prize–winning writer Kenzaburo Oe has written of his and others' astonishment when on August 15, 1945, they heard the emperor speak over the radio. "The Emperor speaking to us in a human voice was beyond imagining in any reverie. The Emperor was a god, the authority of the nation, the organizing principle of reality" (Oe 1995, 103).

The Occupation forces also proclaimed Shinto to be a religion and that because people ought to be able to choose their religion freely it could not be taught in the schools or be supported by state funds. And yet despite this new official ideology, the Sun Goddess Amaterasu continues to be worshiped at the great shrine at Ise. Each time the shrine is rebuilt the ancient mirror that is thought to embody the Sun Goddess's spirit is moved into the new shrine. Six and a half million Japanese visit the shrine each year. Japanese visit Ise the way that Jews visit Israel and Muslims visit Mecca, as a journey to a sacred place.

The precise status of Ise and the nature of the emperor's relationship to the Sun Goddess (if any) became major political issues when Emperor Hirohito died in January 1989. At Hirohito's funeral the following month, the Shinto rites were performed behind curtains, evidently so that visiting dignitaries would not have to acknowledge them. Yet many in Japan criticized these proceedings as tantamount to worship of the emperor and thus a violation of the 1946 Constitution.

Then, in November 1990, Hirohito's son and successor, Akihito, was enthroned. Part of the enthronement procedure is the "great food-offering ritual," in which the new emperor offers special foods to the deities of the heaven and earth and performs a ritual of union of sorts (left ambiguous in official accounts) with the Sun Goddess. The last time this ritual had been performed was in 1928, when the emperor was still considered a god. At Ise he still is thought of as the chief priest of Shinto. There was a great deal of protest from those who considered the ritual to be religious, and thus to violate the Constitution's mandate that state and religion be separated (Weisman 1990).

Similar controversy continues to surround the Yasukuni shrine to the war dead. Prime Ministers regularly visit the shrine, located next to the Imperial Palace in central Tokyo, to venerate the war dead, sometimes in their official capacity. In August 1985, Prime Minister Nakasone with his cabinet made an official visit to the shrine to pay tribute to the war dead. But here Japan's difficulty in facing its wartime history surfaced, because major ("Class A") war criminals executed by judgment of the 1946–1948 Tokyo Trial are among the two and a half-million people listed as gods in the shrine's record book. Furthermore, the Rape of Nanking is among the events celebrated, a fact that led China to protest this attendance. Protests by many Japanese led Nakasone to forgo additional state visits to the shrine. In July 1996 a new prime minister, Hashimoto, tried again, but he too had to back down after domestic and international protests.

Veterans' groups continue to enshrine and deify the spirits of Japanese soldiers, however. In 1988, the Japanese Supreme Court backed up one such group over the objections of the widow of a soldier about to be deified. She was Protestant and protested that the deification violated her religious beliefs, but the Court claimed that her religion had no bearing on the group's freedom to carry out the ritual. The idea of religious exclusivity—that one religion excludes others—is not part of the Japanese legal tradition (Haberman, 1988).

Death practices, indeed, have all along been important elements in the state–religion nexus. The eighth-century ascendancy of Buddhism was accompanied by a change from burial to cremation for emperors and empresses, following Buddhist practice. During the 1600–1868 Tokugawa period, Shinto nationalists were gradually able to reduce Buddhism's official status—after 1654, although burial rites for the imperial family continued to follow Buddhist practices, the bodies were interred rather than cremated. Only at the funeral of Emperor Meiji's father, Komei, in 1867, were all Buddhist elements eliminated from the funeral, and thus one could say that the funeral ushered in the new Shinto-dominated Meiji era. The government prohibited cremation entirely in 1873, as part of its effort to drive out Buddhism, but it was forced to rescind the order as people pointed out that, already, Japan lacked sufficient space to bury intact bodies (*Far Eastern Economic Review*, March 16, 1989, 66–70).

The place of religion in public life, even the definition of what religion is, continues to be the subject of debate in Japan. What *is* clear in Japan is that lines between religions are fuzzy or, rather, that religions are not defined by the individual's exclusive commitment to one set of doctrines as opposed to others. Japan challenges our idea of what religion means for the individual, for the nation, and for the state.

For Further Consideration

*C*an you think of ways in which government policies or generally accepted public practices enforce a particular definition of religion in the United States? Consider that the government accords tax-exempt status only to religious groups meeting certain criteria. In a longstanding dispute with the Church of Scientology, the Internal Revenue Service said that because Scientology centered on sales of L. Ron Hubbard's books, the organization was a business, not a church. The German government refuses to accept Scientology as a religion because of long domination by Christian religions in German society. How does one decide what counts as a religion?

A fine book by Wilfred Cantwell Smith, *The Meaning and End of Religion* (Harper & Row 1978) makes the points that defining religions as belief is a recent approach. For a discussion of the relationship between the Japanese state and religion, see Helen Hardacre's *Shinto and the State, 1868–1988* (Princeton University Press 1989). The film *Shinto: Nature, Gods, and Man in Japan* (Japan Society 1977), highlights the aesthetic side of religion in Japan and explains the relationships between spirits and Buddhas.

For more about Buddhism, there are several excellent ethnographies, general books on the religion, and Web sites. S. J. Tambiah's *Buddhism and Spirit Cults in Northeast Thailand* (Cambridge University Press 1970) is a classic ethnography showing how Thai villagers combine indigenous beliefs and practices with textual Buddhism. Richard Gombrich and Gananath Obeyesekere's *Buddhism Transformed: Religious Change in Sri Lanka* (Princeton University Press 1988) emphasizes contemporary developments in Sri Lanka. A very useful Web site on Buddhism in Japan, with links to specific historical periods and to sites sponsored by particular temples, is found at *http://www.japan-guide.com/e/e2055.html.*

3 *Rituals and Emotions*

eligious practices include those fixed sequences of actions that we often call rituals. People carrying out a religious ritual try to conform to certain rules to get the ritual right. Sometimes they seek a specific end, such as healing, pleasing a deity, or restoring fertility; they perform other rituals out of a general sense of obligation.

In most, perhaps all, societies people mark transitions or life stages by carrying out certain transition rituals or rites of passage. These rituals often have a religious dimension, and they tend to cluster around several points in the life cycle: birth, puberty, marriage, and death. Rituals that mark the passage into adulthood may involve changes in name, membership in a new society of initiates, bestowal of new social rights and duties, or, in the category of religiously competent persons, conferral of supernatural powers. Death is also ritually represented as a transition in most societies; death rituals are usually intended to ease the passage of the spirit to another social state and possibly to another world.

Many other kinds of rituals are concerned with transitions. The beginning of an agricultural cycle or the succession to an office may be ritually enacted in ways that resemble life-cycle transition rituals. Anthropologists have long noticed that such rituals are often structured in three parts. Transition rituals shift actors out of their normal social roles, into an intermediate or "liminal" stage, and then reintegrate them into society. The liminal period provides a time for experiencing, sharing, and representing emotions or ideas not usual to social life, as well as a time for accomplishing the tasks of the ritual process.

Transition rituals often emphasize the creation of life: new persons, life after death, or the soil's fertility. Initiation rituals that move people from an immature to a mature state are of course directly concerned with reproduction and biological fertility. But funeral rituals also may tie death to the regeneration of life, refocusing attention and emotions on life and fertility rather than death and loss.

Second, the content and sequence of rituals shape specific emotions in the participants. Feelings of grief are given well-specified forms of expression, sometimes a prescribed period of mourning followed by a break from mourning, sometimes the reverse: stoicism followed by an emotional release. The promise of new life gives hope after loss, and rituals that structure time support the notion that humans can control natural processes of growth, maturation, and death.

Finally, transition rituals represent the social order in a particular way, often an idealized or partial way, and often as if the rituals themselves produce or shape the social order. Relations and differences between men and women, or superiors and inferiors, may be projected onto a cosmic plane, or produced in the ritual itself, especially in initiation rituals that create adolescent or adult males and females. Initiations often reveal secrets, the mere possession of which is the basis for initiates' claims to supremacy over noninitiates. Secrecy creates status and boundaries across a range of social institutions. From members of initiation societies in Africa and New Guinea, to Mormons and Masons, those "in the know" can claim superiority, power, or at least special status. Death rituals often have a different social design, to restore social order after a loss.

Sequence and the Liminal Stage of Rituals

*T*he sociologist Arnold van Gennep pointed out in 1909 (1960) that transition rituals display a similar sequential structure across cultures. Rites marking birth, puberty, marriage, and death, he remarked, as well as many other rituals of initiation or succession, often are structured temporally as three distinct stages.

The first stage separates the person from the ordinary social environment. It may involve rites to purify the body, seclusion, cutting hair, or simulating death. The separation may be the social recognition of a natural event, such as the onset of menstruation or death, providing a cultural definition for the event. It may create a peer group, such as a group of boys or girls to be initiated. It may define a geographical space, as when Muslims exchange their ordinary identities and clothing for the garb of pilgrims when entering the sacred precincts of Islam in Arabia.

Next comes a stage of marginality, the transitional or *liminal* ("threshold") stage during which the person is outside of normal social life. The liminal person may have to observe certain taboos, or be isolated, or be subjected to beatings and insults, or be elevated to temporary high status. This stage may be as short as a brief baptismal ceremony in a Christian church or as long as certain New Guinea initiation cycles lasting 10 years or more. It is a period of social work, where the liminal person is transformed in bodily or spiritual status.

Finally comes the reaggregation or reincorporation of the individual into society (or into an afterlife society), now possessing a new status. A girl may have become a woman, or a boy a man; a candidate is now a king; the loose soul of a dead man takes up its place in heaven.

The middle or liminal period has key importance to the sequence of events. Consider what happens when a signal event occurs: a girl's menstruation begins; a man dies. The event changes the natural condition of the individual in a way that underscores the limits of society's control over nature. Such events are often thought of as polluting. Ritual removes the person from everyday life and provides time for people to define the event and its consequences; to transform the person in body, mind, and status, and then to define the new state—as a fertile woman, or a soul proceeding to the world of the dead.

Of course, some events that are sequenced as transition rituals are not unplanned acts of nature: the initiation of a group of 10-year-olds, or a baptism, or a pilgrimage. Yet the liminal stage of these rituals, too, provides the setting for a dramatization of the individual's recasting into a new form, a convincing statement that the old has died and the new is born.

Reshaping, Reversing, Communitas

No one kind of process dominates these liminal periods; I mention three here. The first is what Gilbert Herdt (1981, 305) has called the "radical resocialization" of the individual—working the person over until he or she feels and thinks in new ways. Herdt writes of the often violent initiation rituals of Melanesia, which may involve long periods of beatings and abuse of young boys, who emerge shaken, with new psychological and social identities (Poole 1982).

A second process is status reversal, or "ritual of rebellion," when ordinary social relations are turned upside down. An Ndembu chief-to-be is placed in a hut where anyone is free to revile him. "A chief is just like a slave on the night before he succeeds," goes an Ndembu saying (Turner 1969, 101). Such periods may also be part of annual cycles. In fertility rituals held at the beginning of the planting season in some Zulu villages in southern Africa, for example, women reverse their otherwise subordinate roles. Donning men's garments, or singing lewd songs, or milking cows, normally taboo practices. These reversals are thought to increase the chance for a good harvest by appealing to the female spirit associated with the rains and fertility (Gluckman 1963).

Related to these stages are festivals that feature role reversals. In the South Asian festival of Holi, dedicated to the god Krishna, high-caste Brahmans and wealthy people are beaten and chased by low-caste people, such as washermen. Across early modern Europe, rituals held to mark annual feast days frequently featured women (or grotesque female beasts) chasing men, or used floats depicting women dominating their husbands, or had men and women dress in each other's garb. Some of the European rituals, like their African counterparts, were seen as promoting fertility.

Status reversals may have provided an outlet for "unruly" sentiments, as some historians and anthropologists argue, but they also sometimes provided a vehicle for critiques of or even attacks on the ruling order. The historian Natalie Zemon Davis (1965, 121–154) points out that in Europe of the seventeenth and eighteenth centuries, peasants sometimes dressed as women to carry out attacks on government officials, "putting ritual and festive inversion to new uses." Men dressed as women attacked land surveyors and tax collectors, stole the king's deer and tore down his fences. The males were able to distance themselves from their normal roles and responsibilities, but could also exploit the sexual energy dramatized during festival occasions. Ritual thus appears to have fed into politics.

A third, related, characteristic of some middle periods is what Victor Turner (1969, 94–165) called "communitas," a state wherein individuals step outside their normal social roles and experience relative equality and direct sociality with each other, as on pilgrimages or in spontaneous gatherings. (Status reversal may also have this effect.) The Islamic pilgrimage, the hajj, provides an excellent example of equality during the transition stage. The hajj, to be examined more fully in Chapter 13, places all pilgrims in a liminal position once they enter the holy cities of Mecca and Medina. All pilgrims, rich and poor, female and male, wear the same simple white garb as they carry out rituals of submission to God and commemoration of Muhammad's first pilgrimage.

Turner, who wrote prolifically on the subject, argued that communitas was generally associated with liminal stages in transition rituals. (He also saw social life in general as a dialectic of structure and communitas.) But, as the Melanesian initiations mentioned earlier suggest, such an association is not at all a general one. Even some pilgrimages do not support this association, such as that portion of South Asian pilgrimages in which caste distinctions are preserved during the journey. We can best understand the specific form given liminal life in a particular ritual sequence by examining the purpose of the ritual and the cultural context in which it occurs. Liminality does seem to involve the suspension of ordinary sociality, but what replaces that ordinary sociality may vary from a highly regimented, even repressive, order (in Melanesia or in a U.S. Army boot camp) to the spontaneity celebrated by Turner.

Grief and Ritual

*T*ransition rituals marking events such as initiations or death are emotional times. Often the emotions are produced by the rituals themselves. The sociologist Émile Durkheim (1858–1917), stressing the social base for much of religious life, argued that ritual action, especially when in a group, channels and determines emotions. (For more information on Durkheim, see pages 55–58.) Durkheim maintained that although there might be natural emotional responses to death, they are highly subject to social shaping. Is this view correct? How culturally different are those emotions? What role does ritual play in the interior lives, the feelings, and the grieving of the survivors? Do rituals create emotions or do emotions determine what kind of rituals people create?

Consider the contrast between the way two Muslim peoples mourn the loss of a close relative. In Java, where people typically value the control of their emotions, Clifford Geertz (1960, 73) reports a man he knew well distancing himself from the loss of his wife, describing how he kept his emotions inside him. A girl who wept softly after her father died was told she could not participate in the funeral events unless she stopped crying. And yet, in Morocco, another Muslim society, the expected behavior is just the opposite. People in mourning tear their clothes and hair and wail loudly and publicly (Westermarck 1968 II, 34–42).

These marked differences in public behavior are between two people with the same religion. Ritual forms, linked to dominant cultural values, prescribe sharply contrasting patterns of mourning behavior.

But we cannot assume from such publicly observed contrasts that the emotions and the grieving process experienced by the individual are correspondingly different (Rosaldo 1984). Many Moroccans may feel indifference; many Javanese, great sorrow. Yet men and women in each society are expected to act in certain standardized ways regardless of their feelings. Many people in the United States report feeling quite different from what their public mourning behavior would suggest. Some feel guilty at the gulf between their mixed emotions and the expressions of grief that they are expected to display. Others adhere to religions that urge their followers in a different direction, to maintain a hopeful attitude consistent with a strong belief in the afterlife. Mormon services reflect this attitude, and Christian Scientists argue that bereaved people can and should lift themselves out of sorrow through the sheer force of the will. Yet many adherents to these faiths do grieve, and may find their social networks not offering the support they need (Palgi and Abramovitch 1984).

Is Grief Universal?

Perhaps the most devastating loss to an American adult is the death of a child, and here cross-cultural variation is striking. Psychologists (Bowlby 1980) argue that parents in all societies develop attachments to their children and experience grief at the loss of children. The attachment and the grief seem to have a basis in the evolution of social relationships. Both features are found in nonhuman primates as well as humans. And yet in many societies the deaths of newborns are not accompanied by the same expressions of loss and grief as are the deaths of older children or adults. In many societies children are not named until some number of days has passed after birth, and a death before that time is treated very differently than later deaths. Do these practices indicate that parents feel the loss less? How strongly does such a cultural practice shape emotions?

Two studies in anthropology have addressed this question but reach distinct conclusions. Nancy Scheper-Hughes (1992) argues that some poor Brazilian parents do feel loss less than do most middle-class parents. She emphasizes the cultural malleability of emotions—cultural practices shape emotional response. Unni Wikan (1990), emphasizing the distance between public expressions and inner emotions, finds that Balinese people feel strong grief emotions, but that they follow culturally prescribed practices of working on their grief through laughter and sociability. These and other studies underscore the emotional importance of rituals and other practices during the transition stage after a death—and also the difficulties in generalizing about "private" emotions.

Nancy Scheper-Hughes lived, worked, and studied in a very poor region in northeastern Brazil in the 1960s and then again in the 1980s. Many in the area had little to eat, and infant death was common. Mothers, fathers, and siblings developed an attitude of "letting go" toward those infants who seemed near death, often drawing on an elaborate catalogue of symptoms that pointed to an inevitable death.

Scheper-Hughes tried to make sense of the families' emotionally flat responses by challenging the Western view about attachment and mourning. In that view, attachment is a basic instinct that structures relationships between all human mothers and their children. The death of a child triggers natural responses of mourning, that must be worked through if the survivors are to be able to carry on in a healthy way. But Scheper-Hughes (1992, 400–445) argues that many mothers in fact have an ambivalent attitude toward their newborns. When the mother–infant experience is positive, and when nurturing all one's children is possible, parents invest emotionally in their children and feel great loss at a death. But in poor Brazil and some other places a "lifeboat" ethic leads parents to choose, reluctantly, to nurture only those who have a chance at surviving. Cultural practices reinforce this survival strategy: parents delay naming their infants and hold them much less than do middle-class mothers.

Death ritual also plays an important part in this survival strategy. In some parts of Brazil, lower-class men and women treat the death of a very young child as a blessing. The child will be taken to heaven, is already a little angel, they say. The wake held for the little child, who is dressed in a white or blue shirt with curled hair and floral wreathes, includes joyous music and samba dancing. Although much more sober in tone in the community where Scheper-Hughes worked, the "angels" were a "transitional object" for these women, she points out (1992, 421), both because the infant is in transition from life to death, and because the dressed-up corpse and coffin allows the woman to let go of her child by giving her an idealized heaven–child to hold onto. Women told Scheper-Hughes: "I feel free" or "I feel unburdened" after the funeral. Grief seemed absent. For some students of Brazilian society the flat emotional response is a mask, a wall against the unbearable. But Scheper-Hughes takes the responses of these women at face value, arguing that culture and ritual succeed in preventing grief responses. The idea that deaths need to be worked through by a process of open mourning, she says, is applicable only in some societies.

Still, it may be difficult to decide between several possible interpretations of Scheper-Hughes's data—are denials of grief a mask, or are denials accurate reports of feelings? Another study of the same area (Nations and Rebhun 1988) reports very different findings. High rates of infant mortality are found in many parts of the world, and yet women mourn these infants. Finally, we should note that arguments for a universal attachment structure are based on cross-cultural research: the major early empirical work (Ainsworth 1967) was not from the West but from Uganda!

Emotions and Their Expressions

Scheper-Hughes's argument was intended to counter universal theories of death, emotions, and ritual. By contrast, anthropologist Unni Wikan draws on her fieldwork in Bali to oppose culturally relativist theories about the malleability of emotions. In Bali, as in neighboring Java, people are expected to preserve a "face" of equanimity at loss or disaster. Anthropologists had long understood the grace and composure of Balinese as a cultural style that focused on beauty and on distancing oneself from emotions. Balinese selves, wrote the anthropologist Clifford Geertz (1966), are quite different from Western ones; they live in a "dramatistic" world composed of masks, roles, and a stage.

Wikan (1990) argues instead that Balinese think and feel their way through the world in ways that are much closer to European ways than earlier anthropologists believed. She describes several months in the life of one woman, who lost her fiance in an accident. Her friends laughed and joked with her, insisting that she laugh too. During the following months she appeared bright-faced and happy, even to her friend Wikan. After several months Wikan did see her cry, and then the woman began to tell of how devastated she had felt through the whole experience. About the same time her friends began to change their ways of being with her, sympathizing out loud with the distress she must have felt. Her emotions, and their understanding of them, were not all that different after all.

But why did she laugh her way through the first few months, and why did her friends insist that she do so? The key lies in a distinctive set of ideas about the relationship between one's "face"—appearances and behavior—and one's "heart"—emotions and

√

thoughts. For the Balinese with whom Wikan spoke, emotions of sadness and sorrow weaken one's life force. A weak life force opens up the body to all sorts of invasions, but most particularly to attacks from sorcerers. These attacks are always near at hand; half of all deaths are attributed to sorcery. Moreover, these sad feelings can spread from one person to another, endangering the community, so one has a social as well as a personal responsibility to keep sorrow at a distance. How does one do that? Whereas we might think of emotions as having a life of their own—grief inevitably following loss—the Balinese think that behavior, including how one forms one's face and the choice to laugh or cry, shapes the heart and channels emotions. Laughing, then, keeps sadness from welling up, and thereby keeps the person strong against murderous sorcery.

Wikan concludes that Balinese appearances of calm and joy are not due to a theater-like detachment from the world, but rather to their strong fears of sorcery and their ideas about how best to combat it. During the transition period after death these dangers are at their highest and thus when the practices of laughing together are most required.

Wikan, then, affirms the distinctiveness of Balinese ideas and practices but sees them as responses to a universal emotion of loss and grief. Scheper-Hughes claims that the emotions of the Brazilians she studied are quite different from those experienced by middle-class families, but she does so by way of a general theory about the responses of mothers (and others) to infants and to risk. Both underscore the critical role of culturally sanctioned practices designed to shape the emotions people feel when a loved one dies. Balinese laughing and Brazilian "angel caskets" bridge the transition period between death and the reintegration of the survivors into the ordinary routines of life.

Initiation, Secrecy, and Fear

Very different are the emotions shaped by initiation rites, rituals that mark a passage from childhood into adulthood, or those that celebrate the movement from outside to inside a society or association. In contemporary U.S. society these two kinds of initiation rites seem quite different: joining the Masons is very unlike the celebration of becoming a bar mitzvah, a full male member of the Jewish religious community. One involves joining a volunteer association as an adult; the other is a stage in life for those born into a particular religion.

Yet both processes involve new knowledge and new responsibilities. In many societies, passing from childhood into a condition of full social responsibility also involves entering into a religious association and acquiring new knowledge, sometimes secret knowledge. The rituals that mark this transition often draw out the liminal or middle stage of the transition gradually, and sometimes painfully, revealing knowledge that will forever mark the individual.

Hopi Whipping and Disenchantment

Hopi Pueblo rituals fuse secrets, pain, initiation, and fertility in a way found in many societies. Hopi community rituals designed to make the seasons begin and end, or to ensure a fertile crop, or to guard the welfare of the community, involve dances by men dressed as spirits (Gill 1987, 58–75; Parsons 1939, vol. 2, 467–476). In the public portion of these rituals, men don elaborate, colorful masks, paint their bodies, strap on rattles and bells, and dance in the plaza. They represent *kachinas,* spirit beings, whose power is lodged in the dancers' masks. The dances and singing draw on this power and channel it toward accomplishing the ritual's goal.

Each February a ritual is held to encourage the coming growing season to be plentiful. This festival, called *Powamu,* is the occasion for the kachina spirits to return to the Hopi mesas from their winter homes in the mountains. Every several years the festival includes initiation rites, when boys and girls around the age of 10 are inducted into either the Kachina association or the Powamu association. The children are taken to underground rooms called "kivas," where the secret portions of rituals are held. There they are whipped by the kachinas. They then assume a fetal position and watch the men with their masks entering the kiva.

The children now realize that the masked figures were only men, not spirits. The shock they experience is fearful and traumatic. One Hopi woman said, "I cried and cried into my sheepskin that night, feeling I had been made a fool of. How could I ever watch the Kachinas dance again?" (Gill 1987, 63).

The whipping communicates both a threat against revealing secrets, and the power of the association into which the child has been initiated. (Full initiation requires a second ritual several years later.) Religious historian Sam Gill argues that the initiation is about the disenchantment of the magical world. Gill points out that initiation rites in other societies also disillusion children of their former beliefs that masked dancers are spirits. The child is torn away from his or her naive belief that what is seen is real and set to participating in the kachina cult activities as an adult. The adult begins his or her religious life as a reflective skeptic. The Hopi woman who recalled her weeping went on to say (ibid): "I know now it was best and the only way to teach the children, but it took me a long time to know that."

New Guinea Traumas and Homosexuality

Much more severe than the whippings inflicted by the kachinas are the long, painful initiation rituals experienced by young boys in some New Guinea societies. John Fitz Porter Poole (1982) relates that the male initiation cycle in Bimin-Kuskusmin society stretches from 10 to 15 years in a boy's life, usually beginning at seven to 10 years of age. One of its stages takes place in a forest house, where the initiates are secluded, beaten, told they are vile (and that women are vile as well) and tormented. Over succeeding days they are rubbed with stinging nettles, forced to vomit, and beaten. Many actions are taken to firm up their bodies and heighten their masculinity, including rubbing boar blood on their chests. They are also told a series of secret myths and ordered not to reveal them.

The initiators explain that they are making the boys into men. One aspect of that process is teaching them how to control anger, an esteemed quality for a warrior. The boys are furious, reports Poole, but must suppress their anger on pain of further beatings. Throughout the ritual they are deceived by men they had trusted, abused by everyone older than they, and denied maternal support. The trauma is great; some boys go into shock. Some of the initiators express concern, but see the beatings as necessary to make the boys mature. The boys themselves suffer afterward from fearful dreams, in which concern for their body parts is evidenced.

Such processes of "radical resocialization" (Herdt 1981, 305) in this and other societies are intended to wrest the boy from his mother, make his body masculine, his sexuality potent, and his emotional makeup that of a brave warrior. Other New Guinea societies emphasize sexuality more than anger. Gilbert Herdt (1981, 1982) describes the ritualized homosexuality among the Sambia that marks the initiation process. Men are produced from boys in part through the ingestion of semen, which is seen to replace the breast milk they ingested as infants and is intended to wean them from women and make them into men. This form of homosexuality is thus a way of replacing an earlier bodily relation to the mother with a relation to other men and fits with the idea, discussed earlier, that men and women have sharply differentiated but parallel relationships to the social and natural world. Herdt (1982) reports that the boys experience fear, maternal loss, and shame when confronted with the initiated men and when they begin to understand what is expected of them. They share their mothers' fears of male aggression and threats, that are symbolized by secret (phallic) flutes, which stand for male dominance of women and elder male dominance over the young boys.

Female initiation rituals in New Guinea involve less trauma. Girls are separated from younger girls, but not from women. The rituals described by Nancy Lutkehaus (1995) for Manam Island in Papua New Guinea are directed toward cleansing girls of the pollution brought on by first menstrual blood and turning them into fertile women. As practiced generally in the 1930s, and with some girls today, the rites involve a long series of actions intended to isolate the girl from her normal social state and from her bodily state. She is not allowed to touch herself or her food. Once she has bathed in the sea to begin the seven- to 10-day ritual sequence, the young girls who attend her are also forbidden to touch her. Slits are cut in her back with knives and ash rubbed in to raise scars to mark her as a fertile woman. She jokes with other women throughout the process.

Sadness is introduced with mourning songs sung at the start and close of the ritual, signaling that the girl is renouncing the pleasures of childhood and now expects to bear children and to leave her village of birth to marry.

Pain, fear, demands for secrecy—all are strongly remembered experiences that impress the initiate with the seriousness of the social norms and ideas he or she has learned. Strong emotions and newly acquired secrets further serve to reinforce the separation between elders and juniors and between men and women. Children are indeed radically reshaped into new kinds of humans.

Theory in Anthropology: Emotions as Religion's Source

Although the idea that religion springs from emotions is ancient, an important modern argument along these lines came from David Hume, a philosopher of the Scottish Enlightenment. In his 1757 work, *The Natural History of Religion* (1993), Hume argued that religion first came from "the incessant hopes and fears which actuate the human mind." Religion thus offers one way of overcoming anxiety.

Hume's idea was given ethnographic substance by Bronislaw Malinowski (1884–1942), one of the first anthropologists to carry out long-term fieldwork. Malinowski worked in the Trobriand Islands, today part of Papua New Guinea, between 1915 and 1918. He distinguished between the practical, rational knowledge and skills Trobriands employ to carry out their everyday tasks, and the religion and magic they call on to supplement their knowledge and powers. Ideas about the afterlife help people live despite their knowledge that death awaits them, wrote Malinowski in 1926, and funeral rituals add further authority to the idea that something awaits them after death. These rituals and ideas "save man from a surrender to death and destruction (1954, 51)." Ideas about the powers of spells and prayer to change the world also serve a psychological function: they reduce the anxiety that comes from uncertainty, allowing people to carry on their practical life. Religion and magic are thus not "pseudosciences"; rather, they arise in response to deep-seated, innate human fears and concerns.

Malinowski was influenced by the psychologist William James (1842–1910) as well as by Hume. In his *Varieties of Religious Experience* (1902/1972), James defined religion in terms of a set of individual human attitudes, as "the feelings, acts, and experiences of individual men in their solitude, so far as they apprehend themselves to stand in relation to whatever they may consider the divine." James advocated pragmatism in philosophy and science; in his version of this approach, the experiences one accumulates, whether in the laboratory or in everyday life, are the basis for deciding about truth and falsehood. Since belief in God works toward the general good, it is "true." Religious beliefs are validated when they are shown to have beneficial consequences, such as reducing anxiety and fear.

References today to innate or unconscious psychological impulses usually draw on the writings of Sigmund Freud (1856–1939), the founder of modern psychoanalysis. Freud argued that the psyche was more than the conscious. Powerful drives for self-preservation and pleasure often shape our actions and conscious ideas in ways of which we are only half aware. These individual drives run headlong into societal norms, creating repression and neuroses. Freud (1930) held a negative view of religion. Born of infantile feelings of helplessness and society-caused suffering, religion he believed, kept people from rationally critiquing and rebuilding their social lives. But Freud's ideas about the power of religious symbols have been used by some anthropologists to explain why certain objects—hair, the color white, blood—are frequent and powerful in religious ritual.

Other theorists and religious historians have examined how and why certain symbols have widespread power. Some theorists stress the irreducible nature of religious experience. Carl Jung (1875–1961), a student of Freud, saw religion as an experience of awe at the power of the divine, a submission to a superior power, that is later codified into doctrines and rituals. Jung (1964) followed William James and the theologian Rudolf Otto in finding the truth of religion in these religious experiences. But Jung then postulated a "collective unconscious" of humankind that contains all religious symbols. These symbols stem from "archetypes" that are innate in every human being and make possible the translation of religious experiences across persons and cultures. These archetypes—the hero, the earth mother, god—form the basis of the universal religious experience.

Profile

Jonathan Spencer
*The Complexity of
Grief in Sri Lanka*

Most of us in anthropology begin our fieldwork with notions about what "real" funerals are like, how people ought to act towards their spouses, and what an authentic ritual would be. The people with whom we work usually disabuse us of these notions, as happened to Jonathan Spencer during his work in Sri Lanka.

In late April 1982 I had just moved into a village on the southern edge of the central mountainous part of the island of Sri Lanka. According to my diaries I was reading *What Maisie Knew* by Henry James and trying to learn long lists of Sinhala vocabulary. I was going to a lot of funerals.

The first funeral I attended was of a prominent Buddhist monk, and I have hazy memories of an afternoon on a rainswept hillside and a complicated bus journey back to my base. The second was of an old man, a former village headman, who had died at his home about eight miles from where I was living. I was at first reluctant to go. I had never met the man, nor any member of his family—surely they wouldn't want a total stranger intruding on their grief. Not so, I was assured by the young men from the neighborhood who were going. I would be especially welcome. And I should bring my camera.

We were received respectfully at the man's home, and after we had viewed the corpse in its open coffin in the main room, offered warm carbonated drinks, cigarettes, and betel. I was persuaded to take a photograph of the corpse, with members of the family and some of my companions posed around it. Buddhist monks arrived and were also greeted respectfully. The coffin was closed and taken in procession to the cemetery a short way down the road, with weeping family members following. There it rested, its lid reopened, by the waiting grave.

At the cemetery, the monks chanted verses and the senior monk preached a short sermon. The family members gathered to pour water together, an act intended to transfer "merit" to the dead man, ensuring a better rebirth. There were long formal speeches from local worthies, all in a style of high Sinhala virtually incomprehensible to me. Eventually, the speeches ended, drumming began, and the family gathered for the final interment. The dead man's widow and daughters, already highly distraught, were ushered into a group by the side of the coffin. As the lid was slowly and dramatically closed again, the women started to scream, "aiyo tatte!" ("alas, father"). One of the daughters collapsed into apparent convulsions, her hair broken loose from its usual careful pinning and flying around her head. Men of the family had to hold the women back as the coffin was lowered into the grave to the percussive accompaniment of firecrackers.

In itself, this display of raw grief would have been difficult enough to watch. But my ethnographer's composure had already been unsettled by my companions' insistence that I get my camera ready for this moment, which was, they said, the "good bit." I refused: surely it was inappropriate, especially for an outsider, to photograph such a private moment. But my scruples mystified my companions. After all, the family of the dead man had hired its own photographer for the occasion. There he was, in classic wedding photographer style, telling the wailing women to hold back a second while he got the focus right. And they did; gulping back the tears and shuffling slightly closer together to fit better into the photographer's frame. When he gave the signal that all was well, they returned to their screams and moans of grief.

I came away from the funeral, emotionally unsettled and intellectually baffled, with my own expectations about ritual and emotion confounded by the scene at the graveside. The funeral itself was very public, not the quintessentially private event that it would have been in Britain. My presence as a foreigner was not inappropriate, but added a vaguely glamorous luster to the dead man's reputation. The expressions of grief were extraordinarily intense and unquestionably real; yet, they also seemed, as the moment with the photographer demonstrated, somehow self-conscious and staged.

My first thought was to interpret all this in terms of the collective shaping of emotion, and especially through the Greek notion of catharsis, in which the audience at a tragic play transfers its emotions to the protagonist. In this case, the women expressed the grief for the entire company of people at the funeral. I also noted a difference in gender behavior: the men were either calm or actively engaged in holding the women back; the women were the ones expected to display their grief at its most visceral.

But as I talked to other people about my reaction, everything became more complicated. My Sinhala teacher back in the city,

himself a Catholic, told me that the women's display of grief was a "Catholic" practice that had only recently been borrowed by the Buddhists. I also learned that in other parts of the country, especially in poorer, less sophisticated villages, women remained at the funeral house and did not accompany the coffin to the burial ground. Several people in the village where I lived told me they found this new organization of grief and mourning disturbing. What I had seen, then, needed to be interpreted in the context of a rapidly changing religious field, in which issues of class and status were bound up with the diffusion of new ritual practices across the boundaries of religious and cultural "communities."

The women's grief, for all that, was real, and it had taught me an unforgettable lesson about the contingency of my own categories of public and private, the real and the staged. But it had also opened a window for me onto a much more complex and fluid world, in which a moment at a funeral involving a professional photographer and a small number of grief-stricken women forced me to consider how religious practice is refracted by issues of class, gender, and dense local history. ✍

Jonathan Spencer teaches in the Department of Anthropology, University of Edinburgh.

For Further Consideration

*T*hink of a ritually marked transition in your life; can you identify stages in that ritual? Was there an intermediate or liminal period? Did your sense of yourself change after the ritual was completed?

Around the world rituals mark puberty; you can easily collect and compare such rituals. One film that shows four different girls' puberty transitions (in a rather negative light) is *Rights of Passage* (Filmakers Library 1985).

Why do some rituals involve pain and fear? Have you experienced such a ritual? What effect did it have on you? Why have hazing rituals in the military and in college fraternities lived on?

Two books illustrating the changing religious field in Sri Lanka are Richard Gombrich and Ganath Obeyesekere's *Buddhism Transformed: Religious Change in Sri Lanka* (Princeton 1988); and R. L. Stirrat's *Power and Religiosity in Post-Colonial Setting: Sinhala Catholics in Contemporary Sri Lanka* (Cambridge 1992). Students interested in the context for this piece can look at Jonathan Spencer's *A Sinhala Village in a Time of Trouble: Politics and Change in Rural Sri Lanka* (Oxford University Press 2000).

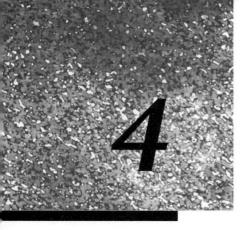

4 *Death, Life, and Debates*

Death Ritual and the Social Order

*I*f initiation rituals underscore conceptions of gender, death rituals make especially visible ideas about the individual and the collectivity. If an individual leaves society, is he or she to remain part of it? In the answer to that question people often highlight their picture, real or ideal, of society and of an individual.

In much of China and Taiwan, villagers conceive of the spiritual world as composed of three beings: ghosts, gods, and ancestors. Each is dealt with differently; for example, offered different kinds of food or money. These three beings are also associated with three kinds of humans. Gods are dressed in the garments of officials and they can punish people and be bribed. They keep records; they are clearly bureaucrats. They are worshipped in temples (Wolf 1974). Ghosts, by contrast, are worshiped outside, with large offerings of food or clothing, and they resemble bandits or beggars—strangers, in other words. Ancestors are, well, ancestors. You owe them a debt for your own life and prosperity, and you feed them as you would feed a human visitor to your home.

This close correspondence between society and supernatural beings suggests that in different Chinese settings people would interpret these beings somewhat differently, and they do: the god who is a police official today may have been an influential country gentleman in the past.

From Spirit to Household God in Japan

In rural Japan, where the individual is thought of as a member of a household and of a community, at death a person becomes a spirit (kami) as well as a Buddha (hotoke). Funerals are performed by Buddhist priests, but death ritual also involves pre-Buddhist ideas of pollution and ritual. A long transition stage allows the spirit to progress from an individual's spirit to one element in the household deity. Death ritual thereby reinforces the notion of spirit collectivity (Plath 1964; Smith 1974).

Death begins a three-stage process of transforming the deceased into a part of the spirit collectivity. At death the body may be cremated or buried; urban Japanese inevitably cremate. In either case, bodily death pollutes the spirit (shirei) as well as the close relatives of the deceased. Death ritual helps to separate the spirit from the pollution. The grave receiving the body is located far away from the residential part of a village and is called the "abandoned grave." In some parts of Japan a second, "ritual grave," consisting of a headstone is built nearer the house. This grave may be tended without encountering the pollution of the dead body. Urban Japanese must rely on funeral parlors. (Today the combined expenses of burial, home altar with tablets, and the services of a Buddhist priest can amount to a middle-class family's one-year pretax income!)

The memory of the deceased individual is preserved for the first 49 days after death. The survivors set up a mortuary tablet on the household altar, together with a photo of the deceased, incense, bells, and other objects. Buddhist memorial services are held for the individual every seven days until the 49 days are completed. The soul also wanders near the house during this period, before leaving on the 49th day.

Sometimes the soul takes some action on its own on the 49th day to settle accounts with the living. In an eighteenth-century puppet play called "The Woman Killer and the Hell of Oil," Yohei murders Okichi, but no one knows that he is the murderer. Yohei arrives on the 49th day of the ritual, just after a rat has run along the rafters of the room, dislodging a scrap of paper with evidence of the murderer's guilt; and the husband of the dead woman exclaims that this was a sign from the dead person. "This I owe to Buddha's mercy," he says.

At the end of this initial period the family holds a series of rituals to transform the spirit of the dead into an ancestral spirit (*sorei*). The photo is put away and the temporary tablet disposed of, replaced by a permanent tablet, usually an upright wooden plaque four to six inches high, lacquered in black or gold, and inscribed with a special posthumous name of the deceased and the date of his or her death. (Buddhist temples provide these after-death names.) This tablet is placed with the other tablets on the altar.

The altar and tablets stands for the house's history (Smith 1974, 1978, 152–165). The household (*ié*) is thought of as a corporate group, the headship of which passes from father to son over the generations. The tablets are the first objects to be saved (standard newspaper accounts of fires say that "flames swept through the building so rapidly that the residents only had time to carry out the altar and tablets"). The tablets are even more important than the Buddha image. As one man put it, the ancestors need help like anyone else, whereas the Buddha can take care of himself.

But the tablet itself is impermanent. After either 33 or 50 years (depending on the region of Japan) the tablet is destroyed and the spirit becomes a god. The spirit is sometimes transferred to the household god in a noteworthy ritual in which the tablet is cast into a river and then a pebble is picked up from the river bed and placed on the household god's altar. This collection of pebbles represents the spirits merged into the guardian god of the household as a collectivity.

Thereafter, services are held for the collective dead, without identifying them singly, both with daily offerings of flowers and on seasonal occasions, in particular: New Year's on January first through third, Obon or the Festival of the Dead or of Lanterns on August 13–15, and the equinoxes in late March and September.

The Obon festival, when the ancestors come down from where they live to their villages, has been celebrated at least since the year 606 C.E. One dedicates temples and recites Buddhist verses and makes offering to ancestors. One category of ancestor is especially grateful for these offerings: ancestors who committed misdeeds in past lives may end up on the plane of existence called *gaki-do,* or Plane of the Hungry Ghosts. They suffer from hunger and thirst, and they alone out of all one's ancestors may benefit from offerings one makes to a holy or virtuous person.

But Obon is the time to make offerings to the ancestors generally. The ritual grave near the house is cleared and a path is swept leading back to the house. The household altar is cleaned and a dance (today in decline) is held in the village. People return to their ancestral villages to participate in the festival and end the ritual by taking lanterns and small boats to the graveyard or to a mountain or river to see the spirits off on their return to their abode. Japanese overseas also celebrate Obon. In St. Louis, where I live, it is the time for a Japanese festival at the Botanical Gardens, with the lighting of lanterns around the lake in the Japanese garden.

The long transition stage to Japanese death rituals supports the idea of a gradual melding of the individual into the collectivity and thus also supports the general cultural importance of the collectivity.

Regenerating Life from Death

Death rituals also frequently feature images of journeys to new worlds, enactments of rebirth, or the disinterment and reburial of bones (Bloch and Parry 1982).

Images of journeys are sometimes the material focus of religious innovations. As Sumatran Toba Batak people left their ancestral homeland for big cities, they began to use their new wealth to build elaborate family tombs back home. These tombs were carved in the shapes of boats and other images of soul journeys, and the tombs kept alive a sense of attachment to the homeland and a promise of rejoining the family for the journey to the afterworld. In Ghana, a man named Connie Kway began to carve elaborate, painted coffins in the shapes of boats or birds during the 1970s. These coffins sold for the equivalent of a year's average wage and were snatched up by the rich. They were an innovation; Ghanians had not used fancy coffins before, but because they dramatized the comforting and spirit-raising belief that the dead were going to a resting place where loved ones would see them again, they quickly became popular and spawned imitators. (In 1996 a museum tour of the coffins swept the United States, where they were competed for as treasured folk art objects.)

Death is often linked to life and fertility in the transition stages. This linking may take different forms. Bloch and Parry (1982, 7) argue that death rituals tend to revitalize "that resource which is *culturally conceived* to be most essential to the reproduction of the social order." The resource may be the land, or human fertility, or some combination of the two. Thus in four African hunter-gatherer societies compared by James Woodburn (1982), social reproduction was thought to depend most importantly on control over nature, and the ritual response to death was to reawaken the productivity of nature.

For the Merina of Madagascar, studied by Maurice Bloch (1982), reproducing the society requires that members of a descent group have their bones buried together in ancestral tombs. Because these related individuals do not live in the same place, they are initially buried where they die. Their bones later are dug up and moved to the ancestral tomb. The initial burial is attended by sadness and mourning, but the subsequent "regrouping" of the body with the ancestors is full of joy and dancing. During this dancing, women repeatedly throw the brittle bones to the ground, smashing them to bits. These actions merge the physical remains of the individual with the ancestral groups as a whole. The ritual also employs the symbolism of birth, entering into and emerging from the tomb as if it were a womb.

Asmat Headhunting and Birth through Death

Consider in more detail the case of the Asmat, a society of about 50,000 people living in the swampy plains of southwest Irian Jaya, the name for the western half of the island of New Guinea that in 1963 became part of Indonesia. The Asmat are best known in the West for the tall *bis* poles, made out of sago palm, examples of which are to be found in many Western museums (Kuruwaip 1974).

The Asmat (Sudarman 1984) call themselves the "tree people." Their environment is wood; stone or metal for tools must be acquired from elsewhere. Canoes, poles, housing are all from wood. Their staple, sago, is also wood. Every four or five days, the men of a clan will spend an entire day finding a large (45-foot-high) sago palm tree in the forest, cutting it down, removing the pith, and then pounding, washing, drying, and roasting the pith into large cakes of sago to be pounded into sago flour. Sago is regarded as a human being. The sago palm resembles a woman: life comes from within it, and the white, milky sago resembles breast milk. When an Asmat man carves a sago palm into a pole he considers his work as very like what he does to help produce a baby. Asmat hold that the father does not cause conception, but molds the child through frequent inter-course into the shape he or she eventually has at birth (Gerbrands 1967).

Much of the Asmat men's time used to be spent in warfare between clans, fueled partly by their practices and beliefs surrounding death. Asmat believe that deaths are due to malevolent actions by others, that people in other clans kill your own relatives either in an observable way (in a raid, for example) or through sorcery. The spirits of the dead demand retribution or revenge for their deaths (Zegwaard 1959). Asmat once took revenge for a death by taking a head in a raid on another clan, thus continuing the cycle of death and retribution. The relative taking the head would have carved for him a long, 15- to 20-foot bis pole. The clan would then drum and dance to entice the spirit into the pole. The relative would dedicate the pole to the deceased, and cry out (for example): "Oh mother, I have killed a man from [place name]." Then the spirit of the dead person, which would have remained in the village until avenged, would begin its journey out of the village and toward a island somewhere off the western coast, later to be reborn as a new human (Kuruwaip 1974).

Today, headhunting is prohibited, and Asmat seem to have abandoned the practice. But they continue to carve images of deceased relatives onto the long poles, to drum the spirit into the pole, and to erect the pole and publicly dedicate it, calling out for the spirit to leave the village.

Through their myths, the Asmat believe the acts of producing sago from palms, carving wood poles, and cutting heads to be situating their lives in the universe. Taking a head reenacts a sacrifice made at the beginning of time. In a widely told story, a being who was both god and man killed his brother and cut off his head, immediately causing

Drawing of Asmat bis
pole, Irian Jaya.

the universe to come into existence, and all of culture with it. (In some versions of this story, the god–man cut off the head of a crocodile in order to create non-Asmat people.) Taking a head thus caused life to emerge (Zegwaard 1959).

In practice, the skulls of the dead help to bring about a new birth. In past times the skull used would have come from a headhunting expedition, and thus the same skull would accomplish two important functions: it would allow the spirit to leave the world, and it would bring a new person into it. Today the skull would come from a relative. A young male being initiated into manhood sits for days in the men's house, contemplating a skull between his legs, pressed against his genitals. Then he is carried out toward the setting sun in a canoe, following the journey made by the spirits of the dead. When the canoe has traveled far enough from shore he lies in the bottom of the canoe in imitation of someone who has just died. Then he is thrown into the water, still holding the skull, to resurface as a newly born initiated man.

Cutting the sago is also likened to taking a human head and releasing energy. The palm is thought to have the same spirit as a human. Men attack the palm, throwing spears at it, and butcher the starch. Asmat also draw on these ideas to project human actions onto the animal world. They see an analogy to headhunting in the behavior of the praying mantis. The insect is seen as human in its movements (think of how its stance gave rise to its English name), and the female bites off the head of the male during mating.

Not only is the mantis's cannibalism like taking a head, but it reminds the Asmat observer of the mock, or part-mock aggression enacted by women toward men in everyday life. For when the Asmat men return along the river with the sago palm, women carry out an attack on the canoes from the village shore. The attack is ostensibly to keep malevolent spirits from entering the village along with the palm, but in practice women throw their spears hard and accurately and, not uncommonly, men are injured.

Drumming the spirit of the dead into the *bis* pole also replicates a mythic event. The very first man on earth was called Fumeripits. He drowned in the sea but he was brought back to life by War, the name of the white-tailed eagle, who pressed smoldering bits of wood against his body. Then Fumeripits built a large men's house and carved images of men and women. He began to drum, and they came to life, dancing. The carvers and drummers of today cannot create life, but they can attract spirits through their carving and drumming, thereby reenacting Fumeripits' deed on the spiritual level.

In everyday life, too, Asmat experience the link between heads and the continuity of life. All adults sleep on skulls, usually skulls of close relatives, and report feeling a continued tie to the deceased through this skull-sleeping. Some men will (or did) sleep on the skull of a powerful enemy, claiming that they absorb some of the deceased's power at night. Carving the pole and cutting heads thus not only frees the spirit from the village (and the village from the spirit) but also signifies to the living that the dead will be reborn and life will continue. The ritual also gives the bereaved a concrete way to care for the spirits of their relatives. And since they practice it together as a social group, a single individual's death strengthens the power of their origin myths.

The ritual as it once was carried out allowed the individual to complete a logical and emotional circle: a death, avenged by taking a head, was completed when the skull of the victim was used to release the spirit from the village and then to cause a rebirth. But now the circuit has been shorted at the point of headhunting. The Dutch (when they controlled the territory) had already prohibited headhunting throughout the region, but they had little direct sway over the Asmat. The Indonesian government has been much more direct in its plans to change Asmat lives and religions: it encourages missionaries to promote the adoption of proper religion, with a book, a creed, but no violence. The missionaries offer salvation through communion (which might be interpreted by Asmat as a different kind of cannibalism) and rebirth through baptism (a different path to rebirth through immersion in water).

Secondary Burial

The "regrouping" of bones practiced by the Merina (discussed earlier) is one example of a widespread practice of secondary burial, or the removal and reburial of a corpse. This practice is intended to provide material signs of the transition from life to an afterlife by permitting people to examine the bones of the dead after decomposition has set in. Secondary burial is relatively rare, but it is found in culturally unrelated areas throughout the world—Greece, Africa, Siberia, Indonesia, the Americas, and in early Jewish practice. Medieval Christian burial in Europe often included the display of bones in an ossuary.

Peter Metcalf (1982) provides a detailed description of the practice from the Berawan society in Borneo. In this society, a body is stored in a large jar right after death. After several days the bones are cleaned of flesh and stored in the longhouse or on a platform outside. Months or years later (Metcalf records a range of eight months to five years) the bones of some of the dead, but not others, are removed and placed in a permanent death monument. For the Berawan, the display of bones stands for the passage of the spirit of the dead outside the community. It confirms that the spirit has reached the land of the dead.

Robert Hertz (1960) wrote a comparative essay on the practice in 1907. Hertz used material from Borneo and Indonesia but also made reference to similar practices elsewhere. Based on his reading of available ethnography, Hertz argued that people take the natural fact of bodily decomposition as the basis for thinking about the process of death, the transition from the loss of soul to the passage to another place. Just as the body decomposes, so the spirit gradually leaves the body, transformed to a new state in which the spirit is definitively separated from the body.

The process of decomposition, then, defines three moments in the death process, each of which serves as a sign of the unobservable process through which the spirit leaves the body and the community. At the moment of death the spirit has left the body. During decomposition the spirit is uncertain as to its final home, and during this period it may haunt the living and roam the community. But when the bones are seen to be clean, then the spirit has left for its new home.

Hertz noted that people have a horror of the corpse throughout the world, but that it is not a physical repugnance. The same people fear the corpse but wash it, sit with it, even drink the wash water. The fear is for two reasons. First, the death tears a hole in the community, and the social fabric must be mended and order restored. The more important the person, the more ritual work needs to be done, so only some bones are subjected to secondary burial. Second, the soul remains near the corpse, and until it has left the community it will remain to haunt the living. The rites of secondary burial enact the finality of the passage out of the community.

This analysis explains why Berawan people evinced horror at the practice of em- balming when Metcalf described it to them. Embalming for purposes of viewing the body in a "lifelike" state is seen by Berawan as delaying the process of decay and thereby retarding the successful separation of the soul from the community.

Similar concerns are found in the official policy on burial of the Greek Orthodox Church. Bodies must not, commands the church, be buried in airtight caskets lest the natural, and God-ordained, process of decomposition be halted. In rural Greece today, relatives exhume the bones of the deceased five years after the body is buried, and remove the bones to the village ossuary (Danforth 1982). If the bones are clean and white, relatives are assured that the soul has passed to heaven. If decomposition has not been completed, villagers wait an additional two years and then repeat the process. Meanwhile they say prayers for the forgiveness of the person's sins; it is these sins that have retarded the soul's passage and the bodily decomposition.

In these and other cases people feel ambivalent about the passage of the soul from the community. People may wish loved ones to remain near them, but they also wish for closure in the process of dying and mourning. Death rituals demonstrate to the living that the dead have left the community, taking danger with them, but also that they remain close by and that they can be called on to help the living. The soul of a Berawan person remains ready to aid the living in times of illness or other need. Asmat send the spirits of the dead away from the community to an island off the coast, but people continue to sleep with the skulls of deceased loved ones and sense that the person continues to remain with them. For people in many societies, death involves desires for both finality and remembrance; death rituals give those desires a material form.

Debates about Death; Debates about Life

Death, then, is fraught with ambivalence—is it to be grieved or accepted? Does the individual remain individual or merge with the group? Can the living aid the dead, and how?

This ambivalence, cognitive and emotional, can become the basis for major debates within religious traditions. As an example, let me reintroduce the Gayo people of Sumatra, Indonesia, to whom I refer from time to time throughout this book. I have spent about six years working with the Gayo since 1978, and, as do other anthropologists for the places in which they work, I tend to ground my comparative understanding of the world in my relatively deep knowledge of their society (Bowen 1991, 1993).

The 200,000 Gayo people living in the highlands of Sumatra have been Muslims for several centuries. Under Dutch rule after 1904, and under Japanese occupation during 1942–1945, they became part of independent Indonesia in 1945. Most Gayo have always lived in small villages, scattered over the steep, mountainous terrain. They have been dependent on springs, rivers, or rain to irrigate rice and rivers. Villagers' relations to spirits have always been linked to their practical needs. Ancestral spirits protect crops and aid in hunting; they and various other spirits heal the sick; angels, prophets, and God are called on for help in all endeavors.

Under colonial rule, some Gayo moved into the fast-growing town of Takèngën, which became the center for new commercial enterprises, schooling, and the colonial civil service. These Gayo came into contact with traders and teachers from elsewhere in the Dutch East Indies. Some of these teachers were part of a worldwide movement for the reform of Islamic practices, a movement that stressed returning to scripture and sloughing off un-Islamic superstitions and rituals. These reformers urged other Gayo to avoid all practices that were not specifically prescribed by God. Other scholars began to defend some older village practices, but not all, on grounds that they were in accord with Qur'ân and hadith, reports of statements by the prophet Muhammad.

The debates between reformers and traditionalists continue today. Some of the debates are about death rituals. For most Gayo women and men, death signals the

Gayo man asks for blessings and aid in rice cultivation from the ancestral spirit of the village founder, Isak, Sumatra. (COURTESY OF J. BOWEN.)

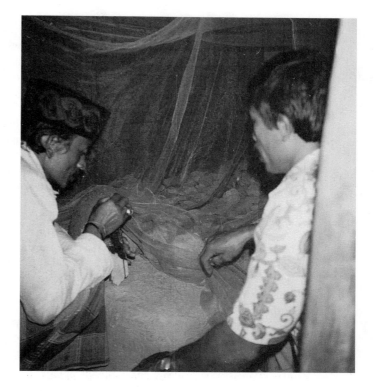

beginning of a series of rituals designed to benefit the deceased—a long transition stage between death and the final disposition of the spirit. Gayo consider the first seven days after death to be the period of most intense death work. The spirit remains near the body. Emotions must be held in check. Debts must be paid off. The bereaved do not publicly mourn; they are engaged in a feverish pace of work, cooking, hosting visiting relatives, and staging rituals. At the end of seven days, an emotional release takes place—only then did I see friends and neighbors cry and mourn their loss.

Some Gayo key this seven-day period to the decomposition of the body in the grave, just as Hertz predicted, without the need to exhume it to check. (They once may have dug up the body, but doing so is contrary to Islamic teachings.) The decomposition and the final release of the soul from the body take place together.

For the first 44 days after death, the spirit continues to wander in the village before departing for "somewhere in the sky," as Gayo say. But the spirit is also near the grave of the deceased. If, for example, you walk by a close relative's grave and you have not recently made an offering to the spirit and fail now to address it, it may attract your attention by giving you a stomachache—"just its way of saying, 'don't ignore me,'" say my Gayo friends. People will hold small meals near the graves of some ancestors, burn incense, and ask for assistance in curing a child's illness, ensuring a good crop, or helping a newly married daughter to conceive.

Teaching the Soul

All these practices imply a continued relationship with the deceased. But more immediate to the death are the rituals right after death that center on helping the soul of the deceased withstand the "torment of the grave." Two practices are notable: the catechism read to the deceased at the grave and the chanting sessions held on successive evenings after the death.

The catechism or "teaching" (*talqîn*) is a religious reminder that is read to the deceased. At the graveside, just after burial, the village religious official kneels in the dirt, grasps a stick inserted near the head of the grave, and reads from a printed, Arabic-language text. He reminds the deceased of the main tenets of Islam. Isak people hold that God returns the soul (required for consciousness and life) of the dead person to the body at the moment the religious official reaches the point in the reading where he utters a phrase taken from the prophet Muhammad: "Every soul will experience death."

The spirit of the deceased, an entity distinct from the soul, has remained near the body since the moment of death and at this moment reunites with the soul to revive the person. He or she feels the edge of the burial cloth, perceives that it has been ripped, not hemmed, and thus realizes that he or she is dead. The deceased then listens to the catechism. After the recitation is complete the soul leaves the body, now for the last time, and the spirit alone remains in the vicinity.

One text describes why the reading is important, thus justifying itself to the listeners, alive and dead:

Hey [Name]! You now have left the world and all its attractions and are entering the next world. Do not forget the agreements that separate this world from the next. Now bear witness that there is no deity but God and that Muhammad is his Messenger. Soon two angels will come, Mungkar and Nakir. Know that these two angels also are creations of God, and do not fear them. If they ask you questions, answer them in a clear voice. The questions will be:

1. *Who is your God? Answer: My God is Allah.*
2. *Who is your prophet? Answer: My prophet is Muhammad, peace be upon him.*
3. *What is your book? Answer: My book is the Qur'ân.*
4. *What is your kiblat? Answer: My kiblat is the Kaba (in Mecca).*
5. *Who are your people? Answer: All Muslim men and women.*
    Answer these questions with a clear voice.

The content of the teaching is basic: your God is Allah, your book is the Qur'ân, and so forth. No one ever claims that the dead would not know these things—indeed, the simplicity of the reminders led one close friend, not sympathetic to this practice, to joke that he would just make sure that he kept a small notebook in his back pocket when he died, so that he could whip it out after death and remind himself of these religious facts. But the reading also reminds the living of the basics of their religion and, their labors on the corpse complete, directs their thoughts and energies to the spiritual destiny of their departed neighbor.

These reminders are of immense and immediate practical importance to the deceased, because shortly thereafter two angels come to pose questions, and if the deceased fails to respond correctly, they beat him or her senseless, so to speak, with the large wooden sticks they carry. For those who recite this text or have it recited, the practice is a moral duty. The reciting eases the torment that the deceased will experience by priming him for his interrogation. The torment is very real, and if we could only hear, I was told, we would know that some souls scream in agony.

Reformers within and from outside the villages attack this practice (which is known throughout the Muslim world) as fundamentally misguided. In popular discussions they criticize it from a commonsense perspective, stating flatly that the practice is absurd. They ask: how can the dead hear? They also quote from the Qur'ân (Chapter 27, verse 80): "Thou shalt not make the dead to hear." Some also refer to newspaper articles written in the 1930s and collected in a much-read book, in which the author labeled the practice of reading to the dead as "the work of fools." "Let corpses teach corpses," he mocked; "let them open schools for corpses." As one local teacher complained of villagers: "Can a stone hear? Of course not. In what book did they read that?" Reformers also argue that there is no reliable evidence (meaning no hadith) that the Prophet Muhammad ever carried out such a reminder, and, following their basic principle, nothing that Muhammad did not himself do in worship should be done by any Muslim.

These disdainful remarks are not well received by villagers, of course, who resent what they see as the cold attitude of those who would not have the catechism read. One villager said about a local reformist teacher that "for him a dead person is just an animal or a piece of wood, to be tossed away. But in fact his soul returns for a bit; that is why we must read the text." And when a reform-minded person enters a graveyard, they continue, does he not say "Hello, spirits of the grave?"

Furthermore, continue these traditionalist scholars, there are several reliable hadith that suggest Muhammad did act on the assumption that the living and the dead could communicate to each other. In one, Muhammad is reported to have passed by a graveyard in Medina, stopped, and placed a leaf over a grave. He then began to pray over the grave. When he had finished, his companion, Abu Bakar, asked him why he had done it. Muhammad replied that he had heard the person in the grave screaming in pain, so he asked God to please forgive the person's sins. Abu Bakar then asked him if the dead person had heard Muhammad. Muhammad replied that he heard better than would persons living on the earth.

Chanting for the Sake of the Spirit

The second practice under debate in Gayo society is a series of night-long chanting sessions held one, three, seven, and 44 nights after the death. These sessions (which, like the talqîn, are found in many Muslim societies), are called "sammadiyah" or "tahlil." At each such session, many men and women sit in the house of the deceased and chant many times some short Qur'ânic verses and some prayers. For most of those chanting, the meaning of the event is that each repetition chanted by each Muslim and conveyed through the evening's prayer leader all add up to a certain quantum of merit, and that

God, pleased by this merit, looks with favor on the spirit of the deceased to a degree corresponding to the quantum. People times repetitions equals respite from torment.

Food is served throughout the evening, and, say some, the deceased's spirit enjoys the essence of the food. Some villagers continue to set out food for the deceased on certain days of the year and may dedicate a sacrificial goat or buffalo to an ancestor on the Muslim holiday called the Feast of Sacrifice ('îd al-adhâ) held during the month of pilgrimage.

These evenings can be extremely moving for the close relatives of the deceased. Aman Bani, the religious official of one Gayo village, remembered the first evenings after his father's death in 1982. His friends and neighbors gathered in his house to chant together, directing the merit generated by the chanting toward his father's spirit. Aman Bani led the chants and could feel his father enter the room to receive the merit. He had difficulty forcing the words out of his chest, so heavily did the presence of his father weigh upon him. By concentrating his imagination he could see his father's spirit, his face. His vision told him that the chants were reaching their destination, that his father's life in the grave would be eased.

These actions of aid for the deceased—the catechism, the chanting, and ongoing attention to the departed spirit—are not only heartfelt and morally immediate but are also part of an ongoing reciprocity of aid between the living and the dead. Ancestors can and often do help their descendants and others. People ask the spirits of powerful healers for assistance in expelling illness from their families. The founding ancestors of communities are able to protect the rice crop from the onslaughts of rats, pigs, birds, and insects. Furthermore, not only do people talk to the dead, but they also cajole rice into flowering, ask the spirit of the hunt to furnish game, and heal the sick with the help of diverse spirits.

Reformers have attacked the chanting sessions as well as the catechisms. For them, these sessions are wrong for three reasons. First, they never were performed by the prophet Muhammad, and in religious matters we may only do what he did. Second, coming to the house of the bereaved to eat and drink at their expense while chanting is to "eat the food of orphans," as some reformers like to put it when in a confrontational mood.

The third objection is the one reformers emphasize, that chanting in order to send merit for the dead weakens the moral accountability of the individual to God. "You cannot redeem the sins of others," said one reformist teacher, "only earn merit for what you do in your own lifetime." If a quick catechism could substitute for religious study while alive, and chanting could compensate for the failure to observe God's commandments, then it no longer would be true that one is judged according to his or her deeds. "It would be easy, wouldn't it," remarked one teacher, "to just wait and let our children substitute prayer for our own deeds during life."

In the 1940s these reformers began to write religious poetry as the basis for spreading their message to rural areas. One long poem ends with a quote from the Qur'ân:

> If you die and your relatives give alms,
>   the merit will not reach you.
> Did you not hear the words of God:
>   "A person shall have only as he/she has labored"?

Through poetry, sermons, and public debates, reformers call on the authority of the Qur'ân and hadith to make a theological argument. But alongside persuasion on the theological level are efforts to transform popular ideas of moral duty and the complex of emotions surrounding death. The reformers seek to shift people's moral and emotional focus from the deceased (and the rituals designed to help the deceased) to the bereaved, the survivors. They do this by, first, stressing the absolute, final character of death and the consequent impossibility of continued talk and exchanges with the dead person. Then they emphasize the plight of the bereaved rather than the need of the deceased for help.

At a 1989 wedding the poet Muhammad Yassin sang a poem about death in which he urges mourners to refrain from adding to the grief of the family after returning from the gravesite:

Don't make work for them when you've returned to their house,
  making it hard on the bereaved.

Here "make work for them" refers to the practice of setting out food and drink for all those who pay a visit to the bereaved and for those who attend the nighttime chanting sessions. Reformers tell stories about families ruined under the pressure to put on feasts. In effect, they say, you are "eating the estate of the orphans" when you drink as much as a glass of coffee at their house. Reformers in fact often exhibit a concern for orphans, running a private orphanage in town and holding meals for orphans on major feast days.

The response of traditionalist scholars here as for the catechism is to point out that in general we do help the deceased. After all, they say, we do recite prayers for their welfare at the close of worship (and reformers also recite such prayers), so why not also help them in this way?

Villagers respond in a more direct way. At a chanting session I attended in 1989 one older man gave a speech midway through the evening, and he said the following:

As long as there are people left on the earth, they have to help the dead. If not why would we repeat the Prophet's statement that when we die we leave behind "children who do pious works"? What good is such a child? A child does pious works by helping his parents after their death. A sibling does the same when he also helps say prayers. We just recited prayers for the deceased. But all our fellow Muslims in Istanbul, Damascus, Syria, Baghdad, Egypt, Jerusalem, America, and Babylon: all their prayers reach us, and all ours, them. You do not have to be close by. Islam requires everyone to help each other. As long as there is Islam everyone is required to help those who are dead.

This vision of religious community as a network of people, all helping each other through prayer, was compelling to many present.

On the scholarly plane, the debate comes down to two ways of thinking about what it means to decide rationally how to be a properly practicing Muslim. The reformers argue a "strict letter of the law" position for matters of worship, that if and only if Muhammad told his followers to do such and such should we do it. The traditionalist scholars argue a "principle behind the law" position, that once we determine the basic principles on which God, through Muhammad, based the religion, then we can use our reason to figure out whether a particular practice is consistent with those principles. Much as with debates about the U.S. Constitution—Do we argue from today's meaning of its words? Or from the general intention of the founders?—these debates about Islamic ritual cannot easily be resolved because they involve very different ways of thinking through the problems.

On the social and psychological plane, the difference between the two religious attitudes is linked to two different sets of everyday concerns. Villagers who continue to value communication with ancestors rely on them for aid in everyday life. Townspeople have other concerns. Their everyday lives and religious conversations include people from other parts of Indonesia, for whom village practices seem terribly backward. The identity of townspeople as modern, rational, learned Muslims is at stake. The debates are about interpretation, social life, and one's very identity.

Catholic Masses for the Dead

The debates in Gayo villages in the 1990s parallel those that took place in fifteenth- and sixteenth-century Europe about masses said for the dead. Late medieval Christianity has been described as "a cult of the living in the service of the dead," because everyone accepted that the friends and relatives of the deceased were under a moral obligation to move them along through purgatory into paradise and that they could do so by having masses said on their behalf. (A few people inserted the names of living enemies into their prayers, hoping that God would soon move them into purgatory as well!)

And yet scripture taught that everyone must be judged according to his or her own works (Bossy 1983). Some church teachers judged that the living and the dead were like a partnership in which one finds both active partners sailing around the world, and "sleeping partners" quietly taking their share of the profits.

Others argued that, no, the individual stood in total separation from others before God. For John Calvin and Martin Luther, leaders of the Protestant Reformation, the lonely dependence of the individual on God was absolute. Taking the story of Job as a key text, these reformers argued that one could not influence God or judge God. After all, they said, He has no need of us, only us of Him. This attitude became the doctrine of predestination, that God has predestined each individual for Election to heaven or condemnation to hell, and that we can neither know of His decision or affect it. (See Chapter 11 for a discussion.)

Debates about death are often debates about the living, about individual responsibility, the nature of the collectivity vis-à-vis the individual, and the sources of life and fertility. Death rituals are in part translations of these ideas into practice, but they also exert their own weight on emotions and thoughts. Transition stages, in particular, structure the temporality of dying: they shorten or lengthen the period during which the living can continue to communicate with or give benefit to the deceased. They provide objects and texts to ease the burden of loss and prepare the survivors for reentry into normal social life. They also extend the reach and knowledge of the living beyond the empirical world, and in this respect join with other elements of religions, such as magic, healing, and forms of explanation.

Theory in Anthropology: Émile Durkheim and Society as Religion's Source

To what extent do religious ideas and practices grow out of the nature of social life? In the previous chapters, I have suggested there were causal, historical relationships between the form of society and the form of religious representations. For example, in Japan deities follow the lines of social organization: there are deities that protect the household, the village, and the nation.

The sociologist Émile Durkheim (1858–1917) saw the birth of religion in the ideas and emotions generated out of collective social action. "Religious representations are collective representations that express collective realities," he wrote (1995, 9). Durkheim's general idea was not entirely original. Aristotle, after all, had declared that "men create the gods after their own image." More recently, the French historian Fustel de Coulanges (1830–1889) and the Scottish scholar of Semitic societies W. Robertson-Smith (1846–1904) had linked social organization to religious ideas in ancient societies. Robertson-Smith argued that the earliest societies had been totemic, that is, they had been organized into clans, each of which had a special relationship to a species of animal—"my clan is a wolf." Sacrificing this animal was a way to communicate and commune with the deities, and at the same time it was a means to strengthen the emotional bonds among clan members.

Durkheim drew from these earlier writers to argue that knowledge in general, and religious knowledge in particular, has a social foundation. His argument was philosophical, against Kant's idea that humans had innate categories of the understanding. But it was also social and moral, and grew out of the concerns of the day (Lukes 1973). Durkheim wrote during great social and moral turmoil in France, when older certainties about God and Church had been razed from public and legal life by the Revolution, but no alternative moral certainties had yet replaced them. The country appeared to be polarized between urban agnostics and rural Catholics. Battles were especially sharp over the future of the school system: should it be secular or Catholic, and if secular, what would be its moral content? No wonder that in his first articles, Durkheim was deeply sensitive to the problem of social cohesion in contemporary society: "A society whose members are not bound to one another by some solid and durable link," he wrote in 1886, "would resemble a loose pile of dust which could at any time be dispersed by the slightest wind to the four corners of the world" (quoted in Alexander 1982, 82). But what are these bonds? And how do they unite people in societies that have not undergone the sort of schisms experienced by France?

As one would expect, given the evolutionary way of thinking in vogue at the time, Durkheim sought his answer in a study of *The Elementary Forms of the Religious Life,* the title of his 1912 book. The book posits an early type of social consciousness in those societies where everyone is for all important purposes alike: everyone has the same status, duties, and roles. In such societies people's feelings are also alike and thus are mutually reinforcing whenever people gather together. Moral sentiments, religious beliefs, and other cultural ideas are all very strong, as are law, religion, and social norms.

Durkheim postulated that religious beliefs and sentiments must correspond to something real; they could not be purely illusory or mistaken, as Tylor and Frazer had concluded. They clearly were false if taken at face value. The problem then was to go beneath the symbol to the reality it represents and that gives it its true meaning. First, however, Durkheim argued that we must understand precisely what is the religion we seek to explain. Rather than defining religion as the "belief in spirits," as did Tylor and Frazer, Durkheim viewed it as involving a fundamental division of the world into "sacred versus profane things." Religion is thus collective, concerning how the members of a particular society divide up the world, rather than individual, what a person believes. But *how* the world is divided into sacred and profane varies greatly from one society to the next.

Durkheim accepted Robertson-Smith's argument that totemism was the earliest basis for social organization and that it was the wellspring of religion. He turned to the religions of Australian aborigines to prove his thesis. In these societies, specific groups perform rituals at sacred sites that are associated either with ancestral spirits or with mythical beings that lived during the ancient "dream time" that came before the time we know. Each group also has objects made of wood or stone engraved with symbols of these ancestors or mythical beings, and these *churinga* objects themselves have sacred powers.

Each such social group also has a special ritual relationship toward certain species, such as kangaroo, or certain natural phenomena, such as rain or wind. Members of the group may have special rules regulating their activities with respect to these species, the group's *totem,* and the group can carry out rituals that increase the species' numbers. These rituals sometimes involve eating an item of the species, and Durkheim thought that this practice confirmed the theory that sacrifice and communal eating were the earliest basic forms of religious ritual.

Durkheim argued that the general idea of spiritual force that underlay totemism emerged before ideas about spirits or souls, and he cited related ideas from other societies, such as the notion of impersonal force or *mana* in Melanesia. (He could have cited the Chinese idea of life force, or *chi,* I mentioned earlier.) This same force, at later stages of development, gives rise to ideas of souls, ancestral spirits, and God, stated Durkheim.

Durkheim set out his argument on two different levels. First, he explained the variety of religious ideas by asserting that particular features of societies give rise to particular features of their cultures and religions. Religion thus represents society. So, there are "societies in Australia and North America where space is conceived in the form of an immense circle, because the camp has a circular form." The early division of society into two halves, or moieties, gave rise to the idea of the cosmos as dualistic. In societies such as the Australian aborigines, where people were organized into clans, people often postulated an animal, or sacred place, or force, as the totem of that clan. These totems were projections of a sense of belonging together in the clan onto a spiritual place. As the society grew and spread over a wider area, giving rise to a sense of a broad social group with shared interests that spilled over the boundaries of the clan, totemic representations synthesized into the idea of one or more gods, "the god being only a figurative expression of the society," noted Durkheim (1995, 227).

This level of argument presumes that there already is a general religious idea that can be shaped by society. So arguing at a second level, Durkheim tried to explain the emergence of general religious ideas and sentiments in the first place. People sense a moral force exterior to them, he argued. This idea is given social content in those moments when people come together in social assemblies—dances, meetings, festivals. These assemblies create a social effervescence out of which religious ideas are confirmed and given stronger emotional meaning. A qualitative change takes place, and people begin to feel themselves transported into an altered state.

Religion serves the function of strengthening social solidarity by communicating specific ideas and sentiments and by regulating and strengthening social relationships. A totem, for instance, reminds you what kind of person you are (a member of a certain clan) and thereby regulates relations among individuals. It also gives you a feeling of strength. Speaking of one Australian society, Durkheim wrote: "The Arunta who has properly rubbed himself with his churinga feels stronger; he is stronger" (1995, 229).

This functional perspective on religion gave Durkheim a way of discussing the place of religion in modern society. Religion is no longer a satisfactory *cognitive* solution to the "problem of meaning," in which science is now the master. But religion continues to be *symbolically* important: cult and faith are essential to any society's social solidarity, including our own.

Durkheim emphasized the cognitive, emotional, and social aspects of religious ideas and practices. His *Elementary Forms* focuses on the social origins of religion via a theory of collective emotions, but there, and in other writings, Durkheim also emphasizes the logical nature of religious classifications. In *Primitive Classification* (1963), Durkheim and his nephew Marcel Mauss (1872–1950) compared the symbolic classifications found in Australian, native North American, and Chinese societies. The Zuni Pueblo people of the U.S. Southwest, for example, assign to each of the cardinal directions (plus center, and the zenith and nadir of the sun's apparent motion) a color, a season, and a kind of weather, together with a general force such as creation or destruction, a specific group, and an animal. Durkheim and Mauss claimed that members of these societies have created totalizing religious systems; these systems unite the social, natural, and cosmological realms. Their comparison of logical similarities across these societies inspired later anthropologists to more detailed studies of symbolic classification.

Durkheim's legacy in the field of religious studies was twofold. First, he connected the religious to the social, leading later anthropologists to look for social origins or functions of specific religious practices and ideas. This strain of his legacy was the foundation for British social anthropology, from A.R. Radcliffe-Brown through Edmund Leach and Mary Douglas. For Mary Douglas, for example, the key to understanding food taboos, whether in the Hebrew Bible or in the societies of central Africa she studied in her fieldwork, is to look for the social functions such taboos may have served. She argued that, by separating the sacred from the profane, and then by restricting membership in the community to those who observed the rules, food taboos make group membership sacred (see Chapter 8).

Durkheim also emphasized the ways that participating in collective religious practices confirm faith, and this insight remains compelling. Consider how many European Catholics find visions of Mary to be central events cementing their faith, or perhaps their hope within their faith. In less spectacular ways, the good feelings of participating in something with friends and neighbors may also make the religion particularly "true." Especially important is the way in which public ritual generates religious commitment. A service, for example, in which many people worship together, can be a wonderfully compelling context, generating a sense of being together and being in the presence of something else. Such feelings, perhaps most startlingly displayed when Christian worshipers speak in tongues, lay behind Durkheim's claim that coming together as a social group gave rise to the earliest ideas of the supernatural. However, most of the time carrying out worship, consulting oracles, or avoiding tabooed foods are experienced as routine actions. It may indeed be that the routine nature of most of religions' demands, the integration of religion into everyday life, provides a social and psychological comfort.

Second, Durkheim connected the religious to the intellectual, continuing Tylor's emphasis. "The essential notions of scientific logic are of religious origin," he wrote in *Elementary Forms* (1995, 431). This statement has broadly echoed in cultural anthropology throughout the world, and most notably in the work of the French anthropologist Claude Lévi-Strauss. The creator of the structuralist approach to myth, marriage, and art, Lévi-Strauss approached the classificatory systems created as part of religions mainly as the product of intense, imaginative intellectual activity. Rather than seeing totems and totemic social organization as a primitive form of identification that then gave rise to higher forms of society and religion, Lévi-Strauss considered them, in his *Totemism* (1963a), as one among many ways of classifying the world in order to understand it. Particular plants or animals are chosen to be totems not because they have utility or excite awe in and of themselves, but because they provide a usable symbolic template through which to make distinctions in the natural, social, and cosmological worlds.

Profile

John Bowen
Studying Culture through Internal Debates

The Gayo have long maintained their differences of opinion about what happens after someone's death. I have found it very productive to begin investigation of a topic by looking at what people heatedly disagree about, on the assumption that the disagreements that are greatly important to them are matters worth studying.

My book on Gayo ideas and practices of Islam (Bowen, 1993) began with an extended account of an impromptu discussion that occurred one day between a tailor and his customer. I happened to be there to ask a question of the tailor about poetry. Their argument, sparked by a line of poetry, ran the gamut of Islamic ritual—from prayer to death ritual and sacrifice—and showed in clear form the major underlying issues dividing Gayo Muslims. One issue has to do with whether we should follow Islamic ritual traditions or start anew by reinterpreting scripture.

It is a basic issue about how humans relate to the past: when do we rely on our ancestors' wisdom; when do we take a fresh look?

What we think about this question often affects how we lead our lives, and is true of the Gayo as well. Reformers, those urging the fresh look at old texts, tend to be townspeople, who mingle with people of other ethnic groups, each with their own traditions. Traditionalists tend to be villagers, enmeshed in older practices, which they see as underwriting the fertility of their crops and the health of their children.

As I study other topics I continue to look for "internal debates," among members of a society as pathways for understanding. By listening to what people are arguing about, you learn what they share and accept as common ground for debate. And you learn which arguments are likely to be effective, because they can be made in that shared ground, and which are not.

For example, it does not get you very far in Indonesian circles to state that the Qur'ân is irrelevant to modern family law. Indonesian Muslims by and large agree that family law ought to be based on Islam. Their disagreements concern what interpretation to make of "Islam." Some people argue that in its general passages about men and women the Qur'ân favors gender equality. They see the unequal gender provisions of Islamic law, such as unequal inheritance shares for sons and daughters or different standards for divorce, as appropriate for Arabia generations ago but inappropriate for today. Others argue that God's commands in the Qur'ân are meant to be taken seriously, in all periods of history, and that we may not always know their rationale. Both sides agree that any changes in family law have to pass by way of the study of Islamic scripture. Outsiders who wish to shape the future of this discussion are best advised to enter into this internal debate on its own terms, that is, as a debate within religion, not one that places the religious and the secular in opposition.

Similarly, in contemporary France, Muslims and others are debating whether girls should be allowed to wear headscarves to school. Both sides agree that state schools are secular places where religious ideas should not be taught nor religious affiliations ostentatiously displayed. They also agree that the headcovering is seen by its wearer and by others as a sign of being a Muslim. The debate concerns the nature of "ostentation." Is the headscarf akin to the small crosses that Catholic girls are permitted to wear on necklaces, or is it more like a poster urging others to convert to Islam? ↩

For Further Consideration

To enrich your understanding of the Asmat rituals you might watch the film *The Asmat of New Guinea* in the *Faces of Culture* series (PBS 1983). A film about Sumba, Indonesia, *Horses of Life and Death* (University of California Extension Center 1991), shows a battle that marks the harvest and a funeral procession and, because it involves a ritual to carry a soul to the afterlife, can be usefully compared with the Asmat ritual.

You might reflect on funeral rituals you have attended. Which elements were most powerful? As a project, you might interview others, possibly family members, about how they responded to a funeral of a close relative or friend. You could discuss, for example, closed versus open caskets, burial versus cremation, or private versus large, public funerals.

5

Gender, Religion, and Ethnography

*O*pen any textbook on anthropology, and without difficulty you will find a section where the authors discuss the universality of gender differences. Since the early days of the discipline, anthropologists have written about ways in which male–female relationships are constructed in different societies. But in the 1970s a new feminist anthropology turned to studying gender and sexuality for answers to pressing political and cultural questions about equality and human rights. They asked big questions about gender and inequality. Michelle Rosaldo (1974), Sherry Ortner (1974), and others observed that wherever one finds inequalities in women's and men's access to resources, it is the men who control more than the women. Why, they asked, should there be such consistent inequality?

Rosaldo, Ortner, and their collaborators argued that the answer lay in a political inequality based on biological differences between women and men. Women, taken up with tasks of raising children, were identified more closely with natural processes than were men. Men, considered relatively more "cultural," were able to grab the public podium and control how social matters were represented and how resources were divided. Although this cross-cultural inequality could be (and, they wrote, ought to be) overcome, because humans are not the prisoners of history, it was nonetheless the general human-historical background against which all such overcoming must take place.

Although these authors were careful to note that they were speaking of the public cultural representations in a society and that they did not believe that only men ever exercised power (Ortner 1996, 139–146), their early formulations were followed by criticisms and reformulations, often made by the same authors. For example, Ortner and Whitehead (1981) pointed out that the earlier approaches had downplayed the wide variation in the ways people think about gender and sexuality. In some societies, people assume that biology strongly determines male–female differences. In other societies, however, biology is subordinated when people believe that practices of nurturing, maturing, or being initiated shape a human into a fully male or female person (see also MacCormack and Strathern 1980).

We can probably safely say that people in all cultures recognize differences between men and women, and, furthermore, that in elaborating their ideas about these differences they point to features of physiology and biology and to different roles in procreation. But that is about as far as we take the idea of physiology and gender, because there are widely differing ideas about gender and sexuality. More precisely, and interestingly, people are not unambiguously sorted into the categories "male" and "female" according to a single set of criteria in every society. The Hua in the highlands of Papua New Guinea, for example, classify people both in terms of their external genitalia and in terms of the amount of male or female substance each person is thought to possess. A person accumulates both kinds of substance through physical contact with others, so one's behavior determines one's substantive sexual identity. Some Hua are considered male in terms of genitalia but female in terms of their substance, or vice versa (Meigs 1990).

These feminist critiques were notably as critical of previous methods of ethnography as they were of commonly held notions of gender. Reinforced by renewed studies of well-known anthropological terrains, feminist anthropology explained why an ethnographer's perceptions may be shaped both by his or her prior assumptions and by the limits placed on the field of action in the society being studied.

Creating Gender through Ritual

*H*ow does religion come into this picture? Religious representations of people add a degree of cultural force to gender ideas, so that people regard them as universal, or cosmic, or God-commanded, or "natural." Each type of representation has a very different consequence, but they all make what appears to be culturally specific seem inevitable because it is ordered by deities, or because it is simply there, in nature. We can call these the *ideological* consequences of religion, when beliefs are linked in some way to the social and political system. Religious ideas also may be sources of strength for both women and men who wish to challenge how society is put together. Religious ritual also contributes to culturally specific ideas of gender because it casts male and female beings in particular cultural terms.

Producing Men and Women

Let us reconsider the Melanesian initiation rituals we studied in Chapter 3 (pages 35–36), this time as ritual means of producing mature and fertile men and women. These initiation rites are understood as creating sexuality; they highlight the distinctions between men and women (Keesing 1982). Men and women are seen as radically different, and the fluids and powers of one are dangerous to the other. Distinctions, separation, and hostility characterize ritual represenations of gender in many of these societies.

But men and women are also seen as creating biological parallels to each other. Semen and menstrual blood are polluting to the opposite sex in Melanesia (whereas female pollution of males through menstruation is a widespread belief). Female rites are centered on removing menstrual pollution to create fertility; male rites on separating the boys from women.

Male rites sometimes imitate those female rites that are closely linked to physiological events. Thus, men symbolically "give birth" to canoes in the Manam society of Papua New Guinea (Lutkehaus 1995). In some Melanesian societies men "menstruate" by spilling blood from their slashed penises. This act and other blood-lettings on one's own body strengthen sexual powers. In these cases the female body and processes of biological reproduction serve as symbols of social reproduction of men and women.

The parallels and the sexual segregation also support notions that homosexuality is required for male growth (Herdt 1981, 1982; Poole 1982). Men are required to "grow boys into men" in some societies. Older males bleed and multilitate younger males, reveal secret knowledge, and provide them semen to ingest, all in order to strengthen their bodies and their reproductive and aggressive capacities. In some cases men also use semen to fertilize the crops.

Some of these practices have parallels in Amazon societies. In both places one finds an emphasis on male mysteries and solidarity, on the use of such specific objects as sacred flutes and bull-roarers as emblems of male exclusivity and power over females, and threats of gang rape against women who view these male cult objects (Keesing 1982, 9). In central Africa, too, people speak of "growing a girl" and "growing a boy" into an adult through the initiation rituals (Turner 1967, 101–102).

Ritual, Fertility, and Culture

Drawing on these and similar examples, some feminist anthropologists proposed a general theory of gender differentiation (Rosaldo 1974; Chodorow 1974) that turns on the ways in which boys and girls are socialized. They argued that, across cultures, women and men differ in the degree to which they require active socialization into their respective gender roles. Girls are oriented toward the domestic sphere, these authors claimed, and thus can remain within it as they mature. Boys, who are oriented toward the public sphere, must distance and differentiate themselves actively from their mothers. Male initiation rituals bring about and represent this differentiation of males from females.

The Chodorow-Rosaldo theory does explain the role of negative emotions toward women that characterize teachings central to male initiation rituals in some New Guinea societies. Their theory of the *reproduction* of gender differences in the development of each individual human was later expanded by feminist scholars (Collier and Rosaldo 1981) into a theory of the *origins* of gender differences in the early history of humankind; this theory also explained the ideas about fertility underlying many representations of gender.

Contrary to the received wisdom of an earlier era, these scholars argue, in many societies of simpler technology it is men, not women, who are credited with promoting fertility (Whitehead 1987). Many societies based on hunting and either gathering or horticulture in Australia, the Americas, and Africa feature rituals celebrating men's powers to create life without women. Why should this be? Collier and Rosaldo (1981) argued that ideas of fertility are really ideas about social relationships, and that it is men's power to bring about marriages that these ideas celebrate. And why do men control marriage? Simply put, the story that explains their control starts with their deficiencies: men rely on marriage to eat. Because men do not have automatic access to the foods gathered or cultivated by women, they have a great interest in marriage. Because men must find a spouse, they must secure social ties to potential parents-in-law and brothers-in-law. Men also seek to have their general sociability recognized as both culturally and biologically important, claiming that fertility is the outcome of their social activities. Whitehead (1987) argues that in New Guinea, for instance, male control of intercommunity exchanges of goods and services allows men to claim fertility as their contribution to society and thus justify excluding women from fertility rituals.

This theory uses comparative evidence to suggest origins story similar, in its logical form, to the classic "social contract" theories proposed by John Locke and Thomas Hobbes to account for the origins of society. The feminist theory was proposed at a time when many anthropologists were looking for new origins stories to counter some of the sweeping, male-centered stories such as "man the hunter" (see Conkey 1991). But like all grand narratives the story can account for only some of the social reality it seeks to explain.

For example, women also undergo initiation, and sometimes the initiation process is intended to make them, not the men, more cultural and fertile. Janice Boddy (1989) describes the practice of infibulation found in many areas of the Middle East and northern Africa, when part or all of a girl's clitoris and labia minora is removed as part of a ritual designed to make her into a woman. Reasons given for these operations include the need to protect a family's honor by preserving its daughters' chastity and to curb women's sexual desire.

Boddy points out that the men and women in northern Sudan both subscribe to the general idea that men acquire more reason or rationality (*aqal*) than women do and that women have more emotions and desires (*nafs*). Men say further that women are less able than men to control their desires, viewing infibulation as part of a larger repertoire of social practices (including seclusion and veiling) designed to control those emotions.

Women take a different view. Although they, too, see women and men as differing in their natures, they make concerns about fertility the most important reason for practicing infibulation. Only by undergoing the practice, they say, can women marry and thus have legitimate children.

Women regard carrying out infibulation as continuing the work that God began by creating humans. Only after circumcision and infibulation do girls and boys become fully gendered. It is then that they are expected to behave as women and men, sleeping and eating separately, and no longer playing together (Boddy 1989, 58–59). In a constricted social world where cousins are one's prime marriage partners, turning kin into potential spouses begins early.

Women see themselves as having the central role in structuring the physical and social reproduction of their community by preparing women for marriage and for giving birth. They consider that their activities make them, and not the men, the guarantors of the cultural order. They see men as marginal to the society, mediators between the village world and the outside world. Women's and men's views of gender and culture start from the same position, then diverge widely. Because men dominate public forums of discussion, women's views are less often heard.

Gender Differentiation and Initiation

It has been demonstrated that initiation rituals represent gender relations and are often seen as producing them. And initiation ceremonies generally underscore ideas of gender found throughout the society or carried by a particular religious tradition in that society.

Hopi society is organized around matrilineal clans, and, as in most such societies, Hopi men and women play complementary roles and enjoy status that is more nearly equal than in many other North American societies. As we have seen (in Chapter 3), the initiations of 10-year-olds include both boys and girls. This is in striking contrast to the New Guinea and Amazon cultures, discussed previously, with strong male–female oppositions in social life and strong ritual symbols of gender distinctiveness such as menstrual blood and semen.

Within any one New Guinea society, rituals construct and represent the male and female orders in different fashion. In Manam Island society (Lutkehaus 1995), boys are initiated in cohorts but girls are initiated individually, attended by other girls. The boys become members of secret male societies, whereas the girls become members of women's networks. In classic Durkheimian fashion, the ritual form depicts the most salient form of sociability toward which each gender is headed. Male domination of women within the society is not only actively promoted during the initiation but is supported by the very existence of the men's houses. Women and children are excluded from the houses, and this "very fact of exclusivity serve[s] to create and perpetuate the politically dominant position of men" (Lutkehaus 1995, 200).

Strong themes of male–female difference also run through many African societies, where the major focus is on male initiation and where boys and girls are initiated by strictly segregated paths into different secret associations (La Fontaine 1985). Along the western African coast, for example (in much of Liberia, Sierra Leone, and the Ivory Coast), men are initiated into the Poro association, women into the Sande. Each association has internal grades along which an individual may advance. Most people do not pass beyond the first grade, but at higher grades men or women gain new secret knowledge. Those in the highest grades of the men's Poro wield considerable power in the society; their control of spirits legitimates their overruling the chief. The main theme of initiation and of the associations themselves is hierarchy: between occupants of different grades, and by the Poro over the rest of the society.

Each society has numerous lodges, so called after the example of Freemason lodges. Indeed, Poro members remark on the similarity of their society to that of the Masons. A Liberian man told one European ethnographer: "It is a pity you are not a Mason, for then I could tell you more. The Poro is just like Freemasonry" (quoted in La Fontaine 1985, 94). Creoles in Sierra Leone, ineligible to join a Poro society because they were not tribal members, indeed became attracted to Masonry because it provided them with the equivalent of the Poro. The association, structured around grades and secrets, had become a cultural type, to which Masonry was assimilated.

In Sierra Leone, initiation into the women's society takes girls and women away from villages and into the bush, where they stay for a week or two at a time, dancing, feasting, and acquiring new knowledge. But the girls also undergo infibulation. Although the operation is always painful and often dangerous, and it leads to health problems later in life, many women reject calls (echoed by Muslim preachers) for an end to the practice. They point to the value of the camaraderie they enjoy in the women's society. "This is a happy time for us," said one just-initiated 16-year-old girl, pointing to the freedom the women and girls feel among themselves (French 1997). The future of the initiation has become the focus for debate in the country about how religion and custom ought to be understood and changed.

Reanalyses through the Lens of Gender

A principal contribution of feminist anthropology has been to show how the gender of the ethnographer may limit in important ways what he or she learns during fieldwork. One well-known study by Annette Weiner (1976) demonstrated how earlier fieldwork carried out by men missed rituals and knowledge held only by women. When Weiner revisited the site of Bronislaw Malinowski's classic fieldwork, the island of Kiriwina in the Trobriand Islands, she found that women carried out a great number of rituals—most importantly, mortuary rituals—that formed part of the overall system of exchange. Though the ethnography of Trobriand exchange was perhaps Malinowski's greatest contribution to anthropology, Weiner was able to show that he ignored these forms of exchange.

Rituals of Reversal, Reversed

An adequate ethnography of ritual meanings takes account of women's and men's actions and understandings and may lead to the reexamination of older understandings of entire types of ritual. As we saw earlier, the anthropologist Max Gluckman argued that a large class of African rituals could be considered as rituals of reversal or rebellion in which women or powerless people held sway for a short, highly ritualized, period of time. One of his main examples was the "Heavenly Princes Cult" of the southern African Zulu people. Gluckman (1963, 114–115) described the society as "patriarchal," on the grounds that in everyday life women were subordinate to men. And yet in rituals, women were allowed to represent life as if women were dominant. Gluckman argued that these and other rituals reinforced the prevailing social order by providing a symbolic release for potential hostility or resentment.

Gluckman's formulation of "rituals of rebellion" has been influential in anthropology (Turner 1969) and (largely through the work of Victor Turner) in other fields as well (for example, Davis 1965). It has been particularly well accepted in studies of gender and ritual in Africa. But as a recent analysis (Sanders 2000) shows, many of these rituals, at first glance suitable for analysis as rituals of reversal, in fact have a better explanation that depends on understanding the complementary roles of women and men.

Sanders studied with Ihanzu farmers living in the dry areas of northern Tanzania, where attracting sufficient rain is a constant concern. Men predominate in public political affairs and own nearly all property. Men and women will sometimes describe the society as male-dominated or patriarchal. Such a characterization should be taken as part of the social reality to be studied, however, and not the end of analysis. Women control grain and they brew the beer that is the basis for everyday socializing. Furthermore, descent in the society is matrilineal (through women).

Rain is normally encouraged through rituals presided over by two royal leaders, a man and his sister; but in the years when people judge these normal rainmaking rituals to have failed, the leaders will decide to hold a women's rain dance. (Trials of "rain witches" may also be held.) The ritual lasts several days, during which women shove anti-witchcraft medicine into the ground, dance naked into the bush and onto special dancing grounds, and visit ancestral caves, usually while shouting lewd songs. Any man caught in their way is liable to be attacked.

Although the ritual is ripe for study as a ritual of reversal, their performance in these moments of danger is better explained by the local understandings of women's attributes. Women's bodies are thought to be "wet" while men's are "dry," and thus it is women who must work to bring on the rains. Moreover, the women are capable of transforming the dry weather conditions by bringing together gender attributes: their own (wet) bodies with the aggression and violence associated with men. Thus the ritual is not designed— or locally understood—as granting women "power for a day" (or several days). It is not a ritual of reversal, but a transformative uniting of male and female qualities.

Articulating Women's Perspectives through Spirits

We have already seen that in many societies women act and reflect on their actions in ways that are sometimes less public than are the deeds and words of their male counterparts and that their actions have often been ignored by male anthropologists. Certain religious practices seem to be used by women in a number of societies as the means to reflect on and improve their position; for example, possession and mediumship as it is found in eastern African societies, from the *zar* cult in the Sudan (Boddy 1989; Kenyon 1995) to possession by *tromba* in Madagascar (Sharp 1993). These cults and practices are both ways of healing the sick and ways of commenting on social life.

Zar Possession

Most people living in the Northern Sudan are Muslims, and Islam, locally defined, provides the concepts and texts for the prevailing discourse in villages. Men control that discourse and what is considered to be central or peripheral to it. But women produce a different set of messages and ideas, in part through their activities in the zar spirit cult. As Janice Boddy (1989) shows, these activities shape both men's and women's perceptions of themselves and their social and moral norms. Furthermore, the cult and mainstream Islam define each other by contrasts, much as we saw for highland Sumatran ideas about sacrificial ritual.

Zar are spirits prone to possess and cause illness in humans. The word refers to the spirits, the illnesses, and the rituals required to propitiate them. The cult is found throughout northern Africa and Arabia. The spirit world is layered onto the human world and spirits may descend into humans at any time, where they remain. The human must then learn how to let the spirit enter her and how to accommodate her requests so that she will not cause further harm.

Boddy describes a healing ritual that occurred over several days (1989, 125–131). The ritual leader, *shaykha,* speaks to the spirits as the women, one by one, let themselves be possessed. Very much like the Candomble trance spirits described in Chapter 6 of this book, these spirits represent cultural types and their human vehicles speak and move accordingly. A Western military officer has her human medium shuffle along in a march-like dance, bob formally at the waist, and request a European-style belt and a radio. Two women who are possessed by a Nomad spirit leap at each other brandishing naked swords. An Ethiopian prostitute behaves accordingly (and requests scanty clothing), while another spirit has the possessed woman move after the fashion of a man who is engaged in Islamic repetitive chanting, *dhikr.* As a result of all these possessions, the afflicted woman for whose benefit the session is held is formally considered to have been healed.

In this Sudanese village possession is widespread among married women—40 percent have been possessed—and rare among men. The distinctive perspective that it gives to experience is thus characteristic of women. Like Wiccan associations in the United States, described later, zar provides a set of practices and ideas that can articulate women's perspectives, power, and problems. Like many religious organizations, the cults function more as organized social groups in the cities and more as networks of women in rural areas. They resemble men's Sufi orders and, like them, provide a social matrix for women in village, town, or city.

Boddy meticulously traces the parallels between wedding ceremonies and possession rituals, noting that possession rituals frequently reverse the order of processes that accompany wedding ceremonies. This reversal shows that the wedding symbolism is not inevitable. For example, the loss of blood accompanying sexual intercourse on the wedding night is countered by the ingestion of blood and the use of blood from a sacrificial animal to annoint the afflicted patient at the possession rituals (1989, 332–334). More generally, by providing a parody of weddings, the ritual suggests that there are realities beyond the one experienced by women as they become wives.

As new problems have arisen for Sudanese women and their families, zar cults have expanded and adapted to deal with them. In the present time of great material need, zar specialists may lend needy women money (Kenyon 1995, 240). Zar has also received increasing attention from the Sudanese government, which has promoted and publicized it as part of "Sudanese tradition." Susan Kenyon (1995, 241) reports that in the capital, Khartoum, men have begun to form their own zar cults, and she speculates that they may try to centralize and professionalize the cult, a step that would represent a break with its current psychosocial functions.

Wicca

Although most of us think of witchcraft as something associated with old Salem, bonfires, and brooms, the term now usually refers to ideas and practices inspired by an ancient religion closely related to fertility, the earth, and goddess-worship. Most often these practices are referred to as *Wicca,* from an Old English word for witchcraft.

Wicca provides an excellent example of how a variety of practices can be packaged as a "religion" in the modern sense of the term, with creed and canons, leaders and followers, and a form of organization something like a church. The historical foundation for Wicca seems to be a long legacy, mostly in England, of crop planting and harvesting rituals. People who grew up in those traditions generally thought of them as merely things that one did, not as part of something called "witchcraft." Margot Adler (1986, 72–73), a true "participant–observer" as both a journalist and Wicca devotee, quotes a Wisconsin woman whose father's parents brought these traditions to the United States from Scotland and Wales. Adler wrote that "to them Witchcraft was a *practice*" (1986, 72); their theology was simply that the earth was the female principle and the oak tree the male principle. As one Witch explained

I was shown how to do certain things, practical things. How do you make your garden grow? You talk to your plants. You enter into a mental rapport with them. How do you call fish to you? How do you place yourself in the right spot? How do you encourage them? (Adler 1986, 73).

Eventually some people in England became more self-conscious about these practices and baptized them as the English "Family Traditions." Writers began to claim that they were part of an unbroken legacy of the Craft, or Wiccanry, traceable back to an ancient time before the rise of Christianity in Europe.

The founder of the contemporary tradition of Wiccanry is Gerald B. Gardner (1884–1964), an English colonial planter and later civil servant. In about 1939 Gardner was initiated into Wicca in England. This initiation would have likely taken place undercover because witchcraft was still prohibited in the United Kingdom. After the last of the Witchcraft Acts was repealed in 1951, Gardner began to write about Wiccanry. He set out what became its standard history and doctrine, claiming that it was an ancient religion, focused on the cult of the Goddess and of nature, that had survived underground in Europe through millenia of oppression.

Gardner's claims that Wiccanry had an ancient lineage provoked a great deal of controversy (nicely set out by Alder [1986]). The basic idea that contemporary Wicca practitioners were reviving pre-Christian, proto-feminist, ecologically sound ideas has survived intact, and has continued to animate most practitioners of the Craft in the United States and elsewhere. Wiccanry leaders have drawn on a number of elements to construct a synthetic version of the cult: the older farming practices mentioned earlier, Masonic and Rosicrucian teachings about mysteries and ancient, pre-Judaic religious practices, the Spiritualist ideas of communication with the dead that were popular throughout Europe and the Americas in the early twentieth century, and popular practices of divination. The basic unit of Wiccanry is the coven, a voluntary association of women and sometimes men, which meets to celebrate its lineage and to perform rituals.

Chapter 2 discussed how the Japanese created Shinto out of elements of ritual practice so as to have a religion that would be equivalent in form and structure to other religions. Wiccanry reflects precisely the same process taking place in twentieth-century United States and Britain. With the rise of the idea that the assorted and diverse "magical" practices found in rural areas were in fact the fragments of an ancient "religion" came the impulse to define that religion's elements. Congresses of Witches were held in different locales in the United States to attempt to define the elements of Wiccanry and a Covenant of the Goddess was signed by 13 covens in California in 1975. A major figure in the formulation of Wiccanry, Aidan Kelly, modeled the Covenant on the charter of the Congregational Church, which offered a decentralized model of church governance.

Despite these efforts to create a religion and an established church of Wicca, Wiccan groups are continually forming and changing, with several distinct ideologies. One is feminist, sometimes called *Dianic*, after the goddess. These groups draw particularly on the writings of Starhawk, a Westcoast coven leader. They stress their links to ancient Pagan religions that worshipped the goddess. Another stream emphasizes the writings of Gerald Gardner, and hence can be called *Gardnerian*. The organizations that follow this stream are the most formalized of all Wiccan groups, and include an idea of succession to leadership positions for women. Janet and Stewart Farrar's book *The Witches' Way* describes the Gardnerian rituals. A third stream is *traditionalist*; its covens consider themselves to be continuing the traditions of specific places of origin, usually Wales, Ireland, or Scotland. Each coven tries to incorporate into its rituals legends from that country.

Starhawk's book, *Spiral Dance,* probably the most influential work among North American Wiccans, proclaims Witchcraft "perhaps the oldest religion extant in the West" (1989, 16). According to Starhawk's history, male shamans and female priestesses presided over European human societies beginning 35,000 years ago. In the name of the goddess the shamans enticed game to their death and the priestesses guaranteed fertility. As agriculture was discovered, the priestesses brought forth the regenerative power of the earth. Nothing changed in the way humans related to nature until the invasion of the Indo-Europeans who brought patriarchy, metals, and war. But the Old Religion lived on in rural areas to become the practices of the Druids. With Christianity, the figure of Mary was regarded as another form of the goddess; and Christ, of her child who was sacrificed and reborn. In the fourteenth century persecutions began, but most witches escaped; some fled to America, some joined with slaves and Indians, finding commonality in their practices. Only recently has the Craft, the Old Religion, Witchcraft been free to emerge and reorganize into loosely organized covens and practitioners (Starhawk 1989, 15–30).

This multicultural history and nonhierarchical approach to the Craft fits the attitude of the most receptive readers in twenty-first-century North America. In the United Kingdom and North America today are a proliferation of organizations and associations difficult to label, reflecting the creativity of Wiccanry. Indeed, Wiccans stress that they are simply reviving and maintaining ancient practices, or the Craft.

Wiccans also emphasize their freedom from doctrine. "It's a religion of ritual rather than theology" wrote Aidan Kelly (Adler 1986, 170). What then are those practices? Contemporary American Wiccanry eschews centrally prescribed ritual form, though there are certain constant elements within a multiplicity of practices. Wicca ritual usually includes hymns, chants or songs that evoke several goddesses and gods and the power of nature. The participants, sometimes nude, meet and often move in circles.

Loretta Orion (1995) studied Wiccanry in the 1980s and participated in the 1983 Pagan Spirit Gathering held at the summer solstice in Wisconsin. Before the central ritual, Orion learned about dowsing and the proper way to ask an herb's permission to be picked. Participants evoked or "drew down" a multitude of Greco-Roman, Norse, Celtic, South Asian, and African deities, sent blessings to Starhawk (who was at that moment leading a demonstration against a nuclear power plant) and, to the accompaniment of drums and flutes, moved in a counterclockwise circle while chanting the names of goddesses, singing, and eventually cheering, howling, and laughing.

The moving circle was followed by the full moon ritual, an elaborate event celebrating the great mother goddess represented by a pregnant woman carried in a chair; she was followed by 12 women dressed as different aspects of the goddess, including Kali, Hecate, Discordia, and a generic Amazon figure. A priestess invoked the full moon and promised fertility and men dressed as forms of Dionysus planted seeds in the soil with a "swimming, squirming, spermlike dance," wrote Orion (1995, 140).

Wiccan rituals combine several ritual elements, as the description of the solstice celebration illustrates. They usually involve movement or chanting designed to create a sense of a collectivity. In this respect they resemble the Australian Aboriginal dances that inspired Émile Durkheim to identify the birth of religion in energetic group dance. Durkheim focused on the moment when collective action creates a consciousness of a collective power. Wiccans themselves speak of the creation of a "cone of power" at these moments (Orion 1995, 128–140).

Second, the rituals invoke pre-Christian deities to connect humans to the natural elements, especially to the earth and its fertility. (Recall the origins of the Craft in agriculture.) The rituals continue the idea of ancient mysteries that have attracted people to Masons and Rosicrucians. The prominance of female deities celebrates many Wiccans' belief in a protohistorical period when women ruled. Wiccans disagree about whether an ancient matriarchal period can be proved, but they do agree that matriarchy can provide an idea of female freedom (Adler 1986, 196).

Finally, Wicca rituals link fertility to human sexuality. Sexuality is more or less present in coven activities but should be understood as part of the total complex of ideas, in which it is seen as a way of liberating oneself from patriarchal Christianity.

Religious Patriarchy and Its Challenges

Wiccans' attention to female powers and to pre-Christian deities reflects the idea that Christianity began a period of male domination that continues throughout much of the world. Some historians and anthropologists also see the lineage of Judaism, Christianity, and Islam as sanctioning patriarchy, though others emphasize the cultural roots of patriarchy and point to the way these religions have provided women with resources for liberation.

Abraham and Sacrifice

Some scholars argue that the major narratives underlying the monotheistic religions take on the force of myth, shaping the way followers think about the world. Do these narratives portray the world in a consistently patriarchal way? In a forceful book on patriarchy and religion, Carol Delaney (1998) argues that the biblical story of Abraham has provided a template for thinking about gender within the three related Semitic religions (Judaism, Christianity, Islam) and that this template has had unfortunate consequences for human welfare.

Delaney finds proof that these three religions are thoroughly patriarchal in their founding myths. In Abraham's choosing to sacrifice his child it is implied that the child is his to sacrifice, and that the child's mother, Sarah, does not have to be consulted. Only the father's decision and his son's submission have religious relevance, not the son's or mother's autonomous wills.

In the Torah, the Gospels, and the Qur'ân, the relevant lines of descent are through males, not females. The relationship through the seed of Abraham, thus through serial fatherhood, defines the religious community. Delaney argues that people raised in the traditions of these three monotheisms have internalized the model of faith through sacrifice set out in the Abraham story and enshrined it in laws and institutions such as marriage and the family. The social consequences have included a tendency to abuse children, she writes (1998, 235–241), because the Abraham story has directly or indirectly supported the idea that children are ours to sacrifice.

Delaney (1998, 238) finds connections between certain contemporary Christian child-rearing manuals that urge parents to "break the will" of a child and the Abraham story. And she cites a disturbing account of a 1990 trial of a man who killed his daughter in a manner that replicated Abraham's near-sacrifice of his son—except that in the modern case the deed was carried out. The man was found insane, but Delaney leaves us with the question: If Abraham acted above the law, can someone working from within a Jewish theological framework condemn this man; can he or she be sure that he was truly insane and not another person who had heard God speak?

Fundamentalism and Gender Roles

Another way to approach the question of gender and the monotheistic religions is by looking at speeches, sermons, and writings connected with particular movements. Susan Harding (2000) undertook this kind of research in her study of Protestant Fundamentalism by listening to the preachers and followers of the Reverend Jerry Falwell to understand the force of the way they speak about the world.

The Fundamentalist religious tradition is known for claiming that women and men have separate natures and tasks. Preachers frequently cite St. Paul's exhortation to Christian wives to submit to their husbands "as unto the Lord" (Ephesians 5:22–24). This basic paradigm invests the marital relation with the same sacred hierarchy that characterizes the relationships of all humans to God. In the 1940s and 1950s Fundamentalist preachers described wives as "the weaker vessel" and decried notions of companionate marriage.

Harding observes that one of the norms embraced by Falwell's Moral Majority movement is the wife's submission to the husband's leadership, but goes on to examine the contemporary sermons and speeches through which this norm is communicated and given more complex meanings. She notes, for example, that Falwell distances himself from those norms and that image in his speeches through the use of irony, confession, and self-deprecation.

By the 1970s and 1980s, writes Harding (2000, 161–181), Fundamentalists had come to think of marriage in terms of companionship and complementarity rather than in terms of command and hierarchy. Evangelical feminists had a great deal to do with bringing about changes in the ways preachers spoke about gender relations. (The term *evangelical* places the emphasis on working to convert others, as distinguished from the tendency of some Fundamentalist movements to focus inward on their own communities.) By the 1980s, more evangelical and Fundamentalist women were working outside the home, and their work began to be publicly valued as part of how a Christian life could and should be built (Harding 2000, 172–173). This was a major change but it was made without ever abandoning a reliance on St. Paul's gender-unequal admonition. It was accomplished by affirming the husband's right to make final decisions in family matters while emphasizing the wisdom of his consulting—and sometimes conceding to—his wife. Some preachers, notably Falwell himself, began to adopt an ironic stance toward biblical text even while affirming it in their rhetoric.

A 1986 speech by Falwell illustrates this stance (Harding 2000, 167–168). A strong attack on America's moral decline, with special emphasis on AIDS and single-parent families, changed into a very different style as Falwell made a confession about marriage. Married 28 years, he and his wife had never discussed divorce, even though "we've had some knock-downs and drag-outs [Laughter]. I've lost every one of them [Laughter]. I tell you, men, the best thing you can do is quickly raise your hands and unconditionally surrender because you're gonna lose [Laughter]. Amen? [Amens]" (Harding 2000, 167–168).

Harding points out that the joking reveals the current flux in marital norms but that it, and the entire speech, was addressed to men and not women (176–177). Fundamentalist public speaking, Harding observes, "implicitly privileges men through its rhetorical forms and in its content, which in many and varied ways create a two-tiered audience with men 'up front' and women 'in the back.' " Public Fundamentalist rhetoric remains directed at men and supportive of men even as they no longer can claim a superior role and a monopoly on extra-household activities.

How was this shift possible? At the height of their confrontation with the growing feminist movement during the 1970s, many conservative Christians argued that to stop following Paul's injunction would be to challenge biblical inerrancy. But by the 1990s many Fundamentalists had been able to adopt a more gender-equal style of family life without renouncing their belief in an absolutely true Bible. As Harding points out, this accommodation has been more a matter of selective emphasis than a shift in doctrine. One does not, after all, have to pay equal attention to all verses all the time.

Harding cites another example to point out how interpretation may change without requiring explicit shifts in doctrine. In the 1960s, defenders of racial segregation sometimes cited passages from Genesis to support their position. In 9 Genesis Noah curses the descendants of his son Ham because Ham had seen Noah naked. For those who believe Ham's descendants were the people of Africa the Bible supports continued policies of segregation and discrimination in favor of whites.

Eventually many Fundamentalists agreed to or at least came to tolerate a change in social policy. The passages themselves were not blocks to the eventual demise of segregation; they "simply stopped being cited" (Harding 2000, 181).

As Falwell began to say less and less about how families should be run, activists began to convey new and broader messages. By the late 1980s a new set of evangelical counselors and organizers had taken on the role of reforming family life around scripture. The most successful has been James Dobson, the head of Focus on the Family. From its headquarters in Colorado come a large volume of videotapes, newspaper columns, books, and radio programs illustrating a certain set of norms for family life. The more the message is aimed at a general public, the less religious and the more psychosocial it becomes. Dobson's widely syndicated newspaper columns are virtually devoid of explicit religious content and treat issues of child-raising in a secular psychological idiom. Other social movements, like the Colorado-based Promise Keepers movement, have arisen with parallel programs.

The Fundamentalist and evangelical conservative Christian movements have changed their approach to gender relations in two ways. One is by playing down while never denying the importance of key biblical texts (such as Paul's statements). The other is by expanding the range of media and activities by which "family values" are conveyed far beyond the pulpit to include mass media and new social movements.

Women and Islamic Dress

*I*n recent years, no single religious image has evoked as many conflicting ideas and emotions about gender as that of a Muslim woman wearing a headcovering. The modest dress, headcoverings, and sometimes face coverings worn by some Muslim women have for many onlookers come to symbolize the (hopelessly) patriarchal nature of Islam.

The best anthropological way of studying the veil and its meaning would be to observe a range of practices in a variety of places. Current dress in Cairo illustrates the variety of "Muslim-looking" dress options available to women, as I observed in Cairo in Summer 2000. A 1982 film by Elizabeth Fernea, *A Veiled Revolution,* carefully documents the range of dress styles and ways of thinking about dress among middle-class women of Cairo, and subsequent studies (Ahmed 1992; El Guindi 1999) have delineated the complex social and religious meanings attached to dress choices.

First we need to discard the word *veil* and distinguish among various types of clothing. The Arabic word *hijab,* or "barrier," is used in many Muslim countries to refer to Islamic dress or modest dress in general. Several types of garments can be combined in different ways within an Islamic dress repertoire, and, further complicating matters, many different Arabic terms are used to refer to various items. The dress may include headcoverings (*khimar, 'abayah*), face covering veils (*niqab, burqu'*), or an all-enveloping

Muhajjaba *in Cairo. Dress form or* jilbab *(loose, ankle-length, long-sleeve, opaque fabric) and color (austere dark solid) show typical Islamic dress for women 1970s and 1980s.* (PHOTO BY FADWA EL GUINDI. COURTESY OF EL NIL RESEARCH © 1995.)

garment (*milayah, jellabah, burga'*). (But these words have different meanings depending on time and place.) And each item comes in a variety of types. A headcovering, for example, might be a simple scarf, a hood-like item, or part of a single garment. A veil may be highly transparent or completely opaque. A long dress may cover all or some of the body or be replaced by trousers and a tunic. It may be accompanied by gloves and socks (El Guindi 1999).

All these items come in a variety of colors and styles, from black through shades of beige, to blue and green, to multicolored, and all have specific associations. Black tends to be worn by lower-class women and is seen by them as the most modest color (as is true in some other non-Muslim parts of the Mediterranean world). Green is believed to be the Prophet Muhammad's favorite color; in some countries (Malaysia, for example) this association leads to a profusion of green, while in some others (Iran, France, and Indonesia, for example), it does not. By the 1980s women in many Muslim societies began to wear "high fashion" outfits of silky materials, with elaborate jewelry and matching accessories.

But women also draw on a repertoire of dress items in different situations. Yemeni women, for example, have two types of headcovering for indoor wear, and two for outdoors (Makhlouf 1979, 30–34). For indoor wear, women can choose between a garment that is draped around the head and that can be pulled down or up to cover the face, and a tied scarf, more fashionable, used for visiting. For outdoors, the *sitara* combines a large scarf draped over the head and a batik cloth covering the face but allowing the wearer to see out. The alternative is the *sharshaf*, a three-piece garment consisting of a pleated skirt, a waist-length cape, and a thin black face covering. The choice among possible coverings is shaped by and reveals social status. High-status women tend to wear the *sharshaf*, lower-status women the *sitara*, with those in the middle alternating between the two. Covering may also be used to indicate a kin relation. In parts of northern India studied by Ursula Sharma (1980), for example, Muslim women marry out of their natal villages into their husbands' villages and mark their new status by their veil. The wife's use of face covering depends on her husband's place in the village kinship system: she covers her face in the presence of men considered to be senior to her husband, such as his older brothers and cousins, but not before his inferiors. And she does not cover her face before men of her natal village.

Fadwa El Guindi (1999, 103–114) points out that women and men often use head or face coverings to indicate status, authority, or respect, noting the specific use of a veil by the widow of the Prophet Muhammad, 'Aisha, who became politically active during the reign of Muhammad's successors. Following the murder of a successor, Uthman, 'Aisha appeared at the mosque in Mecca and, standing on the spot where Abraham was thought to have laid the foundation of the original sanctuary, ceremonially veiled herself and addressed the crowd. Her act of public veiling claimed her a position of political authority, and El Guindi (1999, 112) compares it to the Prophet's act of donning a black headcovering that covered much of his face on his triumphant return to Mecca.

Dress and Feminism in Cairo

The city of Cairo offers illustration of how a multitude of meanings conveyed by head and face coverings have changed over time in the Middle East. Cairo of the 1910s and 1920s was experiencing rapid cultural change, with cinemas, new newspapers, rising rates of literacy, and higher education. Its citizens chafed under British colonial control, and women in particular resented obstacles placed in their way by the colonists. It was the British adviser to the Minister of Education, not an Egyptian, who tried to prevent a woman from obtaining her secondary school certificate. (The Egyptian student finally succeeded in 1908.) Women were contributing to newspapers and attending schools in increasing numbers and were forming intellectual and literary associations. They were also creating hospitals, founding political organizations, and demonstrating against the British. Women were publicly and politically active at the center of nationalist, anti-colonial movements (Ahmed 1992).

Among the leaders was Huda Sha'rawi, who made the lifting of the face covering an act signifying women's liberation. In May 1923, when Sha'rawi and her colleagues arrived at the Cairo train station from an international women's conference in Rome, they publicly and ceremoniously removed their face coverings (*burqu'*), though not their headcoverings. Women of the upper class had already been unveiling in great numbers, but her act gave the trend momentous political and cultural significance by representing women's causes as culturally linked to Europe, despite the women's opposition to European domination.

Two streams of feminism emerged from these activities. One, led by Huda Sha'rawi, urged progress toward a European way of life. The other, led by Malak Hifni Nassef, wanted to place the feminist cause within the struggle for Islamic renovation and reform. Nassef's views were different from Sha'rawi's. Though she equally opposed polygamy and rejected the view that Islam demanded that women cover their heads, she cautioned Egyptian women against slavishly following European ways before they had received the education that would allow them to make intelligent choices. She saw the real problem for Egyptian women as male domination; only education would allow women to overcome their subordination (Ahmed 1992, 179–184). Nassef's early death meant that the former stream predominated until the 1980s, when new Islamic feminist voices began to be heard.

Women advanced to college in record numbers during the 1950s and 1960s and began to move the general program outlined by Sha'rawi into new territory, advocating changes in domestic relations, women's access to contraception, and better medical attention for women. Leila Ahmed (1992) argues that women adopted Islamic dress as a way to combine their feminism with an increase in religiosity that happened during the same period. She points to the rapid rise during the 1960s and 1970s in the number of women who migrated to Cairo, often as children, and received dramatically higher levels of education. In 1953 men outnumbered women in the universities by 13 to one, but by 1976 the ratio had dropped to 1.8 to one. By 1982 women held 26 percent of the jobs in professions and science (Ahmed 1992, 210–211). They trained their new skills on social problems: the maltreatment of women and children, male domination in Arab society (whether Muslim or Christian), illiteracy.

The "open door policy" of the 1970s increased both economic inequality and the visibility of Western consumer products and Western middle-class behavioral norms, particularly freedom of interaction among men and women. But in the 1970s things changed dramatically. In 1967 Israel had defeated Egypt in the Six Days' War. Feeling humiliated and perplexed, many Egyptians turned to religion as a source of strength. Many Muslims joined Sufi orders, which offered activities of chanting and meditating. The most striking event, however, was when many people said they saw the Virgin Mary appear near a Coptic Christian church, under a tree where Mary had rested with Joseph and Jesus in their flight to Egypt. Thousands of Muslims and Christians flocked to the site to see her (El Guindi 1999, 131–132). For these people and many others, the apparition gave a religious meaning to the military defeat, namely, that Egyptians needed to rediscover their piety. Egypt's subsequent military victory over Israel in the 1973 war only added to the growing alliance between feelings of religious piety and national identity.

From then on, it was the "religious movement" (*mitdayyinin*) that developed in Cairo. Students seeking to promote an Islamic model of comportment also advocated Islamic dress for men and women. El Guindi (1999, 134) describes the women's Islamic dress that began to be worn in the 1970s not as a return to any traditional dress form, but as "an innovative construction." The students and other activists made the new garments in their homes. Men and women in the movement wore *jilbabs*, loose full-length, solid-colored gowns of opaque fabric. Men also wore baggy trousers and shorts, and grew short beards. Women wore headcoverings called *khimar*.

These men and women argued that the Qur'ân supported their new dress, citing verses from two chapters of the Qur'ân. In one (Qur'ân 24:30–31), God instructs all female believers to use their khimar to cover their cleavage and to "display their beauty" only to their close relatives. In another (Qur'ân 33:59), God commands the Prophet Muhammad to tell believing women to put on their jilbabs (El Guindi 1999, 139).

Ahmed argues (1992, 222–225) that women and men adopted Islamic dress as a response to a contradiction between their culture of origins and the new urban situation in which they found themselves. Surveys taken in Cairo in the late 1970s showed that these men and women tended to come from conservative backgrounds, with parents who often were less educated and of rural origin. They themselves had achieved university-level education. Adopting an outwardly conservative Islamic dress may have been a way to cope with the tension between the values and norms of the new urban, highly educated classes and those of their parents and helped them deal with their parents' failure to understand their new lives. The new dress styles also helped them feel part of a community of religious-minded people at a time when they may have felt adrift and confused.

In a more positive vein, Ahmed sees both the early feminism of Sha'rawi and the later adoption of Islamic dress as equally the efforts of women to achieve autonomy, under different circumstances and for different social classes. In both situations women have used dress to create a public space for themselves. Islamic dress may offer practical advantages to working women, a point made by the Cairene women who discussed their dress choices in Fernea's film (1982). The women said that when they adopted Islamic dress other men and women accorded them more respect and that they also felt more self-respect. These garments protected them from unwanted advances by men, some said; they were good for working women because one didn't have to dress up, and were more practical for work involving bending down or working on the floor.

These women also saw wearing Islamic dress as a public expression of one's own strong will regarding Islam, keeping the faith, having love for God, preserving Islam. Precisely because they attributed these meanings to the garments, some women said they did not yet feel ready for the burden of wearing these clothes.

Women's Islamic dress can also serve to render more acceptable their roles outside the home. Arlene MacLeod (1991) views this response in a more negative light than does Leila Ahmed, observing that adopting such dress may be a married woman's way of coping with not being able to both work and tend well to her family. MacLeod (1991, 102–107) adds the valuable perspective of working-class women to the story. Before the religious movement of the 1970s, these women wore smocks and kerchiefs, topped by a black overdress when visiting or shopping. But women who reached the middle-class working stratum had generally adopted Western dress, which served as a badge of upward class mobility.

Karima's story exemplifies the conflicts experienced by some working women as part of what MacLeod calls the "new veiling," the revisions of dress that took place from the 1970s onward. Karima was married and had small children when MacLeod spoke with her in the mid-1980s. She also worked in an office. She said that taking on the hijab (*muhajjaba*) after the birth of her first child helped her feel at peace, even as she felt caught between the conflicting, tiring demands of work, child care, and homemaking. "When I wear this dress, it says to everyone that I am trying to be a good wife and a good mother" (MacLeod 1991, 118–124).

Ahmed and MacLeod interpret the meaning of the new forms of dress in slightly different ways. Ahmed, writing mainly about middle-class women, and especially students, emphasizes the autonomy that adopting the hijab can bring. MacLeod's study of lower-middle-class women focuses on the hijab as an expression of the contradictory pull between home and work, conservative and modern social norms. Ahmed points to the instrumental value of the veil in carving out public space, MacLeod to its role in expressing a set of feelings. MacLeod also suggests that it might be seen as an "accommodating protest": protesting even while adapting to their uncomfortable situation.

The differences in MacLeod's and Ahmed's interpretations reflect not only class differences but also the ambivalence many women have expressed concerning the adoption of Islamic dress. The hijab defines its wearer in certain ways that can both promise autonomy and restrict a range of options. The decision to adopt this dress can be felt both as a free choice and as a result of social pressure.

Comparisons

Adopting Islamic dress may have very different meanings for women in other countries and, just as in Cairo, may vary according to social class and religious ideology. In Iran before 1979, for example, wearing the black, fully covering garment called the *chador* was a way for women to protest against the rule of the Shah. It was for them an expression of a desire for freedom, including but not limited to religious freedom. But since the 1979 revolution enforcement of a strict dress code by religious police has made many women ambivalent about these dress forms. Many women now combine brightly colored dresses with more somber outerwear. If Iran continues to liberalize its cultural policies under President Khatami, Islamic dress styles may continue to diversify.

Controversy has arisen in some countries over the wearing of simple headcoverings by girls attending state high schools. In each country the controversy has had different roots and thus different meanings. Indonesia, as we saw in Chapter 2, has more Muslims than any other country and Islam is state-supported. But the state ideology is pluriconfessional, meaning that all citizens are supposed to follow a recognized religion, though one is not favored over another and all are supposed to be subordinate to allegiance to the state. When in the 1970s some girls began wearing headcoverings to public schools, state officials viewed the headscarves as signifying allegiance to Islam taking precedence over allegiance to country, and banned them. (The ban was later lifted.)

In both Turkey and France, scarf-wearing took place in a context of state secularism, but with two very different histories. Turkey came into existence after World War I under the leadership of Kemal Ataturk, who, in abolishing the Ottoman caliphate (the successor state to Muhammad's political leadership) also abolished Islamic law. He worked to make Turkey a European country, outlawed Sufi brotherhoods, and required that worship be in Turkish rather than Arabic. The army continues to see itself as the guardian of Ataturk's legacy, and vigorously opposes any visible signs of Islamic politics, including the wearing of Islamic dress in public schools or in the Parliament.

French politics are founded upon the opposition between the agents of secularism and the Catholic Church, an opposition dating to the Revolution but renewed at the beginning of the twentieth century by laws separating religion from public affairs and by a concerted effort to create a nationwide, secular school system. When in 1989 some Muslim schoolgirls wore scarves to school, their action was seen by some as an attack on the principle of secularism. French law currently allows the wearing of "unostentatious" headgear by Muslims, Jews, and others, but teachers sometimes lead walkouts from schools where girls have taken up wearing scarves.

The hair and the head are frequently invested with important social, spiritual, and sexual meanings, particularly with respect to social transitions. An act such as shaving the head may signal that one enters a state outside of normal social life. In Thailand, for example, men shave their heads upon joining a monastery for a period in their lives and regrow their hair upon leaving. When Muslim men or women have made the pilgrimage, they wear white caps or scarves to mark their passage to the special status reached by the person who has completed his or her religious duties. In other cultures those with long hair may be especially powerful (Samson, forest monks, St. John the Baptist, for example) or less powerful (intellectuals, hippies), but they, too, are different.

Theory in Anthropology: Pierre Bourdieu, from Norms to Practices

We've seen in this chapter that in some societies the public representations of a social event are quite different from the less public reasons given for the event. In the example of infibulation practiced in the northern Sudan, women discuss the practice as creating properly cultural women and future mothers out of unsocialized girls. But it is the male discourse about the practice, one that explains it in terms of controlling female desire, that is publicly aired.

This example is of the kind discussed by the French sociologist Pierre Bourdieu as evidence of the weakness of an anthropology that relies on publicly proclaimed social norms or rules as sufficient accounts of the reasons for actions. Bourdieu set out his "anthropology of practice" in France in the 1970s and has continued to elaborate upon it (Bourdieu 1972, 1990, 1998). He argues that previous work in anthropology and sociology viewed people as following rules or social norms, referring specifically to the structural anthropology of Claude Lévi-Strauss and the sociological tradition developed by Émile Durkheim. This approach, he argued, ignored two aspects of social action: the improvisational, often unconscious character of action, and the fact that it is constrained by the "field of power" in which it takes place.

One of Bourdieu's early and best examples of what is missed by a "rule-following" notion of social action concerns marriage among the Kabyle of Algeria. During his fieldwork, Bourdieu found that men publicly celebrated some marriages as fulfilling the norm of "marriage with the father's brother's daughter," or in anthropological jargon, the patriparallel cousin. These marriages, proclaimed the men, solidified ties through males. But when he looked into how specific marriages came about, Bourdieu found that it was women who made crucial decisions about which marriages should happen and they did so in a way that solidified ties among *women,* not men. As in many small-scale societies with marriages usually happening within the group (what we call "en-dogamous" marriages), kin ties between any two people often can be traced in more than one way. In the cases studied, it was the kin pathway through males that was publicly celebrated and that was said to follow the social norm. But it was the shorter kin pathway through females that seems to have been the one in the minds of the women who effected the marriage. This pathway did not conform to a rule or norm; rather, it defined a social relationship that could be strengthened by means of the marriage.

Thus, the event involved not following a rule, as structuralists would have judged it; but rather, improvising a new social relationship out of ones already existing. "Making the marriage" consisted of taking a series of steps, including casting around for suitable spouses, approaching their families, and so forth, and each step involved quick reactions to new demands or opportunities. But afterward the marriage was publicly interpreted in a field of power defined by asymmetries of gender, where it was men who had the right to define the marriage and to effectively rewrite its history. They held the "symbolic capital" in the society that allowed them to define it as a patriparallel marriage that confirmed the rule.

Bourdieu is best known for his work on France, where he identifies two general kinds of capital, economic and cultural, that together define the field of power and that shape the ideas, aspirations, and strategies that individuals in various class positions take with respect to education, careers, aesthetic choices, and in other domains. But most important for the anthropology of religion has been Bourdieu's earlier emphasis on the ways that rituals or other, more everyday, actions unfold over time, with their practitioners embodying a partly conscious, partly unconscious sense of what to do next. This sense of "what to do next" Bourdieu calls *habitus.* It refers to the knowledge that actors have learned over time and can put into practice without necessarily being able to explain how they do what they do, as when we find ourselves able to walk, speak one or more languages, and play a game, without thinking about how we are walking, the grammar of our languages, or how it is we arrive at certain strategies in our game.

For the fieldworker, this approach to action means that we attend to the microhistory of the unfolding of an event and try to discern why actors take each step that they do take. This event ethnography can then provide the microfoundations for understanding actors' senses of which rituals "worked" and which did not.

Profile 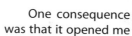 *Studying Fundamentalism*

Susan Harding teaches at the University of California, Santa Cruz, and studied in Spain before turning to the work she describes here. Her account of language and conviction among Fundamentalists is to be found in her book, *The Book of Jerry Falwell: Fundamentalist Language and Politics* (Princeton University Press 2000).

When I went to Lynchburg, Virginia, to learn about the Reverend Jerry Falwell's Fundamental Baptist community in the 1980s, I carried a lot of cultural baggage. I would have preferred to travel light, but my bags were packed for me long before my trip and went with me in spite of my disclaimers. I had a satchel full of negative perceptions about Fundamentalists from my upbringing in a middle-class, post-Episcopalian, NEW YORK TIMES–reading, academic family. My education packed another bag of bents and slants that celebrated liberal values, caricatured or ignored the religious expressions of Bible-believing white American Protestants, and viewed their political activities with horror.

Even my professional training burdened me, given anthropology's origin and shaping by the voices and values of science, reason, and tolerance, against which the figure of "the Fundamentalist" necessarily stands as a negative lesson. But anthropology also gave me the wherewithal, in the form of both skills and dispositions, to unpack my excess baggage. It was hard work, constant, never finished, a little like an ascetic discipline, but it was perhaps the most rewarding dimension of the project.

While I was in the field, my mantra was, "Everything they say is true." Initially, I intoned this mantra in order to counteract the opposite presumption invested in me by my background, but it had two unforeseen, escalating consequences, which I embraced.

One consequence was that it opened me up to hearing the complexity, fluidity, and force of what people in Falwell's community, including Falwell himself, were saying. As a result, I found out that the membrane between born-again belief and disbelief is thinner than we think. I "got caught" in their discourse, not as a believer, but in a space of overlap between belief and disbelief. I did not convert, but I came to know what it meant to have a soul, a sin nature, a heart; to say "God spoke to me" and "Satan is real"; to know that there is no such thing as an accident, that everything, no matter how painful or perplexing, has a purpose. In this psychic intersection I gained access to the vernacular of Bible belief, and it became my primary field site, my focus of study, in Lynchburg.

The other effect of my mantra was that it focused my attention on how things come true, how things are made real, whether or not they are consistent with what Fundamentalists say about themselves or with what others say about them. This was very useful since much of what has been and still is said about Fundamentalists and Fundamentalism is polemical, that is, is part of a huge cultural argument over the validity and public place of Bible-believing white Protestantism in America. Any chance I had of saying something fresh about the people I lived with in Lynchburg depended on my getting out of that polemic. And that is what I did, over and over again, as I wrote my book. For each chapter, I took up a topic—conversion, pastoral authority, fund-raising, revival, jeremiad preaching, pro-life campaigns, creationism, the End Time, the televangelical scandals—that was well-worn by clichés in both the popular and academic imagination. Listening for truth, or, rather, for truth-making, was, in effect, a method of "getting uncaught" from the tangle of polemic and cliché that mired each topic and of placing in the forefront of my writing the complexity, heterogeneity, generativity, and agile force of born-again language.

So in the end my book, like my fieldwork, became among other things a series of exercises in unpacking cultural baggage, Fundamentalist as well as modern, about Fundamentalism.

For Further Consideration

Web sites on Wicca abound, and each makes its point of view explicit. For that reason, this is one topic you can explore by yourself on the Web. A particularly informative site is called, appropriately enough, the Student's Guide to Wicca (*http://home.att.net/~macmorgan_design/guide/whatis.html*). Look for the book *All One Wicca* at the link to "What Is Wicca."

The Web site Maryams Net (*http://www.maryams.net*) has interesting links to articles about women in Islam and to Islamic studies sites. An Internet source for ideas about Islamic dress is an annotated bibliography compiled by Greta Scharnweber called "Barbie in Hijab" (*http://www.georgetown.edu/faculty/armbrusw/Fashion.htm*).

I have found more Internet resources on sexuality and religion than on gender and religion. A useful site for gay and lesbian issues relevant to established religions in the United States is at *http://calvin.usc.edu/~trimmer/religion.html*.

6

Extending Our Powers: "Magic" and Healing

Some scholars, and many practitioners, of religion like to distinguish between "magic" and "religion" (with additional categories of "sorcery" and "witchcraft"). Magic, according to this view, is when we manipulate objects or recite spells for practical ends, whereas religion is when we appeal to deities or God. Sorcery and witchcraft appear as something like magic, except that both involve special powers, and witchcraft involves a special bodily state.

These definitions are useful starting points, but they have one major flaw: they improperly dismiss the extent to which religion is precisely about people using objects, ways of speaking, or states of mind to achieve practical ends. We saw in Chapter 4 how death rituals can allow people to call on ancestors for assistance in life's tasks. Consider as well the mixed motives that bring many in the United States to attend church, temple, or mosque, or to pray at home: along with faith are desires to heal oneself or another person, ensure a place in heaven or help another's departed soul reach that place, make a million dollars, or retain one's standing in the community.

Contemplate also the popularity of faith healing as practiced by and for adherents of mainstream U.S. religions. In a 1996 Time/CNN poll, over one-quarter of U.S. residents said they believed in the efficacy of faith healing, almost three-quarters said they thought prayer could heal others, and nearly nine-tenths affirmed the power of prayer to heal oneself. Healing by laying on hands is an immensely popular practice worldwide, from Christian Scientists, to Baptists and televangelists, to followers of Japanese New Religions, to Muslims in Asia and Africa.

Achieving a practical end such as health or power seems to be a major goal of people who follow large-scale religions and of practitioners of small-scale ones (to which the label "magic" tends to be applied). Put more generally, we all desire to extend our capacity to explain and control the world beyond what our senses tell us, and sometimes in those efforts we draw on ideas of the supernatural. Our efforts also display our culture's concerns about causation and responsibility.

Understanding "Magic"

arlier students of religion sought to identify the fundamental features that lay behind beliefs in magic. The nineteenth-century anthropologists Edward Tylor and James Frazer thought of magic as a pseudoscience, what primitive people did instead of science. Magic for them was just like science in that it sought to act directly on the world, in a technical or instrumental way, but it was empirically false in its assumptions. Magic was a set of spells and techniques acquired with more attention to their effects (the practical side) than their principles (the theory).

Likeness and Contact

In his massive work on myth and folklore, *The Golden Bough* (1981), Frazer isolated two ideas that he saw as the basis for magical thinking: like affects like; and things that come into contact affect each other. The first he called "homeopathy," the second, "contagion." Homeopathic magic makes use of similarities, either natural or human-made, to reach its end. One kind of similarity is in the appearance of an object, so dolls or pictures of a person, when altered in some way, will, because like causes like, cause a corresponding alteration in the target person—the proverbial "voodoo doll" with the pins stuck in it. But there are other ways similarities are drawn on for practical ends. One can transfer the properties of any object to someone for a good or ill purpose. Gayo people use leaves that feel cool to the touch to bring down a fever on the assumption that the patient will feel cool because the leaves are cool.

Actions, rather than objects, can also have efficacy through the logic of likeness. Take the *couvade*, for example, a ritual first remarked in native North America wherein a father-to-be imitates the process of giving birth while his wife is experiencing labor pains. By his enactment of the successful birth he is supposed to push the process along and make it easier. (Perhaps this way of thinking underlies Lamaze birthing procedures in which the woman's companion performs blowing and counting exercises along with her.) A more complex logic underlies the "cosmic balance rituals," long called "increase rituals," in native Australia (Swain 1995, 25–28). Aboriginal groups recognize a particular plant, animal, or other object as their protective totem. They act out the birth of their totemic animal or plant and thereby increase its number. The additional special relationship between totem and people then leads to their prosperity.

The second principle is contagion, that contact between two objects means that action upon one of the objects will produce effects on the other. The hair or nails of a person, or clothing, may be used to work magic on the person. During the beginning of my fieldwork, several neighbors were concerned that I might become the victim of illness-causing magic and warned me not to hang up my wash outside. A shirt could be used to work magic on me, they said. Of special interest to societies around the world are discarded body parts, from fingernail clippings to the placenta. Because it is born along with the child, the placenta is treated in some societies as the child's brother, and how it is treated can affect the child's fortune. Some people bury it, to ensure that the child will always return from a trip; others store it away. The history of contact with the person gives the placenta its importance.

But "magic" is not limited to marginal activities or small-scale societies. The history of the Christian Church is inextricably bound up with what, from the perspective we take here, we would call "contagious magic." The power held by relics of saints, after all, derives from the relic's history as a part of the saint or as something that came into contact with the saint. For several centuries new churches had to be founded on a relic. Certain portraits, such as Our Lady of Czestochowa in Poland, draw special power from the contact with a saint (Saint Luke in this case). And of course the Shroud of Turin's special claim is not its likeness of Jesus but the supposed contact with Jesus's face. From the point of view adopted by Frazer, "magic" is less a type of practice than it is a psychological basis for making certain claims about power and efficacy. We find the ideas of likeness and contact compelling, and so we are especially likely to accept claims made on their bases.

Magic and Anxiety

Frazer's view of magic as replacement for science too neatly divided the world into "primitive" and "modern" societies. "Magical thinking" is in fact part of religious life and everyday life in all societies. The anthropologist Bronislaw Malinowski (1954) argued that science and magic are not substitutes for each other, but in that all societies they cooperate to create a psychologically satisfactory life. For all people, argued Malinowski, our ability to control our environments stops at some point, far short of what we would like. At that point magic comes in. It allows us to act on the areas of life filled with uncertainty, thus reducing our anxiety and allowing us to get on with life.

Contrary to what Frazer claimed, Malinowski said that no people in the world confuse technical or scientific knowledge with magic. People everywhere realize that their knowledge and control over the world has limits. Within the limits of that knowledge and control, practical, empirical science and skill is sufficient, and one does not find magic. Malinowski offered examples from his fieldwork in the Trobriand Islands, part of present-day Papua New Guinea. For Trobrianders, most everyday activities are fully under their control and therefore do not involve magic. A Trobriander knows how to make a basket or a pot with little chance of breakage and how to fish in safe areas, within the lagoon, for example, with no danger and little uncertainty. These activities are not accompanied by magic. On the other hand, activities that do have a certain degree of uncertainty, risk, or danger connected with them are likely to have magic. When Trobrianders venture out into the open sea to fish, they must use more chancy methods of fishing and face much more danger; it is then that they use magical spells to ensure a safe and successful venture.

Malinowski's approach gives us clear predictions of when we will find magic and when we will not. To state the argument abstractly: in any particular domain, activities that involve the most uncertainty are also the most likely to be accompanied by magic, that is, by practices that do not have technically or scientifically apparent effects but are believed by the actors to help their chances of success.

George Gmelch (1978) provides an example from American baseball. There is a clear division in baseball between activities in which players are expected to succeed nearly all the time and those in which they are not. Fielding is an example of the first, where failing to catch a pop fly ball will be counted as an error and not as an expected, common failure.

Pitching and hitting are clear examples of the second category, where players have much less control over what happens. A player who hits one-third of the time is very successful, as is a pitcher who throws strikes only half the time.

Is Malinowski's prediction right for baseball? It appears so: pitching and hitting, where so many things can go wrong, are accompanied by magic; fielding is not. Players practice magic by experiment and correlation. They try wearing an outfit or eating a certain food; if they do well on that day, then the clothes or food become "lucky" and a required part of their daily preparation. Gmelch himself, a former player, ate pancakes on mornings before games after he had won games on pancake days. Or they may decide to abstain from sex (as did an entire Canadian team during the 1996 Olympics), or the opposite, before game days.

Baseball magic can, as Malinowski stressed, relieve anxiety and build confidence. But once a player starts relying on magic he starts to require his magic to keep up his confidence. Magic can create anxiety as well as resolve it—a point made by a contemporary of Malinowski's, the anthropologist A.R. Radcliffe-Brown (1965).

One might say that for Malinowski, magic was a kind of psychology, not science; it arises out of one's awareness of one's own inability to control a situation but a desire to be able to control it. Magic is close to wish fulfillment or daydreaming. Malinowski's approach is an important corrective to Frazer's in providing a richer portrait of why people make use of magic. For example, the couvade, where the father imitates the birthing process, was explained by Frazer in terms of "like affects like." But why do we find magic for this event, giving birth, and not for many others? What drives people to make use of "like affects like" here? Malinowski would say that the couvade gives the father a feeling of participation and accomplishment in a situation in which he otherwise has little to do. In the United States, at least, the joke used to be that the father would be sent to boil endless pots of water, ostensibly to sterilize equipment but in fact to channel his nervous energy. The couvade-like techniques of Lamaze and other birthing exercises are, from Malinowski's point of view, more refined forms of magic.

Crop Magic and Change in the United States

People also change what they practice, and magic is particularly susceptible to change over time, as dominant ideas about causality and knowledge change. Herbert Passin and John Bennett (1943) studied farmers in southern Illinois in the early 1940s. They found that farmers had once planted according to "signs" and that some still did. They observed which planting times seemed to produce the best crops and, like baseball players, followed the results of their experiments as rules to guarantee success. They planted lettuce on St. Valentine's Day, cucumbers during a dark moon, and beans on Good Friday. As with Malinowski's Trobrianders, they stressed that you had to know how to plant, know the science, and also observe the signs, and that neglect of either one led to failure.

Some of these farmers developed theories about the signs, often causal explanations based on analogy. One theory is still widely distributed across the United States: the moon draws plants upward when it is full, and the earth's gravity pulls them downward when the moon is new. The moon's light makes plants "light." Following this theory, plants that grow up (beans, corn, peas) should be planted during the full moon; plants that grow down (bulbs, potatoes, carrots) should be planted during the new moon. These practices were driven by tradition, not theory, however. "We never said why; we just knew," reports one Kentucky full moon planter (who also worked as an extension agent); "the people who did question, they didn't have a crop."

Fewer farmers follow the signs today. After World War I and then the depression, Passin and Bennett's Illinois farmers found it more and more difficult to get by simply by growing their own food. Increasingly they turned to farming large areas of a single cash crop. Because the labor of planting and harvesting now occurred at the same time for most of their land, the farmers had to hire outside labor whenever it was available. They could no longer afford to follow the signs. They dealt with the dissonance between their beliefs in the signs and the new constraints on their farming by downgrading the importance of the signs. Some of them said that traditions about signs often contradicted each other and therefore the signs were unreliable; others contrasted their own "modernity" with the "backwardness" of those who still used the signs. But most had nagging doubts: during one interview, a husband disparaged those who still followed the signs until his wife reminded him that he still planted at the new moon (Passin and Bennett 1943, 103). But many farmers in the United States continue to follow the phases of the moon for planting, consulting the *Farmer's Almanac,* which follows the moon theory in its advice.

Healing and Culture

*M*alinowski did not, any more than Frazer, explain why any one society adopts particular kinds of chants, spells, or other activities. Neither writer incorporated the study of culture into his account, as we must do here.

Giving Birth in Panama and Malaysia

Consider two examples of birthing magic, one from Panama and one from Malaysia. In both, midwives and shamans help the mother in moving the baby down the birth canal and out into the world. But they do so by drawing on very different sets of images and values. Cuna society, in Panama, holds high the culture of heroes and battles (Lévi-Strauss 1963b). There, a shaman, who can be possessed by spirits, sings to help childbirth. He sings a story of how Muu, the spirit that forms the fetus, has exceeded her usual domain and captured the woman's soul, thereby preventing her from moving the baby down the birth canal. The shaman must carve small figurines, the spirits of which he then leads up the birth canal to overcome wild beasts and defeat Muu and her allies. In his song the shaman describes in painstaking detail the events leading up to his own arrival at the woman's house—the woman experiencing pain, the midwife coming to call him, his own arrival—and then the journey of the friendly spirits. The journey is in the same concrete detail as the mundane events and, in Claude Lévi-Strauss's analysis, the woman is thus likely made to feel the entry of the spirits as real. She now can identify her pain with specific, well-described animals and spirits lodged in her vagina. The detail makes the journey psychologically real to the woman in pain, giving her a language for her pain and difficulties, organizing her perceptions and feelings.

Now contrast the chants recited by a healer in a Malay village studied by Carol Laderman (1983). As with the Cuna, the ritual specialist only intervenes when the midwife can no longer cope with the difficult birth. Malinowski's idea that most people work on a common sense basis until they reach the limits of their capacities and knowledge, and only then reach for magic to extend their grasp, thus once again seems to work well. The specialist, called a "bomoh," recites a story about God's creation of the world and of the first couple, and then about the creation of the individual human. These stories follow generally available Muslim lines. They provide a story for the woman that takes place out of ordinary time, placing the woman's suffering also out of ordinary time and giving it a sense of order, naturalness, and harmony. Just as Cuna culture highlights battle, Malay culture stresses the importance of harmony and control.

Even if the woman does not hear every detail of the story, women do know the story's general outline beforehand, says Laderman, and are soothed by its familiar references to the creation story, listing of prophets and mythological figures, and litany of the sequence of days leading to birth.

The story responds to a general cultural emphasis on harmony with the universe. But what happens in the individual? Drawing on work in U.S. hospitals as well as Malaysia, Laderman argues that the psychological response to hearing the story creates a biological response, producing endorphins that reduce pain and also reduce anxiety. Endorphins are chemicals found in several areas of the brain, which appear to be responsible for "placebo effect" pain reduction. Not only do these effects benefit the mother, but because anxiety can prevent proper cervical dilation, the reduction of anxiety may directly lead to more productive contractions, and a quicker, easier birth.

Of course, the ways in which imagery, narratives, beliefs, and emotions affect bodily states, from levels of pain tolerance to changes in the immune system, is a topic under considerable current research. On the one hand, fear can lead to death, as Walter Cannon (1942) observed; more recent research suggests that the "fight or flight" adrenaline response induced by fear, though useful in the short term, is debilitating over longer periods, weakening the heart and the immune system. On the other hand, dissociation (the mechanism involved in trance and hypnosis) and positive imagery reduce pain levels. Just how "magic"—and the many other curing techniques now used in the United States and therefore not so labeled—works on the nervous and immune systems is far from being understood, but it is now widely accepted that such mechanisms do exist.

Faith and Healing in Christian Science

Faith healing abounds in Christian denominations, and a belief in the power of mind over body made a particularly strong entry into bookstores and U.S. minds in the 1990s. This amalgam of religion, science, and self-healing has its longest-lived representative in the Christian Science Church, founded in 1879 by Mary Baker Eddy. From the enormous

Mother Church in Boston emanate the *Christian Science Monitor* and high-quality radio news programs. Adherents are found mainly in the United States and Protestant areas of Europe.

Christian Science healers, called "practitioners," and laypersons can cure themselves and others through prayer and by reading from the religion's two key books: the Christian Gospels and Eddy's book, *Science and Health,* reissued in a new edition in 1996 by the church. This book tells followers that humans are spiritually perfect, though morally far from perfect, and that they only need realize they have the power to abolish sickness. The miracles performed by Jesus are nothing but instances of God's law, available to all humans. Sin, sickness, and death are closely related, and the pure life brings health with it. These beliefs resemble Indian notions of *dharma,* the concept of natural and moral law, where one's moral actions (*karma*) have a direct effect on material events in the world, including one's sickness and health.

Christian Science advocates often relate anecdotes about a recovery through prayer that doctors thought impossible—beginning with Eddy herself, who was inspired by her own recovery from a bad fall on the ice. One writer describes a serious automobile accident in South Dakota, after which he foreswore all medical treatment but called a Christian Scientist practitioner in New York who applied "absent treatment," praying at a distance (Leishman 1958, 127–133).

Science and Health suggests how to pray for health and urges the patient to "mentally contradict every complaint from the body." It contains no secret formulas; but fixed prayers do take on "magical" qualities. The practitioners studied by Bryan Wilson in England recited the following phrase each morning as a defense against the malevolent forces of "animal magnetism":

Malicious animal magnetism does not know where I am or what I am doing: it does not know God's plan or purpose for me, nor the work that God has given me to do; nor can it perpetuate any lies about me; for I live, move, and have my being in God, in Spirit, in the secret place of the Most High (Wilson 1961, 130).

Mary Baker Eddy herself once flirted with hypnotism as a remedy for illness, and later strongly denounced it, leaving a trace in this prayer and in the general suspicion of mental suggestion as a source of illness and sin. Practitioners admit that the common cold may afflict people, but argue that it spreads only if we so believe. We must repel the "aggressive mental suggestion" that colds spread, thereby keeping ourselves from catching them.

In theory Christian Scientists oppose trying to mix medicine with prayer; arguing that the two remedies are so different that they cannot be combined. In some cases Christian Science parents have refused medical treatment for their child. A Minnesota couple and practitioner who let an 11-year-old boy, Ian Lundman, die of diabetes in 1989 were successfully sued for 1.5 million dollars in compensatory damages, an award later upheld by the U.S. Supreme Court. But other Christian Scientists do wear glasses, enter hospitals, seek dental treatment, and allow doctors to treat broken bones and infections (Fraser 1996).

Trance, Possession, and Healing

*H*ealing practices often turn on the idea that a spirit has possessed the patient and is causing the illness. The cure then involves putting the patient (or sometimes a curer) into a trance state, investigating the reasons for the spirit's actions, and driving out the spirit (or *exorcising* the patient).

Afro-Brazilian Trances

In Brazil today, healers draw on Afro-Brazilian religion traditions to carry out their art. Afro-Brazilian religions, variously called "Candomblé," "Umbanda," or "Macumba" (and related to Haitian "Voudun" and Cuban "Santeria"), developed when people living in West Africa were forcibly brought to the Americas as slaves (see Chapter 9). Forced to conceal their own religious ideas and practices, they developed a blend that appeared Catholic but contained elements of West African religion. Today these traditions have changed in various directions, some emphasizing African sources, others native American elements, still others the ties with Catholicism and with European Spiritism (Brown 1986; Goodman 1988, 42–51).

In the Brazilian trance-healing practices called Macumba (Richeport 1985), trance is employed in varied settings to aid in healing. In sessions involving "professional mediums," specialists sit in a separate, cordoned-off part of a room. They are dressed in white and are already in a trance. They each have special "spirit familiars" with whom they communicate. Patients deliver to the staff slips of paper containing their questions; usually the questions are about their own illnesses. The mediums then ask for answers from their spirit familiars and relay these answers back through the staff. These sessions are calm, although sometimes a supplicant will slip into trance, and in such cases he or she may be approached about becoming a medium.

A second type of session involves mass trances. Dozens or hundreds of people gather together for evenings of trance, dancing and music, and consultation. These large-scale sessions also employ mediums, but they walk and dance around on the floor, mingling with other people who wish to attend. Rather than having personal spirit familiars, all the mediums cycle together through several standard spirit types during the evening. Each type represents both a familiar cultural figure of the Brazilian environment and a kind of emotion. When the mediums are possessed by the "old black slave" spirit, they sit, smoking pipes, and dispense this old man's wisdom to those attending (who are often relatives or friends). When they take on the flashily dressed woman called Pomba Gira they are seductive and loose, enjoying this break from normal behavioral restrictions. When they are the child they scamper about eating candy. (There is also an Amazonian equivalent of these sessions in which Indians act the role of whites, drink champagne, and act terribly refined.)

Use is also made of trances at clinics for the mentally ill. Patients are encouraged to enter a trance state and act out their emotions and frustrations; often they, too, take on stereotyped roles such as those mentioned previously.

Shared Healing in Southern Africa

The Kung people living in southern Africa once lived entirely from gathering and some hunting. The great variability of rainfall and thus food in their lands led them to develop norms of sharing and exchange. Sharing distributes risk and gives people a source of food during periods of drought and scarcity.

Healing follows similar lines of thought. The Kung heal those who have fallen ill by assembling in a group at night around a fire and dancing to reach a trance-like state of transcendence called "kai," reached by tapping into the energy, *num*, that everyone has in the pits of their stomachs. About half of the men tap this energy, and about one-third of the women. (They tend to be people whose parents did so. Larger percentages try, and somewhat smaller percentages become active healers.) Num energy is not a limited good, but is given by God to individuals and benefits everyone in the group when people tap it.

Reaching the state of kai can be dangerous and painful. An older healer described the feeling in terms of death and rebirth.

Your heart stops. You're dead. Your thoughts are nothing. You breathe with difficulty. You see things, num things. You see spirits killing people. You smell burning, rotten flesh. Then you heal, you pull sickness out. You heal, heal, heal. Then you live. Your eyeballs clear and you see people clearly (Katz 1982, 45).

When your own num has begun to boil others feel it and they, too, begin to dance.

Kung healing dance at dawn, Botswana. (COURTESY OF RICHARD KATZ, *BOILING ENERGY*, p. 33.)

Healing takes place in three stages. The healer, once his or her num is boiling, can see the num in other healers and the spirits causing illness. Then the healer pulls out the sickness, laying hands on the ill person to put num in and draw out illness, and then shaking the illness out into the darkness. The healer begins to sweat as his num boils; this sweat is the num and he or she rubs it into the patient to forcibly expel the illness (Katz 1982, 106–108).

Then the healer, in a heroic confrontation, does battle with spirits and gods. Usually the illness has been caused by spirits of the dead. Sometimes they have specific complaints about the living person they are bothering; sometimes they are just looking to stir up trouble. But they are also messengers from the great god, Gao Na, a capricious god who may destroy humans should he find them annoying.

Healers may argue with the spirits or even journey to the god's home. Others at the dance hear one side of a dialogue between the healer and the spirits or god, a dialogue of cajoling or threatening. The healer may hurl insults at the spirits or reason gently with them, telling them that they gain nothing from bothering humans.

Kung trance-healing is collective in spirit and in practice because the source of healing power, the num energy, is more powerful the more it is shared.

Modern Magic in Japanese New Religions

*I*n Japan, new forms of healing and worship bring trance mechanisms together with the Japanese cultural heritage to heal patients suffering from what we would call psychosomatic illnesses. These New Religions developed in response to new life situations, particularly in response to the new illnesses and anxieties felt by many newly urban Japanese. Those millions of Japanese who have moved into cities since the 1950s have found themselves cut off from their accustomed places for ritual practice and sources of religious strength. They also found themselves living in a radically new era, with new kinds of pressures on the job and at home.

The New Religions range from the nationally important Soka Gakkai, with its millions of adherents, its own newspaper and university, and its strong ties to a major political party, the Komeito, to smaller sects and cults. Between 10 percent and 30 percent of Japanese are estimated to follow one of the New Religions. But these New Religions and their healing practices draw on elements from Japan's older religious traditions.

One such religion, studied by Winston Davis (1980), is Mahikari, meaning "True Light." It was founded in 1959 when a man of lower-class origins in Tokyo recovered from illness and debt and received a revelation from God that he was to change his name and bring light and health to the people of Japan. This man, now known as Okada Kotama, began to heal people through the use of amulets (a method he had learned from another group), and the sect grew rapidly in popularity. By the late 1970s Mahikari had more than 150 dojos (buildings for practicing spiritual disciplines) and somewhere between 50,000 and 100,000 active members. Close to half a million had received its amulet.

Purification and Apocalypse

The major activity engaged in by people who join Mahikari is called "okiyome," (purification). The process of okiyome is designed to rid the body of spirits that have possessed it. These spirits may be those of ancestors, or of other people, or of animals, especially foxes and badgers. The process involves divination and then exorcism of the spirit.

People generally come to be healed at Mahikari because of a physical complaint, the roots of which are often psychosomatic: cramps, back pains, headaches, and so forth. In their theory of causes of these illnesses, the healers join physical and psychic explanations. Consider one account of illness:

"There is much poison around us," said a Mahikari teacher. (Indeed, in the main river in the city where Davis studied Mahikari, fish introduced to the river die within 3 minutes from industrial toxins!) "We eat poisoned food and the poisons build up inside and cause illnesses. But," he then asked, "why did we eat the poison? Or, given that bacteria can be carried in food and then eaten by us, what led us to eat the infected food?"

The Mahikari world view offers to supplement the scientific world view by bringing the laws of natural cause and effect down to the level of the individual and his or her suffering.

The answer to our suffering is that we are possessed by spirits. Indeed, according to Mahikari, nearly all illnesses are caused by spirits. Each person has an astral spirit, which must burn off its impurities on the astral plane. (Here we see echoes from Buddhism of the planes of existence and the idea of karma.) Burning off impurities is not fun, and many of these astral spirits seek refuge in humans or torment humans for one reason or another.

The power to exorcise spirits derives ultimately from the High God, "Su-God," and also from a Shinto god he created, called Miroku, identified with the bodhisattva figure Maitreya, here called the "Buddha of the Future." Mahikari sees itself as a supplement to other religions. It recognizes that all religions worship lower deities and prophets created by Su-God; some of them have lost their healing powers, however, which Mahikari offers to restore.

The Mahikari ideology also places the individual's suffering on a grand world-historical plane. In its version of history, mankind once was united on the lost continent of Mu, where people existed in five colors. The yellow people were dominant, and within the yellow group, the Japanese. Mu had all the technological advancements of today: telephones, airplanes, and so forth. It was ruined when the races began to intermarry. The present world then developed, but is about to be destroyed.

This story combines an apocalyptic vision of coming disaster with a way out. Because of human wickedness, Su-God has recently put strict gods in power, and signs of this change are to be seen in recent earthquakes, droughts, and so forth. Humankind is to be subjected to even greater torments, and only those possessing the amulets of Mahikari will be saved, to become the "seed people" of the next era.

These kinds of disaster-plus-solution texts appear throughout human history and are often called "millenarian movements" (see Chapter 14). Each of these movements appropriates a set of already widely accepted ideas and traditions—for example, the role of a Buddha or Christ in ensuring salvation—and harnesses them to a small-scale organization, to which are attracted people looking for spiritual guidance or discipline or health. These movements take the promise of salvation seriously, and set out to get it here and now.

Amulets and Ancestors

Consider in greater detail how healing works for Mahikari adherents. People come to the sect to be healed; they learn why they suffer; and the ideas they learn are an important part of the healing process. They learn that their souls are polluted by spirits and by material pollution and that Mahikari offers them both a temporary, personal solution through healing and a way to prepare for future destruction through continued membership in the sect. People are satisfied that they understand why things have happened to them, that it is not their own fault, and that they can do something about them.

The healers diagnose the patient's ills by detecting the auras around their bodies. Bodies give off electromagnetic waves, they are told, and the shape of these waves can be detected by an "aura meter." Auras come in different shapes and colors. Healers can also detect spirits around the body. But the main activity of the healer is to channel energy into the body that will heal and also will ferret out spirits bothering the patient.

The healer wears an amulet, a small locket worn on a chain, with a piece of paper inside that has a symbol written on it. This locket is "plugged in" through the central Mahikari organization to God—indeed, the objective properties of the amulet are explained in ways that draw on electric and electronic imagery. If the amulet gets wet it may disconnect, healers are told, and apology money must be paid to Mahikari for it to be reconnected. Monthly dues must be paid, which are offered to Su-God "to keep the line connected for the next month."

The healer, wearing the amulet, raises his or her hands over the patient's body, concentrating rays from God on the body. The healer begins with the patient's "primary soul" and then looks for parts of the body that seem to need attention, perhaps massaging the body to detect such parts. The healing power of okiyome also works for inanimate objects, such as automobiles or movie projectors. (Of those people belonging to Mahikari who were surveyed, 42 percent had repaired their television sets with okiyome; 29 percent had used it to fix their wristwatches.)

In the case of people, spirits usually are responsible for their ailments. The healer must find out the identity of the spirit and then convince it to leave the patient. The patient must enter a state of trance. The healer chants over him or her, and the patient usually begins to move and cry out in ways indicative of the spirit's identity. The patient's hand movements may be characteristic of a particular animal (serpentine movements indicate a snake, and so on). Or the patient may write out words or names on a tablet.

But the healer usually talks to the spirit as well, asking it if it is human, when it died, and, most importantly, why it is possessing the person. The healer scolds the spirit: "Go back to the other world and leave her in peace."

The most common explanation of specific ailments involves relationships with ancestors. Events may have caused an ancestor's spirit to possess you, for one of two reasons. First, you may have neglected the altar of the ancestors in your house. One man's ancestor came back to possess him because the altar was on a filing cabinet and the spirit was disturbed by the noise. In the Mahikari sect people study proper altar care to avoid these problems. Nothing must be above it (so it must occupy the top story of the house), its flowers must be arranged properly, and it must have proper lacquered tablets and be supplied with food every day. Recall that in rural society the altar was the site of the protective household god, and so the anxiety of ordinary people about neglected altars makes sense.

Second, events that happened to ancestors, or to yourself in an earlier life, may have caused your misfortune and caused you to be possessed by an ancestral spirit. Healers draw on the logic of karma from Buddhism to explain how this works. One woman had been the wife of a warrior (samurai) in a previous incarnation, and when she married he grew jealous and came to bother her. Samurai often appear as the ancestors responsible for possession because they tended to commit all sorts of bad deeds and would be expected to bring misfortune.

But sometimes another kind of spirit is involved: that of a fox or snake, for example. Here, too, there is an explanation of what event caused the spirit to possess the person. One man with cancer of the face was found to be possessed by the spirit of a snake. When he was a boy he had cut off the head of a snake, and the spirit had chosen appropriate revenge.

Trance Psychology

Central to the patient's experience of being healed is the state of trance into which he or she enters. Trance, like any other altered state of consciousness, begins when one dissociates, or withdraws from ordinary states of consciousness (Davis 1980, 132–144). We have all experienced dissociation during daydreaming, when different, sometimes odd thoughts and images wander into one's consciousness. But in the kind of structured trance settings found in Mahikari or elsewhere the patient has been trained to expect certain specific symbols, images, or actions to emerge. Mahikari patients study books of spirit images beforehand; some also rehearse the hand movements of different spirits. They then *project* their fears, anger, sadness, or specific problems onto the symbols that have been made available to them. They respond to questions posed to them about ancestors or animals, and can introduce into their answers their own life problems. Finally comes the moment of release, or catharsis, when the person collapses onto the floor and experiences a strong feeling of relief. (Aristotle used "catharsis" to refer to the moment in a drama when pent-up emotions in the audience are released.)

The psychology of the trance-healing session is not specifically Japanese; Felicitas Goodman (1988) documents trance and possession worldwide. Its particular form in Japan draws on older culturally specific practices, however. One is the duet form of the healing: the process always involves an exorciser and a subject, who then exchange roles (rather than, for example, a single healer and many patients). This duet form is found in much older spirit possession–healing cults in Japan and is familiar to patients. It is especially effective in the way it taps the Japanese emotion of "dependence" on another, *amae.* This emotional relation has its prototype in the dependence of a child on his or her mother, and underlies relations to teachers, employers, and, in the past, the emperor. When the emperor was demoted to the role of ordinary human and state symbol after World War II, psychiatrists (Doi 1986) noted that some people became depressed by the loss of a pole for their dependence emotions.

The healing session helps to draw out longings for someone to depend on, in this specific, highly charged sense, and also longings to be depended on. The alternation of roles allows the person who is missing these roles in everyday life to better assume them. For example, one housewife had become so concerned about pollution in food that she could not bring herself to cook for her family. She then became immobilized out of guilt for not doing so, for no longer being depended on. These feelings emerged during trance, and repeated sessions gave her a way to speak these feelings as well as a new setting for dependence–role playing.

Mahikari combines universal psychosocial processes (such as trance) with culturally specific features (such as the focus on ancestors). Simply by participating in a group, regardless of its content, some people gain a stronger sense of the value of their lives. Members also have a legitimate reason to meddle in other people's lives. But, remembering Malinowski, we might pay special attention to the way the process adds confidence and certainty to the making of difficult decisions.

Take the case of Winston Davis's teacher, Yoshida Sensei, and his wife (Davis 1980, 52–63). Yoshida's father had died in the hospital, even though he had asked his son to take him home to die. Several years later, their daughter died in the same hospital. Later, Yoshida's mother died of a stomach ailment, and Yoshida himself developed ulcers. They joined Mahikari and began to be possessed by a number of ancestors and relatives, and through the exorcism procedure learned the causes of their various misfortunes.

Yoshida's father appeared in the form of a badger. He complained of dying in the hospital and said he had caused the daughter's death as revenge, and added his regret that Yoshida had sold off their land. (Yoshida remembered that he had had trouble selling the land and now knew that his father was behind these troubles.) Yoshida taught his father that he must be a spirit and not trouble them in the earthly world: "Apologize to God and return to the astral world to continue your austerities," he demanded. His father's spirit wept at this. They then agreed that Yoshida could sell some of the land, since it was difficult to farm and surrounded by buildings, as long as he bought some other land as a hedge against inflation. After that the father appeared as a human spirit; he had progressed up the spiritual ladder.

The process addressed the several sources of guilt faced by Yoshida and his wife, explained the series of illnesses, and finally exorcised the guilt by leading Yoshida through a series of emotionally charged sessions. Finally, it legitimated his further action, allowing him to sell off land with a clear conscience.

Who Joins the New Religions?

Women make up 60 percent of the participants in Mahikari; many of these women are unmarried and in the traumatic period after high school during which society views them as in transition to their next state, marriage. Employers still see most women as temporary employees, biding time until marriage. But some women either wish to pursue careers or have not found suitable husbands, and many psychosomatic illnesses occur then.

Healing can explain why marriage is difficult, perhaps because of possession by a jealous husband from a past life, and can also provide an outlet for repressed emotions and desires. Consider several cases discussed by Winston Davis (1980, 161–200): Tanio lived in fear of men. Her own father was often drunk and violent, and she was raised by her mother. In trance the spirit possessing her declared herself to be that of a woman whose husband she stole in an earlier life. Nakata never married because, trance revealed, she was possessed by spirits of aborted children. Eiko was happily married but her family resisted her joining Mahikari. Her own ancestors torment her whenever she worships her husband's ancestors. (Here emerged the classic problem of changing ancestral allegiances.)

These women and men found power in an environment of their own general powerlessness. Inside the sect people experience possession and curing. But outside, as well, they experience miracles. Only 12 of 688 members interviewed said they did not experience such miracles. They found social status within the group. And they found an ideology that explained much of what was happening around them, gave them a way to muddle through it, and promised future salvation.

Whatever we might think about these groups, they are a response to urban ills. Some of them are clearly destructive (and some think even Mahikari to be so). In March 1995, canisters containing the nerve gas sarin exploded in a Tokyo subway, killing 10 and injuring more than 5,000, and the attack was linked to the sect Aum Shinrikyo. Aum Shinrikyo's leader, Shoko Asahara, preaches much the same apocalyptic vision as does Mahikari's Okada Kotama. Aum hands out battery-powered headgear to followers so that they may communicate directly with their leader. (The headgear also attracts recruits from the sciences.) Its teachings combine Buddhism and Hinduism—especially the god of destruction, Shiva. Aum followers had to renounce ties with the outside world and donate all their goods to the cult (Sayle 1996).

The history of state Shinto and its ties to militarism have made the Japanese state very wary of interfering in these sects, even when evidence of criminal actions emerges. In 1989 Asahara was named responsible for killing a lawyer helping to return children kidnapped by the sect. And yet Aum was recognized as a religious body the same year and no steps were taken against its leader. One legacy of state Shinto is thus an extraordinarily lenient attitude toward the new sects.

Magic and Religion

Those practices that we might call "magic" have differing relationships to religion. Some, such as baseball practices, are not based on any belief system whatsoever. Others, such as Trobriand spells, do imply beliefs in spirits but little else. Still other practices, such as healing in Japan, Brazil, and Malaya or among the Cuna of Panama, draw on extensive bodies of knowledge about how spirits work. In all cases some of the older insights by Frazer and Malinowski about the logic and functions of magic can still help us understand why people are attracted to certain practices. Malinowski's notion that all people use science plus magic, with the latter added on to the former, continues to make sense. The forms of magic differ greatly: memorized spells, possession and exorcism, narratives about creation or battles, or about God or the effectiveness of medicine. But each such practice gives the person a sense of control, or understanding, or certainty greater than what was enjoyed before the event. Each practice also seems to reduce anxiety (although once it is relied on, its absence may create anxiety).

These features of "magical" practices all concern their effects. To understand their contents and why Japanese, Brazilians, and Cuna do things differently, we have explored the linkages between each practice and the dominant forms and motifs of the culture in which it is found. Recall the paths taken by healers. Cuna healers seek to reduce a woman's pain by telling a story of battles; Malay healers, a story about cosmic harmony; U.S. healers, a story about breathing techniques and medicines. Japanese healers draw on ideas about the ever-watchful ancestors, the culture form of the duet, and Buddhist religious traditions to construct a convincing combination of texts and practices.

Institutions built on notions of magic can take on functions of healing, religion, and even community. Their practices can provide confidence insofar as they fit general cultural expectations, and this confidence and assurance can cause physical changes in a patient. For better or worse, they can furnish the basis for close-knit relationships in a disorganized world. Far from being merely a set of mistaken ideas, magic continues to be a powerful force in the real world.

Profile

Michael Brown
Studying New Age Religions in the United States

Michael Brown, of Williams College, spent many years studying shamanism among native Amazonian peoples. His study fits the image of what an ethnographer does, which is to study exotica elsewhere. But what about exotica at home? Brown's work on New Age religions, and specifically on channeling, brought curious glances from colleagues. That work is found in his 1997 book, *The Channeling Zone: American Spirituality in an Anxious Age* (Harvard University Press).

My research on the New Age movement was born from simple curiosity. While spending a sabbatical year in Santa Fe, New Mexico,

I found myself frequently encountering people involved in some facet of alternative spirituality. When I looked for published work that could help me make sense of this freeform religious activity, I found only accounts that either promoted New Age perspectives or dismissed them as deplorable expression of irrationality and self-indulgence. Missing were the nuanced reports that anthropologists typically offer after studying the beliefs of people in distant, exotic places. Given the scale of the New Age movement in the United States, I decided that it deserved a thorough study using traditional ethnographic methods.

Thinking about the project was one thing; carrying it out was another. The New Age movement is so widespread and loosely organized that it would have been impossible for me to study all its facets. I decided to use one of its practices, channeling, as a window on the movement's broader goals. Most of the people I observed and interviewed had been involved in other forms of alternative spirituality in the past, so I was able to gather useful information on the links between channeling and other spiritual practices.

My fieldwork proved to be challenging. When documenting workshops and training sessions, I felt obliged to do what my subjects did, whether it involved trying to channel or "getting in touch with my inner child." Although I had few personal experiences one could call insightful or dramatic, my participation helped me to understand the motivations of people drawn to these activities. Another problem was the reaction of some of my professional colleagues who assumed that I had chosen this project as part of a personal religious quest—a suspicion never voiced when I studied Amazonian Indians years before. The New Age is largely a movement of educated, middle-class people that intellectuals seem to find reprehensible and even threatening. Perhaps they are annoyed by its tendency to borrow academic concepts and take them in new and surprising directions. Perhaps they resent its sunny optimism.

Some of my colleagues felt that this was not a subject worthy of dispassionate study. But while I wrote *The Channeling Zone* I was guided by the conviction that the chief purpose of ethnography is to introduce readers to the complexity of other social worlds. The rules I followed govern classic ethnographies: take people's ideas and practices seriously, describe them with care, call attention to what is admirable as well as to what is troubling, and then let readers make their own judgments. This may be an old-fashioned view of anthropology's mission, but it has stood the test of time. ✎

For Further Consideration

*M*ost North Americans have experience with faith healing; you might discuss those together. For information on Christian Science healing, try the long series of radio broadcasts with examples of healing that are available for listening at *http://www.myfreeoffice.com/sbuaa/ce3.html.* A source of writings and broadcasts about Science teachings is at *http://www.endtime.org/.*

For more about Santeria, start with the Practical Guide to Afro-Caribbean Magic, by Luis M. Nuñez (Spring Publications 1992), at *http://www.iac.net/~moonweb/ Santeria/TOC.html.* Caribe.com (*http://www.nando.net/prof/caribe/caribe.com.html*) is building a site devoted to Santeria, which promises to be substantive. Sites devoted to Umbanda are mainly in Portuguese and require more information to place them in context.

The film *Macumba: Trance and Spirit Healing* (Filmakers Library 1985) is an excellent companion to this chapter, and many other films on these religions are now available, especially from the University of California Extension Media Center, including *Hail Umbanda* (1988) and *Bahia: Africa in the Americas* (1988). Books on Afro-Brazilian groups include Jim Wafer's *The Taste of Blood: Spirit Possession in Brazilian Candomblé*

(University of Pennsylvania Press 1991) and Joseph Murphy's *Working the Spirit: Ceremonies of the African Diaspora* (Beacon Press 1994).

Among several other useful films are *Healers of Ghana* (Films for the Humanities and Sciences 1993), which treats healing and witchcraft; and *N/um Tchai* (University of California Extension Center 1966), which shows the Kung healing ritual described in the text.

7

Explaining Misfortune: Witchcraft and Sorcery

*H*ow do we explain the presence of suffering and evil in the world? Is what befalls us our fault? The fault of distant gods? Or is there a malicious element, a sorcerer or witch, in our midst? The notion that someone or something among us bedevils us gives rise to the ideas we call "witchcraft" or "sorcery." The belief that there are certain people who are witches, predisposed to do evil, is widespread; but there are major differences in beliefs from one area of the world to another. The concepts of witchcraft and sorcery are tied to general ideas about society and community, and for that reason they are very sensitive to social change.

The terms sorcery and witchcraft have been used by anthropologists and historians to refer to accusations that others are committing malevolent, destructive acts. (In the United States and Europe today, "white witchcraft" or Wiccanry has quite another meaning, as we saw in Chapter 5.) But, as in the Salem witchcraft trials we examine in this chapter, religious authorities often invented these categories. In such instances "witches" are part of a religious system that seeks to identify and separate the bearers of good and evil in the world. The terms may also apply when people in particular societies seek to explain unexpected misfortune by blaming it on unseen agents sent by other people—sorcerers or witches.

Accusations of witchcraft or sorcery are but one instance, however, of a common feature of religions, namely, seeking explanations for misfortune.

Religion and Explanation

*M*ost likely, all societies provide some way to explain misfortune by postulating unseen forces, either personified agents such as spirits and devils, or abstract forces such as original sin or karma. These unseen forces are usually invoked when more everyday causes are unavailable.

Karma in South Asia

The idea of *karma* is that one's actions in the past, including in past lives, affects one's life today. The idea can be called on to account for misfortune. We saw in Chapter 6 how Japanese healing practices draw on the idea of karma to explain illness—in a past life a patient was a samurai, and his evil deeds are now visited upon him.

The idea of karma is most widespread in South Asia, where it is interpreted in a variety of ways and is subject to debate between social classes. In particular, views held by some religious authorities of the Brahman priestly class contrast with many popular ideas about karma (Babb 1983). In one Brahmanic view, at least, a great deal of the misfortune of life is due not to a deity, who might be propitiated or recruited through sacrifice or worship, but to one's own actions in an earlier life: that is, due to karma. Under this notion of karma, there is little or nothing that a person can do to change what his deeds in his previous life have preordained. Some Brahmans also invoke karma to explain why they are sitting on top of the caste hierarchy.

Other people reject some of these views about karma, though not the idea itself. Unsurprisingly, people of lower castes are skeptical that Brahmans are on top because of their past good deeds. More generally, as with the strict Calvinist views of predestination that we consider in Chapter 11, "just sit and wait" has less popular appeal than "try something." For these reasons, most village Hindu people have modified the Brahmanic view of karma. The idea that you can do something has strong religious as well as psychological roots. Even the classical Hindu literature portrays people who, through their devotion to the gods, are saved from the consequences of their past lives.

Some people view karma as applying to a group of people rather than only to the individual, and as applying mainly to one's actions in this lifetime. In this view, karma implies that certain categories of people will get their just rewards or punishments during their lifetimes. Susan Wadley and Bruce Derr (1989) give the example of a fire in a north Indian village, which villagers blamed on the bad actions of the Brahman landowners. The fire itself was seen as having singled out for destruction the homes of certain offenders: those who were "eating the earnings of sin" by oppressing the landless laborers. Those Brahmans who escaped did so because of their counterbalancing merit, their good deeds.

The idea of a balance sheet kept between merit and demerit does have some support from classical religious texts. It is widespread in popular culture in South Asia. As one Tamil man in southern India told Sheryl Daniel (1983), karma works "like a bank balance" in that good and bad deeds cancel each other out. This particular man worked as a local temple priest, where his frequent acts of worship brought him much merit. But he also had a number of extramarital affairs, which he needed to offset. (His own calculation was that he was still ahead.) But Daniel reports that for most misfortunes people did not invoke karma. Karma instead served as a background set of forces, much like "fate" in some Western traditions, that can be mentioned when no other explanation is at hand.

Much more commonly invoked as causes of misfortune are the actions of sorcerers, who work through deities and spirits, and a notion of simple fate, brought on by ritual omissions or other unknown events. *Fate* implies no moral responsibility on the part of the people concerned, whereas *karma* implies that their past misdeeds led them to either suffer or commit an undesirable act. Sorcery, however, can be delt with directly, by countering the sorcerer's malevolent actions through rituals of exorcism and possession.

These various accounts of an event may be invoked with self-interest in mind. In a case of chicken stealing reported by Daniel (1983), the friends of the accused thieves blamed the event of chicken theft on simple fate, thereby attributing no fault to anyone, whereas the other side, favoring punishment, chalked it up to the bad karma of the thieves.

And of course, Hindus, like people everywhere, rarely hesitate to attribute someone's misfortune to laziness or stupidity. As Lawrence Babb writes (1983, 167), "[t]here is little evidence, in short, that Hindus are any more inclined than other peoples to ignore the evident proximate causes of human fortune."

Suffering as Part of God's Plan

Many Christians explain the tribulations of their lives as part of "God's plan." Nancy Ammerman (1987) studied a Fundamentalist church in New England whose members talked to her about their certainty that God has a plan for them, both as individuals and as a moral community of saved people. They view their lives as an extensive contract with God: if I behave according to his plan, then I will be rewarded. Church members refer to 7,834 promises from God to be found in the Bible, covering everything from personal health to child rearing. As one church member put it: "He makes the decisions for me, and that is great!" (Ammerman 1987, 40–51).

Ammerman describes the ways these Christians attribute some misfortune to the basic sinfulness of humans, on whom the original sin in the Garden of Eden is visited. Satan, too, is present in this world, and sometimes someone who suffers is said to have participated in Satan's activities. If he or she drank or smoked, for example, this kind of account seems reasonable to these people. Moreover, Satan may strike down the most righteous people as well as the obvious sinners.

But when these Fundamentalists cannot find a specific reason for suffering they may despair, and some have turned away from God. Sometimes they recount their own spiritual histories as a despairing in God followed by a returning to God. They mention Christ's experience of suffering as a source of strength for them: "My savior suffered for me; who am I not to suffer?" (Ammerman 1987, 68).

Seemingly random events provoke considerable thought. Once, a freak tornado devastated homes and stores in a nearby suburb (Ammerman 1987, 70–71). What could its meaning have been? The rarity of such a tornado here led people to think that it must bear a divine message, but they could not decide what that message might have been. Men and women attending an adult Sunday school class held shortly after the event pondered this problem, proposing several explanations and then revising them after discussion. One man noted that his store, in the affected suburb, had been spared: God was rewarding him for his own righteousness, he concluded. But then another person mentioned that a righteous woman, recently saved from sin, had been endangered by the storm. This fact forced the first man to revise his story; it could no longer be about God sparing the faithful and damaging the damned. Perhaps, he tried again, his store was saved to give him the chance to witness to others about God's power. This interpretation could not be refuted.

It was very important to these people to find divine purpose in the event. It was not troubling to them that that purpose was hard for mere humans to discern.

Sorcery as a Focus on Practitioners

*M*agic can also explain why things sometimes go wrong. You missed that easy pitch? You must have worn the wrong shirt. But ideas about sorcery and witchcraft are *all* about explaining misfortune. As classically defined in anthropology, the two terms denote slightly different emphases: by *sorcery* we mean practices used by people who are just like other people. They make use of spells and other powers to malignantly affect innocent persons. Sorcery is a lot like magic but it causes illness and suffering. By contrast, the term *witchcraft* emphasizes characteristics of the people rather than the practices. The term picks out a class of persons who cause misfortune by virtue of an evil power they possess.

Sorcery and Leadership in Melanesia

In many societies in Papua New Guinea and on other islands of Melanesia, people accuse others in their own village or kin group of causing illness and death through sorcery (Stephen 1987). In some of these societies, leaders use the fear of sorcery as a way of controlling subordinates.

Why would leadership be connected to sorcery in this region? Melanesia is the home of the grassroots politician par excellence. In many if not most of these societies, a man becomes a leader by persuading others to join him in certain tasks, such as amassing pigs and other food to put on a large feast. Men who are successful at cajoling others to follow their lead become "bigmen." For them, sorcery becomes a valuable weapon of persuasion.

In some of these societies people also believe that witches, people harboring evil entities within their bodies, are responsible for deaths. But witches are abhorred and may be sought out and killed, whereas sorcerers are feared but esteemed for their powers (Stephen 1987). Sorcery has its positive as well as merely powerful side. Sorcerers may also be healers and they use their powers for warfare against other groups.

Two societies on the Sepik River, northern Papua New Guinea, illustrate the very different ways responsibility for sorcery may be understood. The Abelam consider all sorcery-caused deaths to be the work of members of their own community. They do not openly accuse such insiders, though, because the chief sorcerers are the village leaders, the "bigmen," whom ordinary people do not dare to challenge. In this society the sorcerers are known and feared. In nearby Ilahita society, insiders are also thought to cause deaths through sorcery, but they are seen as the mere agents of the real cause, the dominant spirit of the men's cult. Responsibility is thus shifted from humans to a spirit (Stephen 1987, 252–254).

Sorcery ideas play subtle roles in everyday Melanesian life. Karen Brison (1992) shows how people living in a small community near the Sepik River use gossip and innuendo to influence events without having to take responsibility for leadership. In the Kwanga villages she studied, as in many small-scale, face-to-face communities throughout the world, reputation and slander often go hand in hand. People look with distrust at leaders and at success in general. Melanesian leaders sometimes hint at their sorcery powers in order to gain influence, but when they do they may become the victims of the same backbiting tactics.

Distrust and Navajo Sorcery

Similar social dynamics—distrust, sorcery beliefs, and gossip—were described by Clyde Kluckhohn (1967) in his study of Navajo sorcery and witchcraft. Navajos trace the advent of sorcery and witchcraft to First Man and First Woman. Those beings developed poisons and spells that inflict illness and death. Kluckhohn's fieldwork convinced him that most Navajos believed that other Navajos did engage in these practices—and also convinced him that at least a few people did themselves practice some of these techniques.

Kluckhohn asked why such beliefs would persist over time. They make a good story and can explain why things go wrong, but so do a lot of other stories and beliefs. Why, then, the specific beliefs in sorcery and witchcraft? Kluckhohn pointed to the many hidden or latent functions of such beliefs. Few overt hostilities are allowed in Navajo society; but openly hating a witch is approved behavior.

Moreover, accusations of sorcery are regularly leveled against people who become rich and stingy or who succeed too fast and too well. Healers who seem unwilling to heal may be so accused. The beliefs, said Kluckhohn (1967, 110–113), help soften the transition from a familial society to one in which competition has a legitimate place. They do this by making very successful people wary of displaying their wealth or boasting of their accomplishments. Sorcery and witchcraft beliefs thus can be seen to have positive social functions. Kluckhohn also described the social costs: in greater anxiety, in keeping people from assuming leadership, and, in the past, in sanctioning the killing of people as witches.

Witchcraft and Moral Accounts of Misfortune

*I*f sorcery involves practices and techniques aimed at committing harm, witchcraft involves people who by their very bodily or spiritual composition seek to harm others. Witches tend to be persons within the community. They attack people with whom they ought to be allied, typically out of envy, spite, or greed, rather than for material gain alone. Their actions are morally as well as socially condemned.

These characteristics of witchcraft make it useful in explaining misfortune. People in your own community are most likely to know how to injure you and to have reason to do so. Indeed, people accused of witchcraft are often those who are very close to you and yet somehow different: women who marry into the community (and thus lack the blood ties that presumably would bind them to you), your co-wife or your in-laws (very close, and yet often in conflict), the poor and marginal in the community (who, even if related, presumably envy their betters), and, more generally, people like you who have begun to change and adopt new ways (the category of the accused in the Salem trials, discussed later in this chapter). Sometimes specific historical memories are used to identify a category of likely witches: Navajos, for example, consider two groups of Navajos to be particularly likely to produce witches: those who have intermarried with Pueblo peoples, and those descended from missionized Navajos who sided with the Spanish against fellow Navajos.

Likely targets may also include a member of the community who has withheld the demonstrations of solidarity expected from him or her: personal generosity, expressions of loyalty to the group, support for its leaders. Consider how we apply the label "witch hunt" to the Army–McCarthy hearings or the purges within the Soviet Communist Party. Both processes typified the dark side of the 1950s, a period of ideological dislocation and reorientation, fear and perceived threat, loyalty oaths, and pressure to join in condemning others (often the only way to dispel accusations of disloyalty). Indeed, Arthur Miller's play of the period about the Salem witch trials, *The Crucible,* was immediately understood by those who saw it as being really about the McCarthy hearings.

Witchcraft accusations, then, like magic, can be seen as a very general human practice that may take place in a domain marked off as "religious," but may also surface in other domains of everyday life. It can focus on almost anything, from politics to illness. In the early stages of public awareness about AIDS, for example, some people sought to account for the epidemic in terms of widespread moral failings: homosexuality, a breakdown in family values, and so forth. References to "God's judgment" were heard. People of the United States have often formed moral judgments about epidemics throughout this century, whether tuberculosis, cancer, or today's viral epidemics.

Why do we hold such ideas? Well, we can postulate a basic human unwillingness to think of the universe as random. We seek patterns, causes, reasons for things. For events that have moral dimensions—and all disasters and unexpected misfortunes do—we often seek moral causes. Accusations of witchcraft allow us to excuse ourselves, our friends, and our gods from responsibility. But they also give us something more specific, more focused, than "fate" or "bad luck." Just as a healer's spells or the Book of Job provide a suffering person with a text that makes concrete his or her suffering, so witchcraft accusations point to a real, concrete individual as the cause of all that is plaguing us, no matter how vague the plague might be. Of course, a "witch" may also be seen as the representative or incarnation of an evil god, as is Satan, such that a cosmological battle is brought down to earth and made directly relevant to everyday concerns.

Witchcraft, then, is distinguished from magic by making the person, and not just his or her actions, the cause of an unfortunate event. This is a fine distinction and, in the end, is less important than our understanding of how these practices and ideas work in different societies. There are marked regional differences in characterizations of witches. In both modern Africa and early modern Europe, certain people were identified as witches whose supernatural practices were inevitably malevolent. But in Africa, divination of witchcraft focused more on the specific event; in Europe, more on the person of the witch. Southeast Asian notions hold that people who practice sorcery through an inherited power can also practice magic for the good of others. In other words, although these persons are identified in much the same ways as are witches elsewhere, they are not inevitably evil, but "practitioners" who may work for the good or the bad.

Although the distinction is inexact, it is useful when discussing how these notions function to distinguish between "normal" and "pathological" contexts of witchcraft accusation—without implying that "normal" here means "good." In these "normal" situations, witchcraft accusations are resolved without leading to major social crises. They may harm individuals, but they may be seen as (and in fact function as) ways of avoiding social crises by exorcising the society of its problems through individual scapegoats. The witch may confess, may carry out an act that restores the ill person to health, or may be punished. We shall see how a "normal" system of accusations and the restoring of health works in one society, the Azande. Ironically, the very fact that witchcraft is considered a property of a person rather than wholly the result of his or her actions can lead to situations in which the witch is excused or released once he or she has apologized or attempted to make restitution. The witchcraft was an event that happened because of the witch's body, not an intentionally crafted effort to harm others.

But the logic of witchcraft persecution can also make a sudden switch over to large-scale persecutions, the proverbial "witch hunt." The switch from the relatively benign focus on restoring the health of victims to hunting and killing witches may be caused by social dislocations or paranoias or may involve a tipping point, at which the accusations build their own momentum. Especially during periods of stress, the accusations may continue to build up and be directed at a sizable portion of the society. Such periods of stress include the Reformation in Europe or the contemporary history of urbanization in Africa.

Witchcraft as a Characteristic of the Individual

*P*ractices grouped together as witchcraft admit of wide variation, from the idea that certain people carry an evil-causing substance inside them to the idea that the devil or some other external power uses humans for his or her nefarious ends. These ideas are differently distributed around the world: the first idea best characterizes some beliefs in African societies; the second, Christian-influenced accusations (as well as accusations in some other world areas). We look at examples of each in turn.

Azande Ideas of Bodily Substance

Located on the border between the Sudan and Zaire (and over the past 20 years devastated by warfare in the southern Sudan), the Azande society was first studied in the late 1920s by the Oxford anthropologist E. E. Evans-Pritchard. Among his publications on the society was the anthropological classic, *Witchcraft, Oracles and Magic among the Azande* (1937). This book continues to figure in discussions among philosophers and historians as well as among anthropologists for its discussion of the rationality of Azande beliefs about witchcraft.

Azande say that certain persons have a substance in their small intestine called *mangu*, or "witchcraft substance." Sometimes specialists conduct autopsies of persons suspected of witchcraft, and in some of these investigations they produce (most likely after having planted) an oval blackish swelling or bag in which seeds may be found. This substance is inherited, by men through males and by women through females. From mangu come emanations that cause injury, misfortune, or illness. They may happen without the knowledge of the person in whose body the mangu is located, when the person feels envy, malice, jealousy, hatred, or other negative emotions toward the victim.

These ideas thus form a type of witchcraft, in which, far from being the purposive manipulation of magical techniques, the events that cause illness may take place without the knowledge of the person responsible. Moreover, someone may have inherited the substance yet never use or be aware of having it, and Azande, who do not classify people as witches if they have not done witchcraft, are little interested in such cases. Evans-Pritchard was intrigued by this lack of interest, given the European focus on finding and destroying witches and given the beliefs about the inheritance of witchcraft. After talking with Azande about this issue, he concluded that although in theory all men related through males should, equally, be or not be witches, and the same for women, "Azande generally regard witchcraft as an individual trait and treat it as such." Post-mortem autopsies clear or condemn only the close kin of a suspected witch; they are not used to locate a witch lineage. And even when an autopsy "finds" mangu, relatives may claim that the person was not really their blood relative but the result of adultery. (Of course, others are equally free to disregard this claim.)

Although this attitude toward the problem continues to puzzle some philosophers, who pose it as the "problem of Zande rationality," Evans-Pritchard saw it as simply another emphasis within the range of possible emphases we make in the world. It is the event, and the individual who caused it, that is the main focus of Azande witchcraft discussions; determining who the witches are is definitely a secondary, if interesting, concern.

Explaining Misfortune

A wide range of unfortunate occurrences are ascribed to witchcraft, not unlike Western notions of "bad luck"—with the difference that here steps may be taken to find out who caused the witchcraft. Witchcraft is like "illness," says Evans-Pritchard, in that people react to it as an expected part of everyday life, not out of the ordinary.

In particular, witchcraft explains why events are not completely understandable. If one knows what one is doing, and is careful, and obeys all the rules and taboos, then, in a universe undisturbed by meddling witches, things would work out all right. But when things do not work out all right, witchcraft is the only explanation left. In an arresting idiom, it is the "second spear" of explanation, thrown after the first to clinch the matter. Evans-Pritchard furnished the following examples:

A man hangs himself after quarreling with his brothers. Now, he was clearly prompted by the quarrel to take his life, but that explanation is insufficient, because people quarrel every day but only very rarely hang themselves. The "second spear" of witchcraft is needed to explain his actions.

Some people are shading themselves under a granary when the structure collapses, killing them. The cause, to a certain extent, is to be found in the termites who had eaten away the granary's foundations and caused the collapse. But why was it precisely at that moment that it collapsed? Why was it those people who were killed rather than some others, or no one?

In both cases the logic of explanation is that predicted by Malinowski: everyday knowledge plus the "second spear" of witchcraft. In the first case the everyday account is motivationally incomplete; witchcraft occupies a place that "temporary insanity" does in U.S. culture today, or "the devil made him do it" might have in the recent past. (In other instances, when someone kills someone else out of vengeance or commits adultery out of desire, no such supplement is needed, and protests that "witchcraft made me do it" are laughed down.)

In the second case, the everyday account is morally incomplete. Why did it have to be them? We can understand this need for the reason that will respond to the moral dimension; it is precisely what relatives of crash victims ask, when the answer they seek is not in a malfunction or a bomb, but in the conjuncture of events in the universe or in God's mind.

Sometimes an Azande goes the next step and accuses someone of sending out the emanations. These accusations follow predictable social pathways. You accuse people of your own social standing and with whom you have interacted, people for whom feelings of jealousy, envy, and hatred most commonly arise. You do not accuse nobles or influential commoners, not only because to do so is dangerous, but because you probably have not had the daily petty quarrels with them that most frequently engender emanations of mangu. More likely are accusations by courtiers of a prince toward each other, or among neighbors, particularly in matters pertaining to crops.

Witchcraft in Azande society is more an event than a state, the particular act of bewitching rather than the continual quality of being a witch, and in this regard it is quite different from European ideas. Because the emanations from mangu are always brought on by anger, malice, envy, and like emotions, the witchcraft becomes identified with these sentiments themselves, to the extent that people who regularly exhibit ill will tend to be accused of witchcraft. (Although Evans-Pritchard did not explore this aspect of these ideas, the identification of ill will with witchcraft must act as a powerful social control.)

The person who is accused may feel himself or herself quite innocent of committing witchcraft. Azande witchcraft theory has a space for protests of innocence: because witchcraft occurs when an emotion travels down to the witchcraft substance and then emanates outward, it is possible for a witch to be ignorant, at least at first, of his or her actions. But Azande also limit such protests; they say that witches generally are aware of their mangu and that they meet together to chortle over their misdeeds. If someone has been successfully accused several times, thereafter he or she is presumed to know of the emanations and bears the moral responsibility for them.

Consulting Oracles

How is an accusation evaluated? Usually an oracle of some kind is consulted by an expert. Oracles form a hierarchy from the most common (and least expensive to use) to the most tightly controlled (and most costly), but the form of consultation is the same. You have the expert put a question to the oracle. The question might be: "Did so-and-so cause my son's illness?" but it might also be on a non-witchcraft matter such as: "If I build a house in this clearing will I fall ill?" Among widely available oracles are the stones that when rubbed together either stick or glide in response to questions and the termites that eat parts of a stick pushed into their mound. On the top of the oracle hierarchy is the chicken oracle controlled by princes. When this oracle is consulted, a handler, who works for the prince, administers a strychnine-type poison to the chicken. He then poses a question, directing the chicken to die (or live) if the answer is "yes." The chicken then dies or lives. Sometimes the answer is verified by putting the question the other way around (using a second chicken). Thus, the first time the handler asks the chicken to live if the answer is "yes"; the second time to live if the answer is "no."

How does this oracle, the most important and beyond which there is no appeal, work? Presumably, if the oracles gave random answers to questions they would come to be perceived as unreliable. There must then be some degree of positive correspondence between outcomes and what those involved already know or suspect. Part of the answer lies in what is asked of the oracles.

Some questions will concern matters about which most people already have some knowledge and about which there is already a great deal of suspicion, such that either answer, yes or no, will fit what people think they already know. For instance, a couple was accused of a specific act of adultery, and the oracle came out against them. They had protested their innocence (and may have indeed been innocent this time) but were known to have been carrying on an affair for some time. Upon being confronted with the oracle's decision, the man blurted out: "It must have been another time!" Still claiming his innocence of this act of adultery, he surmised that the oracle had detected a previous adulterous act on his part. In his eyes (assuming his outburst reflected his thoughts), then, the oracle was mistaken but not disconfirmed. Other questions cannot easily be disconfirmed. A person might ask an oracle: "If I build my house in such and such a place, will I die?" If the answer is yes, he will not build there and there is no test; if the answer is no and he does build there, chances are low he will die soon. Similar is the question "If I marry so-and-so, will she die within a year?" If they do not marry the oracle is untested; if they do marry, the chances that she will die soon are again low, and were she to die an additional explanation could be sought in, you guessed it, witchcraft!

Even if we assume that the handlers do not influence the result by varying the amount of poison administered to the fowl, then, the oracle will appear not random but in accord with common knowledge. And of course some bias may enter in, although Evans-Pritchard claimed he could detect none.

What are the consequences of being found guilty? They can be quite severe; once, Evans-Pritchard was told, a man could be put to death for certain offenses. Today a person or couple might be put to work for the prince or fined. But even more commonly, the offender will merely be ordered to make things right. How he or she does so sheds important light on what this business of oracles and mangu is all about. For when one is formally accused of witchcraft—one is presented with the wing of a fowl that died—the correct response is to blow out water and say: "If I possess witchcraft in my belly I am unaware of it; may it cool. It is thus that I blow out water."

Today, younger people are counseled by their elders that even if they are sure they are not guilty, they should just blow on the wing to show that they bear no ill will. The matter is not about guilt but about setting things right, smoothing over the hurt. Of course sometimes the oracle is right on the money, or only slightly off, as in the case of the adulterous couple, and then a spontaneous confession may result.

In analyzing the Azande system we are better off considering witchcraft first and foremost as a set of social practices rather than a pseudoscientific system of knowledge claims (as philosophers often do). Individual Azande may or may not be completely convinced of the truth of each statement uttered about witchcraft and oracles, but the overall effect of the way questions are put, the range of responses, and the focus on restitution rather than guilt, is to make the set of practices believable.

This way of looking at it helps to solve the "rationality problem": the set of statements about and practices of Azande witchcraft is a discourse about social problems, one that gives the members of the society a relatively socially harmless way of talking about conflicts and dissatisfactions, bringing them to light, and also resolving those problems. The moment when water is blown by the accused is a moment of catharsis. Tensions between the parties may be released and somewhat relieved. The overall system of power receives an ideological reinforcement, as the prince's oracle has revealed the truth.

African Witchcraft and Social Change

Because ideas about witchcraft incorporate ideas about social tensions (who is most likely to be harming you) and about power (who gets to decide who is a witch and who is not), they have been part and parcel of the rapid social change of the colonial and postcolonial eras.

Even in precolonial times, accusations of witchcraft were made against women much more often than against men. Some cases of rapid social change exacerbated the attacks on women. In Nigeria, for example, the development of the cocoa economy in the 1940s and 1950s led to the rapid proliferation of women traders, many of whom left the traditional patrilocal compound to pursue their activities elsewhere. These women passed on trading capital to their daughters, bypassing traditional inheritance lines that ran from fathers to sons. Local witchcraft ideas already targeted women; the rapid social and economic change in this period led to an increase in witchcraft accusations and to the 1950–1951 Atinga cult of witch finding that accused thousands of women in Nigeria as witches, forcing them to confess, pay a cleansing fee, and eat a substance that would kill them if they ever practiced witchcraft again. In Andrew Apter's analysis (1993) of the movement, newly powerful male traders financed the cult in part to persecute the women traders with whom they competed.

Accusations of witchcraft continue to be a part of modern urban life in many parts of Africa as a way of talking about evil, particularly the evil brought by strangers (Auslander 1993; Bastian 1993). Tabloids and other newspapers carry witchcraft stories across regions of West and Central Africa. Witches in Zambia and South Africa are accused of causing barrenness and AIDS, sickness and economic failure. Witch finders, in southern Africa often associated with the Zionist churches, are recruited by young men to cleanse their villages by identifying the elderly women and men who are preventing the younger people from advancing economically. Witches are not killed but cleansed by having potions rubbed into cuts on their bodies. And yet, an exception to this general pattern, young militants in South Africa have used the "necklace"—the burning tire used to kill suspected informants during the struggle against apartheid—as a weapon against accused witches, leading one chief—significantly, a woman—to create a new town as a sanctuary for the accused.

These African cases highlight the idea of witchcraft as a property of an individual. This idea can be interpreted in different ways: in the Azande case, people focus on witchcraft events rather than persons. In the other cases mentioned, broad categories of suspect persons were accused of being witches. We should bear in mind that beneath the same analytical category—"witchcraft"—are quite different patterns of accusation and conceptions of blame and retribution.

Witchcraft as Satan versus God

In early modern Europe and North America, misfortune was thought of in a dualistic framework, where God and his followers confront Satan and those in his grasp. Witch hunts in various parts of Europe resembled those in Africa today, except that the source of the witchcraft was not the individual but her or his ties with Satan.

In the United States, witchcraft is surely most closely associated with the celebrated 1692 trials held in Salem, Massachusetts. I would argue that witchcraft ideas in New England once functioned much as they do in Azande society, to encourage confession and purge the society of its fears and tensions. But rapid social changes of the late seventeenth century created new fissures in village society that were given strong moral and emotional colorations by Puritan preachers and church members. Much as in contemporary Africa, older tensions were exacerbated and witch hunts grew in importance.

New England Puritans

The Puritans of seventeenth-century New England held strong religious ideas about the church as a community and about the immanence of evil in the world. A church in this society was not a building or even an association to which one could freely belong. In its narrow and most compelling sense it was a community of people who felt themselves elected by God, as "saints," who had joined in a covenant that bound each to the other. Church members were responsible for one another, such that the sins of one person would lead to misfortune for others (Miller 1956, 141–152). As John Winthrop put it in his sermon on "Christian charity" delivered to the Pilgrims onboard the Arabella en route to the New World in 1630: "We must be knit together as one man and must delight in each other, make other's condition our own, rejoice together, mourn together, labor and suffer together, always having before our eyes our commission and community in the work" (quoted in Demos 1982, 299).

This sense of common destiny was reinforced by the constant copresence of church members in a village. You encountered your fellow parishioner in his store, where he sold you bread, or near your fields, where you might get along or be embroiled in a dispute over boundaries or water. Common destiny and a shared life worked tolerably well as long as everyone prospered tolerably equally. But sharp differences in economic and social standing had begun to emerge, along with ideas of individualism. These new and dangerous ideas were, ironically, exacerbated by the opportunity afforded in the New World: the abundance of land and the fragility of new institutions.

Puritans also held that a strong line divided good from evil in the world. Evil was incarnate in the witch. As the prominent preacher Cotton Mather put it: "There is in witchcraft a most explicit renouncing of all that is holy and just and good." The witch showed "the furthest effort of our original sin" (quoted in Demos 1982, 304). Witches' meetings were imagined as inversions of all that was holy, involving trampling on the cross and defiling the Host. (And, indeed, contemporary Satanic cults do practice some of these rituals of inversion.) In this respect, witchcraft served to sharpen and perhaps to strengthen the moral boundaries between the community and Satan's forces.

In this context, in which all actions were to be scrutinized for their good or evil, ordinary people understandably could experience a great deal of anxiety about whether their actions and feelings came from God or Satan. Puritans believed in predestination, that God has damned or saved us before we were born, but not revealed to us His decision. Puritans saw the world as full of signs or marks of God's will, so that one might recognize in himself the signs of Election, or of damnation (and indeed becoming a member of the church required that one declare oneself saved). But Satan could be behind such feelings, trying to induce damned individuals to enter the church. Even the most highly placed church member could not easily escape gnawing doubts as to the reliability of his or her own certainty. One story has it that a woman in a Boston congregation, tormented by her uncertainty, threw her child into a well to seek relief of certain damnation. (Hers was, however, an incorrect interpretation of the strictly un-knowable nature of Election!)

Evil and Accusations

In this context of gnawing doubts, the presence of Evil, and the ideal of a morally as well as socially close-knit community, fears of evil within—the witch—were endemic. Throughout the early modern period in Europe, accusations of witchcraft were an expected part of life. England had somewhere between 300 and 1,000 executions for witchcraft between 1542 and 1736. Accusations fit the general pattern already noted. Most of the accused were women; indeed, in one detailed record for the period 1560–1680 in Essex County, only 8 percent of the persons tried were men. The typical English witch was an older woman, perhaps widowed, from the poorer segment of the community. Often she was a beggar. She was usually accused of bewitching someone not only in her own village but in her part of the village. Witches were neighbors. The historian Keith Thomas argues that accusers were beginning to chafe at the demands of charity, as the ethics of the time gradually became more individualistic. And yet moral responsibility for charity still was preached by the church and probably felt as legitimate by the better-off citizens. Harsh words, even curses, by those whose appeals for financial assistance were denied would have spawned some guilt in the hearts of these newly individual-minded villagers, and to assuage this guilt, argues Thomas, they projected it onto the "witch" (Demos 1982, 298–300).

Witchcraft accusations were brought from England to New England—indeed, in particular from Essex County, England, to Essex County, Massachusetts. In seventeenth-century North America there are recorded 93 witchcraft cases, of which 16 led to hangings, the Salem outbreak excepted. If we count the Salem trials as well, the total rises to 234 cases and 36 executions—an "accusation rate" of seven accusations per 100,000 people in North America, compared to less than one accusation per 100,000 in England, and about 5.5 for the most "active" county in England, Essex. Clearly, then, events in Salem pushed the rate of accusations far beyond their usual frequency (Demos 1982, 11–12).

Accusations functioned in similar fashion to what we observed for the Azande. The activity of a witch could explain why an unexpected event happened, even when the physics of the matter were perfectly clear. For example, a man on maneuvers with his militia accidentally discharged his gun, which ricocheted off a tree and struck another man, killing him. The first man was charged with manslaughter, but people continued to ask why the rather odd accident had happened. In the event, a woman was accused of witchcraft. She had owed money to the deceased and had been his landlord: she was thus close to him and yet in a socially ambivalent relationship to him. But to blame a single individual was insufficient to account for the presence of witchcraft in the community, where everyone was in some way responsible for everyone else. And so, on a subsequent Sunday the preacher widened the field of blame to include the entire community, whose general moral decrepitude, he charged, had permitted Satan to enter among them and do his evil work (Demos 1982, 3–9).

In such a case the matter would rest there, and so it had been in Salem before 1692. Events in that year represent an abnormal, outrageous set of actions. Yet the people involved were ordinary village folk, much like all the other folk peopling the eastern seaboard then and afterward.

The Salem Outbreak of 1692

First, the events. During the year 1691, throughout Essex County in northeastern Massachusetts, young girls were experimenting with methods of divining their futures, especially trying to find out who their sweethearts would be. Some of them gazed into crystal balls with quiet intensity. These girls, repressed young people with few permitted outlets for play, at times projected their emotions, hopes, and fears onto cloudy images, dimly perceived (Boyer and Nissenbaum 1974, 1–21).

In February 1692, several girls in Salem village were using a crystal ball for these purposes with the help of their slave, a West Indies woman named Tituba. For reasons unknown, several of them began acting very strangely: alternately prancing about and hiding under chairs, making strange, "foolish" speeches that no one could understand, and taking to their beds, moaning and complaining about pains. Some of their behavior was liberating in nature, allowing the girls to yell and to speak out in an atmosphere where they were usually supposed to keep silent.

The authorities of the village interpreted this behavior as witchcraft. One of the first girls to act strangely was the daughter of the village minister, Samuel Parris. As she lay on her bed, Parris and others began to question her, thinking that she might be the victim of witchcraft. The questions put to her and to several other girls were in the form of: "Was it so-and-so?" Much as with the Zande oracle, certain names were put forward and others were not. The girls were urged to name someone, and they did name several women, including Tituba. Three women were then questioned by two members of the provincial legislature, who lived in nearby Salem Town. Tituba confessed to having committed witchcraft; the other two denied the charges.

The accusations snowballed, and the public hangings began in June of that year. Between June 2 and September 22, 19 men and women were hanged, including a minister, the Reverend George Burroughs. The hangings were finally stopped by the intervention of Boston-area ministers who were troubled by the willy-nilly hanging, though not by the principle of hanging witches. On October 12 Governor Phips forbade any more imprisonments for witchcraft, and all prisoners were set free during the following year.

The events raise some troubling questions. First, why were the experiences of the children interpreted as the torment of witches? Were Puritans generally likely to make such interpretations? The nature of the experiences was not all unpleasant, after all. The girls' strange speech suggests the speaking in tongues of the Pentecost spoken of in the Bible and known to the ministers. Indeed, in the very same year of 1692 a Boston servant girl exhibited similar syndromes: spasms, outbreaks of strange speech, and, upon meeting some of the accused Salem women, violent behavior toward them. But in this case, Cotton Mather drew on her behavior to form a group that met with her, chanted psalms, and had similar experiences, which began to be seen as a kind of religious ecstasy.

Later, in the early eighteenth century, the same sort of outbreak in Northampton, in western Massachusetts, was interpreted by the minister of that town, Jonathan Edwards, as a sign of the "pouring out of the spirit of God." This movement led to what came to be called the "Great Awakening," a period during which a wider range of religious experiences and behaviors were accepted (Miller 1956, 153–166).

Second, why were the charges believed? The accusers were young girls, and there was only their own testimony to support their charges. Were the distinguished jurors who found the accused guilty themselves imbeciles? How can we understand their findings?

Finally, why, in this instance but not before or after, did the outbreak expand as it did? Several hundred people were accused, 150 imprisoned, and 19 executed. Earlier outbreaks in New England since 1647 had resulted in a total of 15 executions. Those executed were local people, marginal, following the general pattern: accuse your neighbor if he or she is powerless and likely to be suspected by others on grounds of unpleasantness.

The events in Salem might have been just another minor outbreak. By April, only six people had come under public suspicion of witchcraft. But then the number of accusations picked up and were aimed at people of high status outside the immediate community. The accused included the wealthiest ship owner in Salem Town and two of its seven selectmen, two sons of a former governor, themselves prominent public figures, and even Lady Phips, wife of the governor! And unlike all previous outbreaks, most of the accused were people outside of Salem Village, in the nearby village of Andover (Boyer and Nissenbaum 1974, 22–30).

Salem and Disruption of the Moral Community

The historians Paul Boyer and Stephen Nissenbaum have given us an account of the anomaly of Salem based on the peculiar social tensions of the time. In 1636, Salem Village (today the town of Danvers) was founded but was under the control of Salem Town. The town, not the village, levied and collected taxes and set the prices to be charged for farm produce at the village gate. The village was not legally independent at the time of the witchcraft outbreak (Boyer and Nissenbaum 1974, 37–109).

The town had become a major export center, with a rich merchant class. (Many in China thought the greatest naval power of the day was the "country of Salem" because so many ships bore the name.) By keeping the prices of produce down, the town had prospered for 30 years, and because the town's population had been growing, the farmers had been able to prosper as well. But the population of the village outside the town was growing, too, and the average land holdings per household diminished dramatically at the end of the century, from 250 acres in 1660 to 124 acres in 1690. With less acreage and more farmers, a disparity developed between the amount of food needed by the town and the amount being produced. By the early 1690s, the average income of many of the farmers had declined, and tensions developed between the town and the village.

Not all families fared equally well or poorly in Salem Village. Two families who played leading roles on the witchcraft stage were the Putnams and the Porters (Boyer and Nissenbaum 1974, 110–152). Both had arrived in the 1640s from neighboring parts of England, and both soon became prosperous farming families in the village. But by the 1690s the two large groups of descendants of the original immigrants lived on opposite sides of the village.

The Porters had settled in the eastern half of the village, where they operated two sawmills, sold lumber to town merchants, and eventually married into town families. They and others in the eastern half of the village were able to benefit from townspeople's demand for goods and services. Their land was better for farming as well, and they were also close to the road that ran along the eastern edge. Near them were other small entrepreneurs, traders, and shop owners, all of whom increasingly saw themselves as sharing interests and outlooks with residents of the town. By and large they wished to preserve the close relationship of town and village and feared the future domination of an independent village by the local church. Among other fears was that the church might impose restrictions on the movement of produce outside of the village. The Porters were accused of witchcraft, which they denied. The accusers did not dare to confront the powerful Porters directly, and so they tended to target people who were associated with them.

By contrast, the fortunes of the Putnams were tied up exclusively with the village. Their original grant was of lands in the western portion of the village, where expansion could only be further westward. They were landlocked, with no nearby roads, and with poor, hilly land. They tried to diversify in the 1670s, setting up an iron-smelting plant, but the effort failed. They were fated to stay on the farm, but the farm was getting smaller, as by the third generation the remaining plots were each barely enough to maintain their standard of living.

It was this third generation of desperate Putnams that furnished the leaders in witchcraft accusations. Foremost among them was Thomas Putnam, Jr., his wife Ann, and their 12-year-old daughter Ann. They had been deprived of an estate that had been awarded to Thomas's half-brother (who, to make matters worse, had married a Porter). Several of their children had died. Their frustration and rage was vented at persons who could be attacked in the village and then expanded outward to include outsiders, upwardly mobile, who were insufficiently deferential. The Putnams were involved in the prosecution of 46 accused witches. The daughter, Ann Putnam, was the principal afflicted girl and accuser (Boyer and Nissenbaum 1974, 30–36, 133–152).

For the Puritans, self-interest was the enemy within the body of the community. "Our community are members of the same body," said John Winthrop in 1630 to the first Pilgrim contingent. From this perspective, the town, with its taverns and rich merchants, was to be seen as bringing moral danger to the Church and its community. The minister in Salem village, Samuel Parris, had never been accepted by all villagers, and the Porters were among those whom he saw as his enemies. He felt besieged and insecure, and he channeled his frustrations and anger into his sermons on Judas and on the sense of filth and corruption in the community. And he led the charge against the witches.

Within the village, a remarkable geographic pattern emerged that confirmed the importance of social and economic divisions in the witchcraft trials. Of the 25 accused witches who lived in or near Salem Village, only three lived in the western half of the village and four in the center; all the others lived in the eastern half, most of them along its boundary with Salem Town. (By contrast, of the 32 adult villagers who testified against the accused, 30 lived in the western half of the village.) This distribution of accused witches underscores the degree to which the town was seen as a danger to the community by the accusers. Among the accused was John Proctor, a tavernkeeper who was envied by the Putnams for his success and who was also condemned as too worldly, and John Willard, an outsider who married into the village and then began to buy up coveted farmland in great quantities (Boyer and Nissenbaum 1974, 181–189).

The Porters themselves were of too high a status in the community to be accused by people who would encounter them frequently. But those on the fringes of their circle were accused; for example, a man who had recently married one of their sisters. Other victims were marginal to the community in other ways. Several victims were poor women who were judged as being disrespectful to their benefactors. Cotton Mather had warned that those "who through discontent at their poverty, or at their misery, shall be always murmuring . . . witchcraft is the upshot of it" (Boyer and Nissenbaum 1974, 208).

Evidence and Confessions

That these people could be witches was not doubted. Everyone accepted that witches did exist. Satan's struggle for the souls of people was evident in the world, and misfortune always had a moral tinge to it. As the historian Perry Miller has written, Puritanism had no room for failure. When failure came, it was due to the work of Satan in the world, and among his favorite vehicles were witches.

What was the evidence for witchcraft? According to the canons of evidence of the day, several kinds were admissible (Boyer and Nissenbaum 1974; Demos 1982). One was empirical evidence, which included behavioral traits: these could be positive, such as great physical strength, or negative, such as the inability to recite the Lord's Prayer all the way through. These signs were largely upheld through the proceedings. The category also included odd physical markings, such as the supposed third "witch's teat," a third breast on women. Such bodily evidence was considered to be God's message to humans, but it was generally rejected in the Salem case as being unreliable.

Of long-standing evidentiary value was the category called "Anger followed by Mischief," that is, when after a quarrel or even a sharp look someone was stricken with a malady. This evidence eventually was rejected because of the difficulty of ascertaining the empirical links between the "anger" and the "mischief."

Finally and most dramatically, there was Spectral Evidence—in this case, when the afflicted girls saw figures of the accused coming to them and harming them. This evidence could, of course, be produced at a moment's notice. Mary Warren, one of the girls, tried to recant her own accusations against previous witches when the other girls accused her master, John Proctor. The others responded to her defection by immediately seeing specters around *her*. At this threat, she retracted her recantation and returned to their side. But when "respectable" townspeople began to be accused, some of the ministers remembered that Satan was capable of creating specters and images to mislead the God-fearing, and at that point spectral evidence began to be doubted publicly. Increase Mather, the leader of Boston's clergy, condemned the use of both Spectral Evidence and Anger followed by Mischief. Mather said that even when one saw a specter, it could be Satan causing mischief and trying to impune the righteousness of a good person.

Of course, many people confessed before the case could come to trial. Those who did confess, here as elsewhere, were not hanged but released. From the perspective of a modern trial court this course of action seems very odd. Why release confessed criminals and hang those who insisted on their innocence? But from the perspective of comparative witchcraft studies it is what we would expect. As in the Azande case, the confession purged the community of tensions and, in this instance, of the deep guilt it felt for straying from the righteous path. As with the blowing out of water among the Azande, the confession gives a language for conflicts, the language of Satan and witchcraft. (Possibly, although this is not documented, some may also have thought, as do Azande, that it was possible to cause evil through witchcraft without intending to do so, just by being angry with someone.)

Here is another way the Salem events went wrong. The first three women to be accused had confessed but after that confessions virtually ceased. Why? Boyer and Nissenbaum argue that a cultural change was just then occurring in New England, one that gave just enough moral sanction to individual pride and "face" that many people were no longer willing to confess for the sake of community. Now they wished to act on their individual consciences. But the logic of accusation and confession had not quite caught up with their new sense of obligation and responsibility. From this point of view the events in Salem are a terrible result of uneven moral and cultural transition, away from one world view, that of the Puritan, toward another, that of the outward-oriented Great Awakening (Boyer and Nissenbaum 1974, 209–216; Miller 1957, 153–166).

For Further Consideration

The film *Witchcraft Among the Azande* (Filmakers Library 1983) shows how the practices discussed here have persisted despite the conversion of most Azande to Christianity. Also of interest is *Sorcerers of Zaire* (Films for the Humanities and Sciences 1993).

Does this way of explaining why things happen have anything to do with your lives? Have you ever sought to explain some event in terms of religion, or luck, or in some way other than common sense or science? What about this event led you to explain it in this way? Perhaps it seemed random, injust.

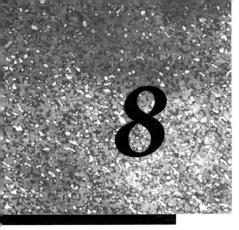

8 Prohibitions and Boundaries

*M*any religions stipulate not just things people should do, such as sacrificing and worshiping, but also things they should not do, such as eating certain foods, wearing certain clothes or coming into contact with people of other religions or of lower status. Prohibitions or "taboos" are some of the most striking features of religions, in part because they distinguish, and often socially separate, people of different religions. They bring religious affiliation into everyday social life, restricting, shaping, and channeling social interactions and behavior.

With the discussion of taboos in this chapter, the focus of this book shifts slightly, from purposive ritual activity to the institutions and forms that characterize particular religions. The remaining chapters consider the relative importance of images and speech in several religious traditions, the meanings conveyed by places and pilgrimages, the role of individuals in religious movements, and the ways modern nation-states assimilate a plurality of religions into public life.

Prohibitions (part of religious law in the broadest sense) are all those norms or social rules that carry some form of sanction. This chapter focuses on the important ways prohibitions or taboos are used to create boundaries between the secular and sacred and between one religious community and another. Religious law may become part of civil or state-enforced law, as when some largely Muslim countries enforce compliance with the fast during the month of Ramadan, or when some largely Catholic countries follow papal proscriptions on abortion or birth control. (Chapter 15 contains a more detailed discussion of religion and state law.)

All religious rules involve a degree of conformity; they lead practitioners to behave in certain ways that mark them off from other people. In his definition of religion, the sociologist Émile Durkheim argued that taboos serve to define the community of practitioners: "A religion is a unified system of beliefs and practices relative to sacred things, that is to say, things set apart and forbidden—beliefs and practices which unite into one single moral community called a Church, all those who adhere to them" (Durkheim 1995, 44).

Durkheim observes both that there is a moral community of adherents, and that their focus or center is a set of things classified as sacred (as opposed to profane), as outside of normal society, and as forbidden, dangerous, powerful. Durkheim found this association between taboo objects and religious community in many societies, most clearly in the use of totems, or sacred objects, to define social groups in Australia and native North America. The group shares a totem—a kangaroo, or a sacred place, or a dream—that enhances its sense of being alike and of being different from others. A turn-of-the-century fascination with totem and taboo led some writers to theorize about the origins of religion—including Sigmund Freud (1918/1989) in his speculative book *Totem and Taboo*. Although these analysts went far beyond the evidence, they were right in pointing to the powerful society-shaping role played by taboos and other laws regulating the behavior of members of a religious community.

Taboos, Eating, and Social Inequality

*T*aboos are preeminently about keeping distinct and apart people and things deemed to be importantly different: men and women, impure people (menstruating women, unclean men) and pure people, high- and low-status people, meat and milk products, and so on. These rules are sometimes just about keeping one's distance, but they also often involve rules about eating. Rules about food—what to eat, when to eat it, with whom to eat it—as well as beliefs about food's special powers, seem to be important in many religions. Indeed, it appears that just about everywhere in the world, rules about what you may eat (particularly, whether you may eat animals or not, and, if so, which ones) are of great social and moral importance. So are rules about how you eat: with whom, using what hands or implements, at what times of the day, with foods arranged in what order of consumption, and so on.

In the several religions of Middle Eastern origin (Judaism, Christianity, Islam), meals serve as key symbols of religious affiliation and as practical rituals through which religious acts are carried out. Consider the Passover seder, for which one must rid the household of all leaven; the Islamic month of fasting, followed by a great feast; the strict adherence to dietary rules by many Muslims and Jews; and the importance of the Last Supper as a central image in Christian traditions.

Elsewhere in the world, food and eating have ritual and religious importance. In rites of passage, for instance, people are often denied those highly valued foods that would identify them as full members of the society. Or individuals may deny food to themselves as a means of seeking a higher level of religious experience. Eating together is a primary means of achieving peace everywhere. But eating together, or even receiving food, is completely impossible between members of certain castes in India, where, according to beliefs about caste and gifts, food is seen as a primary carrier of pollution. In many New Guinea societies, competitive feasting, where people seek to outdo each other in holding a feast, is an important way of creating, validating, or changing relationships between groups.

Eating is, of course, also a central element in secular culture. We tend to emphasize the rights of people to eat what they want and where they wish, but consider the popularity of books on "eating to win," where steak means power, fish means wimpiness, and so forth, or how in the 1960s the refusal of lunch-counter owners in parts of the U.S. South to serve black people became a key symbol of the civil rights struggle.

Rules about food may be especially characteristic of those religions that have spread throughout the world—in particular, Judaism, Christianity, Islam, Hinduism, and Buddhism—because of the concern for defining the boundaries of the religious community. (Wearing special clothing is another such boundary marker: see the discussion of Islamic headscarves in Chapter 15.) Food taboos are a way of maintaining a degree of uniformity in practice as a religious community moves out from a center and disperses among people of other religions. In fact, taboos concerning food seem to increase as a religious community expands or disperses (as the later discussion of Judaism illustrates).

Hawaiian Taboo and Captain Cook

The word *taboo* comes from Polynesia; it was first reported to Europeans by Captain James Cook during his voyages to the Sandwich Islands in the 1780s. The "tapus" observed on the Hawaiian islands, Fiji, and elsewhere involved distinctions between chiefs and commoners, men and women, and sacred and profane times and places. Chiefs levied severe punishments (and promised supernatural harm) against all those who transgressed these distinctions. Chiefs were from the gods; commoners were separately created beings; and to cross that line was to violate the celestial and the temporal order. For a commoner to touch a chief violated the taboo and could lead to death; chiefs were sometimes carried over the lands of commoners lest their touch of those lands prevent the commoner from tilling them.

Taboos were basic to religion and polity; they were the meat of hierarchy. They also structured the year, which led to a curious event in the meeting of European and Hawaiian societies. On Hawaii, the year was divided into the period ruled by Ku, the god associated with sacrifice and the king, and a shorter period ruled by Lono, the god of fertility. During Lono's tour of the island, certain taboos came into force, including a ban on war and on the king's eating of pork, and the king and high priest were secluded. At the end of this period the god Lono left Hawaii, human sacrifice was made to Ku, and the king returned to power. Marshall Sahlins (1985) describes how Captain Cook's voyage to Hawaii in 1778–1779 coincided with Lono's arrival and departure, leading Hawaiians to treat him as the god Lono. But shortly after leaving Hawaii, Cook returned, needing to repair his ships. This untimely return to the island challenged the annual ritual cycle, and, more to the point, the king's supremacy, which led ultimately to Cook's own death.

But the most obvious part of the taboo system, the part that stood for the whole, concerned food and relations between men and women. A set of taboos prevented women from eating with men and from eating certain foods reserved for men. Men took their meals with the gods (at least according to the men), and since their every meal was thus a sacrifice and communion, it would be defiled by a woman's presence. Yet some chiefly women may already have been avoiding these taboos without incurring sanction, thus putting into question the claim that supernatural powers backed up the taboos.

The coming of Europeans upset the system entirely. When Europeans first approached the islands, commoner women came on board the ships and ate with the

PROHIBITIONS AND BOUNDARIES

European men, violating the taboo (and sometimes incurring severe punishment) and testing the authority of the chiefs. Their actions did not yet cause the structure of taboos to collapse, but there were other consequences. Cook's men had been free to travel the islands and in particular to use the temples to heal their sick and bury their dead. But once it was known that they had eaten with women they were viewed as defiled. The chiefs thereafter forbade any European from entering temples.

The flood of traffic with Europeans both strained traditional taboos and gave rise to new ones. Commoners increasingly began to violate taboos on preceding the chiefs in the sea to greet newcomers. Chiefs saw that their own power depended on maintaining control over the new forms of trade; thus, chiefs placed new taboos on commoners' trade in pigs or required that pigs be exchanged only for goods for which the chiefs had need, such as guns and ammunition. Finally King Kamehameha placed a taboo on trade at Hawaii and required that ships proceed to Oahu.

As commoners began seeking to trade for their own benefit, class interests emerged, and they conflicted with the norms of taboo. Women, in particular, continued to eat with these new men, and also to swim out to the ships during periods when a taboo was on such encounters. Cook's men encouraged these violations, because they were sleeping with the women and trading with the men. Even after Cook's death, women, men, and priests of Lono (the god opposed in the ritual cycle to the king's Ku) continued to trade with Cook's ships.

The final abolition of the taboos came about in 1819, when king Kamehameha died. His favored wife Kaahumanu declared that the king had wished her to rule together with his son and heir Liholiho (who was not her own son). Kaahumanu was part of the "Maui group" of Kamehameha's in-laws to whom he had given powerful positions on the other islands as well as key roles in trade negotiations with the Europeans. These affines (relatives by marriage) served as counterweight to his own close collateral relatives (slightly junior first cousins), who were a threat to his power. The Maui affines saw their trade-based relationship with the Europeans as the key to their future power, and decided that their interests were best served by trading in the taboo system, which was already in tatters, for a new class-based set of alliances. So, at a great feast held in November 1819, Kaahumanu and other chiefly women ate forbidden foods, and then were joined, nervously, by King Liholiho. The court then ordered the destruction of idols and profaning of temples throughout the island. Although challenged (by those junior first cousins, whose claims to power depended on the taboo system), the king's party prevailed and the taboos were abandoned (Sahlins 1985; Webb 1965).

In Hawaii, rules and prohibitions had divided the society along several axes, in particular those of chief/commoner and male/female. These taboos were equally "religion" and "politics," and when the conditions for trade and power shifted, so did the system of taboos. The chiefs converted to Christianity as part of their new political economic strategy—religion, politics, and trade continued to be intertwined, but now they were part of a global order of conversion and conquest.

Purity and Pollution in India

In Polynesia, taboos were about internal distinctions, and they structured each society according to a strict hierarchy. In India as well, taboos underscore internal inequalities.

Taboos associated with Hinduism invoke ideas of purity and pollution. They include rules against exchanging food and women across caste lines.

The social hierarchy based on purity and pollution pervades Indian society and is infused with religious meaning, although it is only one dimension of social inequality, along with social class. Hindus belong to castes that are, ideally, all ranked along a single continuum, from most pure to most impure. Each caste in principle belongs to one of the four ranked classes or varnas: the Brahmans, associated with religious learning and priestly craftmanship; the Kshatriyas, from whom kings and soldiers are expected to come; the Vaishyas, engaged in trade and farming, and the Shudras, expected to serve the others. Below these ranks are those without class (avarna) including Untouchables or Harijans; outside of the entire ranking system are people of other religions: Jains, Christians, and most importantly Muslims.

Each of the hundreds of thousands of villages that dot India's agricultural plains has several, perhaps dozens, of castes (Fuller 1992, 75–81). People disagree over the precise ranking of these castes, even to which varna they belong. Sometimes people change the acknowledged rank of their caste, but Brahmans would say that there is a single ranking of every group, and thus of every person. This ranking, or rather the diverse local rankings in particular villages and towns, does, even today, shape a good deal of social life, although some Hindus no longer subscribe to some of its attendant rules. But people generally do marry within a caste, and rarely take on a trade assigned to another caste—though they may and often do take up the many trades not fixed by caste, including most modern occupations.

Hindus refrain from accepting cooked food from people in a lower caste, because doing so would pollute them. People in particular castes also may avoid certain foods, in part as a way of distinguishing themselves from other castes. Many Brahmans do not eat meat, for example. These avoidances are not general to the religion such as those we will consider in the next section. They vary considerably within India and across varnas: individuals and groups distinguish themselves through their food avoidances, but precisely what they eat and what they avoid varies over time and space. In south India, where the distinction between Brahmans and all non-Brahmans is very great (and is the basis for much current political rivalry), Brahmans try to mark themselves off from everyone else by practicing strict vegetarianism. (However, many non-Brahmans also avoid eating meat in the south.) In north India the lines between varnas are more complex and ambiguous. In some places members of the second varna, the warrior Kshatriyas, dominate public life, and they eat meat, they say, to build up strength. North India also has large and powerful merchant castes from the third varna, the Vaishyas, and these castes practice strict vegetarianism as a distinguishing marker. Perhaps because avoiding meat is not so clearly associated with high prestige or with Brahman status in the north as it is in the south, some northern Brahman groups do in fact eat certain kinds of meat and fish, although even in the north most Brahmans avoid meat (Fuller 1992, 92–96).

More generally, among Hindus, substances are pure or impure not in themselves but because they carry the nature of those from whom they come, and thus will pollute if given from a person of lower status to a person of higher status. Your own bodily emissions, from saliva to hair to feces, are polluting to persons or beings of higher status than you, and hence you must bathe before worshiping the gods. You must have people of lower caste cut your hair, launder clothes, and so forth. Cow products, even cow dung, are pure and purifying, as is water from holy places, items used in ritual, and certain mantras. But dead cow products, as with all dead things, are very polluting, hence beef preparation and leather working are done by those without caste or those outside the class/caste system.

Most foods are pure or polluting depending on in whose hands they have been. In general, for those Hindus who continue to follow the food rules, foods are pure if received from a person higher in the caste hierarchy than you, but polluting if received from someone lower than you. Lower caste persons are inherently more polluted and more polluting than are higher caste persons. Food carries pollution because it absorbs something of the bodily substance of the person holding it. Because water quickly absorbs pollution (and thus is an effective remover of pollution when used to bathe), such ordinary boiled foods as rice or vegetables are particularly polluting.

Pollution is thus an ever-present danger. It also adds special urgency and power to the caste hierarchy and serves as a daily reminder to many Hindus of precisely where they stand in the rank-ordering of humans.

Taboos and Community in Judaism

*F*or some other religious communities, food taboos primarily mark the boundaries between adherents to the religion and everyone else. The precise definition of these boundaries—how to tell "us" from "them"—is of more concern for some religions than others. Buddhism, for example, does not have salient markers of this boundary. Someone can claim to be a Buddhist, and have this claim accepted, without having the claim cleared by authorities or undergoing special rites of conversion. The reasons for these fuzzy boundaries were set out in Chapter 2: Buddhism, like many other religions, is not based on allegiance to a single creed or book, nor is it limited to a particular ethnic or tribal group.

By contrast, both Judaism and Islam have shown special concern for maintaining external boundaries. Both are defined around obedience to a set of laws; Judaism also is historically associated with the idea of descent from original tribes.

The Prohibitions of Leviticus

Not surprisingly, then, food taboos are particularly salient markers of membership in the Jewish and Muslim communities. For many Jews and Muslims, the foods that should not be eaten serve as daily reminders of religious obligation and distinctiveness. For Judaism, a list of prohibited foods is found in the Bible, in 14 Deuteronomy, 11 Leviticus, and elsewhere. We find proscriptions on the eating of certain animals: camels, rabbits, mice, crocodiles, and pigs, among many others. The puzzle is: why this particular assortment of animals? Leviticus begins as instruction about the right and the wrong ways to offer sacrifices to God, and then proceeds to list in detail the things and conditions considered pure and impure. The transition is at 11 Leviticus, which begins:

And the Lord said to Moses and Aaron, "Say to the people of Israel, These are the living things which you may eat among all the beasts that are on the earth. Whatever parts the hoof and is cloven-footed and chews the cud, among the animals, you may eat. Nevertheless among those that chew the cud or part the hoof, you shall not eat these: The camel, because it chews the cud but does not part the hoof, is unclean to you. And the rock badger, because it chews the cud but does not part the hoof, is unclean to you. And the hare, because it chews the cud but does not part the hoof, is unclean to you. And the swine, because it parts the hoof and is cloven-footed, but does not chew the cud, is unclean to you. Of their flesh you shall not eat, and their carcasses you shall not touch; they are unclean to you.

The passage continues, prohibiting things in the water that do not have fins and scales; a long list of birds: eagle, osprey, falcon, sea gull, owl; all winged insects that go on all fours, excepting those with legs above their feet (thus, locust, cricket, and grasshopper); any "swarming thing that swarms upon the earth," thus reptiles, but also the mouse and weasel.

Many Jews continue to follow these proscriptions, along with other dietary rules (kashrut) developed by the rabbis, most notably the rules for slaughtering in a way that minimizes pain and for separating all dairy and meat products. In the city of St. Louis, for example, an Orthodox "council of the city" has the authority to decide whether any food or food product produced in the region is permitted (kosher) or forbidden. Their jurisdiction extends to any materials used in making food, such as a chemical release agent made locally for worldwide production of candies or cereals.

Muslims follow a similar set of rules. Early in his prophetic career (622 C.E.), Muhammad, his life endangered in Mecca, fled to the nearby city of Medina. There he was accepted by Jews and non-Muslim Arabs as their leader, and adopted several ritual practices from the Jews, including food taboos. Even after the breakdown of the Muslim alliance with the Jews, certain of these rules were preserved, including the prohibition against eating pig, blood, and carcasses and the requirement of ritually slaughtering animals. Today, Muslims consider observing these dietary rules, in particular avoiding pork, to be one of the most important signs of being a Muslim.

Before the destruction of the Jewish Temple in Jerusalem in 586 B.C.E., Jews regularly sacrificed to God. However, their exile to Babylon made sacrifice at the Temple impossible, and favored a renewed emphasis on each household's obedience to the sacred law. But why was *this particular* set of foods proscribed for Jews, and later for Muslims? Scholars of these religions have asked this question for centuries and have produced a wide variety of explanations. Some have said that it is the very arbitrary nature of the taboos that is important: because the taboos make no immediate sense, following them teaches discipline. Others speculated that the taboo animals were allegories of virtues and vices: for example, the mouse is particularly destructive, so prohibiting its consumption leads us to ponder that particular vice.

These accounts have died out, but many people continue to find convincing the notion that some taboos were motivated by health concerns. Early Jews may have known, through simple association, that improperly cooked pork can transmit trichinosis and other diseases, and that shellfish can concentrate impurities, as do mud-burrowing fish. (The observation about fish is recorded from the twelfth century C.E.) One weakness of this explanation is that anthrax and other diseases were commonly carried by cattle, not pigs, and were much more dangerous at the time.

Moreover, if banning pigs and shellfish was important, why the complicated set of taboos set out in the Bible? Mary Douglas (1966), drawing on Durkheim's theory about taboos and community, argues that prohibiting certain foods was a way of carving up the natural world into the pure and the impure, and thereby create a model for thinking about the purity of the Divine. Indeed, many other prohibitions in the Bible are of things that are partial, maimed, or blemished. Animals offered in sacrifice must not have a blemish; no one who has a physical defect may become a priest; even fields should be sown with only one kind of seed.

For Douglas, the food prohibitions are an instance of a drive toward order within the theology of the times. Certain animals with which people were most familiar served as models of the divine order to be found in nature and to be instituted in social life. Cattle were the typical livestock animal, and people took the fact that cattle have cloven hooves and chew the cud as part of their orderliness, as a "natural" combination of attributes. Animals with only one of these two attributes were judged disorderly. The pig, among other animals, is impure because it is incomplete: it has the cloven hoof but does not chew the cud.

Douglas's account has the virtue of corresponding to the explanation that the Bible gives of the rules. It also is supported by studies in psychology of how we use prototypes to carve up the world perceptually. We think about the category "birds" not in terms of all possible birds, but by imagining a prototype that is something like a robin or a bluebird, not like a pheasant. The ancient Jews, goes this argument, thought about livestock by using the prototype of a cow, not a pig. The pig is marginal, conceptually "dirty," and thus unfit for consumption.

Other prohibitions also have to do with species that fall outside of three main categories of animals: those that fly in the air with wings, those that swim in the water with fins and scales, and those that walk or hop on the land with four legs. The mouse, weasel, and crocodile are on the list because their feet bear an uncanny resemblance to hands. "Swarming" creatures are inedible because they use a different mode of propulsion entirely. Hare and rock badger seem to chew the cud. The biblical focus on order, writes Douglas (1966, 57), makes the dietary rules "like signs which at every turn inspired meditation on the oneness, purity, and completeness of God." Moreover, because pork was highly valued food for non-Jews, its prohibition also reinforced rules against intermarriage and helped preserve the cohesiveness of the group.

The ecological anthropologist Marvin Harris (1974) offers a different explanation of the food taboos. Harris notes that pigs were not well adapted to the arid lands of the Middle East, because they are extremely poor at sweating. Indeed, few pigs are found in the area in archeological excavations. But they are a succulent food, and people might have been tempted to raise them. "Hence Jahweh was heard to say that swine were unclean, not only as food, but to the touch as well. Allah was heard to repeat the message for the same reason: It was ecologically maladaptive to try to raise pigs in substantial numbers" (Harris 1974, 44).

Harris' argument assumes that people were not rational enough to avoid raising pigs on their own, but that the lawgivers were. (He has given a similar account of taboos on harming or eating cattle in India.) It has little to say about the *system* of taboos found in the Bible. Harris notes only that because many of the other prohibited animals were not available or were not common food sources, it was not irrational to forbid them. Here Douglas's argument is more useful in that it offers a logical reason for the system as created. Following Durkheim, she also argues that one would expect some set of prohibitions to mark off the group of Jews as distinct from others. But her account has less to say than Harris's about why it was the pig rather than some other animal that was chosen as a key prohibited animal.

Of course, ideas about pollution and contagion through food are found even among secular people, and taboos may have an underlying psychological base. If this is so then taboos would have a life of their own independent of particular religious doctrines. As we saw in Chapter 6, James Frazer thought that this was so, when he argued that the "law of contagion" together with the "law of similarity" explained most magical thinking in the world. And the psychologist Paul Rozin and his colleagues (Nemeroff and Rozin 1992) have found that both secular and religious people in the United States display reactions to various foods based on underlying "magical" ideas about contagion.

Whatever the psychological roots of contagion and taboo ideas, understanding their role in religions requires us to pose questions not asked by Douglas, to which we now turn. How do people experience living within these systems of taboos? In what ways do the taboos contribute to their religious lives?

Passover and History

Jewish ritual life today contains many references to those historical events of dispersal and survival that transformed ways of worship. The history of Pesach, or Passover, with its central meal, the seder, illustrates how Jewish ritual life was moved from public sacrifice to domestic celebration and observance of taboos (Bokser 1984). Pesach began as two spring festivals. Shepherds would sacrifice a lamb or kid from their flock on the full moon during the month when the animals were born. The lamb (the *pesach*) would be roasted whole and eaten completely during the night. At about the same time farmers would celebrate their early spring harvest by offering unleavened bread, to symbolize the separation of the old grain (in the form of fermented dough used to leaven bread) from the new, harvested grain. (Two other agricultural festivals, Shavuot, "weeks," and Sukkot, "harvesting booths," celebrated the later harvests.)

At some point in early Jewish history these celebrations of harvest and birth merged into one ritual and were given a new meaning, the celebration of the Jews' deliverance from Egypt. The unleavened breads, in the form of matzohs, now became signs of the haste of flight: not enough time was available to leaven the bread before leaving Egypt. And in celebration of this event the book of Exodus (12:19) orders Jews that for this day "No leaven shall be in your houses"—leaven defined for these purposes as contact between grain and water for more than 18 minutes. Sacrifice was still carried out, first at altars throughout Judea, and then, after Josiah in 621 B.C.E. forbade all sacrifices in "high places," at a single gathering at the Temple in Jerusalem. Each family brought a lamb to be sacrificed in commemoration of the lamb sacrificed in Egypt. They killed the lambs around the Temple, gave some of the blood to the priests to be thrown at the base of the altar, then roasted them and ate them with unleavened bread.

After 70 C.E., Temple sacrifice could no longer be made, and the rabbis replaced the earlier focus on sacrifice and harvest with an exclusive focus on the covenant with God and its document, the Torah. Passover was now solely a commemoration of the flight from Egypt, and it was held at home (not at the synagogue, perhaps to avoid implying that the synagogue had replaced the Temple). The matzoh replaced the sacrifice as the main element of the meal, although a piece of meat on a bone remains as a reminder of the now lost practice of sacrifice of the pesach itself.

Ritual Life Today

Jewish lives today combine feast-day commemorations of past events with everyday observance of religious laws, but the different ways Jews interpret law and perform ritual have given rise to several distinct religious categories. About half of the 18 million people considering themselves Jewish live in North America; most of the remainder live in Israel, Europe, and Russia; Jews in each of these places generally regard themselves as either Orthodox, Conservative, or Reform. Orthodox Jews (a category including Hasidic movements) stress observance of legal rules; they hold that the Torah (the Hebrew Bible) and the commandments are God's word as revealed at Sinai and continue to be binding on all Jews. Conservative (or Historic) Jews also recognize the validity of the Torah, but emphasize the historical continuity of the Jewish people and the capacity of the people to change law and practice. Reform Jews (along with the smaller Reconstructionist movement) focus on the spiritual essence of Judaism rather than the idea of an ethnically based nation and have been more willing to abandon older rituals and laws.

What divides these groups is mainly attitudes toward religious law; what unites them is mainly the observance of major holy days. For Jews as for Muslims, people living in different countries and cultures participate, in the same day and in much the same way, in rituals of commemoration. For Muslims, these calendrical rituals are mainly about sacrifice and pilgrimage; for Jews, they are mainly about deliverance and atonement. Muslim rituals are patterned after the acts carried out by Muhammad; therefore, what Muslims emphasize is the importance of precisely following the commands given in scripture. Jewish rituals have changed radically over time in their forms and in their meanings, and Jews emphasize the historical events that the rituals commemorate. Jews consider the Passover celebrations and other holidays as primarily about remembering an event that defined their subsequent travails and identity, and about hoping for the future Messiah.

At Passover celebrations today families read the Exodus tale from a liturgy called the Haggadah. Although brought out in numerous editions with new material, all Haggadah texts recite the story of the persecution of the Jews in Egypt and their deliverance by God. A cup of wine is left for Elijah, whose arrival is supposed to herald the Messiah. And many also celebrate the survival of the Jewish people and the birth of the modern state of Israel as additional holidays.

On other holidays, too, different stories make the same general point, that through their covenant with God, the Jews, despite their persecution, were delivered from evil. Purim, a time of games and merrymaking, nonetheless commemorates the hanging of

Haman and the slaughter of the other enemies of the Jews of Persia through the intervention of Esther. Hannukah, a celebration of freedom, observes the victory of the Maccabees. Sukkot, once (like Passover) a harvest feast, became a period to recall the long journey out of servitude (Schauss 1938).

Jewish festivals have changed over the years to reflect shifting concerns. The fasts and the agricultural festivals of Sukkot and Shavuot have receded in importance, and new holidays, such as those commemorating the Holocaust and Israel's independence, have come into being. And yet ritual preserves a common element of linking the current generation to key events in the past, some of them disastrous events for the Jewish community that nonetheless point toward that community's Covenant with God.

But this history may be interpreted in widely varying ways, and these variations return us to the central issue of boundaries and identity. The Passover Haggadah reminds Jews that "in every generation they rise to annihilate us," and the story of Esther can be read at Purim as chiefly saying one must slaughter one's enemies before they slaughter you. In 1996, between Purim and Passover there occurred terrible suicide bombings in Tel Aviv and Jerusalem, and some Israelis drew on those possible readings of history to argue that continued war was inevitable, peace impossible. And yet others argued that Purim was chiefly about resisting oppression; Passover, about faith in deliverance, and that reacting to the bombings with oppression and lack of faith was in effect giving in to terrorism.

Central to these debates is both history and the Covenant, which is embodied in the Torah, the first five books of the Bible (Genesis, Exodus, Leviticus, Numbers, and Deuteronomy) given to Moses as the Law. At a boy's major rite of passage, when he becomes a "son of the commandments" or bar mitzvah, he shows his ability to read from the Torah. Recently, as we saw in Chapter 5, some Jews have added a ritual for girls, the bat mitzvah. For many Jews, prayer in Hebrew and reading of the Torah remain daily rituals. In daily prescribed prayers the worshiper praises God and petitions him for the restoration of the Temple. Orthodox and Conservative Jews pray in Hebrew; Reform Jews often use vernacular language. On the head and left arm, the worshiper may wear the tefillin, boxes containing biblical quotations to remind the wearer of his religious duties. Although many events take place in the synagogue, home is the center of ritual life. The threshold of many Jewish homes is marked by a small box on the door post, the mezuzah, which contains a biblical passage proclaiming God's unity. "Here O Israel, the Lord is our God, the Lord is One" (Deuteronomy 6:4).

Jews have always felt that correctly applying the Torah to daily life required further writings. Out of a consensus within the Jewish community on the correct understanding of scripture in the second century C.E. came the Mishna, a collection of rules and spiritual teachings. Scholars then wrote further commentaries on the Mishna, and these commentaries, called *gemara*, were joined to the Mishna to form the Talmud—in fact, two Talmuds, coming from scholars in Babylonia and Palestine.

Let us take an example of how scholars explicated the Law. The Torah gives as the fourth commandment:

"six days shall you labor and do all manner of work;
but the seventh day is for the Lord, your God;
you shall not do on it any manner of work" (Exodus 20:9–10)

But the Torah does not tell its readers how to apply this commandment. Questions arise, and arose to Jews trying to observe the Law, and rabbis attempted to arrive at answers. What is "work," and does it depend on where you are? Scholars specified that carrying heavy objects on the Sabbath was permitted in private—that was not work—but not in public places. When in the day does the Sabbath begin and end? Days begin in the evening, and scholars gradually pushed back the exact moment of its beginning. When may one break these rules? Health reasons were listed.

Some scholars have pointed out the resemblance between the multiple cross-references and layers of commentary in these texts and the hyperlinks across computer sites available on the World Wide Web. Recognizing the similarity, in 1996 the historian Eliezer Segal produced sample texts and commentaries in hypertext format. In a different vein, and recalling the role of temple worship, New York City's Temple Emanu-El broadcast its 1996 Rosh ha-Shanah service over the Internet, with the headline "Can't Get to the Temple? Get to the Computer" (Rothstein 1996).

Movable Boundaries

Strict observance of religious laws may require ways to modify the manner in which those laws are carried out. For example, on the Sabbath one may not carry anything except within one's private domain. "Carrying" has been defined to include carrying an infant, or pushing a wheelchair. But what if an invalid needs to attend services, or an infant needs to be carried to the synagogue? One can, decided the rabbis, create a cooperative private domain, called an *eruv,* which might include the houses of a Jewish community and its synagogue. The eruv must be enclosed in some way, for example with posts and wires, as are, often unknown by most residents, parts of some U.S. cities (including an area around the Congress and White House).

Often unobtrusive, eruvs have surfaced in at least one public debate: in London, some objected to placing non–Anglican-Church religious objects in public space—and in particular religious objects that defined boundaries (Trillin 1994). Orthodox Jewish residents of a northern London neighborhood proposed to construct an eruv around their 6.5-square-mile area, using 20-foot posts connected by fishing line, and mainly along existing roadways or rail lines. In the ensuing debate, opponents of the eruv, including some in the older generation of Jews, argued that England's cohesion depended on religious differences remaining private affairs (in a context in which the Anglican Church remains the Church of State, headed by the Queen). A younger generation of Jews, and in particular several Orthodox groups, argued that their religious freedom depended on building the eruv (see further discussion in Chapter 15).

The Lubavitchers of Brooklyn

Devoting their lives to the Law, some Jewish "pietist" movements place special emphasis on correctly observing the many commandments (mitzvot) from God—said by some to be 613 in all, positive and negative. Centuries of persecution, especially in eastern and central Europe, have intensified the desire to maintain internal cultural order through following the commandments. The pietists called Hasidim, who grew in the late eighteenth century under the tutelage of holy men in the Ukraine and eastern Europe, hold that obeying these rules brings the entire cosmos closer to light and goodness.

The most important Hasidic group today is probably the Lubavitchers, whose headquarters since 1940 has been in Brooklyn. The Lubavitchers venerate their leader or Rebbe, the holy man (zaddik) who mediates between God and the world. The Rebbe is specially blessed by God, and that blessedness is passed on genealogically. All seven generations of Rebbes have been descendants of the movement's founder, Schneur Zalman (b. 1745), each a son, or son-in-law (and usually also cousin because of close intermarriage) of his predecessor.

Recent Rebbes have had strong influence in Israel. Lubavitchers, along with some other Orthodox groups, argue that non-Orthodox rabbis (Reform and Conservative) have no standing and the marriages and conversions they perform are worthless. They also hold that only Orthodox Jews, those who maintain the laws of purity and agree that the Torah remains fully active as Law, have the right to return to Israel under the Law of Return, and in 1988 they nearly succeeded in making their view into the official Israeli position. In the 1980s and 1990s the Orthodox religious parties, which often held the balance of power in the Israeli parliament, the Knesset, would from time to time call the Rebbe in Brooklyn to check the propriety of their positions on religious matters.

Many Lubavitchers were certain that the seventh Rebbe, the Paris-educated Menachem Mendel Schneerson (1902–1994) was the Messiah, at whose coming the Temple would be rebuilt. Some flew to Israel at his death to await what they called "the ultimate retribution" for centuries of persecution. In September 1996, two years after the death of Rebbe Schneerson, the then Israeli prime minister, Benjamin Netanyahu, made a special trip to Queens, New York, to say prayers at the Rebbe's grave. (He did not meet with the leaders of American Jewish organizations.)

In her book *Holy Days*, Lis Harris (1985) describes everyday life for one Brooklyn household that belongs to the Lubavitchers. Harris underscores the meaningfulness that the women of the household find in living a life of restrictions and rules. The enforced rest on the Sabbath, when no cooking, not even turning on a light, may be done, gives them leisure and freedom from working for others—an important theme in the context of the historical persecution of Jews. "No one is master of any Jew on the Sabbath" states one woman, Sheina, who married into the community. Such rules "force me to think about the sanctity of the ordinary facts of my existence" (Harris 1985, 125).

Sheina grew up in an Orthodox home, but a personal tragedy and chance meetings with Lubavitchers led her to join the community. She agreed to a marriage arranged by a rabbi, and came to joyfully embrace the many rituals and commandments of Hasidic life. Of the purifying bath in the communal bathing place, the mikvah, not used by most Jews, she said that a community is supposed to build a bath even before a synagogue, so important is maintaining purity. For Sheina, rules that prohibit sexual intercourse between husband and wife for two weeks each month (during and after menstruation) and a ritual bath at the end of the interval make sex more passionate, "like a new bride every month" (Harris 1985, 140).

A similar passion for obeying the Law pervades Sheina's weeks of work before Passover to rid her house of the least bit of leavened food—grain that has come into contact with water for more than 18 minutes. Exodus (12:19) commands that "no leaven shall be found in your houses," and Hasidic housewives labor hard to comply. Sheina cleans her house from top to bottom, replaces the stove top with a special Passover cook top, and brings out an entire set of Passover cookware that is sure to be free of leaven. Her matzohs come from a nearby bakery, where bakers race from kneading the dough to scoring it to baking the matzoh—all in nine minutes, well within the limit! Sheina and her husband also sell all leavened goods—packaged foods and whiskey (made from grain), for example—to a non-Jew, and then buy it back after Passover. The goods remain in their house, locked away, but the transaction means that the Law has been obeyed, because the goods are not theirs.

Sheina's Passover meal, like most such meals, features the foods symbolic of exile and suffering: the meat, of that eaten before leaving Egypt, the egg dipped in salt water and the bitter herbs, of sadness and suffering. But the meal follows hours of discussion about the truth of exile as the Jews' present condition. All those present agreed that the state of exile was permanent until the Messiah should come, and that all attempts at assimilation to the larger world were futile.

What Is the "Jewish Community"?

The Lubavitcher Jews set themselves off from others on the basis of God's command: "I am the Lord your God who has set you apart from the nations." Yiddish continues to be the first language for many, and many avoid what they consider to be unnecessary contact with non-Jews in their midst. But this effort at seclusion also has contributed to tensions in the Brooklyn neighborhood of Crown Heights where many Lubavitchers live alongside others, especially African Americans. Jewish citizens' patrols (called the "Maccabees," after the leaders of a successful revolt in second-century B.C.E. Judea) were accused of harassing local black residents; in 1991 black residents rioted after a black child was killed by a Lubavitcher-driven car, and some Lubavitchers accused the Mayor of anti-Semitism (Remnick 1992).

Lively debates within the Orthodox Jewish movement turn on whether separating oneself from the cultural mainstream is necessary for purity and survival, or a denial of the changing, larger world. Lubavitcher rabbis, through their 1,350 yeshiva schools worldwide, their Chabad houses in many cities, and their active outreach programs, seek to convince other Jews that as "the chosen" they are unique, and will never be fully accepted by non-Jews.

Other Jewish leaders, heirs of the nineteenth-century Reform movement toward cultural assimilation, stress that Jews are also citizens of the countries in which they live and part of modern world culture. German and eastern European immigrants to the United States in the nineteenth century found a world in which no religion was enforced—religion was a matter of individual choice. Whether Reform or Conservative (the latter being more concerned with keeping the Law), synagogues built in the suburbs during the religious revival of the 1940s and 1950s were dedicated to preserving the tradition or civilization of Judaism even for those who did not practice many of the rituals. Some features of ritual were borrowed from the dominant Protestant churches— organ music, men and women sitting together—and social clubs, libraries, and youth groups became at least as important to many Jews as worship. As Riv-Ellen Prell (1989) has argued, as adults became less and less drawn to the synagogue by the obligations of religious law or the force of community, the synagogue focused more and more of its activities on teaching children "how to be a Jew."

In the 1970s, some of these children developed "countercultural" religious institutions, in particular, new prayer communities (havurot). They did so in an effort to infuse their lives with a stronger religiosity, to recapture a lost totality—nostalgically located in the eastern European Jewish town, the shtetl. And yet they created these new forms within American culture. Membership in the prayer groups was as an associational community of free choice. Cultural values of gender equality and democracy suffused their activities. Women as well as men were counted toward making up the minimum of 10 worshipers for a prayer group (minyan). Prayer sessions involved sharing of roles and discussions of proper prayers (Prell 1989).

Mainstream U.S. Judaism and its further offshoots thus developed without the emphases on maintaining boundaries through strict observance of the law found among some Orthodox Jews today, including the Lubavitchers. American cultural ideals of democracy and expressive individualism make a law-centered religious life difficult. Of course, this very difficulty reinforces the notion of being in permanent exile that animates Lubavitcher life.

And yet the centrality of law to Orthodox Jewish self-definition, and the monopoly of Orthodox rabbis over Jewish legal institutions in Israel, means that the question of "who is a Jew?" remains unresolved. The approximately 10,000 conversions to Judaism made each year in the United States are generally performed by Reform rabbis and are not recognized by Orthodox authorities. Nor do Orthodox rabbis recognize marriages conducted under Reform auspices, or civil divorces not accompanied by a religious court's divorce declaration, the *get* (Meislin 1981). Although these cleavages disturb many in the United States, and have given rise to calls for an American religious court, they have particular importance in Israel, where they bring to the fore not only the issue of Jewish identity but also of Israeli identity (see Chapter 15).

We have examined two kinds of rules restricting the actions of a category of people in the name of a supernatural order, or a divine commandment. Some rules restrict what this category of people may do—what they may eat, what they may wear, how or whether they may cut their hair. These special restrictions underline, often conspicuously, their difference from other categories of people. The second kind of rules limits freedom of intercourse between categories of people—who you may marry, with whom you may eat, or even with whom you may have physical contact. Of course these two kinds of rules reinforce each other, for if you may eat only certain foods and must avoid others, your life and the lives of your children are easier if you marry someone in your category.

One clear effect of these rules is to maintain boundaries. But they also may give positive reinforcement to membership in the group. Sheina rejoiced in her search for leaven, and found the confined world of the Lubavitchers to restore a direction and also a pleasure to her life. Of the Muslims with whom I have fasted, many found the deprivations of the fasting month of Ramadan helped to focus their minds on their blessings, or on spirituality. Prohibitions can have multiple effects, inward and outward, on social and religious life.

For Further Consideration

*F*or discussion: What is a "taboo"? Does it need to be a rule you have reasons for following? What about a simple aversion that we feel is natural? What about the negative responses of most Americans to the idea of eating dog; is that a taboo? How is it like or unlike the response of Jews or Muslims to eating pork? Or what about marrying your first cousin; is there a taboo against that? What reasons if any do you know of for these taboos?

I enjoy Lis Harris's book about a Lubavitcher family, *Holy Days* (Collier 1985) because she provides a clear historical background alternating with her own experience of this family and its community. (The book first appeared in *The New Yorker.*) The book *Judaism* by C. M. Pilkington in the "Teach Yourself" series (Teach Yourself Books 1995) is a wonderful short source of information.

On the Web, you can find out more about Reform Judaism on the site sponsored by the Union of American Hebrew Congregations (*http://www.rj.org/*). Many Reform temples have Web sites, allowing you to see how several temples represent themselves and their faith; for example, Temple Beth David of Cheshire, Connecticut (*http://uahc.org/ct/tbd/index.html*). The United Synagogue of Conservative Judaism has an excellent Web site, a bit snazzier than the competitors', at *http://www.uscj.org/uscj01.html.* A quirky, privately maintained Orthodox site called Judaism Resources, with many interesting links, is at *http://trump9.tripod.com/.* A Lubavitcher site, Think Jewish, with many recorded sermons is at *http://www.thinkjewish.com/,* and the Lubavitcher Chabads in specific cities can also be found by searching for *chabad.* Consult also the Israel-based Torah.net (*http://www.torah.net/*).

9 Objects, Images, and Worship

*R*eligions involve actions, ideas, and rules, but they also often provide images and symbols around which religious activity centers and coalesces. We have already witnessed the power of objects, particularly images: in the tall bis poles carved by the Asmat to contain and then release their ancestors' spirits; in the enormous statues of Buddhas constructed and honored by Japanese; in the temple statues in India with which the worshiper exchanges vision, *darshan*. We could add masks used in North American, African, and Melanesian rituals, Northwest Coast poles, and Catholic statuary, to make apparent the range and power of religious images throughout the world.

Not all cultures make visual imagery an important part of religious and ritual lives; in most Muslim and Protestant societies, for example, images of people are downplayed, and instead the sacred word is stressed (as we shall see in Chapters 11 and 13). Often people debate vigorously just what an image means in religious terms—is it itself sacred? Does it contain or attract a spirit? As you read this and the next two chapters, consider the question: What kinds of differences does an emphasis on visual vis-à-vis oral media make for religious life?

Conveying Meaning through Symbols

*A*ll of the media we use to communicate with one another—words, diagrams, gestures, and so forth—are subject to multiple interpretations, but images particularly so. An image, whether a statue, painting, mask, or other object, has meaning in a way different from a statement that we might utter. If I say, "This is a tree," I have clearly said something about an object and a class of things called "trees." A picture of a tree, by contrast, does not say anything. The picture might be a photograph of a tree (in which case it could be taken as evidence that the tree exists, in a court of law for instance), or a very good painting of a tree (in which case it might be interpreted mainly for the skill of the artist or his or her attention to form). It might be a tree housing an ancestor, or a tree evoking memories of shade and protection.

The tree-picture's meanings come from the larger structure of knowledge, associations, and practices in which it is embedded. Moreover, different viewers, with different histories and experiences, might draw from it very different interpretations and associations.

Such images are multivocalic—"many-voiced" or capable of generating many meanings. Recall the Asmat sago tree. The tree's tall form and spherical fruits suggest the human form and head, and the milky, starchy interior suggests breast milk and nurturing powers. The tree evokes myths about the taking of heads and the origins of the cosmos. Many Indonesians view the huge, spreading banyan trees found throughout the country as evoking feelings of protection, and for this reason the tree was taken to be the emblem of the government's political party GOLKAR. The tree now evokes different feelings and thoughts for viewers depending on their political ideas.

In studying the religious meanings of objects we look for associations and resonances on different planes of human experience, from physiology, to culture, to social structure. Certain such associations have a strong basis in body symbolism, such as the sago tree's evocations of heads and milk, or the ideas of danger often linked to the color red. These associations are often widespread, evoking shared human experiences, although they receive different interpretations in different societies. The anthropologist Victor Turner (1967, 28–30) describes these meanings as the "sensory pole" of a symbol's range of meaning. He contrasts these meanings to those clustering around the "ideological pole," which tie the object to socially specific ideas. The same Asmat trees, when carved into bis poles, stand for the unity of the men in the men's house and the needs of the ancestral spirit to be enclosed and then released by the taking of a head. (Men's and women's ideas about the pole undoubtedly differ, but more fieldwork is required to clarify these differences.)

Turner's way of analyzing symbols allows us to consider the interplay of psychological or bodily associations, which tend to be similar in unrelated societies, with those "ideological" associations that are specific to one society or group of societies, or to one religious tradition. Another perspective on meaning, called "semiotics" and deriving from the logician Charles S. Peirce (1972), focuses on three ways in which an object is meaningful: as an *index* based on direct contact or "pointing," as an *icon* based on resemblance, and as a *symbol* based on historically and culturally specific linkages.

The semiotic approach is particularly useful in pointing out two ways that religious objects convey meaning. The first way is through the *history of physical contact* between an object and a spiritual or sacred being. Sacred relics, such as body parts of holy people, masks originating from spirits, or the bis pole once inhabited by an ancestor, are sacred and treasured because of their history of direct contact with a once-living holy person, a powerful spirit, or a revered ancestor. A second way objects take on powerful religious meaning is through their *resemblance* to a sacred or powerful being. Consider how Catholic images of the Virgin Mary are expected (and are seen by some people) to work miracles: to heal, weep, or speak. (The sense of "icon" as "religious image" is one of its standard dictionary meanings, and has given rise to such terms as "iconoclast," meaning "image breaker" in medieval Greek, referring to people opposed to the use and veneration of sacred images.)

Embodying Deities

In many religions, we find combinations of imagery and contact serving as the bases for worshiping gods. Hinduism freely combines several image types, all of which embody a deity. Some statues are highly realistic and anthropomorphic ("representing in human shape") representations of a deity. The focus of the worshiper's attention toward these statues is the eye: the worshiper "exchanges vision" (darshan) with the deity by gazing on its eyes. Power is absorbed through visual contact. Yet other god-objects are not at all anthropomorphic: Shiva, one of the great gods, is often represented by a simple, phallus-shaped stone called a *linga*. The shape underscores Shiva's cosmic creative energy. It, too, is inhabited by the deity.

Japanese religions exhibit a still wider range of image types to represent and mark the presence of a deity. Buddha statues are of particular Buddhas—Maitreya, or Fudo, or Amida. Each Buddha has characteristic markers, such as the position of the hands or the presence of other objects, but the artist still has a great deal of latitude in how the Buddha is represented. But Buddhas are above the world, so they are not depicted as historical personages. By contrast, the spirits (kami) worshiped at Shinto shrines are tied to the world in one of two ways. Some are spirits of ancestors, and so may be shown in paintings as specific individuals with identifiable dates. Others are spirits of locations; they are represented by natural elements such as a waterfall or a boulder. An ancestor is represented by a plaque, which may be converted into a household god through the logic of direct contact: the plaque is thrown into a river, from which a pebble is selected and added to the pile of pebbles making up the household god's altar. Spirit objects are defined by the fact that they are spirits or contain spirits; Buddhist statues, by contrast, must have certain rituals performed on them before they will be said to contain the particular Buddha they represent.

Religious objects play meaningful roles in two very different traditions. The masks and legends of the Dogon people of West Africa represent the creation of the world in dances. Catholic images of Mary, Christ, and saints are intended to focus worship on the universal message of the Church. Both traditions link the immediate and concrete to the universal, and do so through powerful imagery, with multiple associations. The great disparity in scale between these two cases—one bounded in a small plateau region, the other spread throughout the world—shows how similar forms and practices of religion appear in widely differing contexts.

Masks in West Africa

*M*asks are used throughout the world to convey ideas of sacred power. They play particularly important roles in certain regions—a belt across the middle of Africa; Northwest Coast America; Melanesia—but they appear most everywhere. In New Guinea, and along the northwest coast of the Americas, masks often depict ancestors, including primordial ancestors, and they dramatize stories of the creation of humans. The famous transforming masks of the Kwakiutl of the northwest coast enact this creative process in themselves: the face of a bear, for instance, may be opened when the wearer pulls on hidden straps to reveal the image of the human into which the bear was changed.

Masks give a timeless or universal quality to real human beings, and for that reason they are often used to represent the cosmos, or the first people or beings, and then they are used to dance out the primordial creation of the world and the establishment of social order. These dances or other uses of masks then affirm and underscore that order in the face of current disorder. Because they are inhabited by people, almost always men, they also represent the social order in a particular way, especially with respect to gender and age-grade or level of initiation. In many societies, particularly in Africa, women are not supposed to speak of the masks or touch them; they mark as taboo the boundary between control of the sacred objects, in men's hands, and the society of women.

The Dogon people of Mali and Burkina Faso (the former Upper Volta) are famous for their elaborate masks and for the extensive study of their culture by a French ethnographic team (Griaule 1965). The Dogon live from agriculture on a cliff and plateau region, under the authority of a council of village elders. Each village owns a large figure of the mythic ancestor Dyongou Sérou, the first being to experience death. Every adult male belongs to a village mask society, the Awa, charged with guarding the village mask, and he also sculpts his own mask, which may be of animals, Dogon people, foreigners, or other objects. He wears the mask during a variety of rituals, including those designed to accompany a spirit of the dead to its resting place, to ward off spells, or to ensure the fertility of crops or of women.

Seventy-eight different types of masks have been identified for the Dogon, each with multiple levels of meaning that correspond to the four degrees of initiation through which males pass (Imperato 1978). For example, a mask surmounted with a tall lattice work is identified on the first level, and to the uninitiated (including early ethnographers), as "the granary door of Amma," the supreme god. On a higher level it is known to represent the phase in the creation of the universe when Amma's collarbones opened up, and on a still higher level, the "egg of Amma" out of which the first beings were created.

The Dogon consider their masks to be capable of defusing and transferring dangerous sacred powers. In their view, all life forms have a vital force or power called "nyama" (Pernet 1992, 53–62). Nyama can flow from one material being to another, but when it leaves its usual resting place, it changes from supporting life to endangering life. It becomes energy out of place. Masks can be used to transfer such "loose" nyama to a safe place, such as a painting. This process is described in the story about the kanaga mask, which depicts a bird in downward flight. The mask has a vertical piece extending upward from the cap, crossed by two horizontal pieces—the lower one with short extension pieces pointing downward, the upper one with pieces pointing upward. Most Dogon understand the mask as the representation of a story about this bird and its nyama. In the story, a hunter killed the bird and carved its image with wood from a nearby tree. But the spirit of the tree lost its resting place when the tree was felled, which caused the hunter to become ill. The hunter then carved a small figure at the very top of the mask to embody the spirit. In a second transfer, he moved the spirit to a painting in red ochre on the wall of a cave, and his health was restored.

*Drawing of the Dogon kanaga mask,
Mali.*

Men who have reached the higher degrees of initiation interpret the mask in a different way, as representing a story about Amma, the supreme god. Amma had twin children through sexual intercourse with the earth. The children are known as the Nommo. One was female and one male, and both had human forms above the waist and serpent shapes below the waist. Amma had other children, and one committed incest with his mother the earth—an act that led to the introduction of death to the world. To cleanse the earth of this polluting act, Amma sacrificed one of the Nommo (Griaule 1965, 130–137). To the men who know this story, the two arms of the mask pointing skyward represent the sacrificed Nommo and his twin; the two pointing downward, the son who committed incest and his twin. (Various alternative interpretations of the carving on the mask's top have been given to ethnographers.) The sacrifice, like the wearing of the mask, turned dangerous power away from society.

We should note two aspects of the mask and its meaning at this point. First, different people viewing the mask as it is danced around in a ritual event will have very different associations and stories come to mind. The mask is multivocalic. Second, the meanings people bring to their viewing of the mask depend on their own social characteristics, particularly on their gender and degree of initiation. The masks call up diverse images in a way that is highly socially structured.

This socially shaped multivocality also applies to the red fiber skirt the dancers wear (Griaule 1965, 16–23). These fibers contain their own sort of nyama. For some viewers (those who have reached higher degrees of initiation), the fibers also recall the mythic fibers Amma gave to his wife the earth. The fibers were reddened by the first menstrual blood, which appeared after the incestuous union described above. Women obtained them and, wearing them, ruled society. Men then managed to wrest them from the women and by virtue of their possession also took over control of society. When men put on the skirts to dance they are thus calling up a complex set of associations in the minds of viewers. Dogon say that the men are dressing as women when they don skirts. Some viewers will find the fibers calling up images of the sun, menstrual blood, fecundity, and death, with different values attached to these images by different viewers. Others will know various versions of the stories of Amma and the fibers, and these stories will further modify their own understandings of the performances.

The masks also accentuate the line between men and women. Women are not supposed to speak of the masks or touch them, nor may a man discuss them with women. The penalty for infringing these taboos is said to be infertility. Men have the masks and the fiber skirts only because they once seized them from women, and they need be on their guard to keep them in their control.

Male monopolies on masks are widespread, but women's masked societies are found in many societies also (Pernet 1992, 136–157). For example, initiates into the Sande women's societies of Sierra Leone and Liberia wear masks, and when these women venture out with their masks, it is men who must remain indoors.

The masks are used especially for funeral rituals and for death anniversary ceremonies called "Dama" and are intended to appease the spirit of the dead by dramatizing the order of the world (for all viewers) and (for the higher-degree initiated) the story of how the world came into being. The dead person's spirit is reminded of how death came into the world through the incestuous act of one child, but also of how people restored and maintain order.

In many Dogon societies these ritual performances have either been abandoned (especially by those Dogon who converted to Islam) or have been transformed into tourist performances. Even in these, some elements of the original ritual have been preserved, especially when the masks are touched to the ground to ask pardon of the deceased. The National Folkloric Troupe of Mali adapts some of the rituals to theater. Even in those performances the actors retain a sense of the stories and associations found in Dogon villages (Imperato 1978). Yet one can imagine a future in which the masked dances survive only as art, no longer as religion or even as lived culture.

The power and meaning of these masks come from their capacity to evoke associations in different ways and on different planes of life. They evoke powerful bodily events such as sexual intercourse, giving birth, menstruation, and death. They also evoke specific mythic personages and events, and they represent in rituals the division of society into groups and by gender. They convey these meanings through representation, as icons of particular ancestors or objects, and thereby bring viewers into the story being told in the dance. But they also signify a history of direct contact with the power of nyama, and this historical relationship makes the masks themselves powerful.

Images and Offerings in Hinduism

*T*n India, sacrifice, offerings, and devotions are directed toward the gods, of which there are many. About 80 percent of India's 800 million people consider themselves Hindus, and most of them, daily and in countless ways (including sacrificial ways), carry out rituals of offerings and homage to the gods (Fuller 1992, 29–56).

Gods: Few and Many

Some gods are entirely specific to a village or district. Others may have locally specific forms but are also manifestations of pan-Indian gods. Particularly important are Vishnu and Shiva, who stand in a complementary relationship to each other—Vishnu the preserver and Shiva the destroyer, Vishnu the king and Shiva the ascetic (renouncer of worldly pleasures), Vishnu at the center of the world and Shiva outside it. (Brahma, less prominent in worship, is the creator.) Because creation is cyclical—creation following destruction in the cycles of cosmic history—both are necessary elements in the world.

Vishnu is usually worshiped through one of his 10 incarnations, most often as Rama or Krishna. The ancient epic of the Ramayana tells of Rama's life as the king of Ayodhya and represents his life as the model for a righteous king's conduct. The Ramayana is known throughout India (and much of Southeast Asia) in various versions, some emphasizing Rama's divinity. It is read or viewed today in the forms of sacred texts, popular stories, comic books, and shadow puppet plays, and during 1987–1988 it appeared as a hugely popular television series—that also raised popular enthusiasm for Hindu nationalist politics (see Chapter 15).

Krishna is portrayed as a warrior or as a mischievous child. His battles are recounted in another well-known epic, the Mahabharata. But he also transcends mere human warfare. In a section of the epic called the Bhagavad Gita, he counsels his cousin Arjuna to remain above the world even as he is forced to continue his battles. Krishna is also worshiped as a youth and remembered for his romance with the cowherdess Radha.

Shiva has many manifestations. He may be represented by a phallic linga statue, or as a human-looking image. Shiva has sons, Skanda and Ganesha, the latter represented with an elephant head. Vishnu's wives, Lakṣmi and Bhudevi, and Shiva's wife, Parvathi, often are represented by statues in temples, and often their names differ from one temple to the next.

Both Vishnu and Shiva have followers, Vaishnavas and Shaivas, who worship the gods either by these names or in their local manifestations, often alongside other, lesser deities. Each temple in India is, in principle, unique, and each is dedicated to a particular, local form of a deity. For Shiva and Vishnu, this localization of worship means that they are addressed by a distinctive name. In a south India temple devoted to the local

Priest purifies the image of Shiva with water, Shiva temple at Yanaimangalam, Tamil Nadu state, India. (COURTESY OF DIANE MINES.)

goddess–queen Minakshi, for example, Shiva is present as Sundareshwara, Minakshi's consort. At the temple in Benares, Shiva's holiest site on the Ganges in north India, he is addressed as Vishwanatha (Fuller 1992, 37–38).

As with the Virgin Mary, one person and yet also distinct in her many manifestations in the thousands of Marian shrines, these Shivas are many and one. Indeed, some Hindus say the same of Vishnu and Shiva, that they are one, Vishnu–Shiva. Many temples have legends explaining how it was that Shiva or Vishnu came to occupy a spot at that particular temple—after a battle, or a great deed, or to become the consort of a local deity. The idea of one-and-yet-many is thus basic to Hindu religion; however, it is a feature that at least some Hindus find requires an explanation.

The same unity-and-multiplicity is found with respect to the goddess, Devi, who exists in multiple forms. As Durga, she fights off demons; as Kali or Shakti, she is power itself and is supreme over the gods, often shown trampling on Shiva. She manifests herself as a consort of one of the great gods, but also in local forms, where she brings powers of heat, and sometimes disease, but also fertility—all forms of her power, *shakti*. In south India, each local settlement has its own tutelary goddess, known by one name throughout that region. Thus, in much of Tamil Nadu (Fuller 1992, 43) the goddess is Mariyamman: Mariyamman of this place versus Mariyamman of that place—different goddesses and yet also localized forms of the single Goddess.

Hindus also have local deities, and because Vishnu and Shiva, concerned with the cosmos, are unlikely to respond to requests for assistance in everyday matters, worshipers turn to these deities such as the goddess–queen Minakshi mentioned earlier, or still lesser deities worshiped by particular castes. These deities may be ghosts who were enshrined as a means of controlling their powers, or they may be humans, who can be especially relied on to respond to human problems. A village might have dozens of these deities, worshiped by different persons or groups or approached for particular problems.

Thus, some Hindus identify little goddesses (*matas*) that occupy various places in the environment—in a thorn bush, under a three-brick "altar," in a house. They are associated with the Goddess, and their festival is on her day of Navarati, but they are distinct from her. As with the *kami* of Japan, these deities are many and mostly unnamed. They may enter certain men and women and possess them, and through this possession heal a child or answer a vexing question posed by a fellow villager.

At the other end of the deity scale, modern religious and political movements have taken specific gods as symbols for their idea of an all-Hindu India. A prominent Bengali nationalist, Bankim Chandra Chatterjee created a form of the goddess as "Mother India," or "Bharat Mata" (Fuller 1992, 42). In her temple at Benares she is represented not as a personage but as a map of India—a literalistic fusion of the goddess with the nation and the state!

Offerings to Deities

Offerings to deities, or *puja,* may take the form of an informal family rite or that of a village temple festival. You may perform puja to ask a favor from a deity (usually a minor deity; greater ones tend to be above that sort of thing), or when you recite sacred Sanskrit texts about the exploits of a goddess, or when you join a group in singing devotional Hindi songs to Krishna.

A relatively simple puja might be focused on the ancestors of a joint family, of parents, sons, their wives and children (Fuller 1992, 57–82). First snapshot: in a village in Madhya Pradesh, central India, the father regularly worships his agnatic (through males) ancestors in the home. Just before noon he bathes himself, offering some of the water to his ancestors; his wife and sons' wives meanwhile prepare an elaborate meal. He takes a plate of the food, a dish of clarified butter (ghi), and a brass pot with water from the bath, and, in the kitchen, kneels before a piece of flaming cow dung. He sprinkles water around the dung and places some of the butter on the fire. Again he sprinkles water, and this time places some of the food on the fire. After a third sprinkle he bows before the flame, his hands pressed together, touching his forehead. He then joins his family for their meal. Because some of the food has been offered to the ancestors, all the meal now contains the "grace" or *prasada* of the ancestors. Homes also contain altars with images of family deities and teachers; women as well as men worship there daily or occasionally.

Now a second snapshot: in the southern Indian state of Tamil Nadu, in an urban temple a priest is ready to honor Minakshi, the goddess–queen of an ancient kingdom, and her consort Lord Shiva, in one of his many local manifestations. Each of the deities is represented by a two-foot-high movable image set up in the temple complex and draped with white cloth. Musicians play, and their loud drumming signals the close of each ritual stage. A chanter recites sacred formulas (mantras). The priest purifies the

Woman cooking ponkal, *a dish cooked from "raw rice" and suitable for Brahmans, to be offered to the "backyard god" pictured to the left, at Yanaimangalam.* (COURTESY OF DIANE MINES.)

images by rubbing them with a series of liquids, including sesame seed oil, milk, and water that has been infused with divine power through the chanting of mantras. The gods' images are adorned with clothes, jewelry, and flowers, and their foreheads are marked with three stripes of white ash, the mark of Shiva. Food is held out to the deities while water is sprinkled around the offering. The priest waves oil lamps and a candelabra with seven camphor flames in front of the images. People attending the ritual then crowd in to place their hands over the flames and touch their fingers to their eyes and to accept white ash from the priests to place on their foreheads.

This temple ritual may be reduced or elaborated. The images may be purified with water before the ritual, and at its conclusion butter may be poured onto a flame as a final offering. More foods may be offered, and distributed to all worshipers. Or the ritual may be reduced to a presentation of one camphor flame to the deity, with a plantain on the side as an offering. The reduced ritual is still valid (it counts as puja), and the elaborations are not superfluous (they add to what is accomplished).

Forms of offering vary within India and abroad (substantial Hindu communities are found in Africa, Europe, and the Americas, and Hindus make up a large proportion of the populations of some Caribbean islands, Fiji, and Bali). Festivals all revolve around making offerings to the gods. Festivals vary across India but include the springtime Holi,

Worshiper receives from temple priest as prasada *a garland that had been offered to Shiva, Shiva temple at Yanaimangalam.* (COURTESY OF DIANE MINES.)

celebrated in north India to mark the burning of the demonness Holika and the start of the agricultural season, and a sequence of festivals in September and October, especially the festival of lights, Divali, a time for welcoming and escorting departed ancestors.

All forms of offering, simple or elaborate, involve purification, communication, and offering. Purity may adhere to things or procedures. Pouring water over something takes away polluting elements, hence the importance of bathing and sprinkling. Cow products, from butter to dung to the ash of the dung, are pure.

Communication is through multiple channels: chants, music, words, gestures. Before the gods one always shows respect through the gesture called "namaste" or *pranam*, holding the hands together and touching the forehead. It, too, may be succinct or elaborated: a supplicant may merely hold up the hands to the forehead, or may bow down, even touch the feet of the deity. The same range of gestures is used toward people, indicating their relative rank to oneself. Through this gesture one salutes "that bit of god which is in every person." Humans and gods are both arranged in hierarchies.

One also sees the deities—and they see us. This darshan, or vision, is also an exchange of vision, to some people it is the painting of eyes onto the image or a subsequent poke with a chisel that envivifies it. Although the image is not the same as the deity, the deity is in the image and in many different images throughout India at any one moment. Light, the flame, enhances and signals the exchange of vision, and through this exchange the commingling of human and divine essences.

Girl with food that she has offered and received as prasada, part of an annual offering she makes to fulfill a vow, temple to Murukan, son of Shiva, Pattamadai, Tamil Nadu state, India.
(COURTESY OF DIANE MINES.)

The deities may also be dressed, sung to, and chanted over, but they are always fed. The food may be anything that people eat, but it is always offered to the deity, taken back, and distributed to those present—family, neighbors, or temple-goers. It may simply be set before the god, or it may be set on fire—"the flame is the tongue of the gods." The consumed food becomes the embodiment of the deity's power or "grace," one literal meaning of prasada, the food offering. Anything that has been placed in contact with the deity and then returned to humans—ash, water, food, flowers—is prasada and conveys that divine power to the human partakers. (In this aspect of puja its transactional character—something given, something received—is most concretely apparent.)

Relics and Images in Catholicism

Catholic imagery also has been based on different types of meaning and multiple associations in the minds of worshipers. When we think of Catholicism we usually think of elaborate representations of saints, Jesus, and Mary. But Catholic images, like masks in Africa and elsewhere, also draw on other kinds of symbolic meanings to become powerful, multivocalic foci for worship and social life.

A famous example is the Shroud of Turin, a cloth held in Turin, Italy, since 1578 that has on its surface an image of a bearded face, said by some to be the image of Christ. The shroud is venerated by many Catholics, not just because it is a likeness of Jesus but because they think that it was produced by direct and miraculous physical contact with his face, in a fashion similar to the process that produces a photograph. This claim of direct contact generates in many pious people a sense of direct communication between the viewer and Jesus. The arguments about the Shroud's authenticity turn exclusively on this issue of contact, not on its resemblance to Jesus. In fact, the iconic qualities of the image on the Shroud, its resemblance to conventional ideas of what Jesus looked like, are precisely what skeptics point to when they claim that it is only a painting. The relative weight of iconic and indexical meanings is thus of great importance for the Shroud's religious status.

Christianity is, after all, founded on ideas of contact and physical presence, in particular the idea of incarnation, the embodiment of godliness in tangible form as Jesus Christ. The central ritual of the Church is based on the worshiper's direct contact with Christ through eating and drinking of his body. Holy Communion enacts the miracle of the Eucharist, in which ordinary bread and wine are consecrated by a priest and, at that exact moment, turned into the body and blood of Jesus. This countlessly repeated miracle parallels the sacrifice Jesus made of himself for the sake of humanity.

The idea that Christ is in the bread and wine was popularly assumed for centuries. It was finally codified in 1215, when the Fourth Lateran Council ruled that consecration does indeed convert the ordinary substances into Christ, or, in the technical language of the Church, that "transubstantiation" takes place. The Council also ruled that Christ was whole in every particle of bread and wine "under two species." This second idea, called "concomitance," responded to the concern, evidently widespread at the time, that when one dropped crumbs of the bread on the floor one was dropping bits of Christ, that chewing the bread was chewing his bones, and so forth.

The History of Relics and the Host

Relics preserve the history of religious miracles through their own history of physical contact with sacred persons or events. They make up an important part of the history of Catholic religious objects—which is also the history of Catholic politics. Religious objects have mediated between the community and the church hierarchy, between local and universal perspectives, between religion and the state, and between cultures.

The central Church ritual, communion or the Eucharist, is based on a miracle of incarnation. In the early Church the ritual of communion was expansive and collective. The priest said "Peace be with you"; the lay worshipers responded in kind and exchanged the "kiss of peace" with each other (men with men, women with women). Worshipers then brought forward their sacrifices of bread and wine to be consecrated by the priest. Communion was thus the Church partaking of Christ and worshipers communing with each other. Christianity drew on its Jewish roots but also broadened them. Communion widened the bounds of the Jewish seder to include the entire community beyond the realm of one's family and friends. Communion thus modeled socially the universal ideal and ambition of the Church (Bynum 1987, 48–69; Feeley-Harnik 1981, 107–168).

Communion recreates for a brief moment what is in effect a direct physical link to Christ. But Christian churches also relied on other kinds of sacred indexes to maintain a sense of connection among churches and among worshipers. As the Church expanded in Europe and North Africa it created a network of churches under the control of Rome. Churches were built on shrines or as shrines, sometimes near or around cemeteries located just outside city walls, where the buried remains of saints sanctified the ground of the new church. There was a practical consideration at work as well—the belief current at the time was that on the day of Resurrection, the first bodies to be taken up to heaven would be those buried near the body of a saint (Ariès 1974).

A Christian shrine or church usually contained sacred objects, an image or relic that gave the shrine its religious status. A relic was a remnant of a saint—a bone, bit of hair, or an entire corpse—or an object that had been made sacred by contact with a saint (or Jesus). It was movable, and so separate from the place itself. Except in Ireland, where the pre-Christian Celtic veneration of places continued unabated, it was the relic, not the place, that was considered sacred.

Saints' bodies, sometimes partially or wholly mummified, have been favorite relics for churches. In the early churches they were often exhibited to worshipers and pilgrims. Today as well, the faithful consider saints' bodies to be capable of working miracles. Some bodies exude healing fluids, such as a marble sarcophagus in the French Pyrenees that accumulates clear water. Throughout the year the water is collected by individuals and used for healing, and the remainder is pumped out each July 30 at a special ceremony. Soil may be taken from the burial place of a saint and used to heal, particularly in Ireland and the Americas. A small church near Santa Fe contains such a miraculous source of earth. Bones are also used as church relics, today usually contained in elaborately sculpted boxes or reliquaries.

The logic of sacrality through contact reaches beyond body parts and sacred soil. Paintings and statues may acquire sacred status from having once been in contact with a sacred person or object. For example, some paintings of the Virgin Mary draw their religious force from their historical ties to what is called the True Icon (*Vera Icon*) of Mary: a painting said to have been made by Saint Luke and considered to be holy because he, a holy person, painted it, and not because of a property of the representation itself. Paintings that are understood as copies of the True Icon are found in Italy, Spain, and most famously in Poland. Our Lady of Czestochowa, the national icon of Poland, is a painting of a dark Madonna, and it is housed in a fourteenth-century church in the southwestern part of the country. It is the object of the major pilgrimage for Polish Catholics. It is said to derive from the Saint Luke painting. Other paintings or statues are touched to the painting in Czestochowa, and from that contact derive a special (indexical, we would say) power. Copies of the True Icon become as effective as the original in working miracles. (At least by the sixth century C.E. we find stories of paintings carried into battle to ensure victory.)

Images versus Relics

By the late fourth century, a lively traffic in saints' remains had developed across Europe. Remains were sent as gifts, sometimes stolen from crypts in Italy. This traffic was encouraged by the idea that remains could be divided up, and the saint became present in each fragment (analogous to the idea that Christ was totally present in every fragment of consecrated bread). As Theodoret of Cyrus proclaimed: "in the divided body the grace survives undivided and the fragments, however small, have the same efficacy as the whole body (Bynum 1987, 48–53).

During the eighth century a rapid rise in missionary activity led the Church to develop rules for creating new churches. In 787, the Second Council of Nicaea declared that a new church had to possess a saint's relic in order to be consecrated. The new rule further increased the demand for relics. People began to scour the Roman catacombs for bone fragments that could be attributed to early Christian martyrs, and a virtual flood of these bone fragments poured forth from Rome out into northern Europe. The hunger for relics turned major discoveries of bones into momentous cultural events. In the early ninth century Saint James' bones were discovered in northern Spain, and the site of this discovery, known thereafter as Santiago de Compostela, became the third most important Christian pilgrimage site after Rome and Jerusalem (Nolan and Nolan 1989, 160–171).

The propagation of relics not only expanded the bounds of the Church but also provided a firm spiritual foundation for the empire created by Charlemagne. From the ninth century onward, the oath administered to witnesses was taken on saints' relics, and read: "May God and the saints whose relics these are judge me that I speak the truth" (Rothkrug 1980).

During the early years of Christian expansion, there were no official procedures for evaluating relics, or indeed for canonizing saints. A local church could declare someone to have been a saint and then build a church around him or her. The remains would be disinterred and placed on an altar within the church. If the body was found to be intact, or in the language of the times, "uncorrupt," this condition was attributed to its holy qualities, which had continued to reside in the body after death. (Note that in this tradition intact bodies were signs of purity; by contrast in the Greek Orthodox practices discussed in Chapter 4, total disintegration of the flesh is a sign that the soul was received into heaven.)

Many of the relics were, in fact, fakes: countless pieces of wood from Christ's cross circulated throughout Europe, as did chalky stones from the Milk Grotto in Bethlehem said to be colored by milk Mary used to nurse Christ. The market pressures also encouraged theft: one Roman deacon named Deusdona contracted to steal the remains of Saint Peter and to supply them, broken down into small parts, to the Franks. As their authenticity increasingly was doubted, their value declined. (Compare with Gresham's Law in economics: "bad money drives out good.")

The Church responded in two ways. First, it began to exert authority over the status of holy man or saint. It carried out its first canonization of a saint in 993 and gradually gained control over that process. Second, the Church tried to substitute images for relics. Early Christian art (like Islamic art) had been largely decorative. Many people felt that the crafting of human figures would be tantamount to worshiping graven images, a fear inherited from Judaism. In the words of Saint Epiphanius in the fourth century C.E.: "When images are put up, the customs of the pagans do the rest." But popular use of imagery, pictures of saints, developed in the late fourth century and became widespread by the sixth. The Church came to encourage this trend in the interest of promoting universalism. Saints, after all, were many, and their stories often emphasized local miracles and military victories rather than the universal message of Christ that was central to the Church. Basing the legitimacy of a local church on relics underscored the local bases for worship rather than the Church's universalism. To the extent that the Church was able to refocus worshipers' attention toward paintings or statues or other images, it would be able to emphasize the universal figures of Mary and Christ, whose bodies were not available to be relics (Nolan and Nolan 1989, 160–171).

To meet popular objections that only relics were sacred—and the practical point that only relics would share in the resurrection—Church authorities encouraged the crafting of reliquaries: elaborately carved boxes, often with jewels and gold, or statues in the image of a saint that contained minute pieces of the saint's bone. These objects were both relics and images. Images such as paintings or ordinary statues were also said to have had direct contact with a sacred person, or, as in the case of the True Icon mentioned above, to have been painted by a saint, or to have been once physically touched to a painting that was painted by a saint, and so forth, along a historical chain of direct, sacred contact. These efforts drew on popular ideas about contact and sacrality but also promoted universal images.

A More Hierarchical Ritual

The Church's efforts to emphasize its universal message over local sacrality gained momentum in the eleventh, twelfth, and thirteenth centuries, a period of growth in the political power of the Church. What we often call the "age of faith," or, in reference to the great energies devoted to church crafting throughout Western Europe, the "age of cathedrals," also saw a shift in the relationship of people to the institution of the Catholic Church. Rome began to exercise more control over local churches, and in each church priests recast their role vis-à-vis lay persons in a more hierarchical or vertical way.

The eleventh century saw the growth of powerful monasteries, which resisted secular control, the struggle for priority in spiritual affairs over the kings, and the Crusades, which began in 1096. The church became "monumental" in several senses. Doctrine was systematically formulated, most notably by Thomas of Aquinas (1225–1274); the great cathedrals of northern Europe were built; and Rome was able to exert ever-greater control over the behavior of individual churches. It was the great age of pilgrimages to such sites as Santiago de Compostela in northern Spain, to England's Canterbury Cathedral, the site of Thomas à Beckett's assassination in 1170 (and the destination of the pilgrims in Chaucer's *Canterbury Tales*), and the first great Holy Year pilgrimage to Rome in 1300. Many religious orders that promoted pilgrimages—Dominicans, Franciscans, Carmelites—were founded during this period.

All these developments added to the general sense of a Christiandom united by movements of people, the mobilization of popular energies, and a central, controlling power lodged in Rome. In worship itself, these changes led to a great focus on the priest's role, as the representative of Rome, over and against that of the people. Communion and other aspects of liturgy became more centralized, more in the hands of priests and monks. Saint Thomas himself wrote that priests engage in the communion of Eucharist on behalf of others. Saints once had come from the popular ranks, even after canonization became a Church monopoly. Now male saints began to be drawn entirely from the ranks of priests (Bynum 1987, 53–69).

The ritual transformation that most evidently represented this change was the shift from *receiving* communion to *seeing* the Host. By the twelfth century churches had begun to offer communion less frequently and instead to concentrate the attention of worshipers on Christ's presence in the bread and wine at the moment they were consecrated by the priest. Christ could be seen on the altar and adored there. Physical contact was downplayed in favor of, again, the image of Christ, albeit an image of the Host that had become Christ.

As priests emphasized the "adoration of the Host" other changes were made as well. Elaborate containers for the Host, reliquaries, were made and placed so all could see. Holes were made in some church walls so that even horses could commune by viewing the Host. The Host began to be raised up for general view; this practice of "elevating the Host" first occurred in Paris in 1200. Fifteen years later Pope Innocent II declared as dogma the miracle of transubstantiation, the change of bread and wine into Christ's body and blood. In 1264 a new feast day, the feast of Corpus Christi, the "body of Christ," began to be celebrated. By the fourteenth century a new kind of vessel called a "monstrance" ("displayer") was created to display the consecrated Host. As the historian John Bossy (1983) writes, the "socially integrative powers of the Host" were transferred from the mass to the feast of Corpus Christi.

From the twelfth century onward, receiving the Host became something priests did. Already by the eleventh century only priests could take Christ in their hands; others had to receive a wafer directly in their mouths from the priest. The priest once had carried out the consecration of the Host in full view and standing facing the worshipers—after all, in the early church it had been their bread and wine that had been brought to be consecrated. But now the priest celebrated with his back to the people. He took communion for their sake with his back turned. Special "rood screens" were constructed to seal him off from view. In these churches communion became a mystery, a miracle that touched only the priest, who was sometimes venerated precisely because of his privileged contact with Christ. In the words of Saint Francis of Assisi (1181–1226): "He touches Christ with his own hands."

The "two species" of the Eucharist now were treated differently. When communion was offered to worshipers, the consecrated cup was sometimes withheld and ordinary wine substituted. The reason given was that the church feared that a careless parishioner could spill Christ's blood. The wafer now became the focus of this longed-for ritual act. It became a strongly held symbol of the unity of the church and of fears of its being desecrated. Anti-Semitism was often voiced as an accusation that someone had defiled the wafers. Stories circulated of Hosts turning to flesh and bleeding in protest against misuse (for example, by sorcerers) or in an effort to warn churchgoers against an approaching danger (Bossy 1983; Bynum 1987, 53–69).

The Host increasingly became a symbol of the church, rather than a source of redemption for the individual person. Some people protested this church control; these protests included demands to receive the Host "in both species," that is, as consecrated wine and bread. A hunger for the chalice and communion intensified, and ordinary people, particularly women, experienced religious devotions and ecstasies as sensing and eating God.

The central objects that located or founded a church also shifted from relics of saints (with the host as one of many relics) to the general adoration of Christ and the Virgin Mary. In 1150 the pope rejected his former title, "Vicar of Saint Peter" for the new one, "Vicar of Christ," shifting his grounds for authority from the presence of Saint Peter's body in Rome (a relic), to his direct receipt of authority from Christ.

The Church also began to desacralize relics and to replace them with images of saints. It developed the idea of the saints and Mary in the "communion of saints," or "the unity under and in Christ of the faithful on the earth, the souls in purgatory, and the blessed in heaven." Dead souls were enrolled in the new brotherhoods and orders as part of this universal community. This idea of the communion of saints allowed one soul to pray for another. Helping other souls through prayer became a major activity both in church masses and at pilgrimage sites. (Recall the same activity by Gayo Muslims discussed in Chapter 4 and the similar controversies surrounding prayer for the dead.)

Christ Incarnate

The Eucharist, as it became the focus of church activity, is best seen as Christ's incarnation—it gave the worshiper direct contact with Christ. Recall that it was only in 1215 that the Church proclaimed as dogma the eucharistic miracle of transubstantiation. The elevation and adoration of the Host began about then, and Corpus Christi followed in 1264.

These steps addressed what we can think of as the problem of Christ's relics (Nolan and Nolan 1989). After all, according to the church, Christ ascended to heaven 40 days after the Resurrection, leaving no body behind to generate relics. In popular opinion he did leave some relics behind: his blood and the earth that was touched by it; pieces of the cross and nails from the cross; garments worn during the Passion; the Shroud of Turin. The church gradually accepted the idea that his milk teeth, foreskin, and spilled blood could, in theory, have remained on the earth even though he ascended to heaven. Popular pressure was for more relics of Christ, perhaps because of the more difficult access to Christ through communion.

The steps taken by the church in the thirteenth century to promote the worship of Christ may have been responses to this pressure. The doctrine of transubstantiation not only provided an officially sanctioned opportunity for direct contact with Christ incarnate, but it also allowed numerous further miracles, at least in the popular imagination.

Sometimes the Host was said to really become flesh and blood. In at least one shrine, in Lanciano, Italy, are small pellets of blood and a strip of flesh said to have been formed from consecrated bread and water during the celebration of Mass by a doubting monk in the eighth century. Bavaria has a shrine where sacramental wine, spilled on an altar cloth in 1330, formed an image of Christ. Christ could now become real, the object of worship (and sometimes even contact) within a more hierarchical church (Clark 1967, 410–434; Nolan and Nolan 1989, 216–290).

Mary and Marys in European Societies

The church has also promoted the adoration of Mary as Mother of God. This "cult of Mary," which undoubtedly draws on older images and ideas of a virgin mother goddess, first appeared in Turkey in 431 and expanded across the West. At some point a popular idea developed that Mary herself was conceived in her mother, Saint Ann, free from the original sin that everyone else receives by virtue of Eve and Adam's transgression in the Garden of Eden. This idea of "immaculate conception"—conception in the womb free of original sin—spread on a popular level but was not immediately accepted by the church. In the sixteenth century, the Council of Trent declared Mary free of original sin, but only in 1854 did Pope Pius IX declare as dogma that Mary indeed had experienced an immaculate conception.

Marian worship on a widespread, dominant scale dates from about the eleventh century and is due in part to the activities of the Cistercian order, all of whose churches were dedicated to Mary. The popular idea that she was bodily assumed into heaven was officially proclaimed as Roman Catholic dogma in 1950. As with Christ, this doctrine meant that very few relics could be claimed to be available: her sash and veil, a few strands of hair, pieces of milky rock white from her breast milk—slim pickings indeed. More popular were images of Mary, usually as the Pietà, holding the body of the dead Christ.

This image of Mary drew, intentionally or not, on much older notions of a virgin mother goddess who bears a child who later dies in her arms. Inanna, the Queen of Heaven in Sumerian mythology, gives up her son Dumuz to torture and death. The Egyptian Isis nurses and mourns for her son Osiris. (And as we shall see, such pre-Christian images are found in the Americas as well.) Pietà images are especially popular in German culture (70 percent of these images are found there), probably because of the long-standing tradition of imperially founded nunneries. Around 1300, Dominican nunneries began to promote the image of a suffering Mary, a representation of their own direct, personal, at times erotic relation to Christ. The pietà image generally becomes popular during times of sadness and war, because it provides an especially apt image for suffering. For example, many new pietà statues were carved after the trauma of the Thirty Years' War in the seventeenth century, and again after the First World War in our own century (Nolan and Nolan 1989, 191–209).

The numerical analysis of to whom a shrine is dedicated shows how sharp has been the change from saints, usually based on relics, to Mary, always based on a shrine image. In the period before 700 C.E., 92 percent of the shrines formed were dedicated to a saint. That percentage dropped to 20 percent in the "high medieval" period of 1100–1400, and has remained about the same since. The percentage of shrines dedicated to Mary was only 6 percent in the early period, but 73 percent in the high medieval period, and level ever since. Shrines dedicated to Christ have remained at below 10 percent throughout the common era (Nolan and Nolan 1989, 155).

Marian Apparitions and Modern Life

Over the past 150 years, Mary has taken on a new identity in the popular imagination, less as Mother of God and more as an individual who intervenes on behalf of individuals

Pietà of Mary and Jesus venerated at Theirenbach in Alsace, France, c. 1350. (MARY LEE NOLAN
AND SIDNEY NOLAN, *CHRISTIAN PILGRIMAGE IN MODERN WESTERN EUROPE*, p. 200.)

in modern, industrialized societies. She begins to appear in the sky to troubled individuals and to offer solace and instructions. Hundreds of such apparitions have occurred in the past two centuries, but seven were approved by local bishops and gained international attention; these occurred in France, Belgium, and Portugal. These visions include the apparitions of Mary at Lourdes, France, in 1858, and in Fatima, Portugal, in 1917. Both were eventually accepted by the Church; most others were not (Zimdars-Schwartz 1991).

In 1917, in Fatima, three children reported a series of appearances of Mary. One of the three, Lucia dos Santos, later discussed in her memoirs her religious upbringing as well as the events surrounding the apparitions. Lucia took her First Communion at age six rather than at the usual age 10. She tells of how the priest told her to kneel before the image of the Virgin and to ask Mary to take care of her heart; when she did so, she saw the statue of the Virgin smile at her, and she heard the Virgin say she would do this for her.

Lucia was 10 when, together with her friends, she saw the Virgin appear on six separate occasions. Mary spoke to the girls, saying that they had come from heaven, and that she would take them to heaven. All three girls reported hearing the same words. Others came to the place where the apparitions occurred. Some of these other watchers reported seeing a small cloud appear over the tree where the girls saw the Virgin and the tree's branches bend.

At the time, the girls reported hearing three secrets from the Virgin. In 1941 Lucia revealed two of them. The first concerned the nature of hell. The second was a prediction of war unless the world became devoted to her Immaculate Heart. Mary further specified that her followers would need to secure the consecration of Russia to her Immaculate Heart and to convert that country's people. If such steps were not taken, she warned, the world would be annihilated. Lucia wrote the third secret down, and in 1957 her note was sent to Rome. In 1977 Pope John Paul I visited with her (Zimdars-Schwartz 1991, 190–219).

Other reported sightings of Mary followed in the late 1940s, and manifested the worries held by many European Catholics about the general loss of faith and the coming clash with communism (Christian 1984). Marian apparitions provided a kind of collective catharsis, a general focusing and release of these tensions, and have continued unabated through the 1990s.

One of the more recent apparitions has been occurring frequently on a hill just outside Medjugorje, Bosnia, since June 24, 1981. Six girls saw Mary on the first day; since then more than 20 million pilgrims have come for a view. The girls moved the place for their visions into the church, until the bishop ordered them out. Since then some people have reported nightly appearances of Mary (Bax 1991; Zimdars-Schwartz 1991, 220–244).

Pilgrims to the site often return with stories of personal conversions and healing. One Irish woman described her visit as at first just a "holiday." But then she saw the concrete cross that had been built on the site, and saw the sun behind it turn blood red, with a small piece of the sun missing after it had moved behind the cross. On her return home she attended a funeral mass and when the priest held up the Host she saw it as "the image of the sun at Medjugorje and I really believed in the presence of Christ—the sun had been the Host with the piece missing like when the priest breaks off a piece—and I was overcome and cried."

Medjugorje spreads. An Italian family bought a white plaster statue of Mary during a visit to the site, and in February 1995 reported that tears of blood had begun running down the statue's face. Crowds began to flock around the family's home near Rome, and the local bishop had the statue removed. CAT scans of the statue showed no hidden mechanisms; laboratory tests showed the blood to be human; DNA matches with the family's blood were proposed. In the end, the bishop became a believer in the miracle (Warner 1996; Bohlen 1995).

In the United States, an American returned home to New Jersey after a visit to Medjugorje in 1988 and reported that he had been healed of a back injury and hearing loss. Mary appeared to him in his backyard six months later, stating that she had work for him to do. In August 1992 he publicly announced when the second visit would happen, and 8,000 people came to witness the event. About the same number showed up in Cold Spring, Kentucky, when a local pastor predicted an apparition (Steinfel 1992).

The Church has been ambivalent about the apparitions. On the one hand, the apparitions encourage popular faith, and their message is in keeping with the interest of the Church. On the other hand, the apparitions occur outside Church control; they challenge the hierarchy of the Church by providing an alternative source of religious enthusiasm to worship in churches. The Church has given official recognition to the apparitions at Lourdes and Fatima, but not to Medjugorje. There, the local Franciscan fathers, who for centuries functioned as the parish priests, have encouraged people to enjoy the special grace provided by the visions. But the Bishop of Mostar, whose district includes the apparition site, has forbidden worshipers to make the pilgrimage and has called the apparitions "theatrical practices." His ruling has been part of an effort, backed by Rome, to wrest control of the parishes away from the friars, and Mary, here as elsewhere, has become a key token in that struggle (Bax 1991).

Religious sentiments in Catholic Europe have always included some resentment of the power and privileges of the clergy. For those visitors to the sites of apparitions who share these anticlerical feelings, the Church's rejection of visions makes the visions even more attractive. The apparitions usually are reported from marginal regions during times of trouble—Bosnia and southern Italy in the 1990s, economically depressed parts of the United States in the 1980s, post–war Western Europe.

Spanish Shrines

As the Church increasingly came to promote Mary as an object of worship, people have made her into a local protector as well as the symbol of Church worship. In agrarian parts of northern Spain, each valley of herders and farmers contains a number of small villages. Each village parish has its own active patron, whose image is in the village shrine and who protects the village as a whole. The shrine may be an isolated chapel at the boundary of several villages or the parish church at the village center.

In the Nansa river valley studied by the ethnographer William Christian (1989) are 14 such village parishes. Of these 14, one has Christ as its patron, three have the souls in purgatory (*Las Animas*), and 10 have a particular aspect or realization of the Virgin Mary.

Thus, in one village the patron is Our Lady of the Queen's Ford; in another, Our Lady of the Light; in a third, Our Lady of the Bridge; and so forth. Each shrine, each saint, protects a particular territory, a "territory of grace," acting as patron to its inhabitants.

Some of the shrines to Mary are located at boundaries of villages or herding districts. In one district, three statues of Mary are found right at the meeting point of three villages' lands, each facing back toward "her own" village. In local stories, the Virgin is said to choose the spot where the shrine is to be built. In one case a shrine was placed at one spot, but during the next night two oxen came and moved the shrine up the hill to the place where she had desired it to be placed. The Virgin keeps the sheep at home, say local herders, and calls down divine power to protect them. William Christian calls the shrines "energy transformation stations."

One of these patron saints is Our Lady of the Queen's Ford, the patron of the village of Tudanca. The shrine is located in a chapel about five kilometers behind Tudanca. The saint's name comes from a nearby ford, but the patron is also identified as Our Lady of the Snows, an aspect of Mary recognized by Rome and given a feast day, August 5. Over the centuries, celebrations of the feast day have waxed and waned, depending both on the level of nearby economic activity and on the attitude of the parish priest toward the shrine. Currently the shrine is visited only by some Tudanca residents; in other decades, however, it has received attention from people of other villages as well. The shrines patronize and protect their own villages, but they may be appealed to by anyone, especially people from neighboring villages.

In the first week of May each year the image is carried down from the isolated chapel to the parish church in town, where it remains for three months and is the center of church devotions. The period when the image is in the church is also the period of plowing and sowing the fields, and its presence may once have been intended to protect the crops. On the feast of Saint James, July 25, the image is carried in a procession of all the villagers, organized in the following order: children first, then lay men, priests with the image, and women. The villagers thus see themselves as a whole composed of parts. "The villagers for once in the year," writes Christian (1989, 70), "see the village as a social unit, abstracted from the buildings and the location that makes it a geographical unit."

It is the women who continue up the mountain to the shrine and replace the image in its resting place. A woman keeps the key to the shrine, and when, on the patron's feast day of August 5, a mass is held at the mountain chapel, even the priest has to wait for her to unlock it. In other villages, too, special roles in the devotion to the patron are handed down from mother to daughter. Women are the chief worshipers at the shrines.

These patrons are firmly planted in the rural landscape. Each exists and acts on her own. Some of the names are unique, appearing nowhere else in Spain. Others do appear elsewhere, but then are given additional local tags to emphasize their individuality. A shrine to Our Lady of Carmel, for example (a common name for the Virgin Mary), will become Our Lady of Carmel of Cosio, or of another village. These shrines have existed for a long time; some may predate Christianity (when clearly they were known and worshiped by other names).

From the standpoint of these "localized devotions"—worship activities focused on a local manifestation of Mary or a saint—Mary appears as many distinct patrons woven together into a general community of sainthood. The Mary of the Snows is an agent distinct from the Mary of the Bridge, despite the fact that all are manifestations of the one Virgin Mary, Mother of God.

Many in One

Recall a similar feature of worship in India. In south India each local settlement has its own tutelary goddess, known by one name throughout that region. So throughout the state of Tamil Nadu, for instance, once finds Mariyamman of this place versus Mariyamman of that place, as different goddesses and yet also localized forms of the single Goddess (Fuller 1992, 43). This many-in-one is quite similar to that found in northern Spain and elsewhere in the Catholic world. Mary exists in both a highly local and a universal form at the same time in the consciousness of some Catholics, as does Mariyamman (the similarity in names is a coincidence) for Hindus.

The parallel stops at the level below Mary, however, for whereas Hindus have local, lesser deities as well as the major gods, most Catholics have only the major textually sanctioned figures to turn to—Mary, Jesus, saints. In Catholicism the distance between God and local, reachable spiritual beings is mediated by proliferating the number of forms of Mary, and remaining entirely within a restricted pantheon.

There is an irony in the fact that the adoration of Mary was encouraged by the church as a way of unifying and centralizing devotion, but that Mary became the vehicle for differentiated devotions and representations. Of course, even in the universal language promoted by the church one has different names or "advocations" (different forms of a deity) of Mary, a variety that in part stems from the very images the church used: Mary of the Immaculate Conception, Mary the Pietà, Mary of the Assumption, and so forth. Mary is shown in different contexts, and these images become signs of different attitudes or emotions. But it also may be that relying on replicable images as the basis for Catholicism (or any other widespread religion) itself gives rise to this dual character, the "one Mary or many Marys" problem. Once the image takes on any local roots it begins to be thought of as the image of a local individual. The very replicability of the image poses a problem: is it one or many? If one, what are all these other objects? If many, are they different actors?

A Japanese Comparison

Just as Catholics have created "many Marys" to provide nearby, accessible images, so have Japanese men and women turned to deities called "bodhisattvas," or "Buddhas-to-be." These deities, who put off their transition to Buddha status in order to help humans, are nearer to hand when one needs help than are the distant Buddha figures.

Especially important among them is the goddess Kannon, who ensures fertility and safety in childbirth. In India, Kannon was the many-armed god Avalokitesvara, and became (via a gender change) the important Chinese goddess Kuan-Yin, and then the Japanese Kannon. The bodhisattva Kannon is capable of rescuing people from earthquakes, fires, shipwrecks, witchcraft, execution, snakes, and thunderbolts, and of giving a woman the child she wishes, son or daughter. She is sometimes depicted as associated with the waterfall because of her power; her many arms are likened to the many different

Jizo statues set out to atone for an abortion or to ask for safe delivery of a child, at the shrine to Kannon near Kamakura, Japan. (COURTESY OF JOHN RENARD.)

streams of a fall. She also has lesser spirits called *jizo* who act as guardians of travelers and children. Travelers often set out small statues of jizos on their routes, and especially when they are embarking on a pilgrimage. But one may also set out a jizo as a concrete way to take a request to Kannon. These requests are most commonly either for forgiveness for having had an abortion or for safe delivery of a child.

Kannon is both a single goddess and many personal guardians. She can be depicted as a single protector, or as highly individuated. For example, a shrine to Kannon at Kyoto is supposed to contain "60,000" statues of Kannon, one for every face there is in the world; this way of representing her is supposed to guard all the world's people.

A debate has arisen in Japan over the practice of buying jizo statues from a temple to atone for an abortion. Setting out the statue is thought by some to help guide the fetus across the river that separates the world of life from the world of death. These statues, called "water child jizos" (Mizuko jizo), are sold by Buddhist temples for several hundred dollars each. More than 2,000 temples now offer these statues, and temple leaflets warn that failure to appease the spirit of a dead fetus could lead to cancer, heart disease, back pain, rebellion of children against parents, and so forth—a list long enough that anyone who fails to buy the statue will surely find herself victim of the fetus's spirit. Is this service a way the temple serves people's needs or, as one magazine called it, a "business of terror"? Some women continue to visit the statues for years or even decades after the abortion, dressing them up against the cold or pouring water over them to quench their thirst (WuDunn 1996).

Generalized Devotions

Priests entering the Nansa valley have had to work with the shrines already in place, but sometimes they have tried to discourage devotions at the shrine. In most cases, devotions go dormant, reappearing a decade or more later. The priests bring with them devotional emphases of the papacy, and often of a religious order. They try to refocus the devotions of villagers on universal images of Mary and Christ, rather than on her specific manifestations, what one priest called approaching "to the main doors, not the side doors" of the church.

These "generalized devotions," in William Christian's (1989) phrase, are based on the circulation and promotion of images that are highly interchangeable. In homes and in parish churches one finds paintings, lithographs, pamphlets, calendars, and rosaries. These images could be substituted easily one for the other, or replaced with a new batch, without any loss of religious significance. The images are usually of Mary as the Madonna, and sometimes of the cross, and they are used in family devotions. They often come from Rome or from the religious orders currently in papal favor, and their propagation and use is intended to underscore the universality of the Church. For example, the Dominican brotherhoods have promoted the devotion to the Holy Rosary at home using personal rosary beads. The brotherhoods teach people that saying prayers with the beads will allow one to share in all the prayers said by all members of the brotherhood throughout the world. Other orders, including Capuchins and Passionists, have provided images of saints or Mary that correspond to their particular religious emphases.

Mary has played her part in efforts to reuniversalize worship, both through her interchangeable pictures in homes, and through her role in regional and national shrines. Many villages in the Nansa valley have been visited on trips to the regional shrine to Mary, which was approved by the Vatican in 1954, on the 100th anniversary of the papal proclamation of the Immaculate Conception.

Jesus, Mary, and the Nation–State

Of particular importance in changing local worship practices has been the devotion to the Sacred Heart of Jesus, begun in 1673 when a nun in Paris had visions of Jesus Christ in which he urged her to devote herself to his heart as a symbol of his love for humankind. But it was not entered as general feast of the church until 1856, when it quickly became an image to which popes and rulers tried to rally the faithful. In 1899 Pope Leo XIII consecrated the world to the Sacred Heart of Jesus, and King Alfonso of Spain did the same for Spain in 1919, with the backing of a conservative government. Images of the Sacred Heart entered the Nansa valley about that time as well (Christian 1989, 84–85).

Because of its association with the political right, in the 1930s statues commemorating the Sacred Heart became symbols of the Nationalist forces, the right wing fighting under Franco to topple the government. The national monument to the Sacred Heart was frequently "executed" by the Loyalists, and pictures of the ruined monument were circulated by Franco's side to rally Catholic support.

Elsewhere too, the Sacred Heart of Jesus became a symbol of conservative govern-ments. In late–nineteenth-century France the relation of a largely Catholic people to a secular state (and largely secular capital city) was a continuing source of tension. In 1871 many Parisians rose up against the Thiers government, in part because of the state's capitulation to Prussian forces. The government, which had fled to Versailles, brutally suppressed the uprising, known as the *Commune,* and regained control of the city. Shortly thereafter, in an attempt to underscore the central place of the church in French life, the government constructed the magnificent church on the hills of Montmartre called Sacre Coeur—Sacred Heart. Though much loved by tourists (and many Parisians), the association between the building and the suppression lives on in the minds of many on the left. (I happened to be living in Paris in 1971, the year of the Commune's centennial, and I witnessed Sacre Coeur being pelted with tomatoes and stones.)

At the same time, images of Mary surface as symbols of national resistance. In communist Poland, the national shrine of Polish Catholicism dedicated to Our Lady of Czestochowa has for centuries been associated with national resistance against foreign conquerors. The Polish Primate under communist rule, Cardinal Wysynski, mobilized the nation around the shrine image, beginning with the rededication of the nation to this "Queen of Poland" in 1956, and following with hugely successful annual pilgrimages of the shrine to every single town in Poland.

The state's use of religious imagery underscores the changes in how the Church represents itself. In the ninth century, a person was sworn in on relics as the clear chain of direct contact to local sources of sacrality. By the late nineteenth century the state was staking its claim to loyalty on images of and devotions to Mary or, in particular, to Christ. Christ seems more immune to the differentiation process that has made Mary many. Indeed, the role of Mary in Catholicism as a firm local identity goes far beyond Spain, as we shall see.

Relics and Images in Buddhist Politics

Relics and images of the Buddha have played political roles similar to those of the relics of Christian saints. Although Gautama Buddha ascended to nirvana at death, his remains were treated in the way a ruler's would be. They were cremated, and his bones and teeth were converted to relics. The Buddha's relics became both sources of religious power and part of the royal regalia in Buddhist kingdoms. In Ceylon (today Sri Lanka) the relic of the Buddha's tooth was housed in the palace of the King of Kandy and was the key object in the royal heirlooms—both proof of a chain of direct contact with the Buddha and a symbol of the fusion of religious and temporal authority in the Kandyan kingdom (Tambiah 1986, 60–61).

In successive kingdoms in Thailand a statue of the Buddha called the "Emerald Buddha" has played a similar role, and even today the king bathes the statue and changes the clothes that adorn it. The official story states that the statue was fashioned by a monk in Ceylon and brought, along with scriptures, in a boat to the Southeast Asian mainland. The statue's power comes not just from its representation of the Buddha but also from the historical path it traced, from the seat of Buddhist learning in Ceylon to the new kingdom. Its history thus functions in a manner similar to that of the tooth relic, as the material sign of a chain of physical contact between the sacred past and the authority of the present. As the anthropologist Stanley Tambiah (1976, 501) writes, "The Emerald Buddha, like the Tooth Relic in the past indigenous kingdoms of Sri Lanka, represents for Thailand not only part of the regalia of kingship but, more importantly, national sovereignty itself conjoined with the protection and practice of Buddhism."

For Further Consideration

*T*he University of California Extension Center has a number of fine films about masks. *The Spirit of the Mask* (1992) focuses on Northwest Coast societies, one of the most elaborate mask cultures, and gives comparative material. *Behind the Masks* (1973) also covers Northwest Coast material; a film of the same name, *Behind the Mask,* in the series "Tribal Eye," (1975) is about the Dogon masks and rituals described here.

For more information about religion in India, I recommend Chris Fuller's book, *The Camphor Flame: Popular Hinduism and Society in India* (Princeton University Press 1992), and Diana Eck's short book, *Darsan* (Anima Books 1981), as well as the more detailed ethnographic study by Lawrence Babb, *The Divine Hierarchy* (Columbia University Press 1975). You can look at the Web sites created by individual temples, such as the Toronto Shiva temple at (*http://members.nbci.com/shivatemple/*).

A Web site on saints recognized by the Catholic Church is at *http://saints. catholic.org/index.shtml*. It features an interactive discussion site about saints and miracles and a link to the Catholic shopping network. An excellent collection edited by Ellen Badone, *Religious Orthodoxy and Popular Faith in European Society* (Princeton University Press 1990), focuses on the contrasts between priests' ideas and practices and local, popular religion, as does a fine, detailed ethnography of Irish Catholics by Lawrence Taylor, *Occasions of Faith* (University of Pennsylvania Press 1995). Robert Orsi's *Madonna of 115th Street* (Yale University Press 1985) gives a historical account of Catholicism in New York. A film, *Processione: A Sicilian Easter* (University of California Extension Center 1989), depicts a Good Friday procession and presents the public celebration of Christ's sacrifice as an event of collective mourning.

10 *Crossing Cultural Boundaries*

*T*hroughout this chapter we explore a tension central to those religions that have spread to culturally diverse regions of the globe. The list of such religions is longer than one might suspect. The many forms of Christianity, Islam, and Buddhism come to mind first, but the list would also include other religions, each with relatively few followers, but including people from a broad range of cultures. Consider in this light Mormonism, the Bahai faith, and Hinduism, all having practitioners in North America, Asia, and elsewhere. (Other religions, such as Santeria or Lubavitcher Judaism, are, at least as of today, carried by adherents into new environments but less often adopted by people of different religious and cultural backgrounds.)

The history of all of these religions involved the process of *conversion* as people in new environments adopted them. Conversion has required translating religious elements from a language and culture of origin into a new language and culture and also *adapting* the religion to the new environment. Crossing cultural boundaries continues to involve conversion, translating, and adapting as these religions attract an increasingly diverse set of followers.

All three processes create a tension of "crossing" that has strong psychological, social, and theological elements. On the one hand, proponents of each religion try to preserve something of a core message, or set of practices, or allegiance. Failure to do so may provoke retribution or at least prevent recognition as legitimate practitioners. Notions of orthodoxy and orthopraxy, "correct" belief and practice, are regularly brought into play. But on the other hand, converting people in a new cultural environment requires the bundle of ideas and practices that characterizes it to be adapted to emphasize or minimize particular elements. Indonesian Islam does not have the marked gender separation of Arabian forms, for example, and Islam could not have spread so easily in Indonesia if people had not reinterpreted Islam to fit local norms. But that reinterpretation would have been sharply criticized, even within Indonesia, if it had not taken place within the Islamic tradition of acceptable interpretation.

Converting

Converting to a new religion requires one to make some sort of commitment to it. (Although, as we shall see later, conversion may be thought of more as a choice among alternative social rules than as an act of faith.) And commitment to a religion may require, or indeed may itself be, a kind of conversion. The interdependence of conversion and commitment may be understood most easily with regard to children, who are not expected to become adherents and practitioners of a religion without effort. Children are usually required to study in order to become fully accepted members of a religious community, when they may undergo a ritual of acceptance that includes commitment to the religion of their parents. The acts of commitment required of a child are often the same as those required of an adult convert: learning a text by heart, reciting a statement of commitment, undergoing an initiation ritual.

Adult Baptism among the Amish

Consider the Amish, one of several Protestant religions that underwent persecution in Europe beginning in the sixteenth century (others include Hutterites and Mennonites). They were persecuted mainly because they practiced and preached adult baptism, and thus were called Anabaptists ("to baptize again"). They did so because they believed that only someone who had reached the "age of reason" could make an informed and conscious decision to become a member of the Church.

Today, Amish communities are found in many parts of North America, concentrated in Pennsylvania, Ohio, and Indiana. Amish people live in villages and towns, close to non-Amish people they call "English." They continue to learn and use a dialect of German within the community. Their major religious values are submission to God, humility, and openness. They live according to their values by wearing simple clothing, renouncing those inventions that would separate them from the land and from work, and preventing the outside world from intruding on family life.

A commitment to the Amish way of life means staying apart from mainstream society. Boys and girls make that commitment at baptism, which occurs between the ages of 16 and 21. Candidates take a series of classes that stress the strict nature of the Amish social code, the Ordnung. They are told that it is better to not join the order than to join and then break the code. The baptism itself takes place in front of the congregation after a regular Sunday service. Kneeling, the candidate agrees to obey God and his church, and the presiding bishop drips water over his or her head.

The idea of active commitment, of the seriousness of the vows taken, explains a puzzle in their lives. On the one hand, the Amish more than any religious group in America try to keep themselves cut off from the broader society. Electricity, telephones, automobiles, public schools are all suspect because they plug the community in (literally or figuratively) to the wider sociocultural grid. Telephones are one of many subjects of intense controversy because they provide safety and comfort but they also disrupt family and social life. (One solution is to have telephones in separate buildings, so that they can be used if needed but cannot break up, for example, dinner conversations.)

And yet the Amish also permit their teenagers to "flirt with the world" (Kraybill 1989, 138). Indeed, although the Amish churches exercise strict control over the lives of adults, with sanctions that include being shunned by the community, the churches have no direct authority over children and adolescents. Until they are baptized, Amish boys and girls are supposed to be under the authority of their parents.

Amish teenagers typically join one of the several "crowds" of youths in the community (Kraybill 1989, 138–140). A crowd plays sports together, attends films, and travels to cities and to the beach. For their outings they buy and wear clothes similar to those worn by "English" youth. The boys often drive cars and are sometimes arrested for drunken driving or have serious accidents. In the late 1990s several youths were arrested for drug trafficking.

A student of the Amish, Donald Kraybill (1989, 139), writes that this liminal period and tolerated rowdiness serves as a "social immunization" against the subsequent temptations young people face. Having experienced something of the world, they can reject it with knowledge. And though they would find it difficult to leave the Amish world they have been educated for and where their friends live, they believe that they have a choice because they are presented with one. About 80 percent of Amish youth do choose to undergo baptism and remain in the church. There is a psychological soundness to the Amish idea that you can knowingly reject only what you know. For an example of the problem faced by a group of people who have never known such temptation, and are thereby unable to face it with strength when it arrives, one could do no better than to read Mark Twain's classic story, "The Man Who Corrupted Hadleyburg." Hadleyburgians, naive believers in their own goodness, could not withstand the temptation of some easy money to be made through telling a simple lie.

Conversion as Total Social Change

What does conversion entail? It may appear to be merely a matter of changing one's religious allegiance—going to a different place of worship, perhaps wearing different clothes or eating different foods or making different friends. It is, then, an individual choice, accomplished fairly quickly, perhaps with some changes in lifestyle (less likely if the conversion is within Christianity).

This idea of conversion, however, only makes sense for those societies that have an easily detached notion of "religion." If particular spirit beliefs permeate all aspects of one's life, then giving up all those beliefs for some new set will most likely entail leaving the society altogether and changing one's ideas about oneself.

The experience of the Akha people of highland Burma and Thailand offers an example of how, in many societies, conversion can be a process of near-total social change (Kammerer 1990). In the 1960s when their neighbors were converting to Catholicism and Protestantism in droves, the Akha stood out among the peoples of this region for their resistance to conversion. But by the 1980s conversions were occurring with increasing frequency among the Akha. Why this sudden shift?

The answer returns us to our earlier discussion of what the category of religion looks like in different societies. In the Akha language, the word *zah* is the closest to the English *religion,* but it includes much more—the rules for planting crops, holding funerals, healing the sick, and conducting a marriage. For the Akha, their zah defines who they are. Others have their own zah, and those rules define them. One should not, they say, mix zahs from different people. (This sounds rather like the most extreme statements of "cultural wholes" in American anthropology.) Akha have been less likely to marry people of other ethnic groups, and when they do, often they become one of those people, a Lisu, say, rather than an Akha. Custom and culture (including religion) is seen as an all-or-nothing affair.

The Akha were somewhat more insistent than were their neighbors about changing zah, which would logically initially keep them from converting. To change zah would be in effect to change one's overall identity, to become something other than Akha. But we are still left with the task of explaining why, at some point, the balance tipped and the Akha began to convert in large numbers. Here, too, understanding their idea of identity helps us to understand what happened. Akha had begun to attend state schools and learn broader Thai ways, and at some point the intricacies of their older zah became too difficult to learn and practice. Because Akha saw their zah as a unity of practices, and not any better or worse than other people's zahs, it made sense to change zahs entirely, to convert to another kind of people, those who practice "Jesus zah" rather than "Akha zah."

Kammerer (1990) points out that Akha never say they "believe" in new or old zah, Akha-ism or Christianity. For them conversion is a matter of exchanging older practices for new ones, for pragmatic reasons. For the Akha conversion is neither a change of heart nor a sitting on the fence.

External and Internal Conversion

A different case study shows us that conversion may also turn out to be something quite different: not an all-or-nothing choice of social life, but a long-term process of reworking and reinterpreting social practices. John Barker (1993) studied the Uiaku Maisin people of the Oro province in northeast Papua New Guinea. The Maisin people have been Christians since the early 1900s, when they were converted by Australian Anglican missionaries. But Barker observes that conversion continues to take place, and does so in two ways. What he calls "external conversion," associated with the mission station, has to do with trying to acculturate local people to relatively cosmopolitan ways. By contrast, "internal conversion" takes place in villages, where people debate and adapt their ideas to new circumstances. The advantage of Barker's perspective is that it locates distinct conversion processes in two distinct social environments. People have no trouble separating the two, because each addresses distinct concerns.

"From the mission station," writes Barker (1993, 208), "Uiaku appears a Christian community." The church is the center of social life, for sports, women's groups, and for celebrations of saints' days. Bells mark the hours for church and school attendance. Avenues are wide and straight. The church council encourages church attendance, urges people to grow cash crops, and comforts the sick. Councilors fly to other cities in the country to meet with delegates from religious, political, or other organizations.

But village hamlets are organized along quite different lines, one that mark a continuity in social and cultural organization. People build houses near birthplaces. Elders preside over dispute-resolution sessions and have the power to strike through sorcery. Not that things in the village have not changed over the years—villagers added God to the list of powerful spirits in the cosmos, for example. They also stretched older ideas they held to become the equivalents of Christian ideas taught by the missionaries. For example, the term Barker translates as *amity* probably once referred to a peaceful condition that resulted from balance in the exchanges of goods and services between clans. As missionaries taught about Christian "universal brotherhood," people stretched their idea of peace-inducing balance to translate the new idea.

But these stretchings were more than just translations; the new cultural categories, once in place, could serve as moral foundations for criticizing contemporary practices. Barker relates how the extended notion of amity was mobilized by the church deacon (a local man) to condemn some people who allowed the period of mourning to continue too long, so that it was disruptive. In response, some subsequent deaths were met by much shorter periods of mourning than ever before. Villagers understood this change not as an adaptation to Western norms, but as a more consistent pattern of behavior in terms of their own social norms, *their* idea of amity.

This "internal conversion" is thus a kind of moral ironing-out of everyday and ritual practices in terms that are seen as local, but that have been transformed as a result of the process of "external conversion." Villagers participate in both worlds (see Hefner, 1993).

Missions and Civilization in South Africa

Another case study of conversion as a long-term process comes from the work of Jean and John Comaroff (1986, 1991, 1997). The Comaroffs study the dual British colonial project of converting "natives" in South Africa to Christianity and creating a socially modern and disciplined colonial society. They describe how Protestant evangelical missionaries failed to realize their dreams of constructing a unified black Protestant church but succeeded in reshaping the way Africans carried out their lives. Their study focuses on the lives of the Tswana people of South Africa and Botswana and on the activities of the Methodist London Missionary Society beginning in the 1820s.

The Comaroffs point out that Methodist missionaries (and, in varying ways, other Christian missionaries) measured their effectiveness not merely by obtaining formal conversions, but by their success in changing natives' ways of behaving. French sociologists, among them Marcel Mauss and Pierre Bourdieu, have termed the ways an individual acts, responds, speaks, walks, and so forth, his or her *habitus*. South African Methodists were bent on teaching the Tswana the "arts of civilization," which included the arts of cultivation. Missionaries urged the adoption of the plow, which, because only men tended cattle, had the effect of raising the value of male labor relative to female labor. They also taught that natives should live in monogamous households arranged in rows and squares rather than in circles and arcs. The church clock and the church calendar now regulated social life. And as the hourly base for figuring wages, time was now used to measure the value of an individual's labor.

But the Methodist message contained the seeds of destruction for the colonial project. Central to the Wesleyan idea of self-perfection preached in the churches was the equality of people and their freedom to perfect their natures. This message was blatantly contradicted by the realities of mining labor in the nineteenth and twentieth centuries. It also gave ammunition to those within particular churches who would resist any kind of central control, leading to the subsequent proliferation of churches, as dissatisfied factions set out to found new denominations (Comaroff 1985).

The Comaroffs present the encounters between missionaries and Tswana as part of an ongoing conversation. Each side incorporated the other's messages into its own way of thinking, and yet also changed its religious practices slightly as a result of the encounter. The control of water was a matter of survival, for example, but also a political and cosmic matter (Comaroff and Comaroff 1991, 206–213). It was the ruler who brought on rains, and the rainmaking rituals, carried out at his direction, that ensured the rains' arrival.

The missionaries regarded these rituals as the height of superstition and thought they should be eradicated. But they themselves were caught in a contradiction, proclaiming that rain was a matter of nature and scientific meteorological detection, while saying that rain was ultimately in God's hands. The Tswana concluded from this missionary double-talk that their scientific instruments were merely their version of rainmaking devices, which worked through their deity.

Consider how the Tswana people's firm grasp of missionary logic shaped the following dialogue between a mission medical doctor (MD) and the rain doctor (RD).

MD: . . . you cannot charm the clouds by medicines. You wait till you see the clouds come, then you use your medicines, and take credit that belongs to God only.

RD: I use my medicines and you employ yours; we are both doctors, and doctors are not deceivers. You give a patient medicine. Sometimes God is pleased to heal him by means of your medicine; sometimes not—he dies. When he is cured, you take the credit for what God does. I do the same.

The rain doctor is simply calling the medical doctor's bluff: if he really believes, as the missionaries did indeed claim, that all is in the hands of God, then how could he or any other European claim that his human science had cured someone or predicted rains?

The Tswana version of how rain arrives was in fact fairly complex. Rainmaking rituals did not work in some automatic, mechanical way; they required that the community be in a state of "moral recitude, of 'coolness' (*tsididi*)" (Comaroff and Comaroff 1991, 210). Therefore, the ritual expert's primary task was to remove social pollution that might be preventing the heavens from unleashing the rain. It was thus fully within Tswana logic when they later blamed the presence of the Europeans for the failure of rainmaking rituals. For their part, Europeans began to include rain services in the church calendar, the more effectively to combat the natives' view. The conversion effort thus became an extended exchange of and change in the views of both sides.

Translating: Mary in the Americas

We saw in the last example the extent to which projects of conversion also involve attempts to translate across belief systems. Now we look at this translation process from the center outward, and follow the images and ideas of the Virgin Mary as she (and other saints of the Catholic Church) became part of religious complexes in the Americas.

The nurturing and tragic image of Mary has served as a particularly powerful figure in translating Catholicism into other cultures. Not only are there universal resonances with her story, but one also finds very specifically similar stories about a sacred and virgin birth or an assumption to heaven in other cultures.

The story of Mary in the Americas exemplifies the logic of religious syncretism, or the blending of two or more traditions. Syncretism occurs when people adopt a new religion but attempt to make it fit with older ideas and practices. The process usually involves changes in both or all of the traditions. As we saw in Chapter 2, Japanese religious history is virtually defined by syncretism, as Japanese have combined elements from Chinese Confucian political ideology, Buddhist teachings and practices, Christian ceremonies, and the older practices called Shinto. As we have seen in Chapter 9, places already sacred before Christianity became the sites of shrines to Mary. The meaning of the places changed when this happened, because they were no longer entirely local, but linked worship to a larger religious tradition—the images in the shrines were carried to the common parish church for feast-day worship, for example. But the meaning of Mary was also changed, in that she became locally specific and concerned with rendering assistance in local affairs, and not just a remote semi-deity. (More examples of these changes in the meaning of Mary are offered later.)

The Virgin of Guadalupe

In Mesoamerica, today's Mexico and Guatemala, the Mary of Guadalupe has served as a symbol of nation and people, sometimes in opposition to foreign rule. During and after the Spanish conquest of the region, from the mid-sixteenth through the late seventeenth century, the native Mayan people of eastern Mesoamerica organized rebellions. These rebellions soon incorporated the symbols of Catholicism, reworked in Indian terms. The insurgent movements often included figures anointed as Christ or king. In some cases, villagers were visited by the Virgin Mary, who then instructed them to start a new church organization. She would leave proof of her visit in the form of an image that she created either on cloth or as a statue (Lafaye 1976; Wolf 1956).

The two most influential cases involved the Virgin revealing her image to a peasant (in both cases, as it happened, named Juan Diego) during the sixteenth century. The first apparition, in which Mary left her figure on a cloak, took place in 1531 in Tepeyac near Mexico City and became known as the Virgin of Guadalupe; the second, known as the Virgin of Ocotlan, occurred about 10 years later in Tlaxcala state, when Mary imprinted herself on an ocote tree.

The Virgin of Guadalupe was to become the master symbol of Mexico. The Mexican War of Independence was fought under her banner, and her shrine at Tepeyac became the major Mexican shrine. In the official story of the events, the Virgin addressed a Christianized Indian named Juan Diego in 1531, 10 years after the Spanish conquest of the area. The Virgin commanded him to go to the archbishop of Mexico and tell him that she wished a church built in her honor on Tepeyac Hill. Juan Diego tried twice to win the archbishop's approval, but was unsuccessful. Mary then performed a miracle. She told Juan Diego to gather roses in a dry spot where roses never grew, and then to present them to the archbishop. He did so, but when, standing before the archbishop, he unfolded his cloak, there appeared from inside, not roses, but the image of the Virgin miraculously imprinted on the cloak. The bishop immediately acknowledged the miracle, so the story goes, and ordered a shrine built on the spot where she had appeared.

This particular spot was not, however, a random choice. It had once been the site of a temple to the goddess of fertility Tonantzin. Tonantzin, Our Lady Mother, is associated with the moon, as is Guadalupe's image. Indeed, for at least the next 50 years worshipers called her Tonantzin as well as Guadalupe, and this still is the case in parts of Mexico. Stories about Tonantzin continue to be told in Mexico: in one, she intervened when God wanted to punish his children, by challenging him to try to produce milk so she could nourish her children.

These associations or "syncretism" are not unique to the New World, of course. William Christian speculates about preexisting deities where there now are shrines in Spain. In Ireland, in particular, statues of the Virgin often are erected in spots formerly considered sacred because of an unusually shaped rock formation or a sacred grove. And in the Church of Saint Germain in Paris, a black image of the Egyptian goddess Isis was displayed as the Madonna until 1514.

Guadalupe and Mexican Resistance to Spain

In later centuries, rebellions against Spanish control frequently formed around cults of the Virgin Mary. In 1721 in Cancuc (Chiapas), the Virgin appeared to a young girl and asked her to place a cross in her hamlet, build a chapel around it, and offer incense. A local Mayan leader then claimed to have ascended to heaven where he spoke with the Virgin Mary, Jesus Christ, and St. Peter, and was told that the people were to appoint their own officials and no longer had need of the Spanish. This man, Sebastian Gomez, then appointed bishops and priests, all using the symbols of the Catholic Church.

Devotions in the local church had already become "localized" in the sense in which we used the word earlier: worship focused on locally specific images of the Virgin that were understood as protecting the village. Services consisted of giving offerings and prayers to these advocations of Mary and to other localized saints, rather than addressing prayers to God. Gomez and his followers now renamed Cancuc "Jerusalem" and referred to the Spaniards as "the Jews who persecuted the Virgin Mary." Although the movement was suppressed, it illustrates the ways in which local opposition to Spanish rule was elaborated in what were once the conqueror's own images, the sacred images of Catholicism itself.

By choosing Mary and the saints as key images, those local movements that did not reach the stage of open rebellion managed to insulate themselves (and popular religious practice generally) against charges of heresy. The Spanish Inquisition investigated these religious movements and looked for evidence of idolatry, in particular prayers said to images that asked them to directly heal illnesses. The Indians whom the inquisitors interrogated denied that they acted in this way, claiming that they merely appealed to the patron saints and to the Virgin Mary for help. Because the Spanish Church accepted as legitimate both the cult of the patron saint and the possibility of visitations by the Virgin, the inquisitors were unable to find solid ground to prosecute Indian religious leaders (Lafaye 1976).

Why was it the Virgin Mary (and not Christ) who became Mexico's national symbol? The answer is in part due to the way the Church itself portrays Mary and Christ, and perhaps in part due to local family dynamics. The Virgin is associated with struggle and life in Mexico, while Christ is associated with defeat and death. On the religious plane, these distinct associations stem from the crucifixion of Christ, on the one hand, and the nurturing role of the Virgin, on the other. The anthropologist Eric Wolf (1956) argues that on the family plane, the associations grow out of the distinct sentiments the child forms toward his or her mother and father, in both Indian and Mexican families. The child experiences a paradise of closeness to his or her mother, and sides with the mother in her struggle against domination by the father. Mary thus brings out a wealth of early pleasant memories; Christ, the object of struggle. Sentiments formed in the family are expressed in the culture through the symbols of the Virgin and Christ.

On the plane of politics, the Virgin Mary, in the specific advocation of the Virgin of Guadalupe, is associated with the struggle against Spanish military and religious colonization. Many Mexicans interpreted Guadalupe as the goddess Tonantzin who has returned to liberate Mexico. This interpretation follows an indigenous logic of cyclical history, in which gods depart only to return later. Mexico appears as a new paradise, to which came the Virgin to herald independence. In one seventeenth-century text, the Virgin of Guadalupe is linked to the woman portrayed in the Revelation of John, "arrayed with the sun, and the moon under her feet, and upon her head a crown of twelve stars," and who is to realize the prophecies of Deuteronomy. Not coincidentally, the image of the Virgin of Guadalupe in the shrine today is adorned with a sun and moon and the twelve stars.

The Virgin of Guadalupe thus links family (mother), politics (liberation) and religion (salvation). Against the background of these linkages we can understand how it was that in 1810 the patriot Father Miguel Hidalgo y Castilla began the revolution for Independence with the cry: "Long Live the Virgin of Guadalupe and down with bad government."

The political and religious associations have continued in full force into this century. In the early twentieth century, the church, trying to render more uniform the devotions of the faithful, attempted to replace the Virgin of Guadalupe with the Sacred Heart of Jesus from Rome. This attempt was perceived in Mexico as an effort to supplant a Mexican figure with a European one, and it was strongly, and successfully, resisted. And in 1996, the Bishop of Guadalupe, speaking to a reporter in Italy, declared that he considered the peasant Juan Diego to have been a mythical figure (*St. Louis Post-Dispatch,* September 7, 1996). The remark led to his immediate removal from office!

Africa to Brazil: The Role of Images

The example of Guadalupe and Tonantzin suggests that religious imagery can be effective in translating a new religion into an older cultural and religious context: Mary made sense to Mayans who already venerated Tonantzin. Sometimes this process involves a literal translation across deities. Such is the case for religions found in the Americas but derived from West African religions. In Brazil, Cuba, Haiti, and elsewhere, Catholic deities provided useful cover for slaves who wished to continue to practice their own religions, but had been forbidden to do so. As this need for subterfuge decreased, Americans have been free to explore both the African roots of the traditions and the appeal these traditions have to a wide range of Americans, including those of European descent. Known now by the names *Umbanda, Candomblé, Santeria,* and *Voudun,* these Afro-American traditions have formed a distinct religious stream alongside, though at times intermingling with, Catholicism (Murphy 1994). (We examined healing practices within Umbanda in Chapter 6.)

The slave trade brought large numbers of African people to the southern and central portions of the Americas as well as to the colonies in North America. Slavery lasted longer in the southern regions—until 1888 in Brazil. Many of the Africans were taken from what is today Nigeria and Benin. In particular, Yoruba people were brought to Brazil and Cuba, and Fon people were brought to Haiti. Slave traders and slave owners tried to wipe out cultural traditions and mixed slaves from different regions in an effort to prevent Africans from organizing rebellions (Walker 1990).

Because slave owners prohibited the practice of African religions, Africans translated some of the ideas and deities of West African religions into the images and language of Catholicism. Slavers thought that they were imposing Catholicism; Africans understood that they were preserving older traditions.

In Brazil these traditions today are called "Umbanda" and "Macumba" in Rio de Janeiro and "Candomblé" in the northeast region of Bahia. They combine, in different proportions, African qualities, especially in Bahia, and Brazilian innovations, especially in Rio, with Catholic imagery and ideas from a Euro-Brazilian movement called "Spiritism."

In Rio a woman presides over services in a small storefront center (centro) called the Spiritist Tent of Granny Maria Antonia of the Congo, one of many places to which people come to worship and seek help from the spirits (Guillermoprieto 1990). In this center, as in many others, there is a particular "patron" spirit, Granny Maria Antonia. She is understood to be a woman who was born in Africa and was brought as a slave to Brazil, where she died. She is of a recognizable type of Afro-Brazilian spirit, the "Old Black Woman" (and as such replicates the one deity/many deities relationship we have been discussing).

Also exhibited in the center are statues of Christian figures: the Virgin Mary, Jesus, St. George (of dragon-slaying fame), and others. Each resembles corresponding statues in, say, European Catholic churches. But each also corresponds to an Umbanda deity called an "Orisha," and can be traced back to its original in Yoruba society, West Africa. Today people freely offer the Orisha as well as the Catholic name for each image; a century ago any but the Catholic identity would have been strongly denied to outsiders.

In this schema of cross-religious translation, God is Olorun, the creator of the world. The image of Jesus is also identified as Oshala, the creator of human life. Saint George, depicted slaying a dragon, corresponds to Oshossi, the hunter god, and St. Lazarus, protector of lepers, to Omolu, a deity governing disease. Mary is identified with Yemanja, the mother of some of the other Orishas. Furthermore, and here note the parallel with our Spanish valley, other Orishas who are mothers are also identified as manifestations of Mary. These maternal deities are associated with the water and sea as well.

The lifting of the veil surrounding this momentous project of religious translation was not followed by the crafting of new, original statues. In Yoruba and Umbanda, the Orishas have no concrete form; they are forces and principles rather than personages. Thus, the process of rendering African deities in Catholic form added a new visual and individuating dimension to worship, and the Catholic images remain as foci for Umbanda worship.

The identification extends to ritual occasions as well. People observe the Catholic feast days that apply to their "translated" deities, but do so in a way that corresponds to the Afro-Brazilian meaning of the deity. For example, Yemanja (Mary) is identified with the sea, so people flock to the sea on the Catholic feast days for Mary, and once there they offer gifts to Yemanja, wading out into the water and letting the sea carry them away.

Umbanda and Candomblé in fact bring together three religious traditions. Alongside Catholic and Yoruba religions is the doctrine of Spiritism or Kardecism, popular among the elite in Europe and Brazil in the late nineteenth century, and today adhered to by millions in Brazil, either as part of Umbanda and Candomblé or on its own. As we saw in Chapter 6, Spiritism provides a means of healing people from physical and mental afflictions. The doctrine attributes a wide range of events in the material world to the desires and actions of spirits. Sometimes spirits possess people, and when they do they can cause the person to suffer illness. Specialists can communicate directly with these spirits, ask what their wishes are, and restore the person to health.

Umbanda in Rio

Umbanda was in fact born as a revolt against the elitism of Spiritism in Rio (Brown 1986). By the 1920s, Spiritism had become a highly intellectualized and European-oriented set of practices. Lighter-skinned Brazilians (Brazilian color coding of individuals contains many categories, from very dark to very light, rather than a simple black/white dichotomy) controlled the seances. They were speaking with the likes of Voltaire and Plato. If an Indian spirit appeared, possessing a darker-skinned person, they would refuse to allow him to speak.

In the 1920 a middle-class Rio man, Zelio de Moraes, suffered an illness that left him partially paralyzed. His father, a real estate agent, was a Spiritist and took him to his group for healing. There he was visited by the spirit of a Jesuit priest, who revealed that the illness was spiritual, and that he had a mission, which was to found a truly Brazilian religion that would be dedicated to the worship and propitiation of Brazilian spirits.

These spirits included *Caboclos*, spirits of Brazilian Indians, and *Pretos Velhos*, spirits of Africans enslaved in Brazil.

Zelio received additional messages from other spirits. The "Indian of the Seven Crossroads" told him the new religion would be called "Umbanda." Zelio then did as he was told, and founded the first Umbanda center, today called the "Mother House." This center, the Spirits' Center of Our Lady of Piety, attracted a largely white and middle-class clientele. But the spirits that spoke through the participants were those of Indians and Africans, giving them the voice denied them by the Spiritists. The movement grew rapidly, attracting a diverse range of participants.

The social and political role of these movements has changed dramatically in this century. At first tolerated, it was repressed as heretical in the 1930s, 1940s, and 1950s by the Catholic Church, with support from the Brazilian state. State repressions began to loosen in the 1960s, and since 1970 people have enjoyed relative freedom to worship openly. The initial reason for this tolerance was political, as politicians seeking office sought support from the large communities of Umbanda-Candomblé followers. But the change also has been motivated by social and cultural changes (Walker 1990). In the past 30 years many Brazilians have sought their "roots," and some, including many of lighter skin color, have found them in the links back to Africa. Many of these people, mostly of the middle class, have found these links through the experience of possession by an African spirit. In doing so, they have moved away from the Catholicism that once was virtually required of those seeking high social status. Being known as a follower of Umbanda or Candomblé is no handicap to political office, and participation in the movements can be combined with a range of political and social doctrines. The Brazilian Secretary of Public Works in the 1980s, for example, calls himself a "Marxist–Spiritist," believing in both reincarnation and Marxist–Leninism.

These movements also have become part of a broader popular culture in Brazil. On New Year's Day, the major newspapers in Rio run the Umbanda seers' forecasts for the next year. In Bahia state, the home of Candomblé, pop singing groups have risen to the top of the charts with songs based in Candomblé; new wave filmmakers have drawn on the Orishas for their subjects, as in the popular film *The Amulet of Ogun*. The Orisha named Esu, who controls roads and pathways, has been adopted as the patron deity of all communications facilities, and a statue to him stands in front of the post office in Salvador, Bahia's capital (Murphy 1994).

The urban poor are also drawn to these movements. Two million of Rio's 6.5 million people live in squatter settlements called "favelas." For them, "survival calls for imaginative solutions, and Umbanda is nothing if not the triumph of imaginative thought," writes the reporter Alma Guillermoprieto (1990).

Let us return to the Granny Maria Antonia center mentioned earlier. The center is a two-story house located in a lower-middle-class neighborhood in central Rio. A black woman named Stella Soares runs the center. Stella, a former nurse, insists that all who attend don white uniforms; this measure makes everyone more nearly equal, she says. Certain specific spirits visit the center and possess those who attend its services. They are the spirits of individual Indian and African people rather than Orishas. They include the Indian of the Seven Crossroads, the Indian of the Coral Cobra, and the "Indian who tears up tree stumps with his bare hands." They speak; they embody the local identity of black and Indian Brazilians, and through the experience of being possessed the worshipers can experience several identities, several sides of themselves. Her clientele includes dozens of mainly white, middle-class initiates, who go into trance, but also many very poor black clients. "Once they have changed into their white clothes," she says, "you cannot tell the difference."

Are these religions part of Catholicism? Catholic priests call on people to abandon Umbanda, claiming that it has nothing to do with Catholicism, and some practitioners (probably an increasing number) consider themselves to be followers of Umbanda and not, or no longer, Catholics. But many other Umbanda followers claim status as Catholics. They point to a number of close relationships between Umbanda practices and Catholicism. The images in worship are all Catholic. Some Candomblé priests require initiates to be baptized Catholics before they can join in the rituals. The story of how the first center was founded also underscores the connection with Catholicism—it was, after all, the spirit of a Jesuit priest who commanded Zelio to open up his center. Catholic feast days are observed, and many Umbanda practices reinforce the link to the Catholic Church. For example, on August 16, the feast day for Saint Lazarus, Umbanda priestesses drive by churches where the mass is held and sprinkle popcorn on all so that they will receive benefits from Omolu, the deity associated with the saint.

Catholic images, and especially the image of the Virgin Mary, have served to mediate translations of religion across vast social and cultural divides, first within Europe, and then out across seas with the expansion of the church. But the very capacity of the image to carry multiple meanings—what I have called the multivocality of the image—has allowed subordinate groups to contest the dominant meanings. Spanish villagers insist on their own Mary's capacity to protect and nurture; Mexicans, on the Virgin of Guadalupe's role as a national symbol; Brazilians, on Yemanja/Mary's powers over the sea; Christians throughout the world, on Mary's willingness to appear to them and to deliver messages of hope and struggle. Each set of claims to Mary is asserted over and against official counterclaims that underscore the unity of Mary and Christ and the single authoritative voice of Rome.

Adapting: Islamic Sacrifice in New Cultures

*I*slam requires a number of practices of its adherents. Among them is the sacrifice of an animal at the Feast of Sacrifice. This requirement is observed worldwide, but how it is observed and how it is interpreted varies, reflecting the way practice and discourse are adapted to local conditions. The examples that follow focus on the role played by ideas about gender and about ritual efficacy (how a ritual "works") in leading Muslims in particular societies to inflect and reshape the ritual, even if slightly.

As with other ritual events, Muslims see their performance of sacrifice as part of their obligation to submit to God's commands as revealed through the Prophet Muhammad. (Indeed, *Islam* means *submission* to God.) Islam does not have an international hierarchy of religious authorities (as do Catholicism and Mormonism). It is thus striking that the ritual life of Muslims worldwide is as uniform as it is. Muslims everywhere agree on the importance of completing ritual prayer five times daily, fasting during the month of Ramadan, undertaking the pilgrimage to Mecca if they are able, and so forth. This degree of uniformity in the general norms of ritual practice results from the agreed-upon central importance of the Qur'ân, the word of God as revealed to Muhammad, and the hadith, collections of what Muhammad said and did. Islamic scholars base their interpretations, decisions, and law codes on these scriptural texts.

And so Muslims throughout the world often begin an account of why they perform a certain ritual by referring to a place in scripture where God gives a command. For example, we can safely say that all Muslims agree that a Muslim should observe the Feast of Sacrifice (in Arabic, *îd al-adhâ*) each year. The feast day commemorates the willingness of the prophet Ibrâhîm (in English, Abraham) to sacrifice his son at God's command. God's command to sacrifice to him and to him alone is contained in the Qur'ân in Chapter 22 (verses 34–38) and again in Chapter 108, and is the scriptural touchstone for this ritual. Moreover, the collection of reports of the Prophet Muhammad's deeds and statements, the hadith, specify how Muhammad carried out this command during the month of pilgrimage. These reports have become the basis for the annual pilgrimage to Mecca, the hajj.

Now, despite this general agreement on text and command, Muslims have developed strikingly varied ways of observing the command, and sometimes they vigorously debate the propriety of these ways. We start with village practices in the Gayo highlands, then examine alternative practices followed in the nearby town, and finally consider how the ritual is carried out at the other end of the Islamic world, in Morocco. Even when, as in this case, there is a clear and explicit text for ritual, that text may be subject to many interpretations. This multiplicity of interpretations and ritual practices is due in large part to different ideas about the relationship of humans to God, and different ideas about social relationships, especially those between men and women and between rulers and ruled.

Gayo Observances

The Gayo case illustrates how both religious interpretation and social ideas, particularly ideas about gender and family, shape ritual. All Gayo Muslims observe the annual sacrificial ritual. They do so with a keen awareness that they are part of a global celebration. Each year upward of 100 Gayo undertake the pilgrimage, and those who stay behind in their Sumatran highlands homeland often talk about the sacrifices the pilgrims are carrying out simultaneously with their own. I recall in 1989 sitting with a Gayo religious teacher night after night following shortwave radio reports from Malaysia on the daily events of the pilgrimage in Mecca and Medina.

But people also carry out their own personal obligations for each household to sacrifice something on the feast day. In the community of Isak, where I have done most of my work, households sacrifice various kinds of animals: chickens, ducks, sheep, goats, or water buffalo. The person carrying out the sacrifice itself takes care to do it in the correct manner, cutting the animal's throat quickly to minimize pain, and pronouncing the formula, "In the name of God, the Merciful and Compassionate." Just before cutting

Men preparing to sacrifice a water buffalo for the Feast of Sacrifice, Isak, Sumatra. (COURTESY OF J. BOWEN.)

the animal's throat, the sacrificer speaks softly near it, dedicating the animal to one or more relatives, who receive religious merit from the sacrifice. Who actually cuts the throat is not of great importance; a man may delegate the job to someone else, but the ritual must be performed properly, by an adult Muslim. When it is a buffalo that is sacrificed, the animal is first purified by being washed with the fruit of a citrus called the *mungkur* that is thought to rid the animal of its impurities and dedicate it to God.

As in most of Southeast Asia, Gayo gender relations are relatively equal. Women inherit property, manage household finances, and work alongside their husbands in fields, offices, or shops. The household is the unit of production and consumption: all its members work and eat together. Not surprisingly, then, the sacrifice is carried out in the name of the household, not just the male household head. Women as well as men speak of "their" sacrifice, and couples decide jointly on a list of people who will receive its merit. In the case of a buffalo, the beneficiaries usually include parents on both sides, and daughters as well as sons. Widows also carry out sacrifice (without being socially redefined as men), although a man will cut the animal's throat. When a wealthy female trader in Isak sacrificed a buffalo, others tended to speak of it as her sacrifice, not her husband's. She had generated the wealth, although he was part of the household.

Following the sacrifice, households host ritual meals, called kenduri. At each such meal, prayers to God are recited by all present. Depending on whom you ask, blessings, or merit, or just prayers are sent to the spirits of the deceased. These ritual meals are central to many events in the highlands and elsewhere in Indonesia. Sometimes a household will host a meal for everyone who wishes to attend. During each of the four years when I was present for the *îd al-adhâ* in Isak, three or four households sacrificed a buffalo and sponsored such a village-wide feast. At these feasts men and women chanted Qur'ânic verses and statements in praise of God far into the night. These special kenduri were intended to send extra merit to the host's ancestors. Recitations please God, say villagers, who then relieves the torment of these ancestors. (At these events, as at the feasts held after a death that we studied in Chapter 4, the number of guests times the number of repetitions yields the overall benefit.) The learned man who leads the guests in chanting will have been given a list of the people to whom the merit should be transmitted; he then embeds these names in a long prayer (sometimes saying the names very softly), thereby directing the evening's merit to the intended beneficiaries.

Not only do the words sent to God generate spiritual benefit for deceased relatives, but the sheep or buffalo that has been sacrificed by a household also provides a future material benefit. On the Day of Judgment, the persons named as sacrificial beneficiaries will be able to ride on the animal to the place of judgment. Only one person can ride a goat or sheep to this place, but seven can ride on a buffalo. A buffalo sacrifice thus provides the opportunity to bring together parents, children, and grandchildren on the back of the afterlife vehicle, and if they have the resources, most Isak households will stage a buffalo feast sometime during their lives. (With the sands of the Holy Land in mind, they also say they wished they had camels to sacrifice.)

The ritual meals and the sacrifice that precedes them all involve the transmission of a ritually purified animal in the name of God, the communication of an intent that the merit of the sacrifice (and of the chanting at larger feasts) be attached to certain specific persons, and the expectation that God will indeed grant these benefits.

Objections to Ritual Efficacy

But Gayo (and other) Muslim reformists object to these practices. As we saw in Chapter 4, reformists hold that one can only benefit from one's own actions, and therefore ritual meals during which people intend to send merit to a spirit contradict the proper understanding of God's statement: "People shall have only as they have labored." Now, some reform-minded scholars in Indonesia actually support the idea that sacrificing in obedience to God does generate merit for yourself. But Gayo reformists, who tend to live in the town and mingle with non-Gayo people, try to distinguish their own interpretations and practices as clearly as possible from those of the villagers. (Other scholars, who call themselves "traditionalists," defend some village practices.) In part this is because townspeople's identities are based on their rejection of the past—they live as self-styled "modern Muslims"; in part it is because of their own religious convictions.

Certainly religion has been the main idiom for, if not the entire substance of, townspeople's ways of differentiating themselves from villagers. Town friends told me on many occasions of how villagers remained in "pre-Islamic days" (*jaman jahiliya*), evidenced by their reliance on kenduri. They stated that before the coming of Islam people worshiped stones and spirits, not God, and did so by sending them gifts,

Men and women at worship on the Feast of Sacrifice, Isak, Indonesia. (COURTESY OF J. BOWEN.)

sometimes food gifts, in return for their assistance in hunting or sorcery or to achieve other ends.

Village religious practice includes the idea that rituals, often in the form of ritual meals, can send merit, communicate with spirits, and accomplish other practical ends. In order to maximally distinguish themselves from villagers, town reformists have focused their efforts on ridding town observances of any indications that rituals can do these things. In the case of the Feast of Sacrifice they have tried to eliminate any signs that killing and eating together make merit or send blessings to ancestors.

In 1989 I observed the celebration of the Feast of Sacrifice in a reformist stronghold in town. When asked about the purpose of the ritual, town residents invariably referred to God's command in the Qur'ân to follow the example of Ibrâhîm. (Villagers, by contrast, usually mentioned the importance of providing a vehicle for the afterlife.) For these reformists, to follow the example of Ibrâhîm means to adopt his attitude of selfless and sincere devotion, or *ikhlas.* One scholar explained that one receives merit from the sacrifice only if it is done with the proper intent, "for the sake of God and not for a worldly reason." He called the notion that the sacrifice becomes a vehicle for the afterlife "amusing."

In recounting the story of Ibrâhîm, townspeople emphasized his prior decision to give something away in devotion to God, not the moment of sacrifice itself (which would bring up village ideas about the purpose and result of sacrifice). The killing of the goat or other animal was sometimes left for someone else to perform, privately, effectively downplaying killing and eating in favor of other public events: street parades, congregational worship, and chanting in the neighborhood prayer-house.

Townspeople did eat in the prayer-house, but referred to the meals as "eating together" and never as kenduri. Friends of mine gave away food on the feast day, and mentioned prominently the invitation given to town orphans to eat in the prayer-house as proof of the event's real character. The meal was about self-sacrifice and not about creating merit. (The fear of mistaken understandings of what the eating meant sometimes leads to extreme reactions. I recall one teacher who reacted in horror when cookies were passed around a classroom after he had delivered a homily to the students about the meaning of sacrifice.)

Town religious practice has thus developed in part as a reaction to earlier models of sacrifice. Because villagers emphasized ritual meals and the efficacy of the sacrifice itself, town modernists avoid any association between the killing of the sacrificial animal and eating together. The value of selfless sacrifice is instead underscored.

Certain elements of the Feast of Sacrifice, for example, are shared by Gayo villagers and town reformists alike. Women are active participants in the rituals. They may perform sacrifice. They are members of a household unit that is directly involved in the activities: in the villages, when they gather together for a ritual meal (and in images of the family, holding hands, being saved because of their wise decision to sacrifice animals to God); in town, when the family gathers for tearful confessions of their shortcomings and of their love for each other. These elements of female and family involvement are also found in other Indonesian societies and in the writings of Indonesian religious scholars. For example, the possibility for women to carry out a sacrifice is explicitly defended by influential reformist scholars. Are these elements generally true of Muslim societies, or specific to Indonesia? Or to a wider belt of Asian Muslim societies?

Moroccan Muslim Sacrifice: Reaffirming Male Dominance

To answer this question we can appropriately start by searching for the maximal contrasts, the differences that will aid us in constructing a field of possibilities. As it happens, we can begin with Morocco, at the other end of the Islamic world, recently studied for its forms of sacrificial ritual practice by M. E. Combs-Schilling (1989). Here, in contrast to the family-oriented practice and ideology found in Indonesia, patriarchy is accentuated through ritual. Each year on the feast day, the king, who claims descent from the prophet Muhammad, publicly plunges a dagger into a ram's throat, reenacting Muhammad's ritual practice and underscoring his tie to the Prophet. Combs-Schilling shows that the sacrifice also reaffirms patriarchal power in the family and embodies a notion of male fertility. After the king has accomplished his sacrifice, male heads of household throughout the kingdom follow suit. Each publicly kills a ram, the size and virility of which is commented on as a measure of the man's own virility. In village and town settings, the other men of the household stand erect to witness the sacrifice; women and children are either absent or in the background, seated. Women play only the role of passive observers to the sacrifice; after the killing they may dab some of the victim's blood on their faces to "share in the power of sacrifice."

This public enactment of patriarchy accords with Moroccan cultural assumptions about the opposition of male reason versus female passion. More generally, the fixed male/female opposition is just one instance of the belief described by Lawrence Rosen (1989) that one can read from social characteristics of persons to their attendant mental states. The Moroccan view asserts that persons have essential differences in their mental characteristics, depending on such critical social differences as gender and place of origin. This theory underpins not only gender segregation and patriarchy, but also legal processes of determining a reliable witness.

This maximal contrast brings out two major cultural differences between Morocco (and perhaps other North African societies) and Indonesia (and perhaps other Asian societies). The first is the salience of the killing event in the former, but not in the latter. Whether on Java, coastal Aceh, or highland Sumatra, and whether reformist or traditionalist in religious orientation, Indonesians downplay the act of killing in favor of other aspects of the ritual. This tendency tinges all other aspects of the ritual, including the second axis of contrast, that of patriarchy's greater or lesser centrality. As Combs-Schilling emphasizes (and others support her account), the ritual is publicly, officially interpreted in Morocco not just in a gender-segregated way (as one might find in parts of Muslim Asia) but in such a way as to underwrite the domination of women by men.

Other Moroccan Forms of the Sacrifice Ritual

The contrast between Morocco and Gayo (and some other Indonesian) ritual practices thus points toward broad cultural contrasts that also shape, differentially, the way Muslims interpret scriptural commands. This maximally broad contrast is especially important in preventing us from assuming that particular features observed in one place are true of Muslims in general.

But it turns out that within Morocco one finds variant forms of the ritual much as we saw for Gayo society. And, just as with Gayo reformist self-differentiation from villagers, some of these other forms of ritual appear to be constructed in explicit distinction to the public, state-backed patriarchal form of ritual. Abdellah Hammoudi (1993) describes observances in a village near Marrakesh, where women play a ritually central role in purifying the sacrificial victim. They gather its blood not just to share in its power but for use over a long period of time to guard the home and to combat illnesses. Moreover, over the longer ritual cycle (found in parts of Morocco, Algeria, and Tunisia) the Feast of Sacrifice is followed by a series of carnivalesque processions and masquerades in which characters representing women, Jews, workers, and other figures flaunt sexuality and, in classic ritual-of-reversal fashion, violate the sanctity of the sacrifice by wearing the skin of the sacrificial victim. The masquerade highlights the social contradictions between classes as well as those between male and female. These representations of cultural difference contradict the rigor of all-male purity that the sacrifice tries to impose. Stressing the resemblance with European forms of carnival, Hammoudi argues that these rites are part of the overall process by which Moroccans made Muslim sacrifice their own.

The publicly patriarchal character of sacrifice and the explicit links to the Ibrâhîm myth, emphasized by Combs-Schilling, are also documented by Hammoudi. But these public forms now appear as pronouncements that disguise the activities and counter-representations made by women. Moroccan ritual activity, at least in some places, is not the unambiguous proclamation of patriarchy but a structured combination of official patriarchy and other forms, either domestic (such as the healing blood gathered from the victim) or interstitial (such as the masquerades). In these offstage events the socially necessary activities of women gain voice.

Together, the Moroccan and Gayo cases show how Muslims have shaped a particular set of ritual duties in sharply contrasting ways, with cultural foci that do not derive in any direct way from Islamic scripture, but rather, are the products of adapting, elaborating, and transforming scriptural and other elements in directions that make sense locally.

Profile

Jean Comaroff

Fieldwork under Apartheid

Jean Comaroff, often with her husband John Comaroff, has conducted many years of fieldwork in her home country, South Africa, while teaching in England and the United States. This is a particular kind of fieldwork, neither "at home" nor in a society that is totally new to the ethnographer. It is historically-based ethnography, as best exemplified in the (projected) three-volume study of Christianity and colonialism in South Africa, *Of Revelation and Revolution* (University of Chicago Press 1991, 1997).

I grew up in South Africa, and for me there has never been a stark division between "life" and the "field." I was first drawn to anthropology as a way of understanding the contradictory colonial world that surrounded me, but almost from the start, I realized that such understanding also required history, a sense of how current social and cultural formations had come to be as they were. How was it that South African society could both be shaped by grand world processes—like colonization and missionization—yet remain rooted in long-standing, local ways

of seeing and being? Later, when living in Chicago I became fascinated by its own complex past, and I learned that a somewhat obscure local apostolic church, born of the Chicago World's Fair, had had a powerful and enduring impact on the religious life of my native land.

It was these concerns that framed the research that forms the basis of *Body of Power, Spirit of Resistance*. I did my first fieldwork in the town of Mafikeng, in the northwest corner of South Africa, during the years of high apartheid, when there were stringently enforced laws prohibiting the interaction of blacks and whites. Considerable estrangement and suspicion existed across lines of color. One of the few domains in which there was limited interracial contact, and in which Africans were permitted to gather and publicly express themselves, was that of organized religion.

The local independent churches were thus a point of entry for me as a white researcher. The products of a long translocal history, the churches were significant sites within which local people could reflect on their past and act in the present, could voice anger, and strive for healing.

Without a doubt, the gulf that had to be breached before I could communicate with black South Africans on their own terms intensified my fieldwork experience. This was a time of severe repression and clandestine struggle. Confidences could lead to betrayals; fieldnotes had to be guarded from security police. The ur-gency of what was at stake heightened the need for trust on all sides, and charged relationships with a degree of responsibility to which one could never really be equal. After 30 years, I am still in close contact with many of my original interlocutors in Mafikeng. They read much of what I write, and they have contributed generously to my current work on South Africa after apartheid. 〜

For Further Consideration

*M*ost web sites about the Amish are on-line catalogues of their farm produce (which itself is an interesting commentary on how they relate to "the English"). A semi-official Lancaster County, Pennsylvania, site about the Amish is at *http://www.800padutch.com/amish.shtml*. A quite different site, Christian Reality Anabaptist Church History End Times Gospel, to be taken for what it is, assembles voluminous materials and many links regarding anabaptists in general (*http://www.montanasat.net/rickv/#site direct*).

A number of books and films document the forms Catholicism takes in the Americas, among them the film *Flowers for Guadalupe* (Filmakers Library 1995) about the importance of the Virgin of Guadalupe for Mexican women. I have already mentioned a number of films about Afro-Brazilian religions; here I would add *Voices of the Orishas* (University of California Extension Center 1994) about Santeria in Cuba. *Magic and Catholicism* (University of California Extension Center 1975) shows a mixing of Aymara practices with Catholicism in Bolivia.

11

Sacred Speech and Divine Power

*I*t is hard to think of a religion in which set ways of speaking—spells, prayers, recitations—do not play central roles. Humans are talking animals, and we use our powers of speech to understand and shape events in both the visible and invisible worlds. Most rituals we have examined so far have had certain speech forms at their center: invocations of ancestral spirits (in Africa, Sumatra, or New Guinea), stories and spells that heal (in Japan, Panama, or the United States), and pronouncements that channel the meaning of images (in the Catholic mass or Dogon masked dances).

Some religious traditions place particular emphasis on the centrality of the spoken word to religious practice. For the Navajos of the American Southwest, the world was brought into being by the Gods when they spoke and sung it into existence. Speech and song bring this creative power into the present world, for good or evil. So, too, for the Dogon, who understand the world as having been spoken into being. In both Hindu and Buddhist traditions, the word that is spoken and heard has primacy over that which is written and read—in the latter case a direct chain of transmission is broken. It is not only in the European traditions of Moses, Plato, and Jesus that writing has been understood as secondary to speech (mistakenly so, argues the philosopher Jacques Derrida), but in other religions, of greater and smaller scale, as well. Written scripture may play an important role in these traditions—"scripture," after all, means "writing"—but it does so as the written record of what was originally an act of speech.

Certain religious movements portray their own distinctiveness by contrasting their emphasis on the spoken word to the reliance of competing faiths on images. In seventh-century Arabia, Muhammad and his followers contrasted the word of God, which they followed, to the images of polytheists, which they condemned. Moses responding to Aaron's setting up of the golden calf, or Joseph Smith and Brigham Young leading the Mormons across the United States, both condemned the worship of "graven images" and urged their followers to focus on the word of God. Luther chastised the Christians of his time for following the Church rather than scripture, and the "letter of the Bible" has been the watchword for Protestant movements of reform ever since. Each of these leaders has accused other faiths of forgetting or ignoring God's words.

But speech, like images, can be meaningful in more than one way. When we speak we refer to concepts, and through them to things in the world. We also call up associations in the minds of our hearers, associations linked to their memories of hearing such words before, or to the style, rhythm, or voice tone of the speaker. Thus, the way in which a sermon is delivered or a hymn sung can be as meaningful to worshipers as the manifest content of the sermon or hymn. We also understand some speech as directly accomplishing something, as having force as well as meaning: a marriage vow seals a pact; a spell compels a spirit to act. Within a religious tradition people often discuss and debate how best to understand their own speech. Is a sermon better if it is carefully crafted beforehand (as clearly a human product), or is it better if it is spontaneous (allowing the Holy Ghost to offer direct inspiration)? Can a prayer, or a mass, or the recitation of a verse work directly on the universe, or is it only a request to a deity or god?

We consider the relationship between ways of speaking and divine powers in three religious traditions: Islam, in which God's speech sets out a proper path for humans to follow; Navajo religion, in which humans draw on the creative powers of the first beings when they sing prayers of blessing or healing; and several Protestant religions, in which God reveals his word through scripture and spontaneous, inspired speaking.

The Qur'ân as Recitation of God's Speech

For Muslims, speech is sacred and powerful mainly as the source of commandments from God and as the vehicle for carrying out, through prayer and worship, those commandments. Muslims' sacred book is the Qur'ân, a word that comes from the Arabic root meaning "to recite." The Qur'ân is the collection of verses spoken to Muhammad by the angel Gabriel, who conveyed them from God. The revelation of these verses took place between 610 and 632 in Mecca and Medina, in Arabia. The Qur'ân preexisted these revelations as God's speech—indeed, most Muslims regard it as eternal (Graham 1987, 79–115).

The revelations were handed down orally long before they were first written down, and even today Muslims consider it important to memorize and recite these words of God. In its written form, the Qur'ân is arranged as 114 chapters, each divided into verses, and arranged, not in the order in which they were spoken to Muhammad, but, by convention, from the longest to the shortest.

Unlike the Hebrew Bible or Christian Gospels, the Qur'ân is not a collection of long narratives. It contains brief parables and stories but mainly consists of directives and exhortations to Muhammad and his people. Muslims learn the fuller stories of the prophets and of Muhammad's life from other narratives, not from the Qur'ân itself. Much of the Qur'ân is about how Muslims ought to live: values, social norms, and what we generally call "law." These guidelines for living are called sharî'a, "the way." (Law in the narrower sense of enforceable jurisprudence is designated by the term fiqh.)

The following passage, from the third chapter of the Qur'ân, exemplifies the way in which several kinds of messages are typically combined. It reads:

Say: 'God has spoken the truth; therefore follow
the creed of Abraham, a man of pure faith and no idolater.'
The first House established for the people
was that at Mecca, a place holy, and a guidance to all beings.
Therein are clear signs—the station of Abraham,
and whosoever enters it is in security.
It is the duty of all men towards God to come
to the House a pilgrim, if he is able to make his way there.
As for the unbeliever, God is All-sufficient nor needs any being.
(Qur'ân 3:90–92)

A lot is contained in this passage. Muslim children and adults will memorize it in Arabic, learn its meaning in their own language (if they are not Arabic speakers, as most Muslims are not), and then be taught the ways to understand it by a religious teacher. Most Muslim children begin to learn the Qur'ân at a young age, and as they grow up they will likely attend Qur'ân interpretation sessions in the local prayer house or mosque.

The passage is addressed to Muhammad, as are all Qur'ânic verses. It shows him precisely how to admonish and guide the people of Arabia, some of whom had become his followers. God directs him to say a certain passage to the people, a passage that identifies Muhammad's mission as pulling people back to the true path of worship of God from which they have strayed. How that path is identified is important: it is the "creed of Abraham," the same creed delivered to Jews and later to Christians. These people had their own "messengers," similar to Muhammad: the Jews had Moses, to whom was revealed the Bible, and David, to whom was given the Psalms; Christians had Jesus, to whom was revealed the Gospels (in this, the Islamic view of Christ's mission). Jews and Christians are "people of the book," and have been accorded special treatment in Muslim-held territories. Muslims believe that Jews and Christians eventually strayed from pure monotheism (the doctrine of the Trinity is a particular target) but that people of all three faiths worship the same God. *Islam* means "submission [to God]" and is intended as a return to an old faith, not the creation of a new one.

The passage then refers to a historical event, the construction by Abraham of the Ka'ba, the large, cubic, black-draped structure in Mecca around which Muslim pilgrims process during the annual religious pilgrimage. The duty to make the pilgrimage, for those with the means to do so, is based on this passage in the Qur'ân, short though it may be, and the fact that Muhammad made such a pilgrimage in 632, the year of his death.

The final sentence in the passage implies a warning to the unbelievers, those who do not yet accept God, and reminds them that God does not need them, but, it is implied, they do need to heed his call.

The Qur'ân is treated not just as a book to be read, memorized, and studied, but also to be celebrated through song and calligraphy. Contests of Qur'ân melodic recitation are held at regular intervals throughout the Muslim world, in which the beauty of the voice control and melodic interpretation, as well as the fit of melody to content, are the

Islamic calligraphy in the Congregational Mosque in Isfahan, Iran. The inlaid tile design shows both cursive and geometric styles; the inscriptions include Qur'ânic passages and, in this Shi'i setting, invocations of both Muhammad and 'Ali. (COURTESY OF JOHN RENARD.)

basis for judging winners. (Indonesia and Malaysia, two non-Arabic speaking countries, routinely win prizes at the international finals.) Much Islamic art is based on the artistic interpretation of the form of the written Qur'ân, and intricate writings of the names "Allah" and "Muhammad" are found on almost every conceivable surface in Muslim societies. Many Muslims also believe the spoken and written words have the power to ward off evil or heal people of illness.

The Qur'ân is God's major gift to humans, analogous to the presence of Jesus among humans in Christian understanding. It is an exact replica of the words spoken to

Muhammad; therefore, the forms of the spoken and written words themselves take on sacred value. It is also evidence of direct historical contact between God and Muhammad. This direct contact is crucial to Islam's religious foundation, and explains two areas of study within Islam: one that proves that Muhammad was illiterate and could not possibly have created the Qur'ân, and a second that shows the Qur'ân to be inimitable in grammar and rhetoric. These lines of investigation, taken together, prove that the Qur'ân is from God. (Contrast the lack of importance to most Christians of the original sound and shape of the Greek words in the Gospels.)

But Muslims debate among themselves about what the implications of the Qur'ân's divine source are for everyday life. Many Gayo Muslims, for example, consider prayers (*do'a*) that include Qur'ânic verses to be directly effective in healing, or giving one invulnerability, or harming one's enemy. One of my friends, for instance, used a passage from chapter 61 of the Qur'ân as the beginning of an invulnerability spell:

And He will give you another blessing which you love:
help from God and present victory.
Give good tidings, O Muhammad
to believers.

To which he would append a plea ending in the lines:

Let my blanket be from God,
my cloak from God,
my shawl from God.

My friend thought that when he uttered the prayer, God gave him a cloak and shawl, as the material realization of God's promise to give "help from God and a present victory." In his own memory, these divine gifts had served him well during battles fought in the 1950s, making bullets and knives skip off his clothes as he fought. But in the 1980s others pointed out to him that the Qur'ânic passage had been revealed to Muhammad as a message of peace, to stop fighting. One scholar objected to my friend that reciting the Qur'ân could not automatically confer any power on the reciter; that all power came from God and that He knew all that happened in the world anyway and would do as He pleased, regardless of what mumbo-jumbo ordinary men and women chose to recite. All that we can do, he said, is to live good lives and worship God, and then perhaps He will choose to reward us.

The Creative Power of Navajo Speech and Song

*T*he view that speech directly confers power, limited within Islam to one, often criticized view about the Qur'ân and God, flowers fully within Navajo religion. Like Muslims, Navajo place speech at the center of religion, but as the source of creative power rather than as the source of divine commands.

In Navajo tradition, the individual human being has the power to change the world through language (Witherspoon 1977). A person can do so because the world itself was created through language, when First Man sang the song known as Blessingway. Among the first creatures, the Holy People, were Long Life Boy (thought) and Happiness Girl (speech), to whom First Man said: "You two will be found among everything." Indeed, their names are found in nearly every Navajo prayer and song as signs of the powers to create. They also are the parents of Changing (or Earth) Woman, the being who is associated with the earth's fertility.

The sung prayers known as Blessingway tell the story of creation. They also reenact creation each time they are told (Wyman 1970). They may be performed as a separate ritual—for example to bless a house—or be incorporated into other rituals in which, by invoking the events of creation, they endow the ritual with that same creative power. Navajo sand painting also draws its powers from the story of creation. After the Holy People built the first house, they decorated the floor with bits of shale, rock, and mineral dyes. They drew all the forms of life that they eventually were to create, depicting them in the forms of holy people. They then recited a long prayer to these holy people, and in that act created a causal pathway between sand paintings and the sacred powers of creation.

Blessingway and many other prayer cycles identify and associate everyday people and conditions with the Holy People and the events of creation. Blessingway contains many lines that link powers given to the Holy People to powers desired by the speaker, such as:

May the power that enables you to inhale also enable me to inhale.

Let the dark flint which arises to protect you always arise to protect me.

Often these sections of the prayer provide long catalogues of body parts and powers, underscoring the identification of the Holy Person's body with that of the prayer reciter. These identifications are intended to transfer the properties of the Holy People to that of the person who is the object of the ceremony. For example, Navajo singers will help ensure a good birth for an expectant mother by performing a Blessingway ceremony that identifies the Holy People of the Earth, themselves associated with fertility and life, with the mother and child (Gill 1981). The singer will collect earth from a cornfield and water from a flowing stream, both nurturing life, and apply them to the woman. The prayers recited include the Earth's Prayer, which underscores these identifications through passages such as the following:

Earth's feet have become my feet by means of these I shall live on.

Earth's legs have become my legs by means of these I shall live on.

Earth's body has become my body by means of this I shall live on.

Earth's mind has become my mind by means of this I shall live on.

Earth's voice has become my voice by means of this I shall live on.

. . .

It is the very inner form of Earth that continues to move with me, that has risen with me, that is standing with me, that indeed remains stationary with me.

Now it is the inner form of long life, now of happiness that continues to move with me, that has risen with me, that is standing with me, that indeed remains stationary with me, surprising, surprising. (Wyman 1970, 136)

The pair of terms *long life* and *happiness* are the principles personified in the Holy People Long Life Boy and Happiness Girl (Wyman 1970, 19–46). They are linked to all the components of the earth. The effect of these pairings is to transfer to the mother and expected child these two essential qualities, long life and happiness.

Prayers such as these are used for healing when Holy People are thought to have been responsible for the illness. If a person has trespassed on a holy site, the Holy People may place a spell on that person; the Holyway ceremony is designed to induce them to remove the spell. The singer addresses a particular holy person by name and makes an offering of tobacco smoke to him. In the Holyway stories associated with the ceremonies, the holy person is sent tobacco, smokes, and then agrees to help cure the patient. The holy person addresses the patient as "grandson," placing himself in a relationship in which he can be compelled to aid the ill person, his "grandson." The prayer draws on the knowledge contained in these stories by demanding, not requesting, that the holy person cure the patient:

This very day you must remake my feet for me,

This very day you must remake my legs for me.

The prayer ends by asserting that the cure has occurred:

With my body cooled off, I am walking about,
with my body light in weight, I am walking about,

. . .

As one who is long life and happiness I am walking about

Pleasant again it has become,

Pleasant again it has become! (Gill 1981, 128–129)

In this, its concluding section, the prayer performs the act of bringing the patient to health. The verb is in the progressive mode—"I am walking about"—indicating that the patient will continue to enjoy health. Most importantly, the prayer identifies the patient with Long Life Boy and Happiness Girl: he or she has become "one who is long life and happiness."

Speech and Grace in Protestant Churches

So far we have considered ideas about how speech relates to power; now we introduce a third concept, that of the grace of God. Ways of speaking found in many Protestant churches introduce the idea that speech by everyday people can, when accompanied by God's grace, be divinely inspired.

In the sixteenth century, several Christian scholars, notably Martin Luther (1483–1546) in Germany and John Calvin (1509–1564) in Geneva, protested against certain Church teachings. The worship movements that Luther, Calvin, and others established thus came to be known generally as "Protestant" because of this series of protests. Although differing strongly among themselves, these movements shared the dual conviction that, first, people could be saved only through faith and by the grace of God and, second, that scripture, not human institutions, was the ultimate source of religious authority. As the billboard outside the Lutheran Church near my home in St. Louis proclaims today: "Only by Grace; Only by Faith; Only by Scripture."

Protestants make the claim that faith and grace connect individuals to God in opposition to the Catholic claim that the Church, through its sacraments, creates that connection. For the Catholic, the miracle of the Eucharist means that Christ is produced in the bread and water of the Mass. For most Protestants (and, from at least the ninth century onward, for some Catholics), the objects of a mass are signs of, not the substance of, Christ. Moreover, for them the ritual of the Eucharist does not automatically confer merit or salvation or grace on the individual worshiper. Nor do chants said on behalf of the dead aid the dead in their struggle through purgatory to heaven. The individual has free and direct access to God, and God may bestow grace on anyone. The gift of the Word of God thus may reach anyone at any time and place and in unpredictable ways. Faith is all that is required (Clark 1967, 99–115).

In the wide array of movements and churches that followed Luther's break with Rome—Methodists, Baptists, Lutherans, and so on—this emphasis on universal access to God's grace and revelation of grace through speech and hearing led people to develop many and varied ways of worship. Quakers and some Baptists have stressed the universal nature of the minister's role, that anyone may be visited by the Holy Ghost and moved to preach. Charismatic and Pentecostal churches (and certain movements within Lutheranism) have encouraged worshipers to let the Holy Ghost visit them and lead them to speak in tongues, as did the apostles after the death of Jesus. But other movements denied the universal access of people to grace and salvation. John Calvin argued that God has predetermined who is to receive his grace and be saved, and who is to be condemned to hell. This doctrine of *predestination,* held by the Puritans in early North America as well as Calvin's followers in Europe, implied that one's good works had no bearing on one's fate after death.

The Letter and the Spirit of Scripture

The ultimate authority on all religious matters for Protestants is scripture, and not the teachings of a church or pope.

But what is "scripture"? One interpretation of the Protestant slogan "only scripture" (sola scriptura) is that the written text is paramount. Luther was indeed an outstanding biblical scholar, learned in Greek, Latin, and Hebrew, and did argue for the importance of the scholarly interpretation of the text as written. Early Protestant preaching never strayed far from the text of the Bible. What came to be called "Fundamentalist" movements, but might more correctly be called "literalist" emphases on the literal meaning of the text, follow from this focus on the written word.

For some Fundamentalist churchgoers in the United States today, literal truth resides in the 1611 King James Version of the Bible. Some of these Christians call modern translations "perversions." KJV is the Bible "as it is written" (Ammerman 1987, 53). Rather than considering the Bible as a whole, and worrying about contradictions between various parts, Fundamentalists (along with many other Christians) tend to refer to a verse or a phrase, on which they then elaborate, both in sermons and in discussing everyday life. People turn to individual verses that they have memorized, and they also use the language of some of those verses in everyday conversations, speak of their sicknesses as "suffering in beds of affliction" or having "a thorn in the flesh" (Ammerman 1987, 87).

This literalism can lead some Fundamentalists to a point at which they are nearly using the Bible for divination, as in the case of a man who decided to order a tent from Sears and Roebuck Company because he found listed among the permitted foods in 14 Deuteronomy the "roebuck" (Ammerman 1987, 54).

This interpretation of scripture can, of course, be used to underwrite claims of special authority grounded in learning. But these claims are often countered within the tradition of Luther and Calvin by appeal to a second understanding of scripture. Luther, Calvin, and other reformers looked beyond the text to the divine message it conveyed (Graham 1987, 141–154). They placed no special value on the original languages of the Hebrew Bible or the Greek Gospels, and indeed Protestant reformers have encouraged translation as the best way to spread God's word. In this respect they differ from Muslims, for whom there can be only one Qur'ân, the Arabic-language speech of God. (Indeed, most Muslims consider it impossible to "translate" the Qur'ân; English and other versions are usually called "interpretations" or "renderings.")

For the Protestant reformers, then, speech and writing was best thought of as a window to God's word, transparent to its referent. It is the Word, not the particular letters, that is holy. The Bible as preached, translated, interpreted, and witnessed in one's life is the key to the proper understanding of God, not the scholastic analysis of the Hebrew or Greek constructions. The Word of God is thus the meaning of scripture. It can take different forms, including the presence of Christ himself in the world, as the Word made flesh.

God can thus communicate his word in very different ways. Luther underscored the importance of inner communication with God, communication that did not depend on learning. He wrote that "no one can understand God or God's word rightly unless he receives it directly [literally, "without mediation"] from the Holy Spirit." And Calvin wrote that "all of scripture is to be read as if God were speaking," and that the spirit of scripture was more important than the letter of scripture. In their view, God can communicate with ordinary people through many media: the revelations recorded in scripture, the embodiment of the divine in Christ, and the visiting upon any of us of the Holy Ghost (Graham 1987, 143, 147).

Because these inner modes of communication—hearing with help from the Holy Spirit—must accompany the reading of the Bible, Luther linked speech and hearing to the central value of faith:

If you ask a Christian what work renders him worthy of the name Christian, he will not be able to give any answer at all except the hearing of the word of God, that is, faith. Therefore the ears alone are the organs of the Christian person, who is justified and judged a Christian not by the works of any member, but through faith. (quoted in Graham 1987, 141)

The writings of Luther and others thus could be taken to give to individuals the right to hear God's word, no matter what statements were made by the authorities of a church. This radical giving of spiritual rights to individuals surfaces time and again in subsequent history.

Election and Signs

Most Protestant Christians would agree that God bestows his grace where he sees fit. But how and when does he see fit? Can our actions bring on grace?

The struggles over this issue within Christianity trace back to the very roots of the religion. On the one hand, Christianity drew from Judaism. It began, after all, as a sect within Judaism, where obedience to the Law determined the fate of individuals and of the universe. The idea that good works redeemed one's soul were developed by the Church into elaborate doctrines of penance, masses, and salvation. Many Protestant traditions also incorporated such a notion, Methodism among them.

But Christianity became, not a sect within Judaism, but a new religion, and did so in large part by adopting ideas from Hellenism, the world view that pervaded the Mediterranean world (Jaeger 1961). Hellenism included the idea of divine grace that is visited upon humans rather than achieved by them. This concept accorded well with the idea of an all-powerful God, and indeed with the unpredictability of the God of the Hebrew Bible. After all, if God does not need humans he will dispense grace in ways that fit his plans, not our works.

The idea that God's grace is entirely independent of human actions finds its most eloquent exposition in Paul's letter to the Romans, in a section where Paul is distinguishing between the older idea of the Jewish "chosen people" from the Christian idea that God chooses, or elects, some people (and not others) both from among the Jews and from among the Gentiles.

. . . [W]hen Rebecca had conceived children by one man, our forefather Isaac, though they were not yet born and had done nothing either good or bad, in order that God's purpose of election might continue, not because of works but because of his call, she was told, "the elder will serve the younger." As it is written, "Jacob I loved, but Esau I hated."

What shall we say then? Is there injustice on God's part? By no means! For he says to Moses, "I will have mercy on whom I have mercy, and I will have compassion on whom I have compassion." So it depends not upon man's will or exertion, but upon God's mercy. For the scripture says to Pharaoh, "I have raised you up for the very purpose of showing my power in you, so that my name may be proclaimed in all the earth." So then he has mercy upon whomever he wills, and he hardens the heart of whomever he wills.

You will say to me then, "Why does he still find fault? For who can resist his will?" But who are you, a man, to answer back to God? Will what is molded say to its molder, "Why have you made me thus?" Has the potter no right over the clay, to make out of the same lump one vessel for beauty and another for menial use? (Romans 9, 10–21)

Just as the potter may select some pots for greatness, and others for quick destruction, without the pots having the right to answer back, how can we, God's creations, question the will of God, our Creator?

The doctrine of election formed a central part of the teachings of Saint Augustine in the fifth century (Burns 1994). Because original sin cost humans their free will, he wrote, all our fortune, good or ill, is due to God's grace. In the sixteenth century, John Calvin developed this argument into the idea of predestination, which became founding doctrine for the Presbyterian Church. As inscribed in the Westminster Confession of 1647, which the English Parliament accepted the following year, the doctrine was stated in the form that "some men and angels are predestined unto everlasting life, and others foreordained to everlasting death" (Weber 1958, 98–101).

This doctrine left its adherents with a radical uncertainty about their future. Calvin taught that no one can know whether he is saved (although Calvin apparently thought he was), because the damned can have all the mental states possessed by the saved except for the final state of trust in God. So although a strong feeling of faith in God is necessary for salvation, it is insufficient as a source of reassurance about salvation.

This uncertainty has one opening, in the "doctrine of signs," that even if we cannot know with certainty about our salvation, we can see signs of it. These signs could be in one's ability to succeed in the world. Some Protestant theologians argued that one had a duty to assume that one was saved and act accordingly. Individual psychology led believers in the doctrine toward intense worldly activity in the hopes that leading a rational, systematic life for the greater glory of God on earth would itself be a sign that one has been called to serve God—has been elected. Some added an additional tenet that helped close the logical circle: that only the elect had faith strong enough to keep them hewing to this path. Thus, success and profit are themselves signs of election.

Although this line of thinking brought even Calvin's heirs back to a position in which good works counted for something on the religious plane, it was not a return to Catholic doctrine. The Calvinist still has no possibility of absolution; if he is damned then there is still nothing he can do about it. Furthermore, in the idea that a life spent for God was a sign of election, it was the whole life that mattered, and not the individual work, as in the Catholic calculus of sin and absolution.

Max Weber (1958) drew on these religious responses to develop his theory that what he called the "Protestant ethic" provided a psychological push for the development of modern capitalism in Europe. He noted that the pioneers of modern capitalism in Europe were mainly Protestant rather than Catholic, despite the fact that Protestant theologians were far more restrictive regarding what we might call the modern business necessities of interest and competitive pricing than were their Catholic counterparts.

Luther, for example, wrote that "the greatest misfortune of the German nation is easily the traffic in interest. . . . The devil invented it, and the pope, by giving his sanction to it, has done untold evil throughout the world."

Weber's idea was that Protestantism spurred on the development of capitalism, not directly through its doctrine but through the psychological consequences of that doctrine. Men tormented by the unknowability of election were spurred on to succeed in the world, to build edifices of successful businesses as monuments to their worldly success. Weber called this cast of mind "worldly asceticism": denying pleasure to oneself but doing so in a life very much devoted to this world. The capitalist experienced loneliness, since no one could save him and God was distant; had a hatred of material, sensuous life, since it had no positive religious role and tempted people to idolatry; and threw himself into a social life that was solely work for the glory of God.

Weber advanced his thesis by studying the sermons and diaries of Calvinist theologians in the seventeenth and eighteenth centuries. Richard Baxter, for example, served in Cromwell's government as well as in the Puritan Church. He preached hard, methodical work as a religious labor (and opposed sports). The divine quality of this work will be "known by its fruits," he wrote. As a consequence, these men preferred specialization and the division of labor for the greater returns to labor they brought, and thus the greater indication of their own personal election.

The doctrine of election—or "particular election" as it came to be called—was by no means universally accepted by Protestants. An especially widely effective treatise written by Jacobus Arminius in 1608 and called *Declaration of Sentiments* argued that God wishes all people to be saved and gives them the means to do so. Living the good life, stated Arminius, can bring one to God's grace. This position (often called "Arminianism") implied that humans are "perfectible." This argument was taken up in the eighteenth century by John Wesley. The movement he founded was named Methodism for the methodical life he urged Christians to lead. Methodists and other movements accentuated the emotional work required to bring about certainty of salvation and to lead the person into the state of grace.

Baptists gained their distinctive position within the array of Protestant churches through their argument that only those who had gained their faith should be baptized into the church. They thus rejected infant baptism. But Baptists themselves split over the issue of election, with some teaching that Jesus died for everyone; others, that he died only for the elect. Those who held the first view were called "General Baptists" and included the group that left England for Holland in 1607, some of whom then journeyed to Plymouth, Massachusetts, in 1620. Those holding the second view, called "Particular Baptists," founded churches in England and also sent groups to America. Today, some Presbyterian and Reformed churches in Europe and the United States advocate the doctrine, but may place more or less emphasis on it.

Singing and Certainty among U.S. Primitive Baptists

One group of churches that has attempted to remain faithful to Calvin are the self-styled "Primitive Baptists" of the southeastern United States. These churches are scattered throughout the Appalachian mountains, but I draw here on a study conducted in the early 1980s by James Peacock and Ruel Tyson (1989) in the Blue Ridge mountains straddling North Carolina and Virginia. In this sparsely populated region, both elders and other worshipers travel from church to church to worship, often staying Saturday nights with friends. Services include hymn singing, one or more sermons preached by elders, and large meals spread out on communal tables. The churches belong to the Mountain District Association.

The Primitive Baptists adhere to the Westminster Confession, and they actively wrestle with the difficulties the doctrine presents. They attempt to uphold election and reject the idea that we can earn our salvation or have certain knowledge of it. As one preacher put it, "every time you feel inspired, it didn't necessarily come from the Lord." But they also hold to the idea of signs of salvation that one can sense in the world. These signs include the experience of community attained through fellowship and church services, "a sweet meeting," such as one preacher recollected in a sermon in the early 1980s. "Oh, my friends, sometimes we've sung songs here that've lifted us up," he reminds them. And the beauty of their singing is a sign, a foretaste of heaven: "Beyond the little foretastes of experience now, ah, in heaven's pure world today there are angels that sing" (Peacock and Tyson 1989, 112).

"Hymns are small sermons," notes one church elder. Peacock and Tyson describe how, concerned with not overstepping the boundary between faith in their salvation and (mistaken) assurance about it, they choose their songs carefully: "Amazing Grace" and "Guide Me O Thy Great Jehovah" affirm God's absolute sovereignty and "In Sharon's Lovely Rose" expresses hope of reaching heaven, but "Blessed Assurance, Jesus is Mine" is unacceptable because it presumptuously claims assurance of salvation. In their style, too, they express resignation and modest hope, but avoid the joy that could dangerously approach certainty. Upbeat tempos and complex harmonies are avoided; unison singing in a dignified cadence is preferred. Peacock and Tyson recall the tears running down the cheeks of the congregation while singing; their participation in the service is no less emotional than that of their more animated Pentecostal brethren, but it bespeaks a resigned, stoic attitude in the face of God's great and unknowable will (Peacock and Tyson 1989, 114–118).

Sermons pose two related dilemmas for the preacher. Does one prepare an elaborate sermon and risk the sin of pride, or wait for the Spirit to emerge inside one, and risk incoherence? Does one urge people to perform their duties as Christians and risk strengthening the erroneous idea that doing their duties will win them salvation, or refrain from any exhortations and miss the opportunity to guide them along a righteous path?

Preachers do not, in fact, preach from outlines or notes. To do so would be to insult the "Spirit that bloweth where it listeth." Sermons come from the heart. "If I can't feel that power, I ain't preaching the Gospel. I may stand up there and quote scripture and so on, but it ain't the Gospel," remarked one preacher. For, as Luther and Calvin proclaimed, the Bible is the inspired word that emerges in and through humans, not the dead letter of the written book. It was the word of God that produced the Bible and inspires people today as well. Or does not: an elder may rise to preach and after quoting scripture, sit down when he finds he has nothing to say (Peacock and Tyson 1989, 118–126).

In their sermons preachers strive to avoid implying that religious experience is evidence of salvation or that good works can lead one to salvation. Elder Bradley used a sermon he preached in a North Carolina church to trace his own path. His experience preaching and "saving souls" had led him to think that preaching could bring a person to salvation. He realized his error after revisiting the passage in the Letter to the Romans on election. His sermon reminds us how what appears to be an obvious reason for preaching is indeed in error from the perspective of the doctrine of election, and also how the apparent gloominess of this perspective can be in fact the basis for joy:

Finally came to the conclusion that this which I'd been taught, that salvation was dependent upon men hearing the gospel, repenting of his sins and believing on Jesus, that God was using this the preacher to reach the dead sinner, that this was totally contrary to that which was taught in the word of God, but that this salvation depended upon God's own sovereign pleasure and that he made choice of a people in a covenant before time began. And, oh what a joyful sound it was, and how beautiful it was for me then to see things in that order! To see that God planned this salvation, and if God planned something you can rest assured it's not going to come to naught. That which God has planned will be executed. God declared this salvation before men ever had being in himself. (Peacock and Tyson 1989, 122)

The "sweet meeting" that comforts the soul depends on community: preaching, singing, and eating together makes up what these Baptists call "the visible church." But here enters a difficulty: if your group consists of both the damned and the elect, how can you construct a solid community? Two ideas of community have emerged in the Mountain District, roughly corresponding to the contrast between North Carolina and Virginia churches, and these two ideas have consequences for practices of speaking, singing, and gathering in fellowship.

Two Models of Church Authority

For reasons of topography and modes of livelihood, the churches in North Carolina are dispersed in fields and hills, whereas those in Virginia are located in villages (Peacock and Tyson 1989, 87–117). The North Carolina churches are less well attended than the latter group, and worshipers are more likely to live individualistic lives, usually as independent farmers. Charisma, direct divine inspiration, governs the lives of the elders, and it appears in their sermons, which often recount personal experiences. Songs of stoic resignation, sermons about doctrine, moods of individualism, and antibureaucracy sentiments characterize the North Carolina churches.

In contrast to this individualistic structure and attitude, the Virginia churches have created some degree of bureaucracy, and their elders emphasize organization over charisma. The lives of those attending services are more likely to involve work in government civil service or small businesses (although here, too, many farm). Sermons are more likely to dwell on duty. Singing has changed in some Virginia churches, evolving in the direction of mainline Protestant church singing, with major keys predominating and harmonies explored.

Peacock and Tyson recount how the two groups of churches have come into conflict over their differing ideas of authority and community. The North Carolina churches have favored allowing individual churches and members to go their own ways, as the Spirit moves them. Charisma, the gift of grace from God, dominates. Those in Virginia have stressed the importance of following rules and obeying duly constituted authority.

The contrast surfaced in a dispute during the 1980s about the right of a church to exclude some of its members. Churches do exclude members, and members cannot join other churches. Because members and elders rotate where they worship they can effectively keep out the excluded. In this case, one church excluded a majority of its worshipers on grounds that they had associated with a sinner. They had shown themselves not to be of the elect and so had to be thrown out of the church—much as did the Puritan churches of seventeenth-century New England that we read about earlier. The church is responsible for community as a whole, and must exclude sinners.

But the excluded members then formed their own church and asked to be recognized by the Mountain District. The rule-following Virginia churches supported the exclusions and refused to recognize the new church, because doing so would contradict the righteous authority of the church that had thrown them out. The North Carolina churches supported the right of the members to form a new church. They felt called to do so, and who can say they are mistaken in their calling? (Peacock and Tyson 1989, 71–85).

At issue was not just who makes the rules, but who has access to the Word of God. If the Word of God is given to anyone and everyone, at any time and place and in unpredictable ways, then the worship and preaching of anyone should be recognized and attended to. If an individual is called by God, his or her subsequent actions should be respected. But if the right to provide an authoritative interpretation of scripture is held by those persons capable of correctly reading it, then all others should obey that authority. Here the North Carolina churches stood in favor of the availability of God's word to anyone; the Virginia churches, of the importance of a duly constituted hierarchy based on knowledge and the consent of the community acting as a whole.

This tension about authority and community plagues all Christian movements that attempt to structure themselves around the ultimately unknowable grace of God. The Virginia churches have changed as had the Quakers in 1700, toward hierarchy and a "routinized" authority. The North Carolina churches have resisted this pull.

Charismatic and Pentecostal Churches

Other Christian churches in the same part of the United States have maintained an independent stance but have taken different positions on the question of whether we can perceive and experience signs of our own election or salvation.

Many Fundamentalists, such as those in the Northeast U.S. church studied by Nancy Ammerman (1987) doubt that everyone who claims to be saved is so, and they look for signs of salvation, most importantly some outward, noticeable change in the person's life. They should have given up smoking and drinking. They also should show confidence in the Lord; constant worries are signs they have not yet been saved.

Throughout much of the South, Holiness churches are scattered in hills and towns much as are the Primitive Baptists. Preachers and ordinary people often travel long distances to worship. The focus of worship is on the relationship between the individual and God, as in all the movements we have considered so far. But here the role of rather dramatic signs is paramount, for snake-handling is often part of the service. Surviving a snakebite, or a drink of poison, or an electric shock is a sign of God's grace. The women and men who have been bitten sit together in services as the "true believers," or the "true saints." These signs, having survived, are signs, or "charismata" that are given by the Holy Ghost. They are proofs of Jesus' power to save them; cups of strychnine are called "salvation cocktails" (Covington 1995; La Barre 1964).

One church name says it all: "The Church of Jesus Christ with Signs Following." The phrase is in reference to 16 Mark, a key chapter for worshipers at Holiness churches and for many other churchgoers throughout the South—just as the Primitive Baptists and other believers in particular election take their cue from 9 Romans. In 16 Mark, Jesus appears to his apostles and upbraids them for not believing those who said they saw him risen. He then commands them to go into the world and preach the Gospel, and says:

He who believes and is baptized will be saved;
but he who does not believe will be condemned.
And these signs will accompany those who believe:
in my name they will cast out demons;
they will speak in new tongues;
they will pick up serpents, and if they drink any deadly thing,
    it will not hurt them;
they will lay their hands on the sick,
    and they will recover.

Mark continues to relate that these apostles did indeed go forth and do the work of the Lord, and the Lord confirmed the message "by the signs that attended it" or, in the King James Version, "with signs following." Here ends Mark, and from here derives the name of the Holiness church mentioned above.

The relation of speaking in tongues to salvation is further evidenced in 2 Acts, the second key text for Pentecostal and Charismatic churches. It relates, speaking of the apostles:

When the day of Pentecost had come,
    they were all together in one place.
And suddenly a sound came from heaven like the rush of a mighty wind,
    and it filled all the house where they were sitting.
And there appeared to them tongues as of fire,
    distributed and resting on each one of them.
And they were all filled with the Holy Spirit and began to speak in other tongues,
    as the Spirit gave them utterance.

Because these events took place on the Pentecost (the Greek name for the Jewish Feast of Weeks), religious movements that seek to experience what the apostles did are called Pentecostal, or Charismatic because of the adherents' desire to receive the charismata, the gifts of grace visited upon them by the Holy Spirit. Participants in these movements believe that their own speaking in tongues and ecstatic experiences are signs that they are saved—they have renounced the doubt that plagues those who adhere to particular election, and embrace the idea that anyone may be saved—and yet these signs of salvation are still required.

Perhaps it is the strong need to overcome strong doubt that explains the great lengths to which some worshipers go to prove their salvation to themselves and their fellow worshipers. Some handle snakes; others swallow poison. Snakes may have been chosen precisely for the shock the handling delivers to outsiders. "Spread the Word! We're coming down from the mountains!" announced one preacher. The Holiness churches in which snakes are handled date only from about 1900. As with the Primitive Baptists, the churches value their independence. They are usually scattered throughout rural areas and are visited by a series of preachers. They first practiced snake handling in 1909, in Tennessee. Apparently it was not until 1918 that someone died from snakebite, and he was denounced as a backslider, someone who had lost his faith, when he died (La Barre 1964).

Snakes are typically brought out in their cages part way through the service, after a sermon and singing have taken place. Sometimes music continues, usually on a guitar, and worshipers begin to dance and enter trance states, at which time someone may pick up a snake and handle it before dropping it back into the cage or passing it on to someone else. The handling may take place in a more subdued setting, the snake passed from one person to another. Women and men handle the snakes. Perhaps 20 or more people are known to have died from snakebites in Holiness meetings; some state governments have responded by forbidding the use of poisonous snakes.

The Church of Jesus Christ with Signs Following in Alabama received national attention in 1992, when the church's preacher, Glenn Summerford, was accused of attempting to murder his wife by forcing her to put her hand in a case filled with poisonous rattlesnakes. She claimed he was trying to kill her because he could not divorce her and retain his position in the church. He claimed he did it to prove her innocence and that the snake bit her because she was backsliding. He was convicted and sent to jail, and his church, lacking any institutions for succession, disbanded. Other preachers soon began to hold outdoor snake-handling services, however (Covington 1995, 1–63).

But snake-handling is just the most spectacular (at least to date) of a wide range of practices intended to bear witness to the divine presence within oneself. It is itself the most visible sign of the powerful need to bear witness in a striking and public way to God's grace, to the presence of the Holy Spirit in oneself.

Much more widespread than snake handling are practices of speaking in tongues. Even the relatively staid Lutheran churches of suburban St. Paul, Minnesota (near where I grew up), have begun to encourage members to speak in tongues. Some report a sense of release and of grace as the incomprehensible words flow out of them. They do not speak of the experience as like a trance, but as an experience over which they have some control.

Charismatic movements are growing within Roman Catholicism as well, and in 1981 John Paul II met with Charismatic church leaders and gave his approval to their movement. Worldwide anywhere from 50 to 75 million Catholics can be considered to be Charismatic. And Pentecostal churches are growing rapidly throughout the world, particularly in South America and Southeast Asia. In Brazil, where Umbanda and Macumba had become popular as supplements or alternatives to Catholicism, many are finding that Charismatic churches that focus worship on God but offer the opportunity to speak in tongues combine the best of both worlds.

All these movements are seen by participants as bringing the divine into themselves through the mediation of the Holy Ghost. The religious experience provides a material sign that God has accepted the worshiper and that he or she can hope or know of salvation. This particular emphasis on the individual's avenue to grace through personal experience—often spoken experience—is a key characteristic of Protestantism. The individual's relation to God through the inspired Word is markedly different from the idea that contact with God is through the miracle of the Eucharist, itself mediated by the priest. Protestantism relocated God's miracles, his charismata, signs of grace, from communion and the icons of Mary and Jesus, to the individual's ways of speaking. Doing so made possible new forms of community and authority based on those ways of speaking, of which the churches discussed here are but a few instances.

In the religious traditions we discussed in this chapter—Islam, Navajo, Protestant—speech is linked to power through the individual. The speaker who speaks truly and clearly is able to do so because of a relationship with the divine. This relationship is complex and debated, but across religious traditions an idea emerges that sacred speech, in its utterance, places the speaker in contact with the divine. Reciting the Qur'ân is repeating God's own words and can confer power on the speaker. Chanting Blessingway reenacts the events of creation that accompanied the first chanting by the First People. For some Protestants, a true worship service requires speaking in a holy way—in tongues, or when called by the Holy Spirit to preach, or when reading from the Bible in a state of inspiration. This inspirited speaking is in some respects the equivalent of the worshiper's contact with an image—the drawing in of power through an "exchange of vision" with a Hindu statue is probably the closest equivalent. Catholic, Hindu, Japanese, and other traditions also rely on prayer for worship, of course. But the traditions studied in this chapter have taken the spoken element of worship and made it into the privileged element. When this is done—and it is done in different ways in each tradition—the subjective state of the individual also becomes a matter of increased concern. If an object is the center of worship, its objective qualities—its separation from the worshiper—give the process of worship an air if not a doctrine of objectivity: the worship succeeds if certain steps are taken. The Catholic mass is objectively efficacious even if the priest or the worshipers have their minds elsewhere. But once the words uttered by the worshiper become the whole of worship, those daydreamings endanger the very idea of worship. "Thought is the inner form of speech," say the Navajo; "no actions are effective without the correct intention" echo Muslims. Speech is close to thought, or ought to be, and words uttered must be accompanied by the proper state of mind if they are to reach their destination. Subjectivity now takes center stage.

Profile

Gregory Starrett carried out fieldwork on Islamic education in Cairo in the late 1980s and continues to work on that topic in the United States. The results of the Cairo work are described in his 1998 book, *Putting Islam to Work: Education, Politics, and Religious Transformation in Egypt* (University of California Press).

When anthropologist Michael Gilsenan first arrived in Cairo in the mid-1960s, he was struck with a sense of hopelessness, for there seemed no place *small enough* in the bustling city to do fieldwork. Sprawling, crowded, and more interconnected than ever, Cairo, like all the world's great cities, presents a dilemma for the anthropologist, who has been trained to think about fieldwork as a web of face-to-face contacts in an intimate community. There are ways to approximate that intimacy in a city: choose a small neighborhood, a school, a factory as a field site. But for some projects—looking at national political symbols, large-scale religious change, or nearly any element of public culture—traditional techniques can lose sight of the forest for the trees.

Arriving in Cairo in 1988, I intended to collect life-history data in order to find out why Egyptians with similar social and educational backgrounds became attracted to very different sorts of political movements: communist, liberal, and Islamist. I soon found that I was doing a kind of "appointment anthropology" instead of hanging out with small groups to participant-observe. Middle-class Egyptians are just as busy with work and family as middle-class Americans and have little time to humor the odd anthropologist's persistent, naive, and intrusive inquiries. With my attention scattered between different individuals, different neighborhoods, and different workplaces, I had to introduce myself, my project, and my needs anew to each interview subject. There was no group through which news of who I was could spread (usefully, even if inaccurately) by gossip. Furthermore, it was widely assumed that my university—or the American government, who was funding the work—had chosen the topic for me, making the project politically suspect.

Daily life was complicated by the fact that although I defined myself as a long-term resident and would-be "insider" trying to learn the language and culture, ordinary people on the street perceived me as a "tourist" ready to buy things—perfume, tours, and souvenirs—from them. The target of constant sales pitches and occasional attempts at proselytizing, I tried to find ways to appear less foreign. So I grew a beard (a sign of Islamist political sympathy on Egyptians, but not necessarily on foreigners, and thus ambiguous enough to be effective but not dishonest), and carried a copy of one of the local Arabic language newspapers with me wherever I went. These tactics reduced daily annoyances, and were often taken as an outward sign of familiarity and sympathetic interest in Egyptian concerns.

Ironically, my fieldwork a few years later at an African American mosque in the United States was far more traditional. Each week I attend Sunday school classes for children and adults. Sitting at the table, listening to discussions and lessons and answering questions when called on by teachers and imams, I was finally participant-observing! Because I could read and speak Arabic, I was happy to help the children with learning their Arabic alphabet. But because I was familiar in general with Islam and had lived in

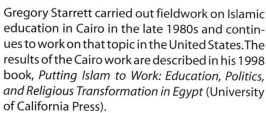

Egypt, some of the newer adult students asked me questions about Muslim theology and ritual practice. I was in a quandary. Not being Muslim, I didn't feel I could appropriately answer—I was, among other things, unfamiliar with the details of this particular group's understandings and expectations—even though as a university professor and educator specializing in Islam, some reasonably expected me to have unambiguous information about their own spiritual practices. So whereas in Egypt I was uncomfortable with the perception that I was either wholly ignorant or necessarily hostile towards Islam, in the United States I became uncomfortable with the perception that I knew or should share more than I did. Whether abroad or at home, the anthropologist's ambiguous position can be a practical liability as well as an intellectual strength.

Doing fieldwork is as much a matter of the ethnographer's own background and expectations as it is about things going on in the field. As Nigel Barley has pointed out, a complex West African system of ancestor veneration might not seem interesting to a Japanese Buddhist anthropologist who keeps a shrine to his dead parents in his living room and carries about a piece of his dead father's leg bone wrapped in a white cloth. What's so unusual?

About midway through my fieldwork in Cairo, I came to the realization that I was dreadfully, desperately bored. Despite having been attracted to the study of Islam as an undergraduate through the almost hallucinatory esoteric journeys of Sufi mystical texts, and then living for months in one of the oldest and most dynamic capitals in the Middle East, it suddenly struck me that there was nothing at all interesting, nothing really *anthropological*, about my research. Here I was, reading and talking to people about the same jealous Semitic God, the same indignant prophets, the same angels and sins and patriarchal sensibilities familiar from my Christian cultural background. Hardly very inspiring, especially for a discipline where, as a British colleague later put it, "people's eyes light up at the news of people with five souls."

But the boredom was a healthy sign. It meant Egypt felt familiar enough that I no longer recognized it as exotic, and I could think in a different way about similarities and contrasts, particularly those that showed how people were altering their religious practices in the face of a rapidly changing world. Still five years before the World Wide Web hit America, I became entranced by the way some Egyptians were adding interactive graphic user interfaces to their religious literature: by producing, for example, Islamic-themed board games and coloring books (and, later, computer software) for children. The use of drawings in a religious tradition historically suspicious of representational art in religious contexts, and of Western textbook conventions in an educational system historically centered on the rote memorization of sacred texts, led me to reflect on the power of the marketplace and the modern school in the reproduction as well as the transformation of Islam. At that time, few people had examined such developments because they were neither traditional in form (as we expect elements of religion to be) nor secular in content (as we tend to expect of "modern" communication forms). ⟨ᔐ⟩

For Further Consideration

One way to initiate comparative discussions about religions is to construct analogies—always engaging even if sometimes misleading. The theologian Wilfred Cantwell Smith suggests that Jesus is to Catholicism what the Qur'ân is to Islam: God's major gift to his people. Could you extend the sequence? What is the Torah to Judaism? What is the power to create through language to the Navajo? What is the analogous power invested in masks to the Dogon?

Or try the game with practices, as I do at the close of this chapter, where I suggest that inspired or inspirited speaking for Protestants is the equivalent of Hindu darshan, in that both represent points of contact between the person and divinity. What would be the best equivalent point of contact for other traditions?

William Graham's *Beyond the Written Word* (Cambridge University Press 1987) offers a very insightful discussion of "oral dimensions of scripture" in several religious traditions. Jack Goody's several books on the subject, for example his short book, *The Domestication of the Savage Mind* (Cambridge University Press 1977), discuss the relationship between means of expression (particularly oral and written) and ways of thinking.

For more on Islam, see the two introductory books by Fred Denny: a lengthy, very good one, *An Introduction to Islam* (Macmillan 1985), and a shorter one, *Islam* (Harper & Row 1987). Richard Antoun's *Muslim Preacher in the Modern World* (Princeton University Press 1989), on Jordan, shows in detail how a preacher works in matters of local community concern together with scriptural references, as does Patrick Gaffney's *The Prophet's Pulpit* (University of California Press 1994), on Egypt.

Some ideas for projects: you might consider taping a sermon, or a testimony ("witnessing"), or any other religious event, and asking of the material, why did the speaker speak in precisely these ways? Some of the aforementioned books can be taken as examples of how to do this method of analysis.

Transmitting Religion

*P*eople not only engage in religious practices and think and talk about religious ideas, they also transmit these ideas and practices to their successors—their children, students, disciples, and other adherents. Part of this transmission process involves communicating religious ideas about what exists in the world, a "religious ontology," along with teachings, scriptures, and histories. Another part of the process, perhaps even more important, is instructing others how to carry out certain practices in precisely the right way. This instruction involves a basic knowledge of religious ideas—you have to know what the spirits are in order to make sacrifices to them or rid sick people of them—but may not require much more. Finally, transmitting religion surely also means getting others to take it seriously. Taking it seriously may be a matter of belief or faith (often so in Christianity and Islam), though it might be more a matter of thinking that if you don't sacrifice a chicken on a particular day, calamities will result, or that you must perform a complex series of initiation rituals as an important part of being a member of a particular group.

A good deal of what we looked at in the last three chapters had a lot to do with transmission. Ritual objects not only provide a cognitive and emotional focus for a religious ritual, they also convince people that what is happening has a kind of reality to it. Religious speaking, singing, and reading brings people into the religious community or strengthens their sense of being part of it. Children (and converts) learn how to "do" religion, and why they should, by participating in these activities. The sources of felt power in religion that we have explored earlier also help explain why and how it is that these ideas and practices survive across generations.

Religious ideas and practices change as much as they are reproduced. As we saw in Chapter 10 people change what they have learned as times change; they adapt and translate their religious ideas. But ideas and practices may also change in the very process of transmission, as people improvise, make mistakes, or select among available ideas, as we will see in more detail.

Improvisation and Variation

*L*et's start by looking at a highly guarded secret rite known to a very few men in a small New Guinea society. Fredrik Barth (1987) studied initiation rituals in the Mountain Ok area of western highland New Guinea. He found that even within a small society each ritual expert had his own ideas about how to carry out the rituals. There were also sharp contrasts in symbolism and rituals between neighboring societies: for example, in the rituals carried out by the Bimin-Kuskusmin people, red paint stands for the virility of the wild male boar and is associated with the final stages of male initiation. But in a nearby society, the Baktaman (where Barth did most of his fieldwork), red is associated with female menstruation. People from one society would be, and indeed were, shocked at the rituals and the meanings found in the other. They do know about each other's practices from visiting each other's societies and, after their initial shock, sometimes borrowing elements of ritual.

Barth argues that these variations are the result of the way in which ritual knowledge is transmitted. One individual teaches another how to carry out each of the initiation rites; often, it is a father who teaches a son. This knowledge is not widely shared, nor are the rituals repeated frequently. Barth describes one initiation ritual that is held only once every 10 years and is limited to men who have already passed through several grades of initiation. During the decade between each performance of this ritual, men might attend similar rituals in neighboring societies. Men who were about to perform the ritual would have to try to remember how a performance was conducted ten years earlier and how elders had instructed them in proper procedure. Barth suggests that although these men say they faithfully transmit the ritual from the ancestors to the present generation, considerable improvisation and borrowing must occur.

Barth points to several specific ways that the meanings of objects in rituals are changed as the ritual knowledge is transmitted. One is based on the "multivocality" of symbols, the fact that many objects can have multiple associations (see also Turner 1969). In the Ok region, for example, water is associated with cold temperatures, with cleansing, the removal of properties, and also with spontaneous generation (from the perception of morning dew appearing as if from nowhere). People might highlight one of these associations at the expense of another. Barth believes that ritual change sometimes occurs when a practitioner highlights, for example, "water as cold" over "water as cleansing." His counterpart in a neighboring society, who may have received roughly the same ritual objects and instructions, might instead make water a cleansing rather than a cooling object in his own version of the ritual. And, indeed, Barth finds the kind of variation among neighboring societies one would expect when objects have multiple associations.

This New Guinea example could stand for many instances of "oral transmission," or the handing down of texts, ideas, and practices by word of mouth from one individual to another and from one generation to the next. The example also illuminates two common features of oral transmission. The first is that people try to make an *exact copy* of the original by learning, remembering, and recreating it. The second is that, in trying to copy the original text or ritual they frequently change it, and if more than one line of transmission is involved these changes lead to *variation*.

Much of what we learn is through seeing what others do and say. The Baktaman ritual specialist Barth describes had watched his father perform a ritual and he had heard him explain why he did each step in the ritual. He had also watched other specialists in neighboring settlements perform rituals said to be the same or similar. Out of all this watching and listening he had (he undoubtedly hoped) absorbed enough knowledge to be able to put together a ritual himself.

In my own fieldwork with the Gayo of highland Sumatra, I watched several specialists in rice ritual and healing magic perform their art. I discussed with some of them how they had learned to do what they did. In all cases, they had watched an older person, sometimes a close relative, carry out these important activities. The learners also asked questions about how to do this or that. Often, and usually late at night, they would explore together the thoughts behind the ritual: how you could tell which spirit was causing an illness; why it was you had the power to make it leave a patient. Some practitioners had little interest in the theory, wanting only the practical knowledge.

From younger apprentices talking with older practitioners came a transmission of knowledge in this Gayo society. Learning about a certain spirit's power came up only in the context of figuring out how to rid the patient of that spirit. Ideas about what God will allow healers to do, if explored at all, were also discussed in this manner. Elsewhere I have explored at length how one healer's ideas about God sending back harmful spirits to their malevolent senders reveal the influence of sixteenth-century religious thinkers (Bowen 1993). The healer's ideas were not transmitted as part of theological treatise, however, but as a means to understand the powers of a healer. And they were not transmitted to everyone. One healer, Abang Kerna, had a rather lengthy version of these ideas about God's powers; others had partial theories consistent with this one; others had no theories at all, just a robust sense of what works and what does not.

In this example, the healers' religious knowledge is anchored to specific practices, relevant only as a means of understanding those practices, and of concern only to some healers. The ideas are thus highly contextualized in the process of learning how to heal. Because there are no public contexts where various theories are compared and critiqued, many greatly varying ideas about God and evil and the reasons for illness can coexist in this society and be transmitted over generations.

New Age "Channeling"

*I*n the examples of the Baktaman and their New Guinea highlands neighbors and the Sumatran Gayo discussed so far, social norms governing how ideas are performed and transmitted determine the possibilities for their variation. Even in these fairly small-scale societies a great deal of improvisation and change takes place. Barth suggests what some of the mechanisms for that change might be; conversely, the absence of regulating institutions, and the absence of a norm of public accountability allows change and variation to persist and be passed on to subsequent generations.

A radically different social context is New Age America, in which a great deal of improvisation and variation is not only allowed but encouraged, and in which a particular idea about transmission has taken hold. The term *New Age* refers to contemporary religious movements in Europe and North America that emphasize individual self-realization, a harmonious relationship with the natural world, and an exploration of both non-Western religious traditions and pre–Christian European ones. New Age movements include card reading, dowsing, crystal healing, and other practices that challenge conventional American ideas of religion (Brown 2000).

New Age movements are the latest in a history of American efforts to improve oneself through religious practices. In the early nineteenth century Methodism achieved enormous popularity by promising its adherents self-perfection and salvation. Today, Christian Science and self-healing books claim to be spiritual companions to medical science. Many New Age movements go beyond perfecting and healing the self to emphasize communication with spirits, which also has deep American roots. In Chapter 7 we noted that in seventeenth-century Salem being possessed by the devil, a very bad thing, was uncannily similar to being possessed by the Holy Spirit, a good thing. It all depended on how the religious authorities of the day interpreted the events. We also saw that possession, unusual speech behavior, and transcendant religious experience continue within contemporary Pentecostalism through practices of glossalalia or "speaking in tongues." New Age movements add some new elements, including a search for sacred places that are centers of energy, often the very same sites considered sacred by native North Americans.

The social organization of New Age religious movements ranges from loose networks and fissiparous small groups to cults, such as Scientology (if one places it in this general category) or the lesser-known Church Universal and Triumphant (CUT) under Guru Ma (Elizabeth Clare Prophet), a cult formed around the charisma of the leader. The apocalyptic message of some New Age leaders can be translated into survivalist actions, as in the case of the CUT, which in the late 1980s stockpiled assault rifles and armored personnel carriers in anticipation of the imminent end of the world (Brown 1997, 126–129).

New Age has also introduced "channeling," seances where humans give voice to ideas and experiences of the long-dead or sometimes the inhabitants of other worlds. For several years in the early 1990s, Michael F. Brown studied channeling. He begins his account by describing the ability of West Coast channeler J. Z. Knight to bring to life the prehistoric man Ramtha. Ramtha delivers messages from another age, which already is sufficient to attract the curious, but he also predicts that, after floods and earthquakes, the world will soon enter a new era in which humans will realize their true potential. He promises that classical American dream, individual self-perfection.

Women are drawn to channeling for the possibilities it offers for imagining other ways of life. Typically, women serve as spirit mediums more often than men across cultures. Brown found that channeling tended to emphasize androgyny, a mixing of male and female elements, in contrast to the women-only emphasis of many Wiccan groups.

Like shamanism and earlier forms of spiritualism, channeling offers direct communication with sources of truth. Distinctive of channeling are the enormous gaps in time and space involved: men or women from thousands of years ago and alien creatures are the commonly invoked speakers. Some channelers enter a trance or trance-like state, a feature which lends them greater credibility and may also increase the attractiveness of the experience for channelers seeking altered states of consciousness. Others operate much less dramatically. Brown describes Bay Area channelers, David and Sarah, with links to spiritual beings called, collectively, "Michael." They work by means of "conscious channeling," which involves the merest hesitations in speech between talking-as-David and talking-as-Michael (Brown 1997, 33–37).

The conscious channelers see themselves as tapping into wisdom shared by everyone—in a sense bringing their own intuition to the fore. In contrast, trance channelers see themselves as relaying messages from a distinct self. We can see these two types of channeling as bringing into this specific practice two distinct streams of American religiosity: the drive for self-perfection, as when the conscious channeler adds intuition to other thought processes, and the contact with spirits.

In their messages to listeners, channelers sometimes borrow ideas from other religions. In the morally relativistic context of the channeling world—everyone doing their own spiritual thing—karma, the idea that some actions will bring about later retribution (either in this or another life), serves as a plausible source of morality, and is particularly attractive because of its non-Western source.

Transmission and Religious Universals

Thinking about the transmission of religious ideas has informed ethnographic and experimental studies of human cognitive processes and has revived an "intellectualist" approach to the anthropology of religion. This approach views religious ideas as the answers individuals pose to vexing questions: Why are there dreams? What is it that leaves at death, and what happens to it? Why is there misfortune, or evil? We can trace this approach back to the work of E. B. Tylor (1970) in the late nineteenth century. It is usually opposed to a "sociological" approach, most closely identified with the sociologist Émile Durkheim, that sees religion as growing out of social life (see Chapter 4).

Recent work that draws from cognitive science offers a theory about the transmission of religious ideas that also claims to explain why we have the particular sets of religious ideas we do have. The cognitive theories resemble earlier intellectualist ones, except that they put the question not in terms of the *origins* of religious ideas but rather in terms of their *transmission*. These theories look like intellectualist ones, that is, they explain religious ideas in terms of operations of the mind, but they are also sociological ones, because they base that explanation on our long-term human experience as social beings. (They are not "sociobiological" theories because they do not posit any specific genetic mechanisms to explain their findings.)

For example, Pascal Boyer (2000, 2001) suggests that we have to explain not just why we have religious ideas, but why we have *these* ideas and not another possible set. He argues that answers will come from knowledge about the ways our minds work. Over the long haul of human experience, he continues, humans would have proposed many ideas about spirits, unseen lands, and mystical causation. Human minds would have found some of these ideas attractive, useful, and relevant to everyday social life and others much less so. They would have retained the former and discarded the latter. In other words, religions are as they are because of selection processes, similar in logic (though not in the precise mechanisms) to those of natural selection in the biological realm.

The selectionist argument begins by noting that spirits resemble humans except for a few differences. For example, consider the following possible ideas about spirits proposed by Boyer (2001, 64–67):

1. *There is only one God! He is omnipotent. But He only exists on Wednesdays.*
2. *The spirits will punish you if you do what they want.*

3. *Some people get old and one day they stop breathing and die and that's that.*
4. *Dead men do not talk (nor walk).*

5. *There is only one God! He knows everything we do.*
6. *We pray to this statue because it listens to our prayers and helps us get what we want.*

Boyer points out that everyone reading this list has an intuition that the first two propositions are bad candidates for religious ideas even though they are about spirits and God; the second two are also bad candidates because they are banal; and the third two are good candidates. Why do we have these intuitions? What precisely is it about them that makes the first two pairs not work and the third pair work as candidates for religious principles? It cannot be that religious ideas are strange or that they "transcend experience," because the first statements also do that, and in any case the people who do pray to statues would say that proposition 6 is very much part of their experience.

Boyer argues that religious representations always preserve certain of our expectations about how the world works and they violate certain, quite specific, other ones. In particular, they preserve expectations about the kind of object the religious object is. The statue that listens is a statue in all respects (it was made by someone, could be destroyed, does not multiply on its own) except that it can also listen to people praying and then relay that information somewhere (or directly grant requests). Gods and spirits are like human beings except that they have special cognitive powers (such as knowing everything that happens) or other powers (such as superhuman strength or speed).

These ideas correspond to the way we think about the world generally. We know the world as consisting of certain kinds of things: persons; artifacts ("things that are made"); animals; trees, and so on. We know many features of each kind. Animals are born and they die; they reproduce; they eat. Artifacts do none of those things; they are made. Each of these kinds has a number of subkinds (artifacts made of wood, or of paper, etc.; animals that are mammals; those that are fish, etc.). These kinds serve as templates for making sense of the world as we learn more about it. When we learn of a new object in the world, a new subkind—say, a human with extraordinary strength, or a two-headed cow—we are able to infer a lot about that new object based on our "template knowledge." We infer from the fact that the two-headed object is a kind of cow that it will have the usual properties of animals, and indeed of cows: that it will reproduce, live and die, eat, and so forth.

Religious ideas add new objects to our existing list, and we understand them by associating them with a particular template. If a spirit or god is a kind of person, but with some unusual characteristics, then saying that it can travel with great speed still allows us to infer a great many other things about that spirit: that it remembers things, that its existence is ongoing, that it perceives things, and so forth. But to say that it exists only on Wednesdays frustrates our normal processes of inference. Could it then remember or even exist in any sense we can understand? Experimental evidence confirms the claim that ideas like a Wednesday-only god are relatively difficult for subjects to recall, whereas all-powerful or all-knowing gods are not.

The reasons proposition 2 fails as a religious idea are a bit different, having to do with the processes by which ideas are adopted and transmitted across generations. We could certainly imagine especially sadistic spirits telling us to do things and then punishing us for doing them, but why would we adopt and transmit such an idea? What humans in fact do, claim Boyer and others, is to work from our moral intuitions, which recent work in developmental psychology shows to be quite basic. "Basic" here means that children and adults think of some actions as being right or wrong in themselves. Boyer argues that we have developed these intuitions as predispositions toward cooperation. For example, we feel outraged when people break in line, even if it is not our line, because they have violated certain rules of social cooperation.

Boyer (2001, 237–240) contends that we then impute moral opinions similar to these intuitions to gods and spirits, with whom we interact, treating their intuitions as similar to ours. We also resent spirits in ways similar to the ways we resent humans. For example, witches may be seen as models of how one should not behave: as beings who act on jealousy, who take but never give, and so on.

The idea that it is our social lives as well as our minds' mechanisms that shape our religious representations also helps to explain other ways we refer to spirits and gods in practice. We may say that God is omnipotent or that he knows everything, but in practice we represent such beings as using their powers in ways that are most relevant to us. People do not think of God as knowing the contents of all the refrigerators in the world at all times, although that is implied by "all-knowing" (Boyer 2000, 207). Rather, people think of God as knowing our thoughts, that is, the ones that pertain to social interaction such as lies, desires, and intents. In other words, God (and gods and spirits generally) know the same sorts of things that we ourselves take into account when we act in society, when we judge the actions of others, and when we judge our own conduct.

This account of religion, then, is based on certain hypotheses about what we are most likely to acquire as children and pass on to others when we are adults. The major mechanism proposed in this account is what we can call *selective retention*; that is, selecting some of the ideas proliferating in a society for transmission to the next generation. The account is analogous to one proposed by Charles Darwin in order to explain the diversity of species and, like Darwin's, it depends on there being a source of variation. In accounts of biological evolution the variation comes from mutations, changes in the genetic code from one generation to the next. In accounts of cultural evolution the variation could come from a number of sources, including error in transmitting ideas (think of the "telephone game"), adaptive pressures, and sheer human inventiveness.

Mimesis and Performance

*B*oyer's concern is with the ways that the content of religious ideas determines the likelihood of their being passed on to the next generation. But the transmission of religious ideas and practices also has a lot to do with (a) how widely they are known and (b) in what form they are stored. The ways in which a Muslim is to perform the key ritual of worship, *salat*, is memorized by millions of Muslims worldwide, and it is written down in books, recorded on cassettes, and depicted on Web sites. There are thus multiple ways of checking to see that the ritual is performed in the same way in different places and from one generation to the next. The possibilities for mutation are thus severely restricted.

People who pass on stories, spells, prayers, and similar kinds of knowledge to others usually see themselves as faithfully reproducing an original text. They are helped in their task by the use of *formulas* in texts. These formulas may be set items that are frequently repeated, or they may be structuring devices, such as the use of parallel lines. Consider, for example, an epic chanted by the people of Roti, an island in eastern Indonesia, as recorded by James Fox (1975):

> *The dogs form a pack*
> > *and the hounds join as one*
> *They track civet*
> > *and they hunt pig*
> *Deep in the woods of Kai Tio*
> > *and deep in the forests of Lolo Batu*
> *The dogs corner their prey*
> > *and the hounds give chase.*

Even from this brief excerpt one can instantly grasp that dog/hounds, civet/pig, and Kai Tio/Lolo Batu form pairs, and one suspects that they will be repeated in much the same way throughout the epic. (They are.) The pairings help the chanter remember the epic: where there is civet, there will next be pig. Sometimes the pairs are simple semantic equivalents, as in dogs and hounds, and sometimes their pairing carries meaning. Pigs and civets are proper objects of sacrifice, for example, when killed together; a different pair, such as cat and civet, would not be. The use of roughly equivalent verbal structures like "form a pack" and "join as one" allows the chanter to make two lines out of one idea.

These and other parallel forms surely help in remembering texts, but they also assist in producing new texts that are recognized as culturally appropriate. The technique is found worldwide. It is basic to the prophetic sections of the Hebrew Bible:

> *They shall beat their swords into ploughshares*
> > *and their spears into pruning hooks*
> *Nation shall not lift up sword against nation*
> > *neither shall they learn war any more (RSV Isaiah 2:4).*

Parallel forms are also used in sermons to encourage the silent or vocal participation of the congregation. Richard Bauman (1983, 76–78) studied the sermons of the Quaker leader George Fox and found that he made extensive use of parallel constructions for this purpose. In one sermon from 1674 one finds the following kind of phrasing:

This is known
as everyone hath received Christ Jesus
*   so walk in him*
there is the gospel order that is the power of God
*   which was before the Devil was*
which brings life and immortality to light
*   the power of God the gospel brings into life*
now in this power in this gospel is the order
*   the everlasting order of the gospel*
which is a mystery.

It is easy to see from even this brief passage not only how Fox employs parallel constructions, but how he repeats familar phrases, building up a general sense and sentiment of "gospel–life–order." Fox also uses the same phrases in subsequent sermons, so that those attending the services would have been ready for the phrases as they came and would have felt they were participating in them.

The use of familiar phrases in parallel structure not only eases the delivery of the stories and sermons, but also makes it possible for others to learn, if not the precise texts, the rules of their production and the grammar underlying each of them. English preachers, Hebrew prophets, or Rotinese tellers of epics could pass on their repertoires to a new generation simply by frequent repetition, always following the same structure.

Some religious practitioners do, of course, place emphasis on the exact copying of texts (spells, stories, prayers, revelations). The Mountain Ok ritual specialists mentioned earlier thought that they were doing this, although their methods of transmission ensured that there would be a great deal of change over time and therefore also variation across space. Other specialists, elsewhere, have created mimetic techniques to try to exactly replicate a text. Greg Urban (1991, 106–107, 126) describes one style with which the Shokleng of Brazil tell or teach their origin myth. The teller produces one syllable of the story, which is repeated by the learner. The teller then says the second syllable, which is again repeated. This teaching-through-dialogue is sending a social message about the coordinated social production of meaning as well as teaching or telling a story. (The story could be told in other styles.)

Probably no set of copying methods is more complex than that followed in India for certain religious texts. The Vedas, the major collection of religious texts for Hindus, must be told, heard, and transmitted without change. Indeed, they are referred to collectively as *sruti*, "that which is heard," as opposed to other, later texts called "that which is remembered," *smrti*.

The oldest of the Vedas date from the second millenium B.C.E. and they have been passed down, generation after generation, through memorization and recitation. Certain Brahman castes specialize in chanting Vedic texts in a way that ensures an exact replication. Each text is memorized in more than one way, much as a proofreader will recite a text backwards so as to focus on the replication of the letters rather than the misleading "sense" of a text. A reciter will memorize the text first in its normal word order and sound, and then a second time without the usual connections between words (as if in English one were to turn all contractions into full forms). On a third occasion the reciter says each word as a pair with the next, and then makes a pair with the second and third words, and so on, in an *ab bc cd* form. It is as if in English one were to move from "John's hit Sam," to "John has hit Sam," to "John has, has hit, hit Sam." In subsequent stages the reciter inverts the pairs ("John has, has John"), doubles the inversions, and so forth, making a possible 11 modes of memorization and recitation (Graham 1987, 72).

One might think that writing and printing would be regarded as a blessing for those concerned with the precise transmission of the Vedas. But remember: they are "that which is heard"; and so the sounds of the texts are the appropriate channel of transmission. The texts may also be written, but in the context of Hindu religion, writing is a second-order channel of communication.

The Qur'ân, Again

Let us consider one particular text, the Qur'ân, in its journey through different modes of transmission. In the previous chapter I underscored the understanding among Muslims that the Qur'ân is a collection of God's words, revealed to the Prophet Muhammad by the archangel Gabriel and then recited by him to others. Indeed, the first revelation began with the command to "Recite!"—a fact often repeated by Muslim and non-Muslim scholars to emphasize that the Qur'ân consisted of oral revelations to Muhammad along with the command that he repeat them to others. The very word *qur'ân* means *reciting*. Each revelation was a chapter (*surah*), consisting of a number of verses (*ayah*). Some chapters are very short; some are very long. As he heard a chapter, Muhammad would recite it to his followers. Each chapter came at a particular moment, and some of them were quite clearly interventions in particular issues of the day. For example, God told Muhammad to realign his worship practices away from Judaism at the moment of conflict with the Jews; at other moments God drew lessons from victory or loss in battle. Repeating such chapters was part of instructing and encouraging Muhammad's followers to continue their fight.

And yet there is another story to be told even at this early point in the Qur'ân's history. The Qur'ân refers to itself as a written, or fixed, book (*kitâb maktûb*), sent down by God to humans in oral form mainly because, had he chosen to simply send the book, "those who do not have faith would say, 'Truly, this is nothing but obvious magic' (Qur'ân 56, 77–80; 6:7)." From this perspective, the oral form of the Qur'ân was a strategic choice made by God. Muslims generally agree that there is such a book in God's hands; disagreements have generally been only about whether the book is eternal or created at a particular moment by God. God had sent down other books before the Qur'ân, namely, the Torah, the Psalms, and the Gospels. The phrase "people of the book" (*ahl al-kitâb*) refers to the Jewish and Christian recipients of those books and indicates their special status as worshipers of the same God.

Those who heard Muhammad recite either committed the recitations to memory or wrote them down. When Uthmân, the third caliph (ruled 644–656 C.E.), tried to create a standard version, he did not assemble the available written versions of each chapter; rather, he brought together the men who had memorized verses upon hearing them directly from Muhammad. In other words, oral transmission held more authority than did written (Graham 1987, 81–95). Oral precedence was partly for technical reasons, in that the written Qur'ân does not have all the vowel markings necessary to determine the precise sense and sound of the verses. In other words, it is only when recited that the verses are complete. But the oral precedence also was and is because the path of transmission—from Gabriel, to Muhammad, to his immediate followers, to the entire Muslim community—is ideally through hearing, remembering, and reciting. In this respect the ideology of transmission for the Qur'ân resembles that for the early Vedas.

Divergent paths of oral transmission continued even after the creation of a standard written text. During the next two centuries they were nourished and developed in different centers of learning and by the third century after Muhammad were recognized as seven authentic ways of transmitting the Qur'ân (Graham 1987, 99–100). When, in Egypt in the 1910s and 1920s, a standard text was produced, it was done not by comparing written versions but by assembling acknowledged authorities in reciting the Qur'ân, just as Uthmân had done many centuries earlier. And, although calligraphic inscriptions of Qur'ânic verses are a prized art form, it is through memorizing and reciting that a young Muslim boy or girl shows that he or she has learned the Qur'ân.

On to Audio

Given this preference for aural and oral modes of transmission, it is not surprising that audiocassettes would be received as a highly, perhaps uniquely, suitable medium for transmitting Islamic knowledge. The Qur'ân should be learned and passed on in a highly precise way. "Precision" means a way of reciting it aloud. Therefore, the written book itself does not serve as a medium of transmission, but a sort of *aide-mémoire*, a useful object to help a living Muslim to teach another living Muslim how to recite. One could, theologically speaking, do without it entirely. Pedagogically speaking, one might be better off with no written Qur'ân. Audiocassettes offer the possibility of listening to correct recitation and practicing it. Throughout the Muslim world one finds cassettes of the Qur'ân, as well as cassettes of sermons, lessons, commentaries, and so forth, in taxis, in the homes of the poor and the rich, in the mosques and the prayer-houses, and in the fields during the planting seasons.

Dale Eickelman (1999) points out that in many parts of the Muslim world, cassettes have begun to replace pamphlets and books as the main vehicle for religious debates. Not only does the cassette have certain practical advantages (you can listen while driving your taxi, for example), but it, or rather the the event it re-presents to the listener, has a religious quality absent from the written page. The cassette has also allowed religious figures to to circulate their sermons and lessons widely without transcribing them.

Consider the current mode of operation of the highest religious authority in Oman, the *mufti*. In the late 1980s, the mufti of Oman preferred to give comments on contemporary affairs in the form of a "lesson" (*dars*), a religious genre of speech in which the authority talks about a particular problem. Lessons are given in small prayer houses or in large halls throughout the Muslim world. The Oman mufti's lessons are recorded on cassettes, which are then circulated to Omanis living outside their country. Sometimes they are transcribed as well. Omanis refer to these recorded lessons to explain their particular brand of Islam to outsiders (Eickelman 1992).

As a mufti, like his counterparts in other Muslim societies, he is also supposed to respond to questions posed to him by rulers or by ordinary people. Each such response, called a *fatwa,* carries the authority of the mufti's office and, even though it has no legal weight in the strict sense of the term, may be very influential among policy makers and ordinary Muslims. In most Muslim societies some fatwas are published, but the Oman mufti prefers to give his responses orally, transmitting them in cassette form. Eickelman (1992, 648–649) reports that on one cassette the mufti responds to a question from an Omani student living in the United States. The student complains that non–Omani Muslims he encounters criticize his beliefs, and asks the mufti for clarification. The mufti also has a regular radio program. Recorded sermons circulate throughout the Arabic world. During the Gulf War of 1990, recorded sermons expressing a variety of views circulated widely, and the preachers recorded on these cassettes showed their own familiarity with the mass media, invoking "such sources as the memoirs of Richard Nixon, the Voice of America, the *Financial Times,* CNN, the writings of George Bush, and contemporary Arab periodicals . . ." (Eickelman 1999, 37).

Replication/ Performance

In many religions one finds complementarity between *replication* and *performance,* but often a tension as well. Replication assigns a high, perhaps the highest, value to transmitting faithfully and fully, generation after generation, the precise words, tones, and perhaps meanings of an initial revealed text. One salient image for replication is the genealogy, where there is demonstrable contact between one replicator and the next, in an unbroken chain of transmission. Replication may be carried out through performance, as in the Amazonian and Indian examples.

But performance can also introduce the independent values of improvisation, innovation, and individuality. A Hindu epic may be unchanging, but it may be performed in many ways (even on television; see Mankekar 1999). Muslims value highly the musical recitation of the Qur'ân, a performance genre called *cantillation.* To be excellent, a cantillation must faithfully reproduce the sounds of the Qur'ân, and the intonation patterns must correspond to or appropriately embody the ideas and sentiments expressed by the words. To win the international contests, however, a cantillator must also bring an individual gift to her or his chanting. Ultimately, a contestant wins only by replicating through a creative performance.

Religion on the Web

S ince the early 1990s, religious groups have been among the more avid users of the Internet and the World Wide Web. Thousands of Web sites devoted to advancing or discussing religious beliefs and practices now exist. (Some are mentioned in earlier chapters.) E-mail lists and chat rooms facilitate long-term debates about religion and society. And Internet users also favor religious Web sites. A 1998 study estimated that of the 100 million Americans online, 25 percent used the Internet for "religious purposes" each month (Leibovich 2000).

Some of those users are looking for information, but most, according to the 1998 study, use the Internet to communicate with other people about religious ideas or experiences. Some sites function as virtual worship sites. Beliefnet (*http://www.beliefnet.com/*), for example, gives users the opportunity to create virtual prayer circles. When Judy Spiegal's father died in 2000, she started such a circle. On the first day, a dozen people of different faiths posted prayers on the site (Leibovich 2000). A temple in Calcutta, India (at *http://www.maakali-kalighat.com/*), offers Hindus a way to worship online, with the option to request different levels of *puja* (offerings), for free, ten dollars, or ninety dollars. As the Web site puts it, "You can thus partake of the holy supplication without actually leaving the comforts of your distant home."

These two examples represent different characteristics of the target audiences—multireligious America, the Hindu diaspora—but they share the basic feature of allowing worship at a distance, anonymously if so desired. The Web sites also create a sense of the network or "community," of those who use the service. Much of Ms. Spiegal's comfort came from the sense that people out there were supporting her. One of the effects of the Hindu temple site is the created sense of a community of worshippers around the world. This virtual community may address specific needs: for example, the Cathedral of Hope in Dallas (*http://www.cathedralofhope.com/*) advertises itself as the "world's largest gay and lesbian church," a claim it can make because of the online participation in services that it offers.

This kind of Web site offers primarily to *mediate*—among individuals (as in the prayer circle) or between individuals and religious institutions (as in the virtual temple and church). The sites differ in the kind of audience they target, from "narrowband" to "broadband." Some sites are linked to specific churches, temples, mosques, or other highly local bodies, and are intended mainly to provide a service (in two senses) for current, potential, or virtual worshippers. Even here there is a good bit of variation, between the site that is merely a convenience for those who physically attend a site of worship anyway, and the virtual religious site. (The Cathedral of Hope is probably halfway between these two points.) Other "narrowband" sites are intended for the followers of one particular religion or set of beliefs (such as the different Jewish sites listed earlier in this book.)

"Broadband" sites attract a wide audience of people with differing beliefs and practices and so they broadcast a fairly tolerant and catholic (in the sense of encompassing diversity) message. Their design varies: some have a menu format (Catholics click here, Muslims there); some offer humor, like The Beliefnet site mentioned earlier, whose December 2000 home page features a picture of the Pope twirling a basketball. The "religions" link on this site takes users to a page featuring columns and discussions about interrreligious issues: interfaith marriages, the place of religion in schools, comparing religions on various topics, and noting the overlapping celebrations of Christmas, Hanukkah, Ramadan, Yule, and Kwanzaa. (Yule refers to the "modern pagan" celebration of the Winter Solstice.)

Here the specific characteristics of Web sites are exploited to good advantage: on the home page one senses the celebration of all religions together, which at times takes on a synthetic "world" characteristic (as in "World Sacred Music," a musical sampler available as a download). But the many links on that page take users to religion-specific sections, some of which are intended to be acceptable to practitioners of each religion. A question-and-answer section features a spokesperson for each of several religions: Father Ted informs fellow Orthodox Christians how to fast; Rabbi David Wolpe urges the Jew who seeks to follow Law not to lose sight of people, and so forth.

The Beliefnet site also takes advantage of the interactive properties of the Internet in two ways. First, it features, as right-hand columns, letters submitted to each of the many linked subsites. Second, it features (center-front, first "religions" page) a quiz in which the user picks his or her religion, and then answers a series of diagnostic questions about beliefs, obervance, behavior, and so forth. Based on the answers, the user is then told whether he or she is (in the Muslim case) a secular Muslim, spiritual seeker, progressive Muslim, or traditional Muslim. The reader who is classified as a traditional Muslim learns that "the Qur'ân plays a role in your daily life as a Muslim" while the progressive Muslim learns that "you probably interpret Islam historically and might believe that *ijtihad* (individual interpretation of scripture) should be reopened." Among the practices that would classify you as traditional is fasting and praying during Ramadan, considering killing Salman Rushdie, saving sex for marriage, and planning on marrying a Muslim.

One has no idea where these correspondences come from. The idea that ijtihad and everyday use of the Qur'ân would be associated with distinct types of Muslim has little relationship to the social lives of Muslims I know or know of. More interesting, perhaps, is the sense of audience implied by this site. Who would take this quiz? Perhaps the Muslim student in a non-Muslim land who feels a need to identify who he is through one of these available labels? Surely not the fellow who threatens Rushdie in a dark alley (the site's scenario). The quiz also suggests books appropriate for each of the four categories (oddly, the traditionalist is referred to a book decrying the influence of "Islamists" in Cairo—perhaps the real intent of the list is to subvert the categories!).

The other current broadband strategy is a more synthetic New Age theology combined with heavy marketing, best illustrated by the new site SpiritChannel.com (*http://www.spiritchannel.com/*), which bombards site visitors with a heavy-beat song about "there's only one religion." (The site's founder is Isaac Burton Tigrett, who created the Hard Rock Cafe and the House of Blues.) It pronounces itself a "for-profit" site, marketing "information, data, guidance, entertainment, products and services related to spirituality and health—all via the Internet, traditional media and in three-dimensional locations."

Creole Spaces

If we think about them in real space and time, then we can profit from Jon Anderson's (1999, 43–44) characterization of many religious Web sites as "creole" spaces. Anderson means that these sites, like the populations in the New World mixing Spanish or French with local languages, mediate between older institutions (associations, governments, churches, schools) and a global public. They are both local, responding to needs, fears, and hopes of a particular group of site creators, and global, in their electronic spatial reach.

Daniel Miller and Don Slater (2000) are anthropologists who have studied Internet use in Trinidad. They found that the religious Web sites are both highly local in their concerns, and yet also attempt to "expand back" (2000, 178), into the larger realm that they see themselves as rightly occupying . What do they mean by this? For the religions they studied, adherents see themselves as part of a much larger community than the Trinidadian one. Trinidad Catholics see the Church as universal, and they have long believed that the common experience of Caribbean peoples makes a regional Catholic theology desirable, something now much more likely to develop through region-wide electronic communication. Hindus on Trinidad see themselves as part of a global network of Hindus, in India, of course, but also in North America, on Fiji, and elsewhere. The Internet makes communication among members of that network vastly easier.

These sites are shaped by very specific, locally grounded networks of communication and influence. The Hindu site is maintained by Sanathan Dharma Maha Sabha, the major Hindu organization in Trinidad. This organization represents the community as under threat from Christians. The major links from the Web site's home page, for example, include texts such as "Jesus Lived in India" and "Hinduism Under Attack." Miller and Slater (2000, 175–176) point out that militant Hindu nationalists, mainly in their North American branches, have actively used the Internet to alert Trinidadians to negative stories about Hinduism, so that they can then negate those stories on their own Trinidad Web site. Internet communication has also instructed Trinidadian Hindus about the differences between their forms of religious life and those found in India, through the decline of caste and the influence of Christianity in the Caribbean. Thus, the site is dynamically located in a network of Hindu nationalism as well as within a network of Trinidadian concerns.

A very different example of the mixing of languages and genres cited by Anderson is presented by MyQuran.com (*http://www.myquran.com*), an Indonesian site for Muslims with an English title and English phrases. It is part of a MuslimNet Ring, a grouping of sites with links to each other, and its content and links are overwhelming. One can hear an entire Surah of the Qur'ân (on December 20, 2000 it was al-Lail) with RealAudio Player, and link to downloads of other chapters. One can also search the entire Qur'ân in one of 15 languages (although some of the attempts reached not yet working sites). A user can download a call to prayer (adzan) with RealAudio and have a choice among calls from Mecca, or Medina, or one by the late Shaykh Muhammad Rifat of Egypt, or from the Istiqlal mosque in Jakarta.

The site's "eMuamalah" (social affairs) section contains Islamic eCards, an Islamic bookstore associated with Amazon.com, and several networks (*jejaring*), including one for academics. I am a fan of Indonesian Islamic music so I went to that link, where I was offered the chance to download about 50 songs by various religious-oriented Indonesian groups, plus the latest songs by Yusuf Islam (the former Cat Stevens) and links to other Islamic music collections. Each visit to the site also pops up a Hypermart window with an ad unrelated to Islam (during my visit, they were for free E-mail, Amex cards, and the latest U2 song).

This site and others like it are extremely user-friendly in more than one way. They have a modern, secular, even consumerist feel to them. They indicate nothing about a particular religious message or orientation. They serve as a portal in a theological as well as technical sense. They communicate a meaning about tolerance toward religion through their very form.

Profile

Pascal Boyer

Supernatural Concepts and Experimental Methods

Pascal Boyer began his career by undertaking fieldwork of the usual sort, in his case in West Africa. His interest in how the people he studied remembered and transmitted their ideas led him to ask about processes of memory and transmission more generally. This shift in question in turn led him to seek ways to combine ethnographic and experimental methods in the study of religious ideas. (You can read more about this line of work in his 2000 article, "Cultural Inheritance Tracks and Cognitive Predispositions: The Example of Religious Concepts," In H. Whitehouse [Ed.], *Mind, Evolution and Cultural Transmission* [pp. 57–89], Berg Publishers.)

What brought me to the experimental study of religious concepts was a paradox familiar to all anthropologists. In most human cultures people have mental representations of supernatural entities—gods, ghosts, ancestors, spirits, magical objects, and so forth. These are different from other mental images because they are not very strongly constrained or fixed. That is, our mental representation of giraffes must include that they are long necks, because giraffes keep displaying long necks that are difficult for our minds to ignore. But gods or spirits are remarkably discrete, individually distinct and varying,

so that our ideas about them are not restricted or specific. So we could expect different people in different places to have extraordinarily variable representations of supernatural entities. But instead we find that such concepts revolve around a number of similar themes: agents with extraordinary physical capacities that go through walls (gods that are everywhere), agents with extraordinary biological properties (gods that never die, virgins who give birth), artifacts with intentional or biological properties (statues that bleed or cry or hear your prayers). Why do we find that human imagination is so repetitive, where it is so unconstrained?

One possibility is that imagination is in fact limited. That is, some concepts may be so much easier to acquire, store and communicate than other concepts that they will spread better and therefore become what we observe in many human groups. Perhaps there is something in the extraordinary features just described that make them particularly good for cultural transmission. I and other anthropologists (Dan Sperber, Scott Atran, Lawrence Hirschfeld) thought that the solution to such questions might be found in cognitive psychology. Psychological experiments show that all human minds have certain fundamental expectations about what sorts of things are around, about the difference between living and nonliving things, between persons and animals, between artifacts and natural objects. So maybe supernatural concepts were constructed by just adding a few counter-intuitive features to these common expectations: a spirit would be just a person plus some nonstandard physical feature, for instance. A listening statue would be an artifact plus some psychological properties.

This made sense of the common themes but raised another question: what is so good about having a standard category (like person or artifact) and adding one counter-intuitive feature, so that you find these combinations everywhere? Justin Barrett and I thought perhaps such combinations were very easily recalled, which would give them an advantage in cultural transmission. This could be tested rather easily: we created stories with key combinations (one fundamental category plus some nonstandard

feature) as well as other material, either odd or unsurprising.

We observed that our special combinations were recalled much better than other material, even if that other material was odd or surprising. After running several studies in Europe and America, Justin Barrett and I conducted replications in India, Nepal, and Gabon, and we found fairly similar effects (with interesting cultural differences that would take a long time to unpack). In none of these places did we use stories or events that were familiar to people. Our results seem to show that people are especially susceptible to concepts of agents and objects that include violations of expectations despite great differences in religious background, literacy, or social organization. Our experiment is only the beginning of such studies; but it seems quite plausible that the solution to the paradox really lies in the way human memory works, that is, in the way our brains are designed. ↩

For Further Consideration

Not surprisingly, New Age movements are abundantly represented both in your local bookstore (the town one, not the university one) and on the Internet. For all you still want to know about channeling, try the site called "What is Channeling" at *http://www.hydrexheat.com/~marina/channel/whatchan.html*. A more general New Age site (*http://newage.about.com/religion/newage/mbody.htm*) offers many topics and links to hundreds of other, related sites.

This chapter already provides a number of references to other Web sites and books. In using the Internet, it is important to identify the sponsors of the Web site and determine where they stand within a range of possible opinions on the topic. This is easy to do if it is the Catholic Church, harder when it is a Hindu temple in Toronto or a Baptist site with no apparent church link. A nice exercise would be to see how many clues you can pick up about the positions of the site's sponsors from statements made on it and links offered to you.

13 *Places and Pilgrims*

*I*n previous chapters we have examined the religious roles of rituals vis-à-vis doctrines, rites of transition, healing practices, sacrifices, taboos, religious objects, and ways of speaking. All these topics involve religious events; they all *take place* in a particular place and time. Such is true of all religions, but some religions give to specific places a special significance. A religious place may be conceived as an origin point for a prophet or people; as a place where gods or spirits reside; or as a spot where a notable event occurred. Places may be unique (Mecca, Jerusalem) or multiple (Mary's many apparitions), or even rather commonplace (graves). They may be natural (a sacred mountain), or made by humans (a holy city), or supernatural (a vision site).

Religious places may organize life far beyond their boundaries. For those whose religion covers a vast territory, the sacred spots may provide a shared orienting direction and thus a spatial sense of community. Mecca is the most striking example, but so are Jerusalem and Benares or, on a slightly smaller scale, the Ise temple in Japan or the Guadalupe shrine in Mexico. But places may also differentiate people into small communities, each with their own temple or altar or ancestral grave. Graves, in particular, link people to place through their dead: the corpse is where ties of descent meet ties to the land. (Some religious traditions, of course, place relatively little emphasis on places, as with most of the Protestant movements examined in Chapter 11.)

Centers and Directions

*W*e find some general associations between features of the natural geography and features of religions that appear in widely scattered societies: that the gods live in mountains; that centers are more powerful than peripheries; that the cardinal directions determine one's fate. But each religious tradition selects and interprets such general associations in its own terms. Consider the cardinal directions. The apparent movement of the sun across the sky creates a natural east–west axis that people use to orient themselves. (The movement of rivers provides another such axis.) The north–south axis bisects this axis to create four cardinal points. This four-way division of the sky provides a handy scheme to sort out many other features of the universe, giving people a sense of understanding and even control over nature and spirits.

For example, the Zuni Pueblo people of the southwestern United States assign to each cardinal direction a season, type of weather, set of animals, color, and social function (Bunzel 1992; Durkheim and Mauss 1963). North has associated with it the winter wind; the grouse, pelican, crane, and the evergreen oak; the color yellow; war and destruction. Some of these associations have natural bases: northern winds are colder and forceful and appear to bring winter, and the evergreen oak is remarkable for its ability to remain green throughout the winter. But other assignments seem more arbitrary and are the result of classifying the world into sets of fours: the colors blue, red, yellow, and white, each assigned to a direction, form the primary colors plus their fusion into white.

These assignments not only appeal to a human love for ordering the world, they also provide a plan for carrying out certain rituals. For example, along with the animals already mentioned, each direction also has a "prey animal": for the north it is the mountain lion (which is yellow, thus fitting animal to color). If people desire to increase their chances of hunting "northern" animals (say, the grouse), they ask the spirit of the mountain lion for help, who then preys along with them. Zuni also divide their social world according to this scheme. Each direction has assigned to it three clans, each of which is named after one of the cardinal animals. Thus, to the north are the clans named after crane, evergreen oak, and grouse. The clan's name animal is also its totem; the clan members stand in a special relationship to it.

Many societies have narratives in which gods or spirits or the first people journey across the natural landscape. These narratives invest sacred power in that landscape. For the Navajo, for example, one of the very first actions taken by the First People was to conduct the first Blessingway ceremony to make the first house, or hogan. They built it facing east, with each of the four directions pointing to one of the four sacred mountains in the Navajo homeland. The directions themselves are not of great significance; what is important is that the creation story locates cosmic events at specific places in the everyday landscape. The directions hold down the cosmos in the world. Narratives about various gods and events always situate their birthplaces, travels, and battles in specific local spots. They also direct contemporary Navajo people about where they will find the correct plants or objects to perform different healing or purifying rituals (McPherson 1992).

The core Navajo ceremonial, Blessingway, contains speeches by gods in which details about each sacred mountain are recited (Gill 1981). The Holy People themselves lived in specific earthly places. For the First Woman the people "made a nice trail leading south from the entrance of First Man's hogan, and along the side of Huerfano Mountain they prepared a nice place for her." Changing Woman orders the people: "at the base of this Huerfano Mountain on the west side you will build a hogan for me, my children, my grandchildren, leaving the entrance toward the west." "At the base of Mount Taylor there is a place called Tree Circle, where Rock Crystal Talking God happened to live." And so on: mythic events, repeated in Navajo ceremonials, can also be located in the everyday world. (One can then understand the vehemence with which Navajo oppose plans to mine ores in the mountains or build new towns along the slopes.)

Chinese Geomancy

Throughout Asia, directions and features of the landscape are thought to shape one's fortune. In China and Korea, experts in geomancy, which in Chinese is called *feng shui* (wind and water), determine the most favorable locations and orientations for buildings based on directional diagrams or compasses (Weller 1987, 147–155). In the ideal configuration of natural objects, mountains and rivers encircle a central place; cosmic energy, or *chi,* will be concentrated in the center and give positive energy to those who reside there.

Cardinal directions also confer good or bad luck: facing south confers and signifies sovereignty, for example. Directions are also associated with animals—the west with the tiger, for example. Landscape features that resemble animals ought to be located in that direction from the place being studied—tiger-looking hills ought to be to the west for luck to be good. The appropriate sites and direction for graves, towns, and temples are determined in this way.

Geomancy is strongly listened to even in commercial Hong Kong. The shipping tycoon chosen by Beijing to run Hong Kong under Chinese rule, Tung Chee-hwa, selected a site for his new government offices only after consulting a geomancer. The feng shui expert considered the placement of doors and windows, the balance of light and dark in the rooms, and even the angles of desks, before approving one place, two floors in an office building. He had earlier rejected Government House because neighboring tall buildings blocked chi from reaching it (Gargan 1997). Not everyone in Hong Kong follows feng shui; one bank publishes an annual list of feng shui predictions that did not turn out.

Japanese Temples and Branches

Japanese religious worship is also directed toward sacred places. As we saw in Chapter 2, spirits, kami, are nearly everywhere. They reside in unusual natural features such as mountains or strange rocks, in ordinary objects such as boulders or houses, and in shrines found in homes and nightclubs, offices and golf courses. But temple complexes are especially important places to make offerings to sprits.

Temple complexes include shrines to kami and statues of Buddhist deities, and visitors stop at both. They usually were built where they were because people believed that the particular place was already occupied by spirits. Rather than spirits (and Buddhas) visiting places where they are worshiped, places of worship are built where these spirits have already emerged into this world.

Each temple complex has a story about how it came to be built where it is. The Narita temple complex story refers back to a ninth-century rebellion against the emperor (Reader 1991, 141–146). The emperor asked the monk Kukai (later to be known as Kobo Daishi and one of Japan's important saints) to carve a statue of the Buddha known as Fudo, and then to seek Fudo's help in quashing the rebellion. Kukai did so and performed the "eye-opening" ritual that infuses the statue with Buddha's power. The imperial forces won. Over a century later another emperor, facing another rebellion, called on a monk to carry the statue carved by Kobo Daishi into battle. Again, imperial forces won, but when the monk tried to bring the statue back he could not move it. Fudo appeared to him and asked to remain there to help the local people. Hearing this request, the emperor built a temple on the statue's chosen site, and this building became in time the Narita temple complex.

The story does not stop there, however, for branches of the Narita temple have been built throughout Japan. Each has as its source of spiritual power an exact replica of the original statue of Fudo Buddha carved by Kobo Daishi, and that is empowered through the same ritual that Kobo Daishi performed in the ninth century. Each statue *becomes* Fudo (just as the many statues of Mary *are* Mary; those of Shiva, Shiva). One branch Narita temple is in Osaka. It was built at the northeast gate of the city because this direction is most unlucky, according to geomancy, and it was hoped that the temple would protect the city. The temple's sponsors also had material interests. They owned the Keihan Railway Company and land in the northeast part of the city; as the area developed, and more people used the company's trains and buses, the owners prospered. Now, the Fudo Buddha is thought to be of particular help to travelers, and today each train compartment and each bus owned by the Keihan company carries a protective amulet that has been empowered at the Osaka branch temple of Narita. Thus, even high-speed travel relies on the powers of a sacred site for its safety.

Dimensions of Pilgrimage

Sacred places also draw people to them as visitors or, especially, as pilgrims, and here we turn to pilgrimage as a type of religious practice. Through the attitudes, ideas, and practices of the visitor one gains a deeper sense of how the place is meaningful.

We can define pilgrimage as travel to a sacred spot for an act of religious devotion. Depending on the attitude and intention of the individual, a wide range of actions might be pilgrimages, from a visit to your grandparents' graves, to a trip to see the Liberty Bell in Philadelphia, to a visit to the Grand Canyon. If a sense of awe and of a reality that transcends the everyday makes an experience "religious," then these events could be considered pilgrimages. But our focus here is on events that are explicitly designated as pilgrimages within the broader context of a religious movement or institution.

Let us consider the various dimensions of a pilgrimage (compare Turner 1974). One might ask, first: What is the primary purpose of the pilgrimage? (There may be a host of secondary reasons, ranging from status-seeking to lunacy, that fall outside the religious domain.) These primary, explicit reasons include general obligations and individual needs. Pilgrims may be responding to a god's command, as when Muslims carry out the pilgrimage to Mecca. Or they may have a specific individual purpose, such as fulfilling a vow or seeking a cure. They may address a more diffuse set of spiritual needs without being commanded or even recommended by religious authorities. Pilgrimages to sites of Marian apparitions fit in several of these categories: people may travel to Lourdes to seek a cure, or to refresh their spiritual lives, or to fulfill a vow made when ill.

Second: Is the primary emphasis the journey itself, or reaching a particular place? We often assume that pilgrimages are usually about going somewhere and then returning, and certainly this is uppermost in most pilgrims' minds when they set out for Mecca, or for Santiago de Compostella in Spain, or for Benares along the Ganges in India. And yet the journey may also be valued, either explicitly within the religious tradition or as part of the broader experience. As the Shikoku pilgrimage described later shows, in some cases the journey may be emphasized, and no particular spot prescribed as the goal. In Western literary traditions that reach back at least to Bunyan and Dante, the pilgrims' wanderings, albeit toward a particular destination, served as an allegory for personal growth and the passage through life. The *Canterbury Tales* concern pilgrims to Canterbury Cathedral in Kent, southeastern England, but are really about the journey itself. Or consider the following from Rabbi Abraham Heschel:

Faith is not the clinging to a shrine but an endless pilgrimage of the heart.

The goal of some pilgrimages contains a mini-pilgrimage within it. As we shall see, the Islamic pilgrimage hurries the pilgrim around the Ka'ba, down the road to 'Arafat, back to Mina and then to Mecca, around the Ka'ba again, and then home. What the pilgrimage is really about is commemoration of Muhammad's actions, not the visit to the holy places, which, unlike the pilgrimage proper, can take place at any time of the year. Some Christian shrines are devoted to the stations of the cross, the path undertaken by Christ that led to his crucifixion, and thus are representations of his own journey.

Finally we should ask about the topography of sacred places. Where is the place located—in the center of a city, or on the periphery of human settlement—and what significance does the location have? How did the pilgrim's goal come to be a sacred place? Consider the classic urban sacred places: the Hindu temples along the banks of the Ganges in crowded Benares city, Mecca at the crossroads of Arabian trade, Jerusalem, and Rome. These places are centers for great institutions: temples, mosques, churches. From these sites come centralized and centralizing claims to authority and knowledge, conjoined with trade and politics.

One also finds sacred places located in remote spots: places where Mary appears to schoolchildren, temples to female Hindu deities, monasteries, centers for Sufi learning, places for lone Japanese pilgrims to wander, forests where Buddhist monks meditate in isolation. These places are sites for marginality: meditating, protecting, reassuring those who are not in power, warning those who are. The distinction between centers of power and its margins is often replicated in the places where pilgrims gather and the faithful worship. (On a small scale, this center/periphery distinction appears in the opposition of parish church/isolated shrine in the Nansa valley in Spain discussed in Chapter 9.)

Let us gain a better understanding of variation across pilgrimages by looking more closely at three pilgrimage traditions: first the Islamic pilgrimage, the hajj, for an extended analysis; then two other examples, the Japanese pilgrimage around the island of Shikoku and the pilgrimages by Hindus to temples in Benares.

The Pilgrimage to Mecca

*E*ach year during the pilgrimage month of the Islamic lunar calendar, more than a million Muslims from throughout the world gather in the holy places in and around Mecca. These men and women have traveled to Mecca to carry out their religious obligation to make the pilgrimage. All the pilgrims must carry out a series of very specific actions, moving and worshiping together, before completing their task and returning home. The principal goal of the pilgrimage is to obey God's commands, as they were made clear to humans through his messenger, Muhammad.

Following the Footsteps of Muhammad

We have already seen that Muslims consider the Qur'ân to be God's major gift to humans, and in this respect the Qur'ân's role is similar to that of the Torah for Jews and that of Christ for Christians. But Muslims also consider as divinely inspired the actions of the Prophet Muhammad—not because he was divine himself, but because he spoke and acted as God's messenger. The collection of reports about his statements and actions are called the "hadith." These reports supplement the Qur'ân as the second basic source for guidance and law in the Muslim community. Much of Islamic ritual as well as everyday life is based on what Muhammad did as contained in these reports, and it is in this way that Muslims developed the pilgrimage, or hajj.

The pilgrimage is meaningful for Muslims in the first place as a repetition and commemoration of the Prophet's actions, "following in his footsteps," as many returned pilgrims said to me. But it was also dictated by God in his revelations to Muhammad. Several years after Muhammad and his followers had fled from Mecca to Medina to escape persecution, came the first revelation concerning the pilgrimage, quoted in the last chapter of the Qur'ân:

The first House established for the people
was that at Mecca, a place holy, and a guidance to all beings.
Therein are clear signs—the station of Abraham,
and whosoever enters it is in security.
It is the duty of all men towards God to come
to the House a pilgrim, if he is able to make his way there.
(Qur'ân 3:90–92)

The house mentioned in this passage is the large cubic structure called the "Ka'ba," which is draped in gold-bordered black silk cloth. The Ka'ba is the centerpoint of the religious world for Muslims. It is toward the Ka'ba that Muslims worship five times daily, and it is around the Ka'ba that they walk when they make the pilgrimage.

In Islamic tradition the Ka'ba dates back to the prophet Abraham, who journeyed to Mecca with his son, Ishmael, and Hagar, Ishmael's mother. (In the Islamic version of the sacrificial trial of Abraham, it was Ishmael, not Isaac, whom he was ordered to sacrifice.) Abraham built the Ka'ba on God's command. The angel Gabriel then brought down a black stone to place in its corner. The stone, it is said, was white, but turned black on contact with the sinful world.

By the seventh century C.E. Mecca had become a trading center in the Arabian peninsula, and it was here where Muhammad was born, grew up, and received his first revelations. His triumphant return to Mecca from Medina marked the victory of Islam over the polytheistic Meccan elites, and his first pilgrimage, in 632, the year of his death, became the model for all pilgrimages since (Peters 1994).

Making the pilgrimage is one of the five ritual obligations, or *rukns* (pillars), of Islam. The pilgrimage has always attracted Muslims from throughout the world, but the development of steamship travel in the nineteenth century and air travel in the twentieth has led to a boom in pilgrimage activity. By the mid–twentieth century about 30,000 people made the journey each year; today about 2 million pilgrims, from the 60 or more countries with sizable Muslim communities, arrive in Mecca each year. Pilgrims come from near and far: the largest delegations are from Nigeria, Pakistan, Turkey, and Yemen, and then Iran, Indonesia, and Iraq. Some pilgrims stay on to study and teach; most return home bringing new ideas and trade goods. Islam was founded by a trader amid vast networks of desert caravans; the contemporary pilgrimage enlarges those networks of trade and communication to the scale of the entire world.

Precisely because these holy cities occupy such a central place in the Muslim popular imagination, they have sometimes been the targets of political movements. During the 1979 pilgrimage, an armed group seized control of Mecca's Grand Mosque and broadcast denunciations of the Saudi government over a citywide loudspeaker system. Iranian anti-American demonstrations at Medina in 1982 led to arrests and revived debates about whether religion and politics could legitimately be separated in Islam. Since then the Saudi government has prohibited delegations from making the pilgrimage when they feared political disturbances (or health risks, as in the 1996 ban on Nigerians during an epidemic in Nigeria).

Although the details of the hajj are taken one by one from accounts of that first pilgrimage, the steps can be sorted into the three stages of rites of transition that were discussed in Chapter 3. Indeed, Victor Turner (1974, 182) argues that in larger-scale societies pilgrimages perform some of the same social functions that are filled by initiation rituals in smaller-scale societies, in providing the place for a religious experience outside the bounds of everyday social life. The pilgrim separates himself or herself from ordinary social life, enters a liminal stage in which distinctive everyday identities are exchanged for the shared identity of the pilgrim, and then returns to the social world. Each transition point is marked by clear religious duties.

Rites of Separation

Although a Muslim may visit the holy places in Mecca and Medina at any time during the year, the pilgrimage itself may be performed only on the eighth, ninth, and tenth days of the last month of the Islamic lunar calendar—the pilgrimage month, Dhu'l-Hijja. (Because the lunar year is 11 days shorter than the solar year, the pilgrimage season cycles back through the solar year.) Unlike pilgrimages made by Christians, Jews, or Hindus to their holy cities, the hajj is a series of ritual actions performed together, simultaneously, by all the Muslim pilgrims for that year (Ruthven 1984, 23–48).

Weeks or even months before these key days, pilgrims have been gathering and departing from villages, towns, and cities all over the world. In Indonesia, as in many other countries with large Muslim populations, each group receives an official send-off from a local government official. As recently as two generations ago, departing pilgrims from the Gayo highlands received a different kind of send-off. They were fed at a ritual during which prayers for the dead were recited on their behalf because most who made the journey were older, and many would not survive the two- or three-month sea voyage. The ritual was held before they left because otherwise they would not receive one.

Travel, whether by land, sea, or air, is for much of the way a secular affair. Only when approaching the port or airfield of Jiddah must pilgrims take steps to enter the state of consecration, or *ihram*. Each pilgrim announces his or her intention to undertake the pilgrimage, renounces shaving, cutting the hair, and sexual intercourse, and changes clothes. The new pilgrim's clothing consists of identical, simple, white seamless garments. Men leave their heads uncovered, and women must not have cloth touching their faces. Some pilgrims even ride roofless buses once they approach Mecca. Each of these measures maintains an unbroken physical link between the pilgrim's head and God, and signals his or her surrender to God.

Moving in the Liminal State

Wearing identical clothing, renouncing normal relationships to their bodies, and concentrating their lives on worshiping God defines the pilgrim's position during the days of pilgrimage. In the liminal state, between their previous lives of various occupations, nationalities, wealth, and status, and their future lives as returned pilgrims, these men and women live and move as equals, sharing some rudimentary Arabic, simple accommodations (for most pilgrims, anyway), and the same daily objectives.

The clothes mark the fact that all pilgrims are religiously equal. As Muhammad's grandson Husayn stated, "The pilgrim offers himself to God as a beggar." Pilgrims mingle with one another even while onboard ship or plane as pilgrims, leaving ordinary social status aside.

Once in Arabia they gather in groups by country and are led through the pilgrimage steps by a group leader, usually someone from their country. For many pilgrims this is their first international experience, rubbing shoulders with others whose language they cannot understand. Arabic prayers and a few short greetings are usually the only form of verbal communication across these groups. Even the American Black Muslim leader Malcolm X (1973, 339) was shocked by this universalism, as he wrote in a public letter to his mosque in Harlem. "For the past week, I have been utterly speechless and spellbound by the graciousness I see displayed all around me by people *of all colors*."

Pilgrims arrive steadily at Mecca. As they do, they make seven lefthand circles (*tawaf*) around the Ka'ba. Indeed, the root meaning of *hajj* is "to describe a circle." Huge masses of pilgrims move slowly around the silk-draped structure. Each tries to touch or kiss the

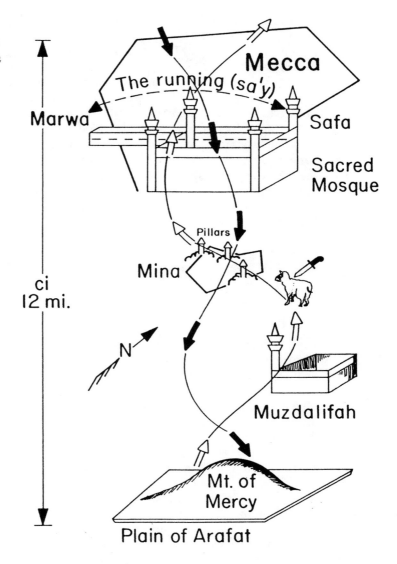

Major rituals and places of the **hajj.** (COURTESY OF RICHARD T. ANTOUN, *MUSLIM PREACHER IN THE MODERN WORLD*, p. 173.)

black stone set into its eastern corner. The Iranian scholar Ali Shariati (1977, 31) described the experience of the tawaf as that of "a small stream merging with a big river. . . . Suddenly, you find yourself floating and carried on by this flood. You have become part of this universal system. Circumambulating . . . Allah, you will soon forget yourself."

The Ka'ba already served as a holy site before Islam, but its guardian was the deity Hubal, whose statue was kept inside the structure. Many other deities were worshiped as well, and the circumambulation was part of worship. Muhammad retained this practice and the veneration of the black stone when he undertook the first pilgrimage, and his followers, though surprised that he did so given the stone's association with paganism, followed suit. The rigorous logic of following the Prophet's actions won out, here as elsewhere.

After the tawaf the pilgrim does the *sa'y,* "running," which does indeed consist of simply running (or, for the older, walking) back and forth, seven times, along a street in Mecca. The running commemorates the time when Hagar was abandoned under a tree at Mecca by Abraham. When her food and water ran out she began to run wildly between two high points, pleading with God for help. When Ishmael raised his hand, there was a well, which became known as the well of Zamzam. The well marked the spot where Mecca was then built. Pilgrims collect water from the Zamzam well and bring it home with them; often diluted with rainwater, it will be used to heal or bless others. The running covers about two miles, and some pilgrims must be pushed in wheelchairs.

The circumambulation, also called the *umra,* is sometimes performed separately out of season as the "little hajj." Travel agencies throughout the Muslim world offer umra packages—a Muslim may travel to Saudia Arabia at any time of year, circumambulate the Ka'ba, visit the holy sites, and return home.

The Hajj Proper

Pilgrims then begin the events that constitute the pilgrimage proper, the events that are performed only on the prescribed days. They must travel to the plain of 'Arafat by sunrise on the ninth day of the month. It is at 'Arafat, a barren plain about two miles from Mecca, where Adam and Eve were reunited after their expulsion from heaven. Here, too, Muhammad delivered his final sermon in 632, in which he set out most of the details of the hajj. A vast tent city is erected on this plain on the days before to the ninth, and there the pilgrims are assigned quarters.

At 'Arafat the pilgrims spend the ninth day in prayer and meditation, gathering around the Mount of Mercy at the edge of the plain. After performing the midafternoon worship, the millions gathered together stand, awaiting sunset, shouting cries of "God is great." This standing (*wuquf*) is the central event of the hajj proper. The special status enjoyed by this rather unspectacular (relative to the tawaf that precedes it and the sacrifices to follow) event comes from its role in replicating Muhammad's final sermon, and from the shared sense pilgrims derive from it of showing humility before God.

Pilgrims then disperse and return toward Mecca, stopping to spend the night in the city of Muzdalifa, where they are to rid themselves of all resentments toward others. There, too, they collect pebbles, which they use the next day to throw at three pillars near Mina, on the return road to Mecca. This *rajm,* or stoning, of the statues is understood to be a stoning of devils. No mention is made of it in the Qur'ân; as with the veneration of the black stone in the Ka'ba, it is performed solely because Muhammad did it on his pilgrimage. As interpreted by most participants, it commemorates Abraham's resoluteness to obey God, for it was on this spot that he prepared to carry out God's command to him to sacrifice his son. The devil appeared to Abraham, and tried to instill doubt in his heart about the sacrifice. Abraham stoned the devil until he fled. After the crowding and rushing of the previous two days the stoning also undoubtedly releases tensions. Some commentators have harnessed the energies visible during the stoning to religious mission; Ali Shariati urged pilgrims to think of the pebbles as bullets used to kill one's enemies.

Pilgrims then carry out a sacrifice in memory of Abraham's submission to God's will. Usually they buy a goat on the spot and arrange to have its throat cut. The meat is distributed to the poor, much of it immediately frozen on the spot by Saudi authorities. The day after this event is called the *yaum an-nahr,* or day of sacrifice, and, as we noted in Chapter 10, it is celebrated throughout the Muslim world by similar sacrifices. The pilgrimage is thus both a duty for all Muslims and the occasion for a worldwide ritual observance.

Reintegration to Normal Life

The pilgrimage proper is complete at this point, and the pilgrims gradually make the return to normal social status. They begin by cutting some of their hair. Women snip off just a bit, but men often have their heads shaved. Now all prohibitions are lifted except for that on sexual intercourse. Pilgrims return to Mecca, perform another circumambulation of the Ka'ba, collect Zamzam well water for the return trip, and now can again engage in sexual intercourse. They are urged to spend several days in "eating, drinking, and sensual pleasure." This urging emphasizes that the pilgrims are now leaving the state of consecration and returning to normal society—the rite of passage has ended.

Those pilgrims who return home immediately find themselves enjoying a new status, that of hajji (male) or hajjiyah (female), someone who has made the pilgrimage and returned to society. Many now wear white for everyday activities or when they attend the mosque to signal this new status. Their status may lead to other achievements: they are probably looked on with greater favor by their local bank; they may be chosen for office. They certainly have much to tell about from their journey. But they also enjoy a sense of religious accomplishment, having fulfilled the most difficult of God's commands.

How Is It Meaningful?

Ordinary Muslims undertake the pilgrimage for a variety of reasons—they are obeying a divine command; they are fulfilling a duty expected of them socially; they may be advancing their own social status. But is this all we can say? In what ways is the pilgrimage with its many component actions meaningful?

The pilgrimage presents a challenge to our usual ideas of the meaning of a religious act. It is not performed with a separate goal in mind, such as atonement or cleansing. The religious historical event that is commemorated in each segment of the ritual is sometimes but not always clear. The only overall, uniting idea of the pilgrimage is that it is made up of actions that were performed by Muhammad on his first (and only) pilgrimage.

Man returned from the pilgrimage proudly displays his new clothing, Isak, Sumatra. (COURTESY OF J. BOWEN.)

Scholars do suggest parallels with earlier rites, either those performed on the same spot as a contemporary ritual and taken over by Muhammad, or parallel rituals within the Semitic ritual tradition that were adopted by Muhammad as properly monotheistic. For example, the wuquf, or "standing," was part of earlier Hebrew practice. Muhammad made the entire plain of 'Arafat a place of standing before God. The *'umra* was originally a sacrifice of firstborn livestock and was held in the early spring, much as with Passover, in the month of Rajab (at that time the lunar calendar was made concordant with the solar, so that Rajab always occurred in the spring). The sacrifice was carried out at the Ka'ba. As late as the twelfth century C.E., local Muslims were still carrying out this older sacrificial 'umra in the month of Rajab.

In fact, although the 'umra is thought of as a little hajj, 'umra and hajj were once distinct events. The essence of the 'umra is the tawaf, the circumambulation of the Ka'ba, while the essence of the hajj is the standing before God at 'Arafat. In origins, the one is sacrificial, the other is an act of submission to God. Muhammad then tied them together in one long series of events.

This kind of explanation may provide a historical account for why certain events became part of the overall pilgrimage. They do not account for the meaning of the rite for those people who take part in it. Muslim commentators have offered several broad lines of interpretation.

One interpretation links the performance of the hajj to the overall meaning of Islam as *surrender*. According to the important twelfth-century theologian Al-Ghazali, devotion to God demands self-abnegation, surrender to his will. Therefore, God has imposed on the Muslim actions that in themselves have no emotional or intellectual appeal, such as the running back and forth between two points, or sa'y.

A second interpretation identifies symbolic or iconic meanings for each individual place or object that the pilgrim encounters. The Ka'ba is the House of the Lord. You will meet God in a seamless shroud, so you meet him today wearing such garments. The tawaf resembles the movement of angels that encircle the Throne of God, which itself is situated directly above the Ka'ba in heaven. Ali Shariati (1977) sees the "running" as standing for purposeful activity on the earth.

A third line of interpretation seems to me to be closest to the ways in which pilgrims themselves interpret their experience. This approach locates meaning not in the events but in their historicity, as commemorations of past events. The running commemorates the moment when Hagar was looking for water for Ishmael and Gabriel created the Zamzam well. The stoning marks the moment when Abraham stoned the devil. The sacrifice commemorates Abraham's willingness to sacrifice his son. At the very least, every event commemorates Muhammad's pilgrimage—and this insight returns us to a key element of Islam, that practices and texts constantly refer back to the life of the Prophet for their authenticity.

And what is the specific goal of the pilgrimage? Despite the fact that worship is always conducted facing the Ka'ba in Mecca, and that "Mecca" has become a shorthand for a central place or goal, in fact the central event in the pilgrimage, the standing at 'Arafat, takes place outside Mecca itself, as does the sacrifice, both in places that are virtually uninhabited during the remainder of the year. Within the hajj framework, for instance, the pilgrim is never still, but is hurried around the Ka'ba, down the road to 'Arafat, back to Mina and then to Mecca, around the Ka'ba again, and then home. What the pilgrimage is really about is commemoration of Muhammad's actions, not the visit to the holy places (which, one should again note, can take place at any time of the year).

Pilgrims expand this sense of historicity from particular commemorations to a more diffuse sense of being in the place where their religion was born, being "at the source." "Everywhere," writes the Pakistani religious leader al-Maudûdî of the typical pilgrim, "he sees the relics of those who lived God, and sacrificed their lives for His sake. Every grain of sand witnesses the glory and grandeur of Islam, and every piece of stone declares: 'This is the land where Islam took birth, and whence God's word rose high'" (quoted in Cragg 1980, 60). As the leader of U.S. Muslims Waris Deen Muhammad said in conversations in St. Louis in 1996, "on the pilgrimage you come near to God; you are visiting Him."

Contrasts in Pilgrimage from Japan and India

The hajj has certain distinctive features that no other pilgrimage tradition shares completely: its script dictated by Muhammad, the temporal limitations on its performance, its decidedly worldwide quality. Two other examples, from Japan and India, illustrate other ways that pilgrimages are constructed and understood, other ways that elements of journey and place, and a variety of motives and purposes, can be combined.

Circling Shikoku

Each year more than a thousand Japanese pilgrims travel around the island of Shikoku in southwest Japan (Reader 1991, 112–116; Statler 1984). The trip takes the pilgrim by many temples and shrines, where requests can be made and spirits venerated. In a society noted for its group characteristics this pilgrimage is highly individualistic: the lone pilgrim may begin anywhere on the island and stop where he or she wishes, for whatever reasons and with whatever goals in mind that she or he might have. Purposes include healing and self-discovery; the emphasis is on journey over goal, and the place itself is very peripheral to Japanese society.

This pilgrimage grew out of a particular movement within Japanese Buddhism called Shingon. The founder of Shingon Buddhism, who also invented the Japanese writing system, was named Kukai, called after death Kobo Daishi (774–835 C.E.). In China he had studied the teachings of Gautama Buddha pertaining to the Buddha Dainichi, who emphasizes the source of salvation to be found inside every man and woman (and the same Sun Buddha who was made the center of the state cult). Salvation may be achieved in this world, taught Kobo Daishi. But the path to salvation is less a matter of accumulating merit than finding an individual path to inner awareness of the true nature of the world.

Shingon Buddhism made ample use of methods for developing awareness that evolved in India and Tibet within tantric Buddhism, whose methods are designed to help an individual better control his or her mind. The writings about these methods were called *tantra,* hence the name for the practices taken together. Some of these practices involved chanting single syllables, called *mantras,* meaning literally, "true word"; meditation; and sexual union. This last practice led rulers to discourage or even persecute tantric groups; but the teachings spread to China, where they became known as *Chen-*

Pilgrims resting near Kyoto, Japan. (COURTESY OF JOHN RENARD.)

yen, the Chinese translation of *mantra,* and this name was carried with the practices to Japan, where it was pronounced *Shingon.*

Kobo Daishi taught that truth had to be reached through inner concentration; it could not be attained through study. (His teachings thus reinforced the general Mahayana Buddhist point that anyone, not just scholars or monks, can achieve salvation.) One of his verses speaks of the ultimate "darkness" lying at the end of study:

Unknowable, unknowable, it is completely unknowable;
about the Buddha and the non-Buddhists, there are
    millions of scrolls.
Dark, dark, it is very dark;
of the Way that is spoken there are many paths.

What is left, when the copying and chanting of scriptures stop?
No one knows, No one knows, and I too do not know.
Though they consider and speculate, even the wise do not know.

The other side of this darkness is the hope that through meditation and concentration one can find enlightenment, find the Buddha-nature that is in everyone, within one's own lifetime. Kobo Daishi personified this path to enlightenment; his legends tell of him covering Japan with temples and shrines and practicing an austere life of meditating and traveling. On the Shikoku pilgrimage the pilgrim not only reenacts part of Kobo Daishi's life, he is also accompanied by Kobo Daishi.

The pilgrimage takes the pilgrim to 88 temples devoted to Buddhist worship, as well as to unofficial places for Buddhist worship and many other shrines to spirits. The thousand-mile journey around the island's circumference, stopping at each official temple along the way, takes about two months for the healthy and longer for men and women who are ill. The pilgrimage is always made clockwise. One may begin anywhere and stop when one has reached the initial point, closing the circle. The circle has no beginning or end (although the temples are numbered 1 through 88); making the circuit the point of the pilgrimage. The pilgrim is fed and housed in the temples and receives alms from people he or she passes on the way. About a thousand people each year make the journey on foot; many thousands more take two-week package bus tours or travel by train or car. Others travel to the island intermittently, eventually visiting all the temples.

Because the saint Kobo Daishi accompanies each pilgrim, alms given to the pilgrims generate merit for the givers. A gift made to a pilgrim is a gift made to the saint. Indeed, the pilgrim, embodies some of Kobo Daishi's saintly qualities in his physical contact, so that people will ask a pilgrim to lie down on their bedclothes so as to physically bless them. (The pilgrim is a kind of walking, temporary relic of the saint.)

But the purpose of making the pilgrimage is not to earn merit but to purify and better understand oneself. "The path is the goal itself." Pilgrims give a variety of reasons for making the arduous journey, but they all have to do with self-improvement. Many are seeking better physical or mental health, either from the Daishi, or from specific deities enshrined at temples along the way. The nature of the ailments has changed. As one priest put it: "In the old days many who were ill made the pilgrimage; lepers, for instance, were numerous along the path. [Indeed, some came to die on the journey.] Nowadays the physically ill go to hospitals. But these are times of strain and mental illness, and so today the benefits of pilgrimage are greater than ever." Today victims of corporate down-sizing are more likely to be found on the path. One such middle-aged former computer management worker made the journey in 1996 to decide what to do after being fired. He made the journey relatively quickly, in 32 days, and resolved during his walking to spend more time with his family (Pollack 1996).

Like the Muslim pilgrim, the person who circles Shikoku is temporarily leaving this world for a liminal world. Also like the pilgrim on hajj, he or she wears the white garments that serve as burial shrouds, signifying both a willingness to die on a pilgrimage and a temporary renouncing of the normal world.

But the elements of the two pilgrimages also point up important, general contrasts in the two religious traditions. Notice how "circling Shikoku" differs from "circumambulating the Ka'ba." The Islamic practice is prescribed, collective, and fixed on a center point that lies directly under heaven itself. The Japanese practice is optional, individualistic, and has no center, or even starting and ending points. As a lesson in how wrong we would be to generalize from supposed facts about a culture to its religion, ponder the highly individualistic Shikoku pilgrimage in a Japan known for its orientation to the corporate group, and contrast it with the highly collective Islamic pilgrimage in an Arabia known for its argumentative style and qualities of schism and fission.

Indeed, it may be precisely because Japan is as society- and group-oriented as it is that individualistic religious practices emerge as essential to human spiritual growth. Not that these practices are asocial—the pilgrim often makes his journey to become a better member of society. But they do respond to a value of self-cultivation that suffuses all Japanese religions, old and new. The ascetic, who undergoes severe deprivations to purify himself and to find merit and spiritual power, is a central figure in the Japanese popular imagination. Monks at a Buddhist center near Kyoto practice a thousand-day austerity, each of those days making a 20-mile journey, living on little food, and depriving himself of sleep. The ordeal ends in a nine-day total fast during which he must refrain from sleep entirely. Having drawn near to death, the ascetic has thrown off his former self and become one with the Buddha figure Fudo. Many ordinary Japanese practice lesser austerities, such as bathing in ice water or fasting. Waterfalls located along the pilgrimage routes are favorite places for cold baths; these baths purify the pilgrim and augment his or her spiritual powers (Reader 1991, 116–128).

Bathing at Benares

If the Japanese pilgrimage stresses self-discovery on a journey as a counterpoint to a collectivist everyday sociability, its Hindu equivalent, similar in many respects, emphasizes multiple power-bringing visits to temples. The pilgrim's goal is to have "exchanged vision" (darshan) with the gods many times in many places. Pilgrimage in India thus involves multiple goals strung out along a journey. Each site is called a "crossing place, ford" (*tîrtha*) to somewhere beyond; a pilgrimage is *tîrthayâtrâ*, journey to a ford (Fuller 1992, 204–223).

The prototypical goal is Benares, in north central India (Eck 1982). Called by Indians "Kâshî," the City of Light, Benares lies alongside the Ganges, a river said to have descended from heaven to earth. More than 70 landings, or *ghâts*, line its banks, some containing temples to Shiva, who makes Benares his earthly home. Benares has always been an earthly crossing, the place where the old northern Indian trade route crossed the river Ganges. As with other places of pilgrimage, it is also a spiritual ford, where earth and heaven meet. Here the dead may be assisted in crossing over the Ganges to the condition of *moksha*, liberation from rebirth, the ultimate goal of the Hindu. Here, too, the gods may descend from heaven to earth. Shiva lives in the city's many temples but also in its ground and buildings: "The very stones of Kâshî are Shiva," goes the popular saying.

The gods descend and pilgrims cross at many other fords, throughout India. Of the thousands of places where Shiva, or the hero Rama, or the goddess Durga have emerged to split rocks or have crushed enemies, a few cities are particularly favored. Some are associated with Rama, and in particular his capital at Ayodhya (the recent political importance of which we consider in Chapter 15). Others, including several associated with Krishna, are on mountains; still others mark the four corners of India.

Benares is the most widely acclaimed of all, however. To many Hindus it is the center of the universe (as is Jerusalem to some Christians, Mecca to some Muslims, Beijing to some Chinese)—located directly under the heavens. Benares also encapsulates worship in India: temples from other parts of India, from the Himalayas to the southern tip of the subcontinent, have replicas in Benares. One may visit these temples and exchange vision with their deities without leaving the city. The city has absorbed their power. And in one new temple the devotion is of Mother India, Bharat Mata, represented in the form of a relief map inside the temple where the image would usually be. The map shows the major pilgrimage places, which pilgrims can view (and "exchange vision" with) all at once! Benares is itself replicated elsewhere: hundreds of temples called "Shiva Kâshî" are scattered throughout India, and at each one a pilgrim or other worshiper exchanges vision with Shiva (Fuller 1992, 208–209).

Our notion of "goal" or "site" thus has to be rethought for Benares: deities are here, in this city, but they are also elsewhere—gods, and God, the spiritual force behind all the gods—is indeed everywhere. (One pilgrim, longing for the black stone dedicated to Shiva near his village home, remarked: "I miss God.") Nor does any deity command pilgrims to visit Benares.

To understand pilgrims' purposes we must return to the way in which Hindus approach the image of a deity. Contact between the deity and the worshiper is exchanged most powerfully through the eyes, through seeing or darshan. When Hindus go to the temple, writes Diana Eck (1982, 20), they do not say "I am going to worship" but "I am going for darshan." And in the temple, in the city, the Hindu sees many images, all of which act as lenses through which he or she can perceive divinity. (Recall the many-in-one quality of sacred images that we discussed in Chapter 9.)

When Hindus travel on a pilgrimage they are engaged in "sacred sight-seeing," a rich process of exchanging vision with deities—and with sacred places themselves. For places are dwelt in by deities, as Benares is by Shiva, so by "taking in" the city's sites they are also "taking in" Shiva himself.

Benares also attracts pilgrims to bathe in its particularly sacred waters and to cremate their dead. The variety of alternative activities and places for worship distinguishes the Benares pilgrimage from the highly prescribed and channeled activities of pilgrims to Mecca, and the focus on the journey itself for pilgrims around Shikoku.

The pilgrim's first duty is to bathe in the river on one of its many landings. Pilgrims bathe in the Ganges to partake of its purifying powers, brown and replete with ashes and bacteria though it is. Indeed, usually they take the popular "Five Fords" trip along the riverfront, where they bathe at each of five landings, or *ghâts*. At each stop, the pilgrim recites a statement of intention, that he or she is undertaking this pilgrimage, and if the pilgrimage is made to fulfill a vow or with a goal in mind (which is not necessary) a statement to this effect is added, such as, "I am making this pilgrimage in hope of bearing a son." Each stop has stories of kings and gods associated with it, and nearby are temples, or phallic linga statues devoted to Shiva, or even a mosque (Eck 1982, 211–251).

The last bath is taken at the landing of Manikarnikâ, at the center of the three-mile-long waterfront. This bath is the most important. The site has a cremation ground and a large sacred well nearby. Shiva is in the temple, but Vishnu built the well as the world's very first tîrtha. And a manifestation of the Goddess, or Devi, here called "Devi of Manikarni," guards the well. This site is called the "burning landing" because when seen from the river one sees the plumes of flames from the crematorium located among the temples.

Those who die in Benares are cremated by the Ganges and their ashes are scattered over the waters. Some who die elsewhere have their ashes brought, or even mailed, to Benares. When one's ashes lie on the Ganges, one's spirit crosses over from earth to liberation. But failing this, pilgrims will say prayers for the dead, offering balls of rice while saying their names. These rites ensure that the ancestors will dwell in heaven. So important are these rites that when long-lost ashes from the cremation of Mohandas K. Gandhi's body were discovered nearly a half-century after the event, they were carried to the Ganges to be poured into the waters (Burns 1997).

Newly arrived corpses are placed by the river's edge before being dipped into its waters for their final bath and then hoisted onto the funeral pyre. The eldest son circumambulates the pyre, lights it, and when the burning is finished, walks away without looking back. Members of an untouchable caste in charge of the cremation ground throw the ashes into the river, where they are gradually carried downstream.

But just as Shiva is present in many places, so are there other tîrtha that can claim the same effectiveness and power as can Benares. Unlike, say, Jerusalem or Mecca, no one spot in India can claim unique attraction. Temples to Shiva elsewhere are just as suitable as places to worship him as is his Benares temple—but those other temples are likely to exhibit pictures of Benares, attesting to the Ganges site's quality as the prototype.

The religious importance of seeing sacred places and images helps us understand why a rapid bus tour of a large number of sites would be a heightened religious experience for Hindus and not just a way to be the active tourist. Pilgrimage is the major reason Hindus travel, and they do so by the millions every year, on foot, by bus, or by train. They value the journey itself: joining others in travel, making merit by giving alms, "seeing" (darshan) many deities, getting away from normal routines, and experiencing another realm—both another part of the country and a glimpse into the beyond. Hardship may itself be felt as proof of merit earned through the journey, even if not explicitly sought out.

Or pilgrims may choose a bus tour that, without the hardship of journeying on foot, offers a greater number of chances for darshan with deities. The anthropologist Ann Grodzins Gold (1988, 262–298) traveled by bus with a group of pilgrims from northwestern India to the eastern coast of Orissa. The pilgrims were from different castes, and came from town and village settings. The villagers included Brahmans (the order, or varna, associated with the priesthood), Rajputs (traditionally a warrior caste and of the second-ranking Kshatriya order), and people from farming, gardening, and other miscellaneous castes. The pilgrimage did not erase these distinctions; indeed, the castes stayed apart; "the fact that we were sharing a pilgrimage did not act as a leveler of rank" (Gold 1988, 269).

On the road, pilgrims sang songs about the deities Ganesha and Rama and about the Sun King, from whom a woman in the song takes darshan each morning. They stopped at one site after another. When reaching a pilgrimage place, a *tîrthayâtrâ*, they would bathe in the waters, view the images in the temples, make gifts to priests and beggars, and occasionally perform a short offering ritual. They traversed the country where Lord Krishna had spent his childhood and observed darshan tableaux of his babyhood. They made a whirlwind tour of Benares's many temples, which left a colorful blur in their minds. The deepest and most favorable impression was made by the sea. "These Hindus had seen countless icons in their lives," remarks Gold (1988, 284) after one pilgrim, emerging from the famed temple at Puri, said with a shrug that "Well, God is God." But, she continues, they had seen "only one sea."

What did the pilgrimage mean to them? None of Gold's fellow pilgrims thought that bathing in sacred waters would cleanse them of bad deeds. Rather, and in a more diffuse way, the entire experience of getting out of everyday routines, taking many powerful darshans of gods, enduring the hardships of the road, and giving alms to beggars would be good for the soul. Hitting the road and seeing the gods lightens the pilgrim of goods and attachments and concerns, bringing her or him nearer to "the deity within himself." Approaching one's inner divinity prepares oneself for the moment, perhaps in some future life, when one will finally attain release or liberation—*moksha*. "Sweeping the road ahead," suggested one widow.

While some pilgrims thought that pilgrimages causally improve one's chances of eventually achieving moksha, others were more skeptical. The differences of opinion resembled the debates we have studied among Christians and Muslims about whether rituals can change God's mind. One pilgrim told Gold (1988, 288) that traveling and bathing could not affect what God determines, although he would reward giving alms: "From what does moksha come? From his own hand, God's, that's from whom. It does not come from wandering. Whatever you give, in whatever place give it. From this comes moksha. What kind of dharma is dirtying the water? But dharma is giving-and-taking."

In scholarly debates as well, Hindus are of two minds about the benefits pilgrimages bring. On the one hand, some commentators on the classic texts assure the pilgrim that "Even if a man be a sinner or a rogue or irreligious he becomes free from all sin if he goes to Benares." But others equally clearly say the opposite, that it is the inner self that must be purified through meditation. After all, observes one scholar, "Fish are born and die in the water (of tîrthas); and they do not go to heaven, for the impurities of their minds are not purified."

The village pilgrims did agree that giving money as alms lightened the soul and brought them merit. Pure giving is easier on the road than in the village—in the latter, one will usually receive tangible or reputational goods in return for a gift, making the gift less pure.

As in the pilgrimage around Shikoku, for many Hindu pilgrims the goal is the journey, and the personal, inner transformations that happen along the way. Indeed, for all pilgrims, in all societies, the journey is important, even where, as in the case of the Muslim's hajj to Mecca, the main emphasis is on performing specific actions. Separating oneself from everyday life, focusing one's attention on the divine, is virtually the defining element of pilgrimage to anywhere.

Profile

Ann Grodzins Gold

From "Sorrows of Simplicity" to "Shared Blessings" in Ghatiyali

Ann Grodzins Gold teaches in the Departments of Religion and Anthropology at Syracuse University. Her work on pilgrims was published as *Fruitful Journeys: The Ways of Rajasthani Pilgrims* (Waveland Press 1988, 2000), and among her writings about field collaborations is the article by Bhoju Ram Gujar and Ann Grodzins Gold, "From the Research Assistant's Point of View" (*Anthropology and Humanism Quarterly* 17[3]; 72–84, 1992).

I cannot write about India without also writing about fieldwork, as I did in *Fruitful Journeys* (2000 [1988]), my study of Hindu pilgrimage. When I first arrived in the village of Ghatiyali in 1979 I was an embarrassed, tongue-tied stranger. Everyone asked me who I was and why I was there, and my answers and demeanor radiated the self-doubt I harbored. I captured my fieldwork persona in those early days with the words of a village woman who pronounced of me, "It is sad to be so simple in the world." As I have returned multiple times, some of my initially awkward relationships with Ghatiyali's residents have grown into lifelong bonds of love and kinship. When I sought to convey the essence of my 1993 fieldwork, I chose the phrase "shared blessings"; this understanding I also credit to Rajasthani women.

A formula that closes women's rituals asks God first to satisfy the whole world, and then to give the speaker satisfaction. Thus women acknowledge desire, but pray against the grain of selfishness that permeates so much of human life. In fieldwork, we enter a community with a cerebral consciousness of research aims that rarely make much sense to our hosts. But what we do is live with people. We are dependent on their generosities, which are often staggering; we also must respond to their demands for mu-

tuality and reciprocity. In both situations—as on the pilgrimage road—some kind of grace beyond transactions may occur.

I have especially close links with one household in Ghatiyali belonging to my former research assistant and present co-author, Bhoju Ram Gujar. Bhoju went with me on the pilgrimage to Puri described in *Fruitful Journeys*. Perhaps that month-long bus trip and close research collaboration set the pattern for almost two decades of deep friendship and intense intellectual synergy. In 1997 I lived in Bhoju's home with his parents, wife, and four children, and they incorporated me into their household in the most literal sense of the word. I can only describe my life, enmeshed in this family's expansive care for my well-being, as pampered—despite what would strike many urban folks as myriad physical hardships including no running water, indoor plumbing, or refrigeration.

I had an experience the day I left that is difficult to describe. I was happy to be on my way home to my husband and children. Bhoju's mother, Raji, disapproved of this, because in India a daughter going to her husband's house is supposed to look glum, not radiant. When I went to part from Raji, I felt a sudden, forceful blow of grief right in my heart, and tears began to seep from my eyes, tears her daughter leaving ought to shed. Later I pondered her personal power—the parting gift of tears meant more than any other, as it physically validated our kinship and my belonging. I am convinced that such moments of intimacy illuminate whatever knowledge anthropology has to offer. Living in this household and working on a painful history of power, I learned to see hierarchies—whether of caste, wealth, gender, or literacy—as only part of far more complicated human stories. ✍

For Further Consideration

*F*or more comparative literature on pilgrimages, consult the excellent collection of articles on Christian pilgrimages in various parts of the world, *Contesting the Sacred*, edited by John Eade and Michael J. Sallnow (Routledge 1991), and Victor Turner and Edith Turner, *Image and Pilgrimage in Christian Culture* (Columbia University Press 1978).

The film *Saints and Spirits* (Films Incorporated Video 1979) documents pilgrimages to the tombs of local Islamic saints in Morocco. Another film, *Holy Places and Pilgrimages* (Films for the Humanities and Sciences 1991), discusses Judaism, Christianity, and Islam. *Huichol Sacred Pilgrimage to Wirikuta* (University of California Extension Center 1991) concerns the pilgrimage and peyote hunt of the Huichol people of western Mexico. *The Shrine* (University of California Extension Center 1990) features a place sacred to Catholics in northern New Mexico, a small church the dirt from which is said to heal. An excellent site for the Muslim pilgrim is the Al-Hajj commercial site at *http://www.the-webplaza.com/hajj/index.shtml.*

Oliver Statler's 1984 book, *Japanese Pilgrimage* (Pan Books) offers a first-person account of the Shikoku pilgimage discussed in the text. A film also documents the Shikoku pilgimage, *Between Two Worlds: A Japanese Pilgrimage* (University of California Extension Center 1994). A guide to the pilgrimage route around the island of Japan is available at *http://www.kagawajc.ac.jp/~steve_mc/shikoku/index.html.*

14 Saints, Visions, and Prophets

*W*e have encountered figures of authority, and struggles over authority in all the preceding chapters: the individuals who founded pilgrimages and New Religions in Japan, rabbis of and converts to Hasidism, and preachers in Quaker and Baptist churches; as well as struggles over who had the authority to interpret texts on Islamic sacrifice, to declare someone a witch, or to certify as valid an apparition of the Virgin Mary.

The beginnings of a religion often lie in the personal authority generated by an individual: a prophet, or saint, or holy man who is treated as truly exceptional among humans. Such authority we call "charismatic." This term originally referred to God's gift of power as understood in Christianity and as evidenced in such gifts of the spirit as miracles, faith, and speaking in tongues. The sociologist Max Weber (1978, 400) used the term in a broader way, as a universal category. In contrast to traditional authority, which relies on inherited characteristics (such as birth order), and legal authority, which derives from characteristics of office (such as a priesthood), charismatic authority rests on the intrinsic attributes of a leader.

Such leaders may draw their authority from different kinds of sources and claims, and we have discussed many sources of authority in previous chapters. Some may be considered to have special ties to spirits, or to be powerful sorcerers, such as the New Guinea leaders discussed in Chapter 7. Speaking in tongues is a sign of God's grace for some Protestants.

Shamanic healers, discussed in Chapter 6, may claim to be possessed by spirits or deities, and to derive their power from this possession. The speech of spirits that leaps from their mouths brings together the individual needs of the patient with the general norms and values of the society. In some societies these healers may become community leaders. In the Wana society of Indonesia they become the poles around which people gathered to form settled communities. In urban Japan they become the nuclei for new religious organizations that meet social and psychological needs of their followers. Healing may also involve other types of internal power or access to the divine. Mary Baker Eddy's popularity and the success of her Christian Science movement, discussed in Chapter 6, rested on her claims that all humans had within them the power to heal themselves.

This chapter examines the role of individuals in initiating religious movements, and the relationships between individuals' sources of authority and the history of new religious movements. First we consider the roles of the saint as a moral exemplar to others and as a source of power and assistance. Then we explore the diverse social forms religious prophecy can take, from Oceanic "cargo cults" to large-scale revivalist movements. We look at two examples—The Mormon Church of Latter-Day Saints and Islam—to illustrate the problems of leadership and continuity in religious movements as they expand over time.

Saints as Exemplars and as Sources of Assistance

One kind of religious authority is the saint, or holy person, who provides an example of how to live a holy, or virtuous, or religiously focused life. The saint is an "exemplar" (P. Brown 1987): a model of the ideal way to live, which may be appropriately reflected on by everyone, even if living the ideal is beyond the reach of most people. Many religious traditions have stories about such exemplary people—Christian martyrs, Jewish holy people, or tsaddiqim (such as Hasidic rebbes), Muslim walî, "friends of God," the followers of Gautama Buddha in India, or of Lao Tze in China. In a broad sense, stories about virtuous ancestors in any community serve the same purpose of instructing the living on how best to live.

In some traditions the exemplary life *is* the major teaching. Christianity is in many ways about Christ's lived example; Islamic teachings rely on Muhammad's life as well as on God's commands. *How* the religion's prime exemplar lives in some respects defines the major thrusts of the religion. Gautama Buddha's turning away from the world to find enlightenment through meditation became the paradigm for the monk and the lay person, especially in the Theravada Buddhism of South and Southeast Asia. By contrast, the exemplary life of Confucius in China is based on harmony within the community and is defined through the relationships people have with others in their families and with their immediate society and in their relationship to the state. This ethic of harmonious worldly involvement defines the virtues to which everyone should strive.

The idea of harmony or balance is also the basis for Haitian Vodou. Karen McCarthy Brown (1987) views the ritual practices of Alourdes, a Vodou healer who lives in New York, as providing a moral exemplar to others in her community. Alourdes's role is, in the eyes of participants, passive, as the "horse" ridden by the spirits who possess her. The spirits embody conflicting aspects of life for these Haitians: courage and childishness, or caring and capriciousness. Alourdes dances among different such spirits, being possessed by one after another. Her possession performances intensify and clarify the clash of such forces in the world. For those who watch her, writes Brown (1987, 167), "the moral problem is not evil but imbalance, both within and among persons." In her possession by different deities, Alourdes exemplifies how to maintain such a balance.

Vodou reminds us that spirits and deities can also serve as moral exemplars, and that as a plurality of beings they can define different points in a moral space, different aspects of the moral universe. Alourdes dramatizes this plurality of spirits and ways of acting, as does the polarity of Vishnu and Shiva in Hinduism, with Vishnu as the preserver and king; Shiva as the destroyer and ascetic. Christianity provides not only the polarity of God and Satan, but also the different kinds of examples provided by Jesus, Mary, and distinctive saints. Gayo Muslims, like Muslims in other societies, not only tell of the lives of prophets, but also understand the world to be populated by good and bad spirits, who live in societies resembling human societies. These spirits embody "good" and "bad" traits more definitively than do complex human beings. They also illustrate the virtues of community: the good ones cooperate and thrive; the bad ones quarrel because of jealousy and hatred.

Saints and other kinds of holy persons provide *practical assistance* as well as moral examples to ordinary people. People pray to Christian saints for help, or they place the medallions of those saints in homes or automobiles. Muslims and Buddhists also ask the spirits of holy people to help in a variety of ways. Living saints, such as the Buddhist and Hindu examples discussed below, may produce talismans or amulets, objects containing some of the saint's power, for people to take home with them. (Writing can also serve as a talisman; Jewish and Islamic scriptures may be placed in a position to guard the home.)

The power to help wielded by saints and by talismans is a secondary power, deriving from their intermediate role between a deity and an ordinary person. Muhammad, Mary, or the healer Alourdes all serve as intercessors and go-betweens. Because saints do not own their power, they can distribute it to others, through prayer, talismans, or dreams. In this respect they resemble the shamanic healer who channels the power of a spirit through his body and voice, or the group of Kung people gathered to boil their internal energy together, through dancing, and heal the entire community.

The holy man's ability to receive and distribute power may come from his personal disinterest in it. The ascetic, the individual who renounces worldly pleasure for the sake of spiritual enlightenment, is a figure in many religions, from St. Francis of Assisi to the forest-dwelling Buddhist monk, to the Nuer prophet Ngundeng of the Sudan, discussed later. Ngundeng's trance-like behavior and eating of filth placed him outside of ordinary society and gave his words added force. Mohandas Gandhi innovated saintly asceticism (Fox 1989) by drawing both from traditional Hindu ascetic practice and from international exemplars, including Jesus, St. Francis, and Tolstoy.

The holy man as renouncer, as ascetic, illustrates how the two features of sainthood—example and assistance—can present a paradox or tension. In the Hindu and Buddhist climates of South and Southeast Asia, the saintly man cuts off contact with the mundane world in order to achieve salvation. But others flock to this saint precisely because he is powerful (Tambiah 1976). Furthermore, he comes to depend on the offerings given by these devotees. How can a world renouncer also be the leader of a movement? This paradox is even more acute today, when some "renouncers" attract millions of followers, not only in South Asia but in Europe and North America. Two examples of these saints are a forest-dwelling Buddhist monk in Thailand and a Hindu "god-man" who uses jet arline transportation but also urges followers to return to Hindu traditions.

Acharn Man, a Buddhist Forest Dweller

In Thailand, monks are known as either "forest dwellers" or "town dwellers," with the first specializing in meditation and the second in book-learning. (Many monks combine aspects of the two categories.) Some forest monks become known as "perfected saints," or *arahants* (Tambiah 1987). Although their powers come from having turned away from the world, they also bless commercially produced talismans distributed to the lay masses. The king and queen of Thailand, along with generals and rich bankers, seek out these forest monks to absorb some of their moral powers.

From where do these powers come? In the Buddhist teachings consulted by monks and royalty, meditation and renouncing material possessions allows the ascetic to ascend to higher than ordinary levels of consciousness and to find there superior powers, or *iddhi,* which enable him to vanish and then reappear, to hear far-off sounds, and to recall his own past lives. But the monk must refrain from enjoying these powers lest in his worldliness he is impeded in his quest for salvation.

The complex life of the saint can be illustrated through the biography of Acharn Man (1870–1943), the most famous exemplar among Thailand's contemporary monks. As with Sufi orders in Islam and lineages of rebbes in Judaism, Buddhist monks trace their spiritual lineages, their sources of inspiration and powers, to earlier monks. Most forest monks today trace their own lineage to Acharn Man.

Man's biography shows him wandering alone throughout Laos and Thailand, but also attracting disciples whom he encouraged to form small monastic cells. In a story analogous to that of Gautama Buddha, Man went through periods of wandering, followed by seclusion and meditation, instructing disciples in villages, and pacifying tigers in the forest. To his disciples Man was primarily an exemplar, but to his circle of lay followers, he was mainly a "field of merit" (Tambiah 1987, 121). Donations of food or other gifts to Man brought the donor religious merit and blessings in return.

After Man's death, some of his disciples joined lay followers in promoting the cult of talismans stamped with his image. Others became forest dwellers in their own right. The talismans are metal medallions with the image of Acharn Man on one side and the lay person or organization that contributed funds for the medallion on the other. A follower of Man blesses the talisman by holding one end of a cord that lies on a pile of the objects, and then engaging in meditation to transfer some of his own powers to the medallion.

Acharn Man's charismatic powers thus continue to be radiated outward to the public through a chain of spiritual transfers. This chain starts from his own person and image, through his followers who themselves have gained higher powers, through their direct physical contact with the metal talismans they bless, to the consumer of the talisman. (Note the similarity to the chains of direct contact created by Christian relics.)

Sathya Sai Baba, a Jet-Age Holy Man

India's contemporary saints are of several types. Some are leaders of large devotional orders, many of them directing worship toward the god Rama. These saints inherited their leadership position from their own teachers, and so on back into time, in a fashion similar to the spiritual lineage of the Buddhist monk. The orders preserve these genealogies of teachers, which tie today's leader across the centuries to the founding saint. One Hindu order, the Ramanandis, dedicated to Rama, consists of both ascetics—some of whom renounce all worldly interests and wander, near-naked—and temple dwellers—who pursue the devotion to Rama through chanting. (These movements have played an important role in current Hindu political activity, as we shall see in Chapter 15.)

While many of these devotionalist orders are centuries old and make their antiquity their warrant of legitimacy, a new kind of saint, the "god-man," makes miracles to show his power and promises salvation to today's middle class. Some of the god-men have attracted large international followings; in the United States these include Bhagwan Rajneesh and the Maharishi Mahesh Yogi. But in India the most famous of these figures is Sathya Sai Baba. He has attracted large followings in the large cities. Some Buddhists in Sri Lanka have also become followers of Sai Baba, seeing him as the Maitreya Buddha.

Sathya Sai Baba's appeal is especially to the English-speaking middle and upper-middle classes, and he is often en route by plane or automobile to meet with his supporters. As Lawrence Babb (1986, 159–201) explains, Sathya Sai Baba is worshiped as a "descent" of God to earth, an *avatâr*. Indeed, his followers refer to him as Bhagavân, "God." At 13 he underwent a prolonged seizure; emerging from it months later he explained that he was the incarnation of an earlier holy man, Sai Baba, who blended Hindu and Muslim traditions. Twenty years later he added, after another seizure, that he was also the deities Shiva and Shakti. He said that after him would be another incarnation of Shiva—this new holy man would be his successor. (He thereby solved the problem of succession ahead of time.) His miracles also became more tightly associated with Shiva: he would materialize sacred ash, a symbol of Shiva's powers, at festivals to Shiva, or materialize lingas (phallus-shaped places of devotions to Shiva) inside his own body, which he would then eject through his mouth.

His followers frequently refer to his miracles as evidence of his divinity. He cures apparently incurable illnesses, raises the dead, accomplishes surgery at a distance, changes sand into religious books, foretells a devotee's thoughts, and, his own particular specialty, materializes objects out of thin air. He apparently can produce any object, but he most often materializes sacred ash, about one pound per day, for devotees to take away with them. He is also said to leave ash footprints in people's houses without every having entered the premises.

This god-man's cult has no formal boundaries, no membership lists, and no centers. It is a loose collection of those who consider themselves his devotees, centered on him alone. But the trusts that exist in his name receive large amounts of donations and use the money to maintain devotional centers, publish books and magazines, and build Sathya Sai Colleges, eventually, according to plans, one in each state. The trusts also sponsor charitable activities, including feeding the poor and working as relief agents during floods or other natural disasters. None of these activities proscribe any special religious rites, and the followers include Hindus and some Muslims. At devotion sessions they sing songs devoted to Sathya Sai Baba and engage in worship at an altar; they may also purchase pictures of the holy man, recordings of the songs, or even life-sized plaster replicas of his feet.

Sathya Sai Baba has special appeal to educated, often rather secularized urban people (and white New Agers) in the United States, and this appeal is at first glance puzzling. These people should be the first to reject magic. But, as we saw in Chapter 6 regarding the followers of Japan's similarly magical healing sects, it is the people who have left many older religious and social practices behind who often feel most in need of new ways to solve personal crises. In India, these people include city dwellers who accept the new conditions of secularism and egalitarianism but worry about the loss of an older life. They find it difficult to maintain religious obligations and find older patterns of authority broken down. Those who come from high castes worry about the pollution they experience in their new lives, where they mingle with people from lower castes in what feels to them to be a disordered way.

The often disorienting conditions of modern life may have led many of these followers to discover their own cultural and religious identity in need of supplement. At times of crisis—illness, loss of employment, family discord—they may be attracted to a new kind of immediately available healing power. Sathya Sai Baba's teachings reinforce their fears at the same time that he offers remedies. He blames Western values and national disorder for much of what ails people, and urges adherents to return to the study of the older Hindu texts. As D. A. Swallow (1982) shows, Sai Baba dramatizes the continuing power of Shiva to deal with pollution and sickness, to overcome pollution and restore health. He embodies Shiva, reassuring his followers of the continuing presence of the god even in this secularized world. His devotees find a way to recover the very religiosity they have left behind, through the visible magic the holy man performs. His cult is not demanding—people can participate in the magic merely by buying a portrait, or reading a magazine—and it may offer something of their more religious past. Indeed, he claims that wealth and liberation go together. He can be experienced as combining the best of old and new: Shiva, health, wealth, and social work.

Prophets and Social Change

When spiritual leaders claim to be entrusted with divine authority, and begin proclaiming divine messages, we call them prophets. Some prophets are also saints; they stake out a path to enlightenment by setting an example, and it is this personal example that remains behind as their primary prophetic legacy. Such was the case for Gautama Buddha in India, and for Kobo Daishi in Japan (the saint in whose name Japanese undertake the Shikoku pilgrimage described in Chapter 13). Max Weber (1978, 447–451) called this type the "exemplary prophet" and contrasted it to the "ethical prophet," whose role is based on the claim to bear specific messages from divine authority. Muhammad, prophet of Islam, and Joseph Smith, prophet of Mormonism, said they were ordinary individuals through whom God relayed a call to return to the proper ways of worship. Moses, of whom we know little, was also an "ethical prophet," revealing commands from an ethical, law-giving deity.

These distinctions are general ones, instances of what Weber called "ideal types." In practice, followers attribute many diverse qualities to prophets. Some Muslims treat all of Muhammad's actions, from the color of his clothes to the manner in which he ate, as if they provided a divine example for humankind. This view moves the figure of Muhammad closer to the status of saint. Others take a different view, considering only certain of his actions—how he conducted the pilgrimage to Mecca, for example—to have been inspired by God and thus intended as examples or models. They emphasize his ordinary human qualities precisely in order to underscore the belief that the Qur'ân came from God, not Muhammad. Such terms as *saint, prophet,* and *charisma* can therefore only be taken as indicators of types of roles and tendencies within religious movements, not clear-cut descriptions of individual leaders.

The Problem of the Prophet's Continuity

Sathya Sai Baba's teachings emphasize a return to older scriptures. But when a prophet has a new message to deliver, how can he or she transmit the prophetic authority and message beyond immediate surrounds and to the next generation? The power of the prophet may be embodied in portable objects (such as the powerful statues found in both Japanese Buddhism and European Catholicism). The message may be transmitted and transferred through verbal reports, or even songs, as with the Nuer people of the Sudan.

These orally transmitted messages may be considered as more authentic than written messages. (Such is the case for religious traditions in India, North America, and in Islam, for example.) When prophetic messages are transmitted, they become subject to radical change, as in the example of the Paiute Ghost Dance we will see later. Variant versions of the original message arise. In many religions, the fact of having many versions of "the same" sacred narrative does not pose a problem. Navajo narratives of the world's origin are told in many ways and in many contexts, and this plurality of versions suits the many uses to which the narrative is put. The story of Beautyway, for example (see Chapter 11), describes world origins and the close ties between speech and thought. Narrating the story brings to life the power of creation and the power of words, to be used in healing or blessing. Different versions of the sacred story can accomplish these goals.

In other religious traditions, however, the nature of the narrative makes such diversity problematic. If, as in Islam or Christianity, the religious message stresses the importance of conformity to divine commands by the community as a whole, then disagreement about those commands will likely lead to divisions in the community. If religious leaders perceive this danger, then they will likely act to create a single version of scripture, commit it to writing, and repress alternative versions of scripture. (They will also likely act to expel religious dissidents.) The creation of a written Gospel, with its four distinct versions of Jesus's life, and of a written Qur'ân, occurred long after the revelations and miracles related in the narratives. In both cases the narratives had been transmitted orally, and in several versions. In the case of the Qur'ân, when the verses were collected in an authoritative version, other written versions were ordered destroyed. In Christianity, books not included in the Gospels were labeled "apocryphal."

This passage from the individual holy person, to multiple memories of his or her life, to an authoritative scriptural text, involves the emergence of a centralized religious authority, and in some cases to state-enforced religious law. Authority becomes less personal and more bureaucratic. Max Weber called the process of transforming religious authority the *routinization* of authority, by which he meant the creation of routine ways of arranging succession to the leadership, structuring the religious organization, and resolving disputes. Even when "routinized," most religious movements are forced to come to terms with other claims to authority, either claims within the movement or assertions of superior authority by external political institutions, especially by states.

The routinization of a movement is one way for religious authority to be transferred. One example of this change of authority is that of seventeenth-century Quakers. The Quaker prophet George Fox had been able to keep the movement together in its early years by virtue of his personal powers of persuasion, but the very ideas that animated early Quakers worked against any centralized control. The spirit, argued the early Quakers, inspires those persons whom it would inspire, so that speaking at meetings, or other social behavior, should not be regulated. The resulting Quaker tendency to pose stark and shocking challenges to established authority—from using "impolite" speech, to refusing to take oaths of loyalty to the king, to going naked as a sign of innocence before God—led to state repression and to turmoil within the movement itself.

Quaker elders eventually came to routinize authority in order to preserve the movement. They established firm rules about how meetings were to be run and how individual Quakers were to speak with other people.

The Birth of Prophecy in the Sudan

Although the Nuer people of the southern Sudan have given rise to many types of leaders and magicians, a new type of "ethical prophet" first emerged in the late nineteenth century. His message has been preserved, transmitted, and used to diverse ends, through the media of song and radio.

Douglas Johnson (1994) calls Ngundeng Bong (d. 1906) the first prophet, the first "vessel of divinity," among the Nuer. As a young man, Ngundeng began to exhibit strange behavior, including wandering alone in the bush, fasting, and eating cow dung. His relatives interpreted this behavior as evidence that he had been "seized" by a divinity— much like the way Sathya Sai Baba was "seized" in his youth. They sacrificed oxen in the hope of propitiating these divinities. After these sacrifices, Ngundeng became normal once again. He reported that he had indeed been seized by a deity, the divinity Deng. He began to teach people prayers to this deity.

Earlier, Nuer had frequently sought help from clan deities, but Ngundeng declared that Deng was a deity for all the Nuer. Many people agreed with him, not because of a crisis in Nuer society, argues Johnson (1994, 327–329), nor because the clash with British armies led Nuer to search for a new leader—indeed, it came before the impact of colonial rule began to be felt. Johnson points instead to the general increase in mobility and dislocation in the late nineteenth century in this part of Africa as the cause of Ngundeng's success. In a way similar to the effects of social mobility on religious consciousness in the first millenium B.C.E., these social changes may have made the idea of a general divinity more appealing to many Nuer. Nuer already were imputing a more active role to clan deities in causing good or bad fortune than they had before, and they were concerned about the power of magic possessed by other groups. Ngundeng's claims thus fit with general changes in religious and social consciousness.

Ngundeng built up his influence and authority through a series of successful acts of religious sacrifice. Before a critical battle with another Nuer group, Ngundeng sacrificed an ox to Deng. His side won the battle. Ngundeng soon gained a reputation for having power over life and death. Merely by looking at him, he caused the death of a relative who had denied him meat. Others who refused his demands soon died, without his having to say or do anything. (Recall from Chapter 7 the related idea among the nearby Azande people that one's witchcraft substance can cause harm without human action.) He was also credited with making many barren women fertile by making sacrifices to Deng. Upon the outbreak of smallpox in 1888–1889, he sacrificed oxen and urged everyone to leave their houses; the incidence of smallpox among the people who followed his urging was relatively low. (One doctor who was present at the time said that the extra meat produced by the sacrifices, together with the act of inducing people to spread out, probably did contribute to a reduction in susceptibility to the disease.)

But Ngundeng was a prophet, not a sorcerer. He was able to turn other prophets and magicians into his disciples. He mediated feuds between clans, usually through sacrifices. He was able to bring together many clans through his prophetic activities, citing messages from Deng. Soon after the smallpox outbreak, he began work on a large earthen mound, said to enclose all evil and disease inside it, and mobilized thousands of Nuer to work on it for more than four years. Sacrifices at the mound were intended to benefit all Nuer, not just the particular clan who had brought the ox. The idea that a religious act or a deity could give general benefits to all Nuer was an innovation over earlier ideas and practices.

The prophet spread his message widely through the hymns and songs he recited, which he said had been created by the divinity Deng. These songs urged Nuer to reconcile with each other and with their various enemies. Even after British raids on Nuer camps in 1902, one of his, or rather Deng's, songs pleaded:

I reject the fight you bring
Divinity and the prophet do not quarrel.

The Nuer have not enjoyed peace in recent years. Relations between the Islamic northern part of the Sudan and the non-Islamic, mainly Christian south, have been violent. Southern rebels have often sung Ngundeng's songs in support of their struggle. He was said to have predicted the wars against the north. But his songs were also sung by Nuer opponents of the rebels. Some of the divisions among Nuer have also pitted Nuer groups against members of a neighboring group, the Dinka. In 1988 these factions finally joined forces against the north, and announced their reconciliation publicly in another Ngundeng song:

Nuer and Dinka
even if you hate yourselves
There will come a time when you will recognize me as your father.

✓ The rebel radio broadcast Ngundeng's songs right after the announcement of the reconciliation, and the legacy of his prophecy continues to animate southern resistance against the north.

Revitalization Movements: Messiahs, Millennia, and Revivals

*M*any prophets hold out the promise of a "new heaven, new earth," a new kind of world in which the trials and problems of this one are replaced with a just and perfect order. Their promises sometimes lead to movements of people seeking to overturn the present order, or converting others to their beliefs, or simply awaiting the promised transformation. Such movements may develop and grow particularly in times of rapid social change and perceived threats to older ways of life, but they also offer innovations, not just reactions to change.

✓ We find such movements throughout time and throughout the world, and called by many names. Judaism, Islam, and Christianity are all built on such a promise of a future redemption and the return of a messiah. This hoping for a future redeemer can be called "messianism" and such movements "messianic." In the histories of Judaism, Christianity, and Islam there have been other persons claiming to be messiahs or perceived as such by followers, such as Joseph Smith, the founder of Mormonism; the Lubavitcher Rebbe; and the Imam Mahdi of the Sudan. These figures and followers fit squarely within the tradition of messiah-beliefs.

Many Christians believe that Christ will return to the earth and reign for a millennium before the Last Judgment. The belief is called "millenarianism," and it is based on a passage in the book of Revelation (20:1–10) describing the imprisonment of Satan and the "first resurrection" of righteous souls during this period, a great battle with Satan, the Judgment of all souls, and then the creation of a "new Jerusalem," a new heaven and earth.

There are further refinements of this belief, discussed later, but the term has been used to describe beliefs and movements in Christianity and in other religions in which leaders promise a world transformation. Such movements have particular appeal to those people who believe that the entire society needs to be changed and that some great event is needed to accomplish these changes. Contemporary U.S. society produces such figures and their followers at near-regular intervals—David Koresh, or Jim Jones, for example. But so do other modern societies: Mahdis or Imams in Islamic societies, or spiritual healers in Japan. Millenarian movements developed in one context often spread to others, as when the Zion Church of Chicago became a basis for a "countercultural" church in colonial South Africa (Comaroff 1985). Other examples of these movements include modern Melanesian "cargo cults," movements based on expectations of social transformation when native peoples acquire the same wealth or "cargo" as owned by Europeans, and the Chinese T'ai-ping Rebellion, a late–nineteenth-century rebellion against the Ch'ing dynasty that was inspired by the vision of a new Heavenly Kingdom close at hand.

In the discussion that follows I use the relatively neutral term *revitalization movements,* taken from Anthony Wallace (1956, 265). Wallace defines such a movement as "a deliberate, organized, conscious effort by members of a society to construct a more satisfying culture." Although his definition imputes a singular psychology to such movements, it aptly emphasizes that such movements are creative, and aimed toward social and cultural improvement. The term revitalization movements, then, may describe the general category of religious movements that promise a radically changed future. Other terms refer to specific features of such movements. "Millenarian" applies to movements that envisage a thousand-year reign of Christ; "messianic" covers a wider range of reference.

Land, Wealth, and Religious Visions

Even where something short of a millennium was prophesied, a wide variety of revitalization movements arising in colonized parts of Asia and Africa have drawn on the imagery and language of the book of Revelations, often associating it with the power and wealth of the colonizers (Burridge 1969; Trompf 1995).

Throughout the Pacific Islands, colonization brought rapid and often radical changes to local ways of life. Three transformations stand out. Colonists seized lands that had belonged to local people. Missionaries built schools and hospitals, and through conversion created new divisions among people. Europeans also brought new manufactured goods and encouraged or demanded of locals that they grow cash crops and purchase these goods.

Local responses to these dislocations highlighted the three issues of land, trade goods, and religious innovation. Their particular emphases were shaped by specific local conditions, but they usually featured creative combinations of European and local ideas and practices. Some responses drew on Christian paradigms; others blamed their own neglect of their gods as responsible for current troubles and emphasized the revival of customs or rituals. One variety of these Oceanic revitalization movements was based on the premise that if local people engaged in some European religious practices, then they would receive European trade goods. These movements came to be called "cargo cults," from *cargo,* the neo-Melanesian word for trade goods.

Maori Prophecies in New Zealand

European settlers in New Zealand drove large numbers of Maori people off their lands in order to create room for new colonial settlements. Maori swidden agriculture (crops grown on land recently cleared of vegetation) required large tracts of land to lie fallow for extended periods, and the people gathered important foodstuffs and other materials from the forests. Colonists converted vast areas of fallow scrub land and forest into permanent grassland for grazing their sheep. Depriving Maori of their land also deprived them of the signs of their worth and power, or mana. Maori responded by attacking settlers, and the result was protracted conflict throughout the 1850s and 1860s. Maori united behind a new king, but settler attacks and reprisals continued, and in 1862 there emerged a new movement, this one based on prophetic leadership.

The new movement, named "Hauhau," was led by the prophet Te Ua, who claimed to have been given new revelations by the angel Gabriel. The movement illustrates two conflicting pressures in many revitalization movements: awaiting God's actions versus taking matters into one's own hands. Te Ua advocated remaining peaceful and letting God destroy the settlers on behalf of his chosen people—here the prophet assimilated the plight of the Maoris to the Biblical plight of the Jews. Te Ua instigated religious rituals in which he and his followers chanted hymns around a mast salvaged from a British ship.

But Te Ua also reported a revelation that uttering the word *hau* would render them invulnerable and mobilize the many angels waiting to help the Maoris drive the Europeans into the sea. The hymn-chanting also included barking out the word *hau* as they circled the mast. Te Ua staged raids on British military camps. Miraculous powers began to be attributed to him, and his movement gathered supporters from Maori alarmed at the European usurpation of their lands. After some skirmishes, Te Ua surrendered in 1868. Hauhau became a church, and it still survives till today.

The Hauhau adherents linked their loss of land to missionaries' activities. As one man put it in a speech to villagers: "These men, these missionaries were always telling us, 'Lay up for yourselves treasures in heaven'. And so, while we were looking up to heaven, our land was snatched from beneath our feet" (Burridge 1969, 19).

Cargo Cults in Samoa and New Guinea

A movement in Samoa during the 1830s and 1840s was largely motivated by the desire to possess the power and control—mana—that some Samoans associated with European trade goods. Here emerged a cargo cult, intended to produce new material wealth, but also based on a new combination of religious ideas. Siovili, the leader of the movement that bore his name, was an early convert to Christianity and traveled widely on European ships, visiting Tahiti and Australia, among other places. He was subject to trances and traditional forms of spirit possession (Burridge 1969, 22–27).

Upon his return to Samoa, Siovili began to claim that Jehovah and Jesus Christ spoke through him. Some of his followers thought he was Christ. He stated that those who joined him in following these religious practices of the Europeans would share in the European goods. But his movement was also religious, one of many cults found in Samoa in this period that emerged out of the various missionary teachings and immigrants from other islands. Chiefs competed for the manas that the new religious ideas might bring them. Other Samoans joined churches and cults for a variety of motives.

Siovili's followers built churches, brought various books to service, and recited words over them in the hope that these acts would bring Jesus with his material gifts (Trompf 1995, 174–175). One of Siovili's followers claimed that she had become possessed by Jesus Christ and announced that Christ was about to revisit the earth, at which time the dead would arise from their graves. She ordered other Samoans to throw out the crops growing in their gardens, walk down to the sea, and there await Christ's arrival. Christ would cause abundant food and goods to fall from the sky. This woman's followers did wait on the beach for three days, after which time they returned to their gardens to see if they could rescue any remaining food (Burridge 1969, 15–27).

Cargo cults are especially common in Melanesia, the area that includes New Guinea and Fiji, perhaps because of the importance of prestige goods in these societies. Political leadership and social prestige in many Melanesian societies result from success in accumulating and redistributing food and other goods. But the revitalization movements in Melanesia were also religious movements, inspired by new religious ideas and practices.

One Melanesian movement that attracted a particular degree of foreign attention was called the "Vailala Madness," a series of events occurring among the Elema people along the Vailala River in New Guinea from 1919 to 1922 (Worsley 1968, 75–92). As with the Maori, the "Vailala Madness" grew out of a particular conjuncture of resistance to colonial land control, religious innovation, and the desire for new material wealth. Just prior to the "madness," the Anglo-Persian Oil Company had begun drilling for oil in the region; both this company and plantation owners took Elema men away as indentured laborers. Many of the workers died of dysentery. Meanwhile, European authorities were extracting agricultural revenue from the district by ordering the Elema to pay a head tax and to grow rice for sale. Elema had no desire to do either.

The local mission church authorities, from the London Missionary Society, supported the colonial cause but also urged Elema churchgoers to transform their lives through spiritual experience. These Elema did just that: they began to speak in tongues and be possessed by the Holy Spirit. Although church authorities interpreted their behavior as spiritual growth and enthusiasm, colonial authorities came to view the behavior as a dangerous "madness." One observer described local people "taking a few quick steps in front of them, and they would then stand, jabber and gesticulate, at the same time swaying the head from side to side; also bending the body from side to side from the hips" (Worsley 1968, 75). People so possessed said they had been given special powers by the ancestors to divine and to cure.

The leaders of the movement were men who had traveled out of the district; many had been pressed into service in the oil fields or plantations. They abolished traditional practices, burning sacred objects and substituting their own prophecies. The prophet Evara foretold the coming of a new order without the colonizers. Ships would bring back the spirits of dead ancestors (including those who had died while laboring for the Europeans) and considerable cargo, material goods. He and other leaders told their followers to engage in actions that would bring back the spirits. Tables were set up in the villages, with flowers on them, around which the relatives of dead persons would sit, dressed in European style. Some leaders contacted ancestors through the village flagpoles, perhaps on the model of the Anglo–Persian Oil Company's wireless (Worsley 1968, 85). Leaders ordered strict moral codes to be observed, including observing Sunday as a day of rest.

Although after many years the movement gradually died down, some living in the area remembered it as having produced real miracles: messages *had* been received via the flagpoles; the steamers of the ancestors *had* arrived; "the ground shook and the trees swayed" (Worsley 1968, 90–91).

The Ghost Dance in North America

Similar to the Oceanic movements was the Ghost Dance that was begun by Paiute Native American prophets and then spread across the North American Plains. Born in conditions of repression and starvation, the dance has continued its existence as part of a political and cultural heritage for some Native Americans, though with a changing message.

First introduced in 1870, the dance was revived and its message spread widely by a Paiute prophet in western Nevada, Wovoka (c. 1856–1932). During a solar eclipse in 1889, Wovoka fell into a trance, during which, as he later reported, he rose to the other world, where he saw God. God instructed him to remain on peaceful terms with white people and to dance a special circle dance that would place dancers in contact with the spirit world; hence its name. Dancing the dance would hasten the time when the people would be reunited with the dead, he taught. Euro-Americans would be wiped out, and Native Americans would return to their earlier state of plenty. (European manufactured goods would remain behind for Native American use.)

Wovoka's prophecy was spread both by word of mouth and by delegations sent to see him from other Native American groups. Some delegates returned reporting that Wovoka, as "the messiah," had done wondrous things: made animals talk, descended from heaven on a cloud, and conjured up a vision of the spirit world.

As the message spread into new areas, with different cultural backgrounds and different relationships to the Euro-Americans, it was transformed. In Wovoka's message, the destruction of Euro-Americans was to happen automatically, and less as a punishment than as a means for Native Americans to regain their earlier ascendancy. His prophecy stood in a tradition in this part of North America of myths about the dead returning to life and inaugurating an age of plenty.

In Dakota Territory, however, the Sioux interpreted the teachings in a different context. The culture as well as the economy of the Sioux had revolved around the buffalo: buffalo furnished food and materials for houses and bedding and were the objects of many rituals. The art of hunting was a central part of life. All this was lost when Europeans wiped out the buffalo herds. During the 1870s and 1880s, the Sioux were confined to smaller and smaller territories until, in 1890, they occupied a particularly barren part of the Dakota territory, where, deprived of buffalo, they were supposed to live from crops, cattle, and government rations. In 1888 the cattle were destroyed by disease, and the following year the crops failed, followed by epidemics of measles and whooping cough. In 1890 came another crop failure and a reduction in government rations.

In March, 1890, Sioux delegates returned from seeing the messiah, Wovoka, and within a few months most Sioux had begun to practice the Ghost Dance. In their version of the message, the Spirit had sent the Euro-Americans to punish them for their sins but had now returned to their side and had made European bullets powerless against them. To prepare for the coming catastrophe, Sioux must rid themselves of European things, they said. No metal of any kind was allowed in the Sioux dances, and people began to wear "ghost shirts" of buckskin or cloth. Nor was any weapon carried in the dance. (The ghost shirt was not part of the Paiute dance and was disavowed by Wovoka.)

In October 1890, Sitting Bull began to practice the dance at his camp, claiming that he had received a direct message from the spirit world to do so. He urged all Sioux to gather in one place and dance, to advance the coming of the great change. Although he did not urge the dancers toward violence, publicity about the Ghost Dance movement exacerbated Euro-American fears of renewed fighting with the Sioux. Government soldiers were sent to arrest Sitting Bull, and they killed him in his camp. Shortly thereafter occurred the massacre of a band of Sioux at Wounded Knee. Some Sioux killed at Wounded Knee wore the ghost shirts, believing them to be impenetrable by bullets.

After these events, and the failure of the expected resurrection to take place, Wovoka, in Nevada, began to alter his message, stressing the importance of proper living. Other groups picked up the dance and the messages, now shorn of the predictions of a coming apocalypse. In Wyoming, the Shoshone combined the Ghost Dance with a ceremony of thanks to God. During the ritual, shamans would report visions of the dead waiting in heaven to return to earth. The Ghost Dance occupied a place in subsequent Native American religious and political life. Later, Christian converts among the Sioux reconceptualized the messiah of the Ghost Dance as Christ. In the 1970s, as Wounded Knee became, for some Native Americans, a symbol of U.S. repression, the American Indian Movement revived the dance.

Christian Millenarian Movements in the United States

Many early Christians expected the Second Coming in their lifetimes, and millenarian movements flourished in western Europe in the medieval and early modern periods (Cohn 1970). Today as well, some Christians consider the millennium to be near. Believers hold one of two ideas about the millennium, however, and the difference between the two ideas, fine as it might seem on paper, has important implications for the role of the believer in the world. Since the 1940s, the two ideas have defined two different groups of U.S. churches (Casanova 1994, 135–145; Wuthnow 1989).

One group, which includes Seventh-Day Adventists and most groups calling themselves Fundamentalists, follows the idea of "premillennialism," that Jesus will return to reign before the millennium. Before he arrives, the world will grow increasingly corrupt, until finally those who are truly saved will be taken up to heaven in a "rapture," leaving the others to face a time of tribulations. These groups keep separate from the sinful world, as we saw in Chapter 8, building their own schools and universities for their children.

By contrast, "postmillennialists" hold that Jesus will come after the world has experienced a millennium of harmonious existence. For most people in this group, which includes many Evangelical Christian denominations, the task at hand is converting as many people as possible to Christianity, in order to prepare the world for Jesus. Led by Billy Graham and others, and emphasizing conversion, large rallies involve healing and speaking in tongues and worldwide crusades. Jimmy Swaggert, for example, regularly tours the world to address crowds in soccer stadiums and other large venues. In Brazil, during the 1980s the work of these U.S. evangelists led to new conversions from Catholicism or Afro-Brazilian religions to an Evangelical church on the order of 10 million (Riding 1987).

The tendency of Fundamentalists to separate from the world was challenged in the 1970s, when the Moral Majority movement led by Jerry Falwell urged Fundamentalists to work to change the world. José Casanova (1994, 156) argues that Falwell and others realized that fundamentalism "cannot survive in a world devoid of shared moral meanings and standards, in a postmodern world in which it would become just another quaint subculture, like that of the native Indians or the Amish, to be added to the 'gorgeous mosaic' of American cultural pluralism."

Mormon Prophecy and Authority

*T*he history of the Mormons shows both how a movement changes the nature of its authority from charismatic (in this case, prophetic) to bureaucratic, and how it adapts to demands made by an encompassing political structure (in this case, the U.S. government).

Joseph Smith, Prophet

The Church of Jesus Christ of Latter-Day Saints, commonly known as the Mormon Church, traces its origins to a man Mormons consider a prophet, Joseph Smith (Anderson 1942; Shipps 1985). In the 1820s Smith received divine revelations concerning certain records that had been written on golden plates and buried near his home near Palmyra, New York. According to his own account, Smith unearthed the plates and translated them "from Reformed Egyptian" to English with the aid of two translation stones. By 1829, two years after he found the plates, Smith had completed translating them. He had kept the plates away from the vision of others, working on one side of a curtain while his scribe—initially his wife—remained on the other. He was then given further directions through divine revelation, and in particular he was directed to found a new church of Christ. In it, he would speak as a prophet and would initiate others, who would also speak God's words. The church would baptize people in a new covenant with God, augmenting the earlier covenants delivered through Moses and Jesus Christ.

Smith published the translation as the Book of Mormon in 1830. Smith was thoroughly familiar with the King James Version of the Bible, and the Book of Mormon is written in the same style, with a similar organization into books and sections. The Book of Mormon tells of a tribe of Israelites who, in about 600 B.C.E., sailed to the Americas. There they built cities and temples and continued to obey the Law of Moses. They were visited by Jesus Christ after his death and resurrection. Christ performed miracles and organized a new church with 12 disciples. But the Israelites fought among themselves. In a reprise of Cain versus Abel, one group, the Lamanites, who had become hunters, disobeyed God's word, but it was they who prevailed over the other group, the peaceful farming Nephites. (The Lamanites' descendants are said to be today's Native Americans.) The last remaining Nephite prophet was Mormon, who wrote an account of the travels and struggles of these Israelites on gold plates and passed them on to his son, Moroni. Moroni buried the plates for discovery by the people who could restore the church that had once existed in America. It was Moroni's angel who revealed to Smith the location of the tablets. The "Latter-Day Saints" of the church are those who respond to the new direct revelations from God, the first revelations since those delivered through Christ. In the Mormon view, Christianity was misled soon after its founding. God had decided to reestablish his true church, with Smith as its prophet.

Soon after the book's publication, Smith began to attract a small group of followers, a few of whom attested to having seen the gold tablets. The group grew over time, and eventually followed Smith from New York. His success as a prophet must be seen in the religious context of his place and time. In the northeast United States of the 1820s, a diversity of religious faiths and movements abounded. This diversity was due in part to the intensity of the religious emotions following on the Second Great Awakening, a period of religious revival throughout the region that had begun three decades earlier. The revival encouraged religious experimentation and the questioning of established churches. (Adventism also began in this region during the same period.) Many people sought more direct forms of contact with Jesus Christ than those offered through standard liturgies. Joseph Smith himself said he was confused by the diversity of religions open to him, and his first revelation was mainly a message from a divine figure telling him not to join any of the existing churches, but to recover the authentic form of Christianity. As with Islam, Mormonism began as, and remains today, a call to return to the purity of the early worship of God.

Smith's part of New York State was also replete with Native American populations and mounds of ancient origin, and the Book of Mormon responded to a deep curiosity about the origins of Native Americans and the identities of the mound builders. (This curiosity also spurred on early archeological speculation in North America.)

Smith himself already had a reputation as a person in touch with the unseen. Before he received the revelations, he had found a "seerstone," a smooth, egg-shaped stone used to locate lost objects. Indeed, he and his father worked as treasure hunters, benefiting from generally accepted beliefs in the powers of seers. After his first revelation, members of his family stopped attending the local Presbyterian church, and joined him in waiting to found a new church of apostles of Christ.

Relatives and neighbors began to accept Joseph's claims, not despite his reputation as a practitioner of magical arts, but *because* that reputation supported his claims to have found a true treasure. Soon the church had 40 members, with Joseph as its Prophet, Seer, Apostle of Jesus Christ, and Elder.

In 1831 Smith moved the church to Kirtland, Ohio, which he proclaimed was on the eastern edge of Zion, the church's ultimate destination. There he attempted to construct a communal form of economy based on sharing, the legacy of which is the tithe, one-tenth of one's income that members are expected to pay the church. Financial difficulties and local hostilities led Smith to move some of the Ohio Mormons to Missouri. Their partial economic success in Missouri, their perceived socialism and the large numbers of immigrants they attracted, led to local attacks on the Mormons (Leone 1979, 11–16). Smith at one point made explicit the parallel to Muhammad's experience of a call for religious purity followed by persecution, when he publicly proclaimed, "I will be a second Muhammad." This parallel hardly improved his image locally, and in 1838, after renewed attacks on the community, the Mormons moved back across the Mississippi to an Illinois town they renamed Nauvoo.

In Nauvoo, Smith rebuilt the church around the divine revelations he continued to receive. These instructions included the doctrine, written down privately in 1843, that God intended males to take more than one wife. This doctrine, announced publicly from Salt Lake City in 1852, was part of a new vision of the afterlife, in which marriages properly conducted by the church would be for eternity, and a man with his wives and all his progeny would move on to rule new worlds. Taking plural wives would mean a larger retinue of progeny, and it followed the example of the Hebrew patriarchs Abraham, Isaac, and Jacob (Foster 1981, 123–180).

Smith attracted many additional adherents, most of whom, poor, had left unprofitable farmlands or poorly paid factory jobs, and were attracted by the utopian message of the Mormons. The community grew into tens of thousands, with Smith as its leader, now declared to be King of the Kingdom of God. He became increasingly despotic, and in 1844 he destroyed an opposition press, an action that led to his arrest. On June 27, 1844, a mob stormed the jail where he was held and lynched him.

The New Prophet and Conflicts with the United States

As with most prophet-led movements, Smith's death left no automatic successor. Struggles for leadership produced several factions. In particular, two lines of reasoning emerged. One group argued that the Smith's descendants had inherited his right to rule. This group followed members of Smith's family back to Missouri, where they established the Reorganized Church of Latter-Day Saints. This church is headquartered today in Independence, Missouri. A second group, the majority, continued the leadership of Smith's church, arguing that the followers had the right to choose their leader. They chose an elder, Brigham Young, to become the new Prophet and Elder. Young led the community westward, across the Great Plains, to the Great Salt Lake in what is today Utah. (A similar debate over succession, at the break between charismatic and "routinized" authority, occurred in Islam, as we shall see in the next section.)

By 1849, Brigham Young had established an autonomous, theocratic (religion-ruled) state on the lake called Deseret. Hundreds of small communities sprung up in orbit around the lake, extending into today's Arizona, Colorado, Nevada, and California. The need for cooperation in creating irrigation provided a material base for authority in these new communities; the church held them together through an intricate hierarchy of leaders and through its ownership of numerous enterprises.

In 1850 the territory came under U.S. rule, and tensions quickly mounted between the Mormons and a U.S. government toward which Mormons had always felt uneasy. For its part, the government feared that the Mormons might refuse to acknowledge U.S. sovereignty. During the 1850s, armed conflict occurred on several occasions between Mormons and "Gentiles" (non-Mormons), and in 1857 President James Buchanan sent an army of five thousand troops to try to occupy Utah. Polygamy, now made public, become a symbol of the conflict, and in 1862 Congress banned it (Firmage 1991). In 1879 the U.S. Supreme Court upheld the U.S. statutory ban on polygamy, declaring it not to infringe religious freedom but rather to protect the vital social institution of monogamous marriages. In 1890 the Court upheld additional, severe legislation that dissolved the Mormon Church as a corporation and confiscated most major church properties. The Mormon Church president responded to these assaults by advising his followers not to contract plural marriage or polygamy. However, he did not characterize the directive to be a revelation, as most other important directives had been and would continue to be characterized. Some Mormons continued to practice polygamy. By statehood, in 1896, the church was deeply in debt. Mormons had become part of a larger economy of the Western states, characterized by industries of mining, livestock, timber, and railroad, all bankrolled from the East. But since the 1930s the church has regenerated its wealth, building on its tithing requirement, and Mormons have become successful capitalist entrepreneurs.

Authority and History Today

The Book of Mormon continues to serve as a sacred book to today's Mormons, who number nearly 5 million in the United States, and about 2.5 million overseas. The Mormon following expands both through extensive missionary activities and by encouraging large families—children are said to incarnate already existing spirits and to advance one's own standing in the next world. Beginning at age 12, every Mormon male passes through several grades in each of two orders of priesthood. At about age 18, most men also go on a two-year mission for the church and are rewarded by passing into the second, adult priesthood order.

Mormons are grouped into wards of about 700 persons; 10 wards make up a Stake of Zion, headed by a president. The center of Mormon activity is Salt Lake City, where the Quorum of Twelve Apostles manages the church. The senior apostle becomes the church's president on the death of the previous president. Mormons attend local chapels and at intervals also attend services at one of the temples found in different parts of the United States and overseas. Chapels hold Sunday services, centered on a form of communion that is quite similar to that held in Lutheran and some other Protestant churches. Lay persons preside over the service and do most of the talking. Rituals held in the larger temples are kept secret from non-Mormons, but they include services held both for the living and for deceased ancestors of living Mormons.

Mormons attach great importance to the long-term historical record. They do so in part because of their ideas about salvation, and in part because of the particular historical account provided in the Book of Mormon. First, Mormons see themselves as capable of saving the souls of deceased persons. Ancestors of Mormons who lived before the advent of Mormonism may be baptized into the church, with a living person standing in for the ancestor. These souls may then be taken through the successive temple rites that move persons up the ranks of the priesthood. These ancestors may be very far removed, and in theory those who can be aided include a large percentage of the world's people. But to do so one must establish the connection to a living Mormon. Therefore, Mormons carry out extensive research into the family trees of, in theory, everyone in the world. The resulting vast holdings of genealogical records, located in Salt Lake City, are available to non-Mormons as well as to members of the church.

Second, history matters because history underlies the church's claims to authority. The Mormon Apostles see themselves as the direct heirs of God's message to humankind, through the media of the buried tablets and succeeding direct revelations to the church's prophets. The rationale for these revelations lies in the saga of Israelites fleeing Jerusalem, founding a new community, witnessing Christ, and establishing a new covenant with

God. Though the community was eventually destroyed, it left its message for the latter-day prophet, Joseph Smith, through whom God's communication with his people was reopened.

History thus provides the rationale, the reasonable account, of why it was that Joseph Smith became a new prophet. The historical record of continued revelations to his successors depicts them, too, as prophets. In the eyes of the outside analyst, the charismatic authority of Joseph Smith was replaced by the bureaucracy of the church in Salt Lake City. In the eyes of the church leadership, however, Smith's successors continue to serve as prophets, seers, and apostles. They continue to receive charisma, divine blessings, from God, in the form of revelations. Charismatic authority is changed but not lost.

This historical account does, however, present Mormons with dilemmas in everyday life, especially in their attitudes toward Native Americans. Believed descended from the Lamanites, the ancient people who disobeyed God and wiped out the obedient Nephites, Native Americans are nonetheless also descended from Israelites. They are thus of the same origins as are Mormons, and for a group that places great emphasis on genealogy this connection gives Native Americans a special status. They are entitled to convert and become full members of the church, a privilege long denied to African Americans. Mark Leone (1979, 174–177) describes a service in an Arizona chapel at which a missionary couple described their experience living for several years on a Navajo reservation. The couple spoke from their experience in business about how Navajo were like anyone else. The couple's talk encouraged their listeners to put aside conflicting attitudes toward the Navajo and to get on with their twin concerns of commerce and conversion.

Muhammad and His Successors

When Joseph Smith announced that he would be "a second Muhammad," he was referring to the special role played by the Prophet of Islam vis-à-vis previous religions. Muhammad, like Smith, saw himself as God's vehicle to perfect and complete the work of revelation. In the views of both men, Judaism and Christianity were indeed the results of God's revelations, but the two traditions' leaders had strayed from the original message.

Islam was also born against a background of polytheism, however, and the statement most often pronounced by a Muslim, called the confession of faith, begins with the dictum: "There is no other deity but God." Islam began in the central desert area of the Arabian peninsula in the seventh century C.E. Trade and social life were organized by tribes, without central authorities. Power resided in one's lineage connections. Arabs worshiped many deities, although trade with Syria had also brought the monotheistic ideas of Judaism and Christianity.

Muhammad's own tribe, the Quraysh, dominated the city of Mecca by its control of the caravan trade. Mecca became a religious as well as a trade center; people came to the city on pilgrimages to its shrines, which included the Ka'ba. Several verses of the Qur'ân berate the Meccans for worshiping many gods and for letting the Ka'ba, built by the prophet Abraham (as we saw in Chapter 13), degenerate into a site of pagan worship.

Monotheism remains one of the central emphases in Islam. This emphasis makes especially sensitive the appeals routinely made by many Muslims to other entities (spirits, saints, or prophets) that they intercede with God. These appeals are often branded as polytheism by other Muslims, who cite the Qur'ânic texts originally directed at the merchants of Mecca.

Muhammad as Messenger and Prophet

The second part of the confession of faith reads: "and Muhammad is his Messenger." Muhammad was born about 570 C.E., and was orphaned early in his life. He married an older woman, a trader, and managed her caravan. He began to receive revelations when he was 40 years old, in 610 (Peters 1994). The first verse of the Qur'ân to be revealed reached Muhammad when he was in a cave. The archangel Gabriel appeared to him and said: "Recite, in the name of the Lord who created, created man from a clot." (The first word of this verse is sometimes translated as "read," and quoted as evidence that God intends people to educate themselves.)

Muhammad then began to warn the Meccan people of the errors of their polytheistic ways. A few men followed him; most threatened him, and in 622 he fled or made the emigration (*hijra*) to the nearby city of Medina. The emigration marks the beginning of the lunar Islamic calendar. In Medina, Muhammad became the leader of the community through his skill in arbitrating between its several populations. He joined with the Jews of the city in praying in the direction of Jerusalem; verses revealed during this time stress the similarity of the two religions. (These verses include the dietary laws, for example.) Muhammad's growing group of followers engaged the Meccans in several battles, most notably those of Badr and Uhud, and his victories finally won him the right to make the pilgrimage to Mecca. He died after making the pilgrimage, in 632.

The place of Muhammad in Islam is both as the Messenger of God and as the Seal of the Prophets. As Messenger of God, Rasulullah, he brought a new collection of God's revealed word to humankind. Other messengers in the past had brought other books: Moses, the Torah; David, the Psalms; and Jesus, the Gospels. This lineage of revelation makes Jews and Christians, along with Muslims, "people of the book." (Hindus were later included in this category because of their use of sacred texts.) Because of their special status, members of these two religious communities were accorded special, protected treatment in Muslim-held territories.

As a prophet (*nabi*) Muhammad is the last in a long series of prophets, including the earlier Messengers. Among the prophets mentioned in the Qur'ân are Abraham, Noah, Hud, Salih, Lot, and Shu'ayb. Hud, Salih, and Shu'ayb do not figure in the Hebrew Bible, but appear in various stories, often as specifically Middle Eastern personages. Shu'ayb warns his people against dishonest business practices, as Moses warned the Pharaoh against preventing the Israelites from going free.

Muhammad was thus human, a normal human being granted the role of God's mouthpiece. What is sent are words, and not Muhammad himself. Because all messengers are said to have this status, Muslims strongly deny the claim that Jesus was the son of God. Nonetheless, many Western commentators on Islam continue to make the error of presuming that the place of Muhammad in Islam is analogous to that of Jesus in

Christianity. (Islam once was called "Muhammadanism" in the West.) It would be more accurate to draw an analogy between Jesus in Christianity and the Qur'ân in Islam, in that each is held by the religion's adherent to be God's major gift to humans. Similarly, the Gospels, the accounts of the life and statements of Jesus, are best compared not to the Qur'ân but to the hadith, the record of Muhammad's life and statements.

Who Rules after Muhammad?

Muhammad's authority in the early Muslim community came from his direct ties to God. He was a prophet but would have to be succeeded by someone who was not a prophet. Who was to rule after his death? On what principle should he be chosen? Or in Weber's terms, how was Muhammad's charismatic authority to be converted into a routine mechanism for selecting leaders?

Muhammad had neither designated a successor nor suggested a way of doing so. He had no male heir, but had there been one, it is not clear that this person would have succeeded him. As it happens, upon Muhammad's death in 632, his closest followers in Medina gathered and chose one among them, Abû Bakr, to be the first caliph (*khalîfa*), "deputy" of the Prophet. He in turn was succeeded by another close follower, 'Umar, under whose able rule Muslim armies conquered the rest of Arabia and moved on to Egypt. 'Umar realized the need to create a regular procedure for choosing rulers, and convened a council (shûrâ) to select a new caliph. This action legitimated the idea of reaching decisions by council, and the process continues to be followed in the Muslim world. 'Umar's committee chose a weak candidate, 'Uthmân, an early convert to Islam, who was assassinated in his own house by dissident soldiers.

The Development of the Shî'î

The next caliph was 'Alî, one of the key figures in Islamic history. 'Alî was the son-in-law of the Prophet and also his cousin and had a great deal of support because of his kin ties. He was the closest heir available to the community. But he failed to punish 'Uthmân's assassins and revoked some of his decrees and thereby provoked the ire of 'Uthmân's own kinsmen, a powerful Meccan aristocratic clan called the Umayyads. Their own leader, Mu'âwiya, challenged 'Alî's leadership. He called for a new council to select a caliph, and met 'Alî in battle (the dispute was arbitrated). 'Alî's rule began to crumble and he was assassinated in 661. His son Hasan abdicated in favor of Mu'âwiya, who began a new period of Umayyad dominance. But 'Alî's other son, Husayn, grandson of the Prophet, became the champion of dissident Muslims who began to see themselves as the "party of 'Alî." In 680 an event occurred that was to mark the Muslim world forever after: en route to the Iraqi city of Kûfa, Husayn was ambushed and his entire company massacred by Umayyad forces at a place called Karbala. His head was taken as proof of the defeat.

The Karbala massacre became the pivotal event in the emergence and identity of the party of 'Alî. Now known as the Shî'î, or "party," this group conceived of legitimate authority as forever charismatic. The spiritual and temporal authority of the Prophet was handed down through his grandchildren to a succession of spiritually perfect leaders called *imâms*. Born in opposition to the regime in power, the Shî'îs, or Shiites, have continued to stress the chasm between political realities and a longed-for truly Islamic world. Shiite populations, most importantly in Iran, Iraq, and Lebanon, formed communities of teaching and learning divorced from the regimes under whose control they had to live. The date of the Karbala massacre, the tenth of the month of Muharram, 680, is commemorated annually in *ta'ziya,* or martyr plays, that feature the assassination of Husayn. Sometimes the events include processions of men striking themselves with chains to participate in the pain and sadness that characterize the Shiite community's historical self-understanding (Momen 1985).

By contrast, the Umayyads and their successors saw themselves as the majority party and the continuers of the Prophet's ways, calling themselves "Sunnîs," after *sunna,* (the Prophet's) custom or practices. Sunni conceptions of authority return to the first council that chose the caliph. The entire Muslim community, or umma, inherits political authority, which they then bestow on a leader through a council. This way of routinizing authority drew on Arab tribal ideas of succession and loyalty, and also was effective in incorporating new peoples as part of the umma. It has meant that Sunni spiritual leaders have tended to play roles in political life.

Notice how the split in the Muslim world over succession fell along the same lines as did that affecting the Mormon community centuries later. One party elected a leader to follow the prophet, while another chose to follow his descendants. In both cases the "kinship party" refused to lose the charismatic quality of prophetic leadership; they repudiated the routinization of authority. In both cases this party proved to be the minority one.

Masters and Disciples in Sufi Orders

A third type of authority, alongside the council and kinship, is that possessed by the Sufi master toward his disciples. Sufi orders offer paths to greater spiritual awareness and closeness to God, through prayer, chanting, and poetry. Each such order offers a specific *tarîqa* ("way" or "method"). The current teacher or master in the order traces his authority back along a spiritual lineage to his teacher, that teacher's teacher, and so forth, usually back to the Prophet Muhammad and, through him, to God (Eickelman 1976).

The first order was founded by the Persian scholar Abdul Qâdir al-Jîlânî (1078–1166). Abdul Qâdir's influence as a preacher grew so large that followers established a special retreat for him, where people came to study and listen. He taught that to approach God, people would first need to divest themselves of worldly goods; that these goods acted as veils that came between them and God. As in other Sufi orders, he urged people to practice *dhikr:* "remembrance" of God by chanting phrases either aloud or in one's heart. Dhikr chants vary from one order to the next, but often include multiple recitations of "there is no deity but God" (*lâ ilâha illâ 'llâh*), the first half of the confession of faith, and of praise phrases such as "glory be to God" (*subhan Allâh*). These activities of remembrance may also be enhanced by music and dance, such as those performed by members of a Turkish order called the "Mevlevi" (dedicated to the Persian poet Rûmî) and known in the West as "whirling dervishes" (Schimmel 1973).

After Abdul Qâdir's death, people began to ascribe miracles to him, and consider him a saint. His sons, and their sons, and so on, succeeded him as heads of the Qâdirî order. As the order spread throughout Asia and North Africa it gave rise to suborders, each linking themselves back to Abdul Qâdir. These orders were an effective way of converting people to Islam, offering as they did spiritual activities and a well-organized religious structure. Each present-day Qâdirî order has its own spiritual genealogy, detailing the transmission of knowledge back to Abdul Qâdir (and continuing on to Muhammad). These spiritual genealogies connect Muslims in South and Southeast Asia, the Middle East, northern and western Africa, and Europe into an international network of Sufi practice and worship.

The movements we have examined here vary greatly in size, complexity, and purpose—from the Buddhist forest dweller and his followers to revivalist movements of many types, and from Ngundeng the Nuer prophet to the large-scale movements begun by Joseph Smith and Muhammad. In each case we have seen adherents grapple with practical problems of continuity and with their relationship to the outside world. Some have had to ask in the face of crisis, "How shall we continue?" Their answers have involved the creation of routines and bureaucracies, a process remarked upon by Weber, but some answers also involve genealogies and talismans. Alongside the routinization of authority there often continues its charisma: in Acharn Man's medallions, in the powers of the Qâdirî teacher, in the Mormon Elder's revelations, in Ngundeng's songs, which continue to ring out over southern Sudanese radio.

Religious movements and authorities of all forms today are part of modern nation-states, in which they invariably live side by side with others of different faiths and practices. Our discussion of the Church of Latter-Day Saints already touched on the problem of maintaining a religious vision that runs counter to that of a nation's majority; in the concluding chapter we encounter this problem head-on.

For Further Consideration

Several studies of revitalization movements include two excellent books on Melanesia: Peter Worsley's *The Trumpet Shall Sound* (1968) and Kenelm Burridge's *New Heaven, New Earth* (1969), both from Schocken Books. Norman Cohn's *The Pursuit of the Millenium* (revised edition 1970) from Oxford University Press is a study of early European millenarian movements.

To further explore the role of holy men in India, Ann Gold's book on pilgrimage earlier mentioned (*Fruitful Journeys,* 1988) is useful, as are several films, including *Hindu Ascetics* (described by its title) and an interesting three-part series (each 52 minutes) titled, *Sadhus: India's Holy Men.* Both are from Films for the Humanities and Sciences.

The distinctions among pre- and postmillenianists get quite complicated; Garry Wills' book, *Under God* (Simon and Schuster 1990) is a very readable account of religion and politics in the United States, with a great deal of attention to these issues. A good case study is in James Tabor and Eugene V. Gallagher's account of the massacre at Waco,

Texas, called *Why Waco?: Cults and the Battle for Religious Freedom in America* (University of California Press 1995). Tabor and Gallagher emphasize the religious roots of the Waco movement, and especially the importance of the Book of Revelation to many religious movements in the United States. A short film from Films for the Humanities and Sciences, *Religious Fundamentalism,* also explores these topics.

Looking for a project? There may be several different Protestant churches in your area and you could develop a conceptual map of them. Have any of them split off from others? What is the denominational affiliation of each? How does the leader of each see his or her church in relation to others? Which other churches does this one most closely resemble? What distinguishes this church from similar churches? You might select some churches for a quick sociological analysis: Where is the church located? What indications of ethnic and class composition can you find? (Look for the approximate value of cars parked in the lot for a quick class index.) Some churches also have their own Web sites.

15 The Place of Religions in Modern Nations and States

*T*he modern world is a world of states and nations, but in many parts of this world, "nations" and "states" sit in uneasy coexistence. Some states, like Japan, claim to be composed of one people, to possess a single national identity incorporating all, or nearly all, of its citizens. But these claims usually are made despite important internal differences in identity—think of the many Japanese of Korean descent or the sizable Christian (and even Muslim) minorities in the country. In other states, from Sri Lanka to Turkey to Bosnia, large minorities are fighting to create their own separate nation–state. Some states, such as Indonesia or the United States, are defined by the coexistence of different religious and ethnic groups, but even in those countries groups are struggling over national identity.

Religious identity and religious differences often enter into these debates and conflicts. Most countries today include several significantly large religious communities, and this *religious pluralism* is increasing. Muslims are becoming increasingly numerous minorities in countries where they never before played public roles. In the United States they already outnumber Episcopalians and are expected to overtake Jews within the next decade. In France they form the second-largest religious group after Catholics. Protestant Christians are rapidly increasing in numbers in Japan and Brazil, as well as in other countries.

Religious pluralism poses sharp and often divisive questions for the public life of a country. What contribution should each religion make to public political and social life? Can a unifying national identity coexist with publicly celebrated religious differences? If so, can a country avoid preferring one religion to others? From where does one select elements of a shared, civic morality and a common legal framework? These questions concern matters of public policy; other questions are matters of empirical study. What steps, if any, do minority religious communities take to conform to national models of religion or culture? To what extent are such minorities able to win recognition as valid religions or cultures? What changes are made in religious doctrines, or practices, or in the boundaries maintained between their members and others?

Religions play several different kinds of public roles. Religion may become identified with the *nation,* even if it does not play a direct role in government. In the largely Catholic countries of continental Europe and Latin America, church institutions have played major roles in public life, at times claiming to serve as the guardian of the nation. These claims have engendered conflict with citizens seeking an independent definition of the nation. Hindu nationalism in India and Buddhist nationalisms in Sri Lanka and Thailand (as well as movements of Protestant Christian nationalism in the United States) have similarly sought to define the nation around adherence to the religion and around key figures in its history.

Religion may also contribute directly to *state-enforced law.* Israel is defined as a Jewish state, with the enforcement of Jewish law, and many states with Muslim populations enforce Islamic law. We may find state-backed religious courts even in countries where the nation is not defined in religious terms, as in Indonesia, Kenya, and South Africa.

Finally, if we switch perspectives and consider the situation of religious minorities, we find that they must find ways to coexist with what José Casanova (1994) calls "public religions," religious traditions that do not form explicit parts of nation or state, but which nonetheless color public life. Muslims consider themselves to be minorities in the United States and Europe because the dominant public culture is strongly shaped by a Christian (and to a much lesser extent, Jewish) heritage. Around the world, European colonialism often left residues of Christian missionization that local peoples had to either join or resist. But public religions also exist on a smaller scale and place pressure on minorities. Protestants living in Hopi and Mayan communities in North America have had their rights to participate in public community life curtailed. Even if their formal rights were protected by the larger legal structure, their roles in "civil society" have been diminished.

We conclude the chapter with a more detailed look at the U.S. experience, where the separation of religion and state institutions is particularly emphasized.

Religious Nationalisms

We have already seen the ways in which Japanese rulers and others have drawn on Buddhism and Shinto as elements in a state ideology. But it is only since the late nineteenth century that the most thoroughgoing effort has been made to equate a state religion of Shinto with the shared identity of the Japanese people as a nation. This equation continues to underlie the ideologies of new religions in Japan, which stress the biological, social, and religious uniqueness of the Japanese people and the continued enshrinement of war dead as national deities.

What we may call *religious nationalism* involves the construction of an idealized nation in religious terms and the construction of an idealized religion in national terms. The identification of religion and nation is not ancient or primordial; it is part of the recent history of modern nation–states. It involves active efforts by religious and political leaders to convince people that national identity is essentially that of a particular religion, against alternative conceptions of the nation as secular or multiconfessional (with several, equally legitimate religions).

Among such efforts are the invention of religious practices that encompass a national territory. Religious identities are shaped through ritual practices; national religious identities, the sense of oneself as part of a national religion, are shaped through practices that give the actor the sense of being part of a nation. Processions of icons from border to border, pilgrimages to different religious sites within the country, and public speeches that define the nation's territory as religious territory all contribute to a sense of being part of a religiously defined nation. Religious nationalisms also often project backward in time an image of the nation as a long-lived entity that always was intertwined with religion.

The examples of Poland and India illustrate ways in which religious nationalisms can be forged and maintained. In both cases, religious nationalism draws strength from a shared opposition to a perceived foreigner. Poland's identification of the Catholic Church with the nation is in part the product of a history of foreign rule; India's movements of Hindu nationalism feed off of hostility between Hindus and Muslims, even as they maintain and exacerbate that hostility.

Church and Nation in Poland

The Polish people have a long history of struggle against foreign conquerors. Prussia, Russia, and Austria each incorporated parts of the Polish-speaking lands, and in the 1870s German Chancellor Bismark threatened the cultural identity of Poles by pushing for Germanization of all German citizens. Poles also battled against Nazi invaders and a communist state. The cumulative effect of these struggles was to fuse all elements of Polish society together with the Catholic Church. The Church was the only institution capable of cutting across the divided Polish lands. As José Casanova (1994) argues, during the nineteenth century Polish writers developed an ideology of national identity that incorporated Catholic identity. In the twentieth century the Church never became identified with the state—unlike its counterpart in Franco's Spain. The Polish Church thus remained untainted by collaboration, and retained its identification with the nation as a whole.

This argument—that outside oppression supported the identification of church and nation—receives confirmation from the experience between the two world wars, when in the independent Polish state the Church did side with one political party and thereby alienated supporters of other parties. Chauvinism also appeared in the form of oppression of Jewish and Ukrainian minorities. In this experience surfaces the perennial problem with any religious nationalism, namely, its difficulty in adopting tolerant (much less welcoming) attitudes toward religious and ethnic minorities. The religious underpinnings of nationalism may make it more intolerant of people of different faiths, while the nationalist side of religion locates it within a particular territory and may make it more intolerant of people of other origins or countries.

Nazi and communist rule returned Poland to the early situation of a strong church–nation alliance. In part this was because the massacres of Jews and deportations of Ukrainians left Poland in the late 1940s a predominantly Polish and Catholic nation. Also, because of the evident dependence of the communist state on the Soviet Union, there appeared to be no leader representing an independent Polish nation. Given the situation, the head of the Polish Church, Cardinal Wyszynski, could draw on a centuries-old tradition that designated the head of the Church as a temporary leader of the nation in the absence of a head of state. He, in effect, played that role during the years of communist rule.

Equally critical in forging religious nationalism, however, has been the fact that Polish Catholicism is highly public, and could not be forced into becoming a private religion of at-home worship. Even more than in many other Catholic societies, Polish Catholicism centers on large-scale public rituals, including pilgrimages, processions in celebration of the feast of Corpus Christi, and passion plays. These rituals involve the entire territory of Poland and all its Catholic inhabitants. Particularly effective were the Cardinal's series of celebrations involving the national image of Mary, Our Lady of Czestochowa, or the Black Madonna. This shrine, writes Casanova (1994, 98), "serves as the national shrine of Polish Catholicism and as the symbolic fortress of the nation against foreign invasions." After he was released from imprisonment by the communist state in 1956, Cardinal Wyszynski rededicated the nation to the Black Madonna at the 300th anniversary of King John Kazimierz's vows, thus projecting the church–nation union back three centuries. Throughout the 1960s and 1970s he engineered an annual procession of the Black Madonna image to every town in Poland, this impressive achievement keeping salient the linkages between national territory and religious territory.

The Church urged that Poles accept the state's right to rule (it was this agreement that led to the cardinal's release from prison in 1956). However, Cardinal Glemp, the head of the Polish Church since 1981, was also advocating the creation of a confessional Polish state and the repeal of constitutional separation of church and state. The Church had indeed allied itself with the nation, but it also had designs on state power. The dangers of church–state identification in the modern world are best exemplified by Spain, where civil wars in the nineteenth and twentieth centuries became religious wars, with one party backed by the Church. The last of these religious wars, the Spanish Civil War of 1936–1939, served as a proving ground for fascism.

Casanova (1994, 107–113) notes that the Polish Church may well remain on its current course of involvement in public affairs as a player in civil society, not in politics per se. He argues that the direct relationships between churches and political parties in the Europe of the mid–twentieth century (best illustrated by the power of Christian Democratic parties in several countries) is now evolving into a separation of civil society, in which religion plays a public role, and political society, where parties are no longer tied to specific churches and therefore are free to pursue solutions to political problems flexibly, free of church dogmatism. Many Poles agree that the number of pilgrims making their way to Czestochowa each year has declined recently, and that the role of the Church as a political guide has passed (Brzezinski 1994).

Hindu Nationalism in India

Looming over India since its creation in 1947 has been the problematic relationship of the two major religious communities, Hindu and Muslim, to the ideas of "nation" and "state." Although India was created as a secular republic, its birth was accompanied by that of Pakistan and also by massive and blood-stained migrations of Muslims to Pakistan. Today Muslims constitute 12 percent of India's population, and the vast majority in Pakistan and Bangladesh (Bangladesh itself having emerged out of a division within Pakistan). Conflicts between Hindus and Muslims in India today are bound up both with the history of partition, migration, and violence, and with the continuing tensions between India and Pakistan. To some Hindus, Muslims and a Muslim state play the same role of foreign threat that successive conquerors did in convincing Poles of the internal links between church and nation.

The 1980s and 1990s have seen mass conflicts between Hindus and Muslims in India. Are these conflicts religious? Consider the continuing conflict in the north India city of Ayodhya, Rama's birthplace (van der Veer 1994). Ayodhya is a holy tîrtha, a ford over the holy river Sarayu and a place for the pilgrim to "cross over" from the mundane world to make contact with Rama. Most of the city's temples are controlled by members of the Ramanandi order mentioned earlier.

However, some Hindus claim that the Ayodhya mosque, built in the sixteenth century, stands on the spot where Rama was born. This "Babar mosque" (after the Muslim Mogul ruler who built it) has become the focus of increasingly hostile Hindu–Muslim confrontations. Hindus launched attacks on the Babar mosque during the celebration of the Feast of Sacrifice in 1912 and again in 1934. The conflict intensified after the 1947 Partition and the flight of many Muslims to Pakistan. In 1949, a statue of Rama appeared in the mosque. Hindus and Muslims naturally interpreted this event in very different ways. For the Hindus, Rama had appeared in their midst, giving them a sign to liberate his birthplace from the Muslims. For the Muslims, their mosque had been defiled. Riots ensued, and the army was called out. The government closed the mosque, and it remained closed to both Muslims and Hindus until 1984, when national politics came to a head in the city.

By the mid-1980s there had emerged a strong Hindu nationalist party, the Bharatiya Janata Party or BJP, which garnered support from Hindu nationalist movements and in particular from the Vishva Hindu Parishad (VHP). The VHP was an attempt to create a united Hindu organization. Given the diversity in religious practice and beliefs we have examined—diversity by region, by caste, and by class—creating a unified Hinduism would be a daunting task. What Hindus plausibly shared, however, was a belief in certain sacred objects and symbols. One was the sacred river, the Ganges, and in 1983 the VHP organized a drive to symbolize Hindu unity based on shared water. Large trucks were sent throughout the country, each carrying enormous bronze pots with water from the Ganges. This water was given to villagers en route, and the pots were replenished with water from local sacred sources, symbolizing Hindu unity—and also giving the VHP a way to firm up its local support network. Just as the processions of the Black Madonna throughout Poland emphasized the claim to a religion–nation unity, the water trucks' journeys underscored claims that all Indian territory, not just Ayodhya, was sacred Hindu territory.

Hindu unity of course also means opposition to Muslims, and the VHP also called for mosques to be removed from several sacred spots, including Ayodhya. By 1989 the VHP had begun to mobilize support for building a new temple in Ayodhya. In November, just before Indian general elections, Hindus were urged to send or bring bricks for the temple, and bricks poured in—from Hindus in Europe and the United States as well as from throughout India. The VHP was eventually stopped from building the temple by the ruling Congress government, but the flames thus fanned led to massacres of Muslims and numerous Hindu deaths in north and eastern India.

One year later violence erupted again, this time brought on by the political party, the BJP. The BJP joined forces with the VHP in part to oppose the government's plan to reserve a greater number of jobs and positions for lower-caste people. (In its mass support and vote-getting, the BJP appeals most to urban, upper-caste people.) Despite police bans, some volunteers bent on rebuilding "Rama's temple" made it to Ayodhya, where many were killed. In December 1990, to further dramatize BJP support for the Hindu nationalist cause, the party leader L.K. Advani began a "chariot"-led procession to Ayodhya, perhaps because the Ramayana had been serialized on television a few years earlier (Mankekar, 1999). Advani decked his party out as Rama's army. His chariot, drawn by an air-conditioned Toyota, was carved and gilded to recall Rama's chariot. He carried the bow of Rama, brandishing it to ward off his enemies. Supporters, marching alongside, were decked out in warrior garb and handed bows as well. We might note the parallel to the way that the Polish Cardinal timed his processions with the Black Madonna to emphasize the antiquity of church and nation in Poland.

The procession began from a place in Gujarat, in western India, widely associated with the tenth-century destruction by a Muslim ruler of some beautiful Hindu temples. This choice of starting point reinforced anti-Muslim sentiments. The procession moved across India before being halted in the eastern state of Bihar, where Advani was arrested—an arrest that then led to the collapse of the fragile coalition government. Mass strikes and riots followed; all trains and buses that passed anywhere near Ayodhya were canceled, but many people were killed.

A little over a year later the mosque was destroyed. In 1992, supporters of the BJP/VHP drive rushed to Ayodhya and demolished the temple. The riots that ensued led to over one thousand deaths, mostly of Muslims (van der Veer 1994).

Though religious sentiments were front and center during the campaigns and riots, we would err in thinking of these conflicts as the emergence of "primordial" or traditional sentiments in opposition to the nation–state. The conflicts and riots developed out of a modern idea of a Hindu nation–state, itself with roots in colonial constructions of religious communities and postcolonial electioneering. In the nineteenth century the British created the idea of a "Hindu majority"—and a Muslim minority—through the census. They interpreted these categories as native Hindus versus foreign Muslims. This view has had an effect on later Indian notions, promoting the idea that one's primary loyalty as a Hindu is to the "Hindu community" or as a Muslim to the "Muslim community," rather than to local communities or leaders. And it was on these notions that Advani and other Hindu nationalist leaders drew to mobilize support for Rama and anger against Muslims. Although Hindu–Muslim tensions predate colonialism and independence, the kind of violent religious nationalism exhibited in this case (and in many other places) is to a great extent a modern creation.

And for most Hindus, as for most people anywhere, nationalist claims have little to do with the practical bases and emotional pulls of religious practice. "Ram is supposed to dwell in our hearts, not in a temple" said one north Indian villager (quoted in Fuller

1992, 261). "We don't need to learn about our dharma (duty) from politicians seeking votes."

The contrast between Poland and India shows that religious nationalisms may have quite different outcomes. In Poland's case the foreigner was the communist state, and the result of the church–nation alliance seems to have been to promote the creation of an independent state with a relatively well-developed civil society, the church now adopting a lesser role. The contrasting case of India shows how a movement that identifies the foreigner to be a fellow citizen can produce intolerance and violence. The difference is not a matter of religious doctrine—the violence in Catholic Spain and the ambiguous, at best, role of the churches in Nazi Germany belie any notion that one religion develops more socially positive forms of nationalism than another (as does the relative intolerance of the Polish Church during the inter–world war period). The difference seems to lie rather in the extent to which a civil society, in which open debate and deliberation may take place, is part of a particular religious nationalism.

Does the existence of a live civil society require that religion and state (as distinguished from religion and nation) be kept separate? Several other societies allow us to test this notion.

Religion and State Law

*M*ost religions, perhaps all religions, carry with them positive and negative commandments or rules. For many religious people, it is these commandments that distinguish between people like them and people who are fundamentally different. Religious commandments also can enhance the meaning people derive from everyday life, such as we saw in Chapter 8 for one Hasidic woman's attention to Jewish dietary rules.

In many countries today, some religious communities have judicial bodies that enforce some of their own commandments. In the United States, although neither state nor federal laws may grant privileges to one religion over others, the Constitution protects the right to freely exercise religion. In some cases the U.S. Supreme Court has interpreted that right to grant special legal rights to some religious communities. The Amish, for example, enjoy exemption from some state laws. Many Native American communities have their own judicial bodies with special legal status. Other communities have their own tribunals, such as the Jewish Bet Din, that act as binding arbiters among adherents of the religion.

In some other countries, religious law is enforced by the state at the national level. In Israel, state-supported rabbinical courts enforce Jewish law, *halakah*. In many Muslim countries (as well as in Israel), Islamic courts have jurisdiction over family law matters, and their decisions are backed by state authority. In these countries, religious authority has become part of a modern state system, with courts, police, and other enforcement agents. Do these arrangements have consequences for people of other faiths who are citizens of these countries? Are there other consequences for social and political life?

Jewish law in Israel, and Islamic law in Indonesia show similarities in the processes of integrating religious law to a modern state system and to local cultures. In both cases, religious courts predate the independent state. Since their independence following World War II, both Israel and Indonesia have tried to create religious court systems that could coexist with a secular legal system. Both experiences continue to raise troubling questions for the citizens of these states about the role of religious law in the modern world. These questions concern how laws are to be interpreted and enforced. Can the religious community agree on a single way of interpreting the law? Or does the existence of a religious court inevitably divide the community? Should everyone who identifies himself or herself as an adherent of a particular religion automatically be subject to religious law, or should it be a matter of individual choice? What areas of social life should be governed by religious law and which by secular law?

Gender and Marriage in Israeli Jewish Law

Although in some respects Moses holds the place in Judaism that Muhammad does in Islam, in fact the lives of the two prophets play very different roles with respect to modern authority and law. Muhammad's life casts a very direct and very specific shadow over daily decisions made by jurists, who base their decisions on his statements and actions. Moses delivered the first five books of the Hebrew Bible to his people as the original Torah, but at that point his life made no additional contributions to Jewish scripture. The Torah has since had a life of its own, accruing layers upon layers of commentary. Indeed, the term *torah* today can refer to the first five books of the Hebrew Bible, or to the entire Bible, or to both the Bible as written Torah and the "oral Torah," further commandments handed to Moses and embodied today in biblical commentaries.

As we saw in Chapter 8, each commandment in the Torah requires elaboration to make it specific and exceptions to adapt it to changing conditions of life. For example, the commandment to do no work on the Sabbath has required jurists to specify which activities count as work and which do not. The consensus today has it that certain activities, such as carrying an infant or pushing a wheelchair, constitute work when in public but not when in private. Because most Jews consider these particular activities essential even on the Sabbath (when babies and older people also attend worship services), authorities have created nominally private spaces, called *eruv,* within which the activities may still be carried out without violating religious law.

For some Jews, then, understanding Torah and living a religious life requires the interpretive intervention of religious authorities. For certain matters, such as resolving disputes and performing marriages, Jews living in many parts of the world have long had recourse to religious courts. In the Ottoman Empire, Jews had rabbinical courts, empowered to decide matters of marriage and divorce as well as such ritual issues as "carrying on the Sabbath." The courts continued to hold this authority under the British Mandate (1917–1948) and in the post-1948 state of Israel. Israel has continued the Ottoman practice of providing a certain degree of legal autonomy and distinct religious courts to each religious community, including Jews and Muslims.

The place of Jewish law remains contested, however (Edelman 1994). Officially, Israel is a nonconfessional state, meaning that no religion enjoys exclusive state support.

The parliament, or Knesset, has final authority over all matters, including religious ones. The law regulating the rabbinical courts, passed in 1953, stipulates that marriage and divorce of Jews will be handled by the courts "in accordance with Jewish law." But who is to interpret Jewish law? Prior to the creation of the Israeli state, political leaders had already committed themselves to granting this authority to Orthodox rabbis, who controlled the courts. In 1947, the executive body preparing for statehood entered into an agreement with an Orthodox body, the Agudah movement, stipulating that the new state would respect the Sabbath, require observance of dietary laws (*kashrut*) in all state institutions, maintain the authority of the rabbinical courts over matters of personal status (especially marriage and divorce), and establish religious schools.

How the remainder of social life would be regulated was left open, and the issue continues to inflame passions on both sides. Many Orthodox Jews see Israel as too secular and try to change social life through direct intervention, some even blocking off streets to traffic during the Sabbath to ensure that Jews follow the law. These men and women see most secular Jews as threatening Israel's distinctive character as a Jewish society. Most of Israel's Jewish citizens indeed consider themselves nonreligious, and they want the freedom to dress as they wish and to drive and visit restaurants and theaters when they wish, including on the Sabbath. They see the Orthodox rabbis as threatening their freedoms. Most of them think that Israel should retain its Jewish character as long as individuals may choose not to observe certain religious rules. What should the character of public life then be? The issue remains subject to debate and, at times, public confrontations.

The same tension emerges over the law to be applied in courts. The Knesset has ruled that the rabbinical courts must decide certain matters, such as the age of marriage, in accord with the statutes passed by the Knesset. Civil courts recognize all marriages conducted outside of Israel if they are in accord with the laws of the land, even if they are not conducted in accord with Jewish law. The rabbinical courts have responded to these pressures by becoming less flexible in their interpretations of religious law, especially on matters of marriage and divorce. Israel has no institutions of civil marriage, and Jews may only be married by an Orthodox rabbi. Jews may not marry non-Jews, nor may they marry people not properly (according to Orthodox rabbis) divorced.

Two resulting problematical questions in Israel (and among Jews in the United States) are: Who is a Jew? and What is divorce? Orthodox authorities accept as Jews only those persons whose maternal lineage (ties through women, starting with one's mother) contains only Jews, or those persons who converted to Judaism under the guidance of an Orthodox rabbi. Thus, many U.S. converts are not recognized as Jews in Israel, and children of Jewish fathers whose mothers either converted or are non-Jews are similarly denied Jewish status for purposes of marriage. But the Israeli government itself recognizes as a Jew anyone sincerely and plausibly identifying himself or herself as a Jew.

This disparity in definition has led to anomalies, such as the treatment of the 35,000 Ethiopian Jews airlifted to Israel in 1984 and 1990. These men and women were granted Israeli citizenship as Jews under the 1950 Law of Return. But the rabbinical courts refused to marry them unless they underwent conversion (and, for the men, recircumcision) on grounds that in the past their ancestors may have married non-Jews. The Ethiopian issue was further complicated by accusations of racism. At one point it was revealed that the blood banks had thrown out all blood donated by the Ethiopians for fear it was tainted with HIV. Finally, the rabbinical courts created a special court to allow Ethiopian Jews to marry among themselves, but still refused to permit them to marry other Jews (Edelman 1994).

Divorce presents additional problems in the gendered nature of Jewish law. Israel recognizes no civil divorce. Jews can obtain a divorce only from the rabbinical court, and the court recognizes divorce only when the husband presents his wife with a document called a *get*. The document, written in a combination of Hebrew and Aramaic, proclaims the husband's act of "releasing" his wife from the marriage. The court must authorize the divorce but cannot deliver the get in the husband's name. (They can imprison a husband if he refuses to grant the divorce but he may still refuse to do so.) If both parties agree to the divorce, then no problem arises. But when the husband refuses to grant it, the wife is unable to remarry. In other countries, including the United States, the Orthodox wife is placed in an anomalous status: she may obtain a civil divorce and legally remarry—and some women do so—but then she is considered by the rabbis to have committed adultery (Breitowitz 1993; Meislin 1981).

Religious Minorities and Public Religions

*E*ven when religion does not become intertwined with nationalist projects or state legal institutions, in both colonial contexts and contemporary nation-states one particular religious tradition may dominate public life or is able to exert power over religious minorities. In colonial contexts, very often Christian missions and schools became the main avenues to power and participation in government. Some people responded to the colonial challenge by converting; others resisted, presenting their own customs and beliefs as of equal worth.

Recall the case of the Wana from Chapter 2. A small people at the margins of Indonesia, Wana religious practices have centered on shamanism: healing and divining through direct contact between shamans and spirits. But as citizens of the modern state of Indonesia, the Wana are pressured to "enter religion," which means to affiliate with one of the five recognized religions (Catholicism, Protestantism, Islam, Hinduism, and Buddhism). Partly to counter such pressure, partly to win recognition as people with a worthy culture, Wana have changed the way they talk about their beliefs to make them comparable with beliefs of Islam and Christianity. They speak of God and heaven—they also do so in a way that promises rewards for them and misery for the Muslims and Christians who administer their region and control trade.

Like the members of prophetic movements, including the millenarian movements and cargo cults discussed in the previous chapter, the Wana have borrowed from the religion of a dominant group and used these borrowed ideas to predict their own eventual supremacy. But (as with the Ghost Dance of the North American Plains), they also drew on their own traditions and continue their shamanic practices. This dance of conformity and resistance is one strategy for preserving cultural distinctiveness in a world dominated by others.

Kwaio Strategies for Recognition

In the case of the Kwaio, on the island of Malaita in the independent nation of the Solomon Islands, religion has been central to struggles for recognition and power (Keesing 1982, 1992).

The spirits of ancestors figure centrally in Kwaio religious practice. The uplands Kwaio people studied by Roger Keesing observe many taboos regarding eating, drinking, menstruation, urination, and the proper and improper places for men or women to go in the village or woods. Kwaio consider major infractions of these taboos to be offenses against the ancestors, which, as we saw in Chapter 9, must be recompensed through a pig sacrifice. Ancestors are important to magic, curing, and successful childbirth.

The British brought colonial domination and missionaries in the early decades of the twentieth century, but Kwaio have continued to recognize the power of the ancestors. Some Kwaio have left the hills and converted to Christianity, thereby, in their eyes, neutralizing the power of the ancestors (Keesing 1982, 231). The important Christian missions have been sponsored by Seventh-Day Adventists and the nondenominational South Sea Evangelical Mission. Both groups recognize the power of ancestral spirits but interpret the spirits as agents of Satan in his war against God. They have urged Kwaio to reject the old taboos and adopt new ones against swearing, stealing, and working on the Sabbath. The Adventists also enforce biblical food taboos. Some Kwaio have converted to find help in Jesus against sickness and death in the highlands (some of which was caused by British colonial invaders). The Kwaio have become aware that converts have been able to violate taboos, such as that against menstruation in houses, without being struck down by the ancestors. They have attributed this success to the power of the Christian God (Keesing 1982, 233–235).

About two thousand Kwaio people have resisted conversion, however. Some converts turned against the missionaries on the grounds that the Europeans were converting them but not giving them the education that would truly empower them. Other "pagan" Kwaio simply wished to preserve the traditional system, with the satisfactions of living in a well-known physical landscape of their ancestors (Keesing 1982, 237). These Kwaio insist on their right to apply their own customary laws, which they call *kastomu.* Many Kwaio have been making lists of customs, genealogies, and taboos in order to preserve them in a form recognizable by the government. Many believe that doing so will prevent their lands from being taken away by others (many have lost lands to logging operations) and also will keep Christian evangelists from invading their territory (Keesing 1992).

Initial Kwaio resistance to Christianity in the 1960s focused on a Seventh-Day Adventist hospital built on the northern coast. Some Kwaio thought that the hospital had acquired the land illegitimately, and Kwaio men killed the first administrator. Because of the way the land was obtained and because of the way "unclean" (menstruating and birthing) women were mixed with men in the hospital, Kwaio considered the hospital to be polluted. But the hospital stayed, and a Christian community developed around it, with banking and mail facilities and a store.

The very idea that writing down customs would protect the Kwaio against the outside world derived from watching Christians. Because the written Bible plays a central role in Christian practices, the Kwaio assumed that they, too, needed a written book to have something of the power held by Christians. It was about this time, when the idea that "writing brings power" was gaining ascendancy, that the anthropologist Roger Keesing arrived in the Kwaio pagan areas. They saw his coming as the fulfillment of a prophecy, made earlier by one of their leaders, that an American would come to write down their customs. (The Americans were remembered as the people who had driven off the Japanese in 1943.)

But *kastomu* and *customs* mean very different things, though they overlap. For Keesing, *customs* included how Kwaio behaved in everyday social life, as well as the meanings of rituals and taboos. For the Kwaio, the neo-Melanesian term *kastomu* refers to relationships with the ancestors, in the forms of ancestral genealogies, lists of shrines and lands, and ancestrally enjoined taboos with their penalties. Customs were behavior and the rules that govern it; kastomu were relationships with ancestors and the rules that derive from them.

But these lists were also understood as local equivalents to *loa,* or law, that would correspond to Kwaio ideas of propriety better than did the British-derived laws used to fine and imprison them. In 1989 Keesing obtained written documents from the son of Fifi'i, the Kwaio leader who had been working on his own to codify custom. These documents begin with the claim that the project was authorized in 1945 by a Kwaio council of chiefs. Fifi'i clearly saw the documents as representing in written form an unwritten Kwaio Constitution, which would have legal standing "besides National Laws" (Keesing 1992, 197). Their content concerns taboos and fines.

The outside world has thrown up strong challenges to Kwaio autonomy. First there was Christian missionization. The market economy led to the primacy of money in determining status. And the state gives power to the courts to jail and fine people for offenses Kwaio consider minor. The Kwaio response has been "not in confrontation but in compartmentalization" (Keesing 1992, 199). Kwaio pagans have tried to preserve older ways of exchanging shell valuables in marriage by prohibiting people from purchasing these valuables with cash. They realized that the ability to buy valuables would quickly inflate their price and make it impossible for Kwaio who did not earn cash through labor to marry. They have drawn sharp lines between the polluted Christian areas and pagan settlements. They have demarcated plantation areas, where taboos can no longer be observed, from the domain of the ancestors, where taboos continue to be observed. By the 1990s each of the two communities had come to define itself against the other, and to some extent acknowledge the power of each other's gods.

The Kwaio thus developed a double-edged strategy as a cultural and religious minority in a colonial setting dominated by Christianity. First, they demanded that the British, and later the rulers of the independent Solomons, acknowledge their own ancient constitution, the legitimacy of their claims to authentic law and custom. Second, they drew religious boundaries to prevent encroachment by polluting and threatening powers.

But the Kwaio strategy only worked, to the extent that it did, because of the relative isolation of the settlements and the willingness and ability of some Kwaio to not enter into direct social relationships with the rest of the colony and the nation-state. Most other minorities do not have that option, either because they are already in direct, face-to-face relationships with others, or because they must or wish to participate fully in the institutions of the larger society.

Protestants in the Pueblos

The reverse relationship between Christianity and an indigenous religion emerges when a minority of members of small-scale societies converts to Christianity.

In some Pueblo societies of New Mexico, for example, tribal governments are also religious hierarchies; the societies are "theocracies" or religious states in this sense. Pueblo social life involves compulsory performance of a number of duties, including religious rituals. Some Pueblo members converted to Protestantism, and thereafter withdrew from those community activities that they considered to be religious rituals and thus in violation of their new religious principles. In response, the tribal governments denied them some benefits enjoyed by other tribal members, such as rights to housing, or the right to use a community threshing machine to thresh wheat. Members of the community also ostracized them, avoiding them socially.

The Pueblo case has figured prominently in recent debates about individual rights and community rights (Kymlicka 1995; Svensson 1979). Were the civil rights of the Pueblo Protestants violated? Or do these communities have the right to perpetuate their way of life by requiring members to participate in communal activities?

Catholics in China

Beginning in the 1950s, China's communist leaders tried to repress Catholic religious practice and beliefs by creating a state-run Catholic Patriotic Association and persecuting those Catholics who sought to continue worshiping on their own. In the 1980s, the state permitted some churches to reopen. But in the late 1990s, with President Jiang Zemin evincing concern over a decline in socialist enthusiasm, officials began to prevent Catholics from holding Christmas celebrations. In early 1996, paramilitary police and helicopter units descended on a tiny village in the northeastern province of Hebei and destroyed a Marian shrine to which more than 100,000 Chinese Catholics had made pilgrimages during the preceding year.

At the same time, the estimated numbers of Christians in China have shot up. Perhaps 8 to 10 million Chinese are Roman Catholics today (the official number is 4 million). The number of Protestants has grown from about 1 million in 1949 to about 20 million today. Richard Madsen attributes the surge to the moral vacuum left by the collapse of communism as a "quasi-religious ideology" (Tyler 1997).

Minority Religions in Europe: Toleration or Public Recognition?

European states have maintained a general attitude of official toleration toward minority religions, due in some part to the historical memory of the disastrous religious wars of the seventeenth century, in which Catholics and Protestants fought and slaughtered one another over their religious differences. European toleration of differences within Christianity remains, in one form or another, the public religious tradition in England (which has its official Church of England) and in most of continental Europe.

French Secularism versus Headscarves in Schools

France, however, is a decidedly secular state. In theory, at least, the public life of French citizens in schools, or in governmental roles, is to be kept free of religious markings or preferences. Of course, the historically dominant religion in France was Roman Catholic, and before the French Revolution this was the religion of the state. But the Revolution was based on opposition to the privileges accorded the Catholic Church as well as the nobles, and this secularist idea of the state continues to lie behind public policy.

This idea has recently been tested by religious groups, including Orthodox Jews and Muslims, who claim the right to exercise their religious values in public roles (Moruzzi 1994). As was briefly discussed in earlier chapters, one recent case has most famously tested the degree to which religious affiliation may be displayed publicly. In October 1989 three Muslim French girls of North African parentage wore headcoverings to their public school. The school authorities ordered the girls to take off the scarves and dress like all other girls; the girls and their parents refused, on grounds that wearing the scarves was part of their religious practices. The issue arose in other schools around the country and in November 1989, the government ruled that the girls did have the right to express their religious beliefs in public. But in 1993 new cases arose, and in September 1994 the new Center-Right coalition in government decided to ban the wearing of headscarves in schools. This decision has since been reversed, but the issue remains unresolved in the minds of school superintendents, teachers, and pupils.

At issue was not a matter of taste or of disruption in the classroom. The students and their parents argued that this manner of dress was required by their religious beliefs in covering the female body. Some of the scarfwearing students also refused to attend biology class on grounds that the teaching of evolution of species contradicted their religious beliefs, and physical education class on grounds that the mixing of boys and girls also violated their religious principles.

Nor was the decision to ban wearing the scarves merely a morally cramped response to pressures from the political far right, which in France lays blame for most social and economic ills on North African Muslim immigrants. In fact, banning the headcoverings was seen by many as required by the logic of French citizenship and it was supported by many on the political left. France grants full citizenship rights to the children of immigrants, but in return requires that they be educated to become culturally French. School is an instrument of the secular state for educating future citizens, and in the official French view students must see themselves as absolutely identical, differentiated only by achievement. This identity is weakened if some students represent themselves as fundamentally different from the others, and (because of the militantly secular character of the state) especially so if these differences are religious. In practice, students have been able to wear necklaces with Catholic crosses—this inconsistency shows how violations of rules often are noticed only when they also transgress what has come to be seen as "normal" behavior.

But in the particular schools where the "affair of the scarves" led to a confrontation, local officials had already tried to exclude Arab children from day care (free and state-funded in France) and a group of Jewish children had protested against the state's requirement that they attend classes on Saturday mornings in violation of their Sabbath. The school principal evidently feared that allowing the headscarves would add legitimacy to other calls for respect for religious principles. (The principle was an active politician on the right, and soon thereafter became a representative to Parliament.) National politicians of the left as well as the right opposed the initial decision to permit the scarves—one article called the decision the "Munich of Republican education" (referring to the capitulation of the British government to Hitler's early annexation of territory).

Why did this affair arouse such strong emotions? Some conservative Catholics, and some antiracism activists, supported the girls and the government; many on the extreme right wing and much of the left opposed the decisions. Two lines of argument dominated the debates. First was the claim that secularism was challenged by the scarves. The French left sees itself as guardian of the secular anti-Catholic tradition founded at the moment of the Revolution. Public education was seen as the way to combat the power of the Church. Many of the same figures also claimed that the scarves were the symbol of the oppression of women. Putting on jeans is an act of freedom; putting on the scarf is an act of submission (Moruzzi 1994). The political right chimed in for this second argument, but placed it in a totally different context: the battle between Christianity and Islam and the general threat to French identity posed by immigrants.

The problem from the French position is that toleration is limited to the private sphere, in which cultural differences have free reign. The public domain is subject to universal rules, and people should appear there as "just citizens."

The National Church in Britain

French policy on religion may be familiar to U.S. readers accustomed to a principle of the separation of church and state, but in the European context France is an unusual case. All other members of the European Union make available some state funding for religious organizations. In some European countries, political parties have links to particular religious denominations.

Britain, for example, has an established church, the Anglican or Episcopal Church, in which all state weddings and funerals take place. Other churches and religious organizations are allowed, and some even receive state support, but they take second place to the Anglican Church.

Some Britons recently have urged that the Church be disestablished, deprived of its official status. Non-Anglicans, including many Muslims and Jews, argue that for all British citizens to enjoy full citizenship, they all must enjoy an equal capacity to shape the public culture. Such an equality implies that the public culture cannot favor one religion over another, as it currently does.

However, some Jewish and Muslim leaders have come out publicly in support of the continuing establishment of the Anglican Church (Modood 1994). They argue that when there is a national religion the followers of that religion feel comfortable about their place in the society and therefore exert less pressure on minority groups to convert or conform. They also argue that Anglicanism is less threatening than secularism to Muslims and Jews, because at least it supports other religions' continued existence. By contrast, secularism contains an anti-Islamic sentiment. These people cite the example of France, where strict secularism makes it more difficult for some people to accept the public religious self-identification by Muslims.

The Crucifix in Bavaria

German attitudes toward public religion are still further away from French secularism than are British ones. Recent controversy in Germany has not concerned the wearing of religious dress in schools but, rather, whether the state of Bavaria may make compulsory the display of the crucifix in schools (Caldwell 1996).

In France the normal state of affairs had been, at least in theory, the absence of any religious markers in the classroom, and the signs of religious difference, the Muslim headscarves, introduced into the classroom clashed with secular state officials' expectations. In Germany, and especially in Bavaria, the normal state of affairs was quite different. The state required that all primary school classrooms prominently display a large crucifix.

In 1995, however, the Federal Constitutional Court responded to a suit from a non-Christian ("anthroposophist") family and overturned the Bavarian regulation. The decision set off a storm of protest. The court ruling did not require the crucifixes to be removed, only that schools would not be obliged to hang them. But the furor was intense. Even Chancellor Helmut Kohl objected that the state had an obligation to pass Christian values on to children, and numerous commentators compared the federal court's decision to the Nazis' acts of exchanging crucifixes for swastikas. Some politicians called for disobedience of the court order.

To explain the reaction it helps to consider how these key religious symbols give public solidity to boundaries between "Us" and the "Other." In France, the Other is either Islamic fundamentalism or religion taking over the state. In Germany, it is the denial of Christian values under Nazi and communist rule. In the United States, it is persecution of religious dissenters by a state-backed church.

The place of religion in Germany traces back to the aftermath of religious wars in the seventeenth century. The German lands adopted the principle that a ruler could determine the religion of his subjects, a principle that tolerated princes, not subjects. It provided for shared practices and beliefs throughout the realm.

This principle continues to claim legitimacy. In 1918 Catholic Bavaria demanded protection against the potential persecution of Catholics in a Germany now two-thirds Protestant. In response, the framers of the Weimar Constitution granted to the German states the right to administer public education. They also gave all registered churches the status of public corporations, to be supported by taxes. These articles were adopted into the 1949 Basic Law, the West German Constitution. The Basic Law continues to be interpreted as the expression of German values that the state should take active steps to promote. The furor over the Bavarian cross decision was thus aimed at a court seen as violating its obligation to promote Christian values.

German attitudes toward religion continue to be shaped by the idea that states could choose between established forms of religion, which meant in practice the Roman Catholic or Lutheran Churches. This historical background has led some Germans to strongly oppose the presence of new religions, or sects such as Scientology. These Germans see Scientology's claims to religious status as a cover for attempts to extract wealth from converts and have led state governments to limit the development of local Scientology branches. By the late 1990s the controversy had reached international proportions, with Scientologists taking out full-page ads in newspapers in the United States and elsewhere to protest German state suppression of religious freedom.

Religion, Nation, and State in the United States

The German Constitution and the general attitude toward public religion and the state in Germany stands in marked contrast to the dominant interpretation of the U.S. Bill of Rights as a set of specific restrictions on the powers of the state. But U.S. history on religion, nation, and state is more complex than the phrase "separation of church and state" might imply.

Running through the history of debates and laws in the United States about religion and public life are two contradictory but strong lines of argument. One stresses the constitutionally mandated separation of church and state and the dangers to freedom posed by government entanglement in religious affairs. The second stresses the historically dominant role played in U.S. public life by Christianity—or more narrowly Protestant Christianity, or more broadly a Judeo-Christian tradition.

The first argument stresses rights and laws and echoes something of the French attitude. The second argument stresses historical tradition and shared values and resembles the German approach. Each has its claims to an antique lineage: the first, to Christian suspicion of government as inevitably corrupting (a view held by Saint Augustine, for example); the second, to the tradition of civic republicanism, where the state ensures that the community follows a set of moral, including religious, norms (Taylor 1990). The European cases discussed above remind us of other possible approaches to ensuring religious toleration, such as offering state support to all religions. They also remind us that other, relatively tolerant societies do in fact have an established church, such as the Church of England.

The rights argument for separating religion and state is based on the first 16 words of the Bill of Rights, which reads: "Congress shall make no law respecting an establishment of religion, or prohibiting the free exercise thereof." Many heated debates in our recent history—by the courts, in legislatures, among ordinary citizens—turn on how these 16 words are to be interpreted. Does the first clause, the establishment clause, prohibit all federal or state aid to religious schools, or all public displays in government buildings of religious symbols? Or does it more narrowly prohibit only laws that give special privileges or powers to a particular church? Does the second, the free exercise clause, protect the rights of schools to set aside a moment for silent prayer? Or does this practice run afoul of the first clause? What rights do parents have to further their children's exercise of religion? To what extent may Christian Scientist parents legally withhold medical aid from their children on religious grounds? May religious communities withdraw their children from school before the legal minimum age? Certain of these issues, such as the right to withdraw children from school, involve finding the right balance between the Constitution and the legislative power of the states. Other issues, such as silent prayer in the schools, may be seen as requiring a weighing of the two clauses against each other.

Religion in the Early Centuries

The emphasis on limiting the powers of government over religion was motivated by the colonists' experience of religious persecution (Berman 1990). This persecution occurred not only in Europe, but also in the colonies. The same religious groups that fled persecution abroad soon practiced it in their new homes. Authorities in New York and Massachusetts expelled Lutherans and Quakers along with Catholics and Jews. Even the relatively tolerant colony established by William Penn forbade deists to live in the colony and kept Jews from holding office.

The main purpose of the establishment clause was thus to prevent that kind of intolerance from developing at the federal level. The strongest advocates of the clause, James Madison and Thomas Jefferson, were fresh from their struggle to disestablish the Anglican Church in their home state of Virginia. Few other churches had universal pretensions; most were organized along *congregational* lines, meaning they were governed by the local congregation for the local congregation, and did not aim to become a universal church. Indeed, most residents of the colonies were Puritans, whose religious leaders were far more concerned with reserving church membership for the saved than they were with expanding their rolles.

The framers of the Constitution went further, preventing the federal government from supporting all Christian churches equally through taxation. As James Madison argued in 1785: "Who does not see that the same authority which can establish Christianity, in exclusion of all other Religions, may establish with the same ease any particular set of Christians, in exclusion of all other Sects?" (quoted in Frankel 1994, 27). This sentiment lay behind Thomas Jefferson's famous phrase that there should be "a wall of separation between church and state" (Berman 1990, 40).

There was, however, no single state and no single church in the United States, then as now. Rather, there were many different governments and many different ways in which people pursued religious beliefs. The Constitution only affected the powers of the federal government, and prevented it only from passing laws that would infringe upon the free exercise of religion or that would establish a church. It did not forbid officials from acting on their religious beliefs in passing other laws, nor did it keep them from effectively making one set of religions dominant in public discourse.

Nor did the Constitution say that religion was a matter for individuals to decide. As the legal historian Harold Berman argues (1990), for Americans of the 1780s and 1790s, free exercise of religion meant the freedom of religious communities to regulate family and social life, not the freedom of the individual to do as he or she pleased. Such was clearly true for the majority of American Puritans, for whom religious membership was seen as a binding social covenant, but true as well for denominations we now think of as highly individualistic, such as the Unitarians. One Salem Unitarian church even records that in the seventeenth century it flogged and sold into slavery some Quakers who refused to contribute to a new church building! In the late seventeenth and early eighteenth centuries, states aided parochial schools and all public schooling was explicitly intended to further Christianity. Well into the twentieth century, marriage was considered to be religious, and divorce law was derived from English ecclesiastical law (Berman 1990). The authority of the community, embodied in its church, was taken for granted by most citizens of the early Republic, and it is this set of experiences that those arguing for maintaining public religious tradition cite.

Balancing Rights and Tradition in a Pluralistic Nation

In the two centuries since independence the United States has changed from a nation dominated by Protestant, and particularly Puritan, Christians to a nation of diverse major religions, including Catholicism, Judaism, and Islam, and of many citizens not affiliated to a major religion. From a nation where most people thought of religion in terms of community norms as well as private faith, the United States has become a nation where most people think of religion in terms of individual beliefs alone.

In 1800, nearly everyone in the United States belonged to a Protestant denomination; Catholics, Jews, and other faiths taken together amounted to perhaps 2 percent of the population (Hunter 1990). Then came the enormous migrations of European Catholics at midcentury and again at the turn of the twentieth century, along with migrations of Jews and Asians of various religions. By the 1990s, Catholics constituted about 25 percent of the population, and Jews and Mormons each about 2 percent. Protestants of various denominations made up about 56 percent of U.S. residents. And within each of these large categories are more religious-based diversities than before. Whereas once the major divisions among Catholics were their countries of origin (especially among Irish, Italians, and Germans), today the major divisions concern the stands taken on doctrinal issues and on the authority of the pope. The severe cleavages today among fundamentalists, evangelicals, and others within the many Protestant denominations as well as between these denominations is paralleled in the nineteenth century only by the hostility exhibited by most Protestants against Mormons and Adventists. Nor was there an explicit "secular humanism" such as is professed by many today.

The relation between governments and religions has changed as well, but arguments for rights and those for tradition continue to have their strong supporters. Only in the 1940s did the Supreme Court explicitly hold that the Fourteenth Amendment prevented states from enacting laws establishing religion or preventing free exercise. In a 1947 case, *Everson v. Board of Education of Ewing Township*, the Court emphasized Jefferson's "wall of separation between church and state," and stated that states as well as the United States could not favor one religion over another. (Ironically, this broad doctrine was declared in a case in which the Court upheld a state law that gave state aid for buses used to take children to parochial schools.) The Court distinguished between aid to children and aid to schools, approving the former. In subsequent decisions the Court has upheld laws aimed at granting children equal opportunity, for example, the right for a deaf child to have a sign language interpreter in a parochial school when that right is already granted to public school students. But the Court struck down as illegitimately "advancing religion" state permission for a Hasidic Jewish group to form a public school district that included only their own adherents (Frankel 1994, 96–107).

Despite these decisions, to some degree law and public discourse in the United States continue to give special status to Christian religions. Christian prayers in the White House and Congress are a reminder of the tendency to mix Christian symbols into public life. In 1997, the second inauguration of President Clinton began with a prayer by the evangelical Christian minister Billy Graham.

Public prayer continues to be fought over in the courts. The current law of the land is that school-sponsored prayers violate the establishment clause. But this apparent consensus is tenuous, based as it is on a series of close decisions. For example, in the 1992 case *Lee v. Weisman,* the Supreme Court decided five to four that prayer delivered by a rabbi at a public school graduation was unconstitutional. The majority opinion stressed that any school-sponsored prayer, whether in the classroom or at an assembly, engendered social pressure on those not subscribing to the majority faith. But the dissent argued that graduation prayers were a tradition, the idea of coercive social pressure was fabricated, and that Americans have always thanked God for their blessings.

Some recent decisions have emphasized the argument from historical traditions. A 1984 case, *Lynch v. Donnelly,* upheld the right of a city to display a nativity scene, and in 1983, in *Marsh v. Chambers,* the Supreme Court upheld the right of the Nebraska legislature to pay a chaplain to open sessions with public prayer.

Although today a majority Court opinion would probably not state that "this is a Christian nation," as one did in 1892; nonetheless, judges and politicians from time to time continue to refer to the United States as a Christian nation or Judeo-Christian nation. Moreover, apparently neutral laws, such as laws mandating a "moment of silence" in schools, may be seen as discriminating in practice by stigmatizing students who do not adopt prayerful attitudes or who find the dominant model of "silent prayer" to be in fact a Christian model. Muslims, for example, carry out obligatory worship or ritual prayer (salat) at specific times of the day and in doing so stand, bow, and prostrate themselves—none of which actions can be performed during the "moment of silence." The Supreme Court recognizes this problem in general; in the *Yoder* case (406 U.S. 220) discussed below, the majority stated: "A regulation neutral on its face, in its application nonetheless offends the constitutional requirement for governmental neutrality if it unduly burdens the free exercise of religion."

One contested area concerns whether only beliefs, or beliefs and practices, are protected by the free exercise clause. In 1879, in a decision (*Reynolds v. U.S.*) that upheld a law against the Mormon practice of polygamy, the Court held that religious practices were not themselves protected: while laws "cannot interfere with mere religious belief and opinions, they may with practices" (98 U.S. 166).

But in 1972, in the landmark case *Wisconsin v. Yoder,* the Supreme Court ruled that a state had to prove a compelling interest before it could constitutionally compel a community to obey a state law that conflicted with its religious practices. In that case, an Amish parent had been sued by the State of Wisconsin for violating a law requiring school attendance until age 16. The parent had removed his child from school after finishing eighth grade and claimed that continuing in school would unduly subject the child to the influence of the secular world and would thereby endanger her salvation.

The Court found that the state did not show the required compelling interest in this case. Spending the years after eighth grade at home, learning the skills that would serve children best on the farm, was not obviously inferior to continuing on in school. Compelling school attendance would infringe on the Amish religious way of life, so the Court ruled that the law violated the free exercise clause.

Justice Douglas dissented in *Yoder,* noting that the Court did not know the wishes of the children, and that many children do leave the Amish community and are disadvantaged if they do not have the years of high school education required by the state.

Under debate in these cases is not only how best to interpret the Constitution but also what weight to give the perception of an inherited religious tradition. As the country has become more religiously diverse, can the lengthening string of relatively well-represented religions be merged into a generic monotheism? The change from "Christian nation" to "Judeo-Christian tradition" leans in that direction; will it become "Judeo-Christian-Islamic"? The end point in this direction is Indonesia's state ideology of "belief in one God" and sanctioning of five religions as putatively monotheistic (Islam, Catholicism, Protestantism, Hinduism, and Buddhist).

An alternative direction is a public discourse around moral values, such as family. This direction poses several problems: that it allows the reemergence, albeit in a new guise, of confessionally specific values. This reemergence is evidenced in 1996 debates about same-sex marriage, where the argument that marriage is religious in origin is intended to mean Christian, allowing the quotation of biblical passages against homosexuality. In these instances phrases such as "family values" serve as general categories to be filled by those specific religious views that have the most sustained voices in public debates.

We began this book in a church in the United States and a village in highland Sumatra. The two places can again illustrate the range of answers to the question: What role should religion play in public life in modern nation–states? The Sumatran answer emphasizes religion's role in public life. As a Muslim resident of a village or town one is expected to participate in collective religious rituals, from burying the dead to worshiping together on Fridays. As a citizen of the Indonesian state, one's legal standing may depend on one's religion, for example, when turning to a court for a matter of family law. As a member of the Indonesian nation, one is assumed to belong to one of a set of five recognized religions. The values and practices of those religions are part of public national life, celebrated on television, in speeches, and in public ceremonies attended by the president. The U.S. answer has been quite different, though here, too, religion has its public face. On any one street in most U.S. towns and cities live people who attend a variety of churches, temples, or other places of worship, or do not attend any such places at all. In principle, neither one's legal entitlements as a citizen nor one's standing as an American are affected by religious beliefs or practices. And yet, it is Christmas, not Hanukah or Ramadan, that receives public notice in lights and exhibits, in the pattern of public holidays and school vacations, in speeches and newspapers. And vast, nondenominational U.S. Christian organizations (such as the multimedia empire Focus on the Family) distribute Christian videos, books, newspaper columns, and radio programs throughout the world. Christianity continues to play a strong, if contested role in public life, even as courts and legislators maintain the "wall of separation" between religion and the legal activities of the state.

The study of religion as practice helps us understand the different forms that public religion can take. At issue in current controversies in France, Germany, the United States, as well as Indonesia, India, and Poland, is not the correctness of religious doctrine, or the beliefs of individual citizens, but the range of *public practices* that are appropriate. What messages are conveyed by exhibiting a cross or menorah in a state-supported building? Does wearing a headscarf send a challenge to dominant ideas of citizenship? Is setting aside a moment for silent prayer in a school an instance of religious freedom, or is it an implied endorsement of those religions that include such kinds of prayer?

These questions, and the controversies around them, turn on how different people interpret the practices of others, from wearing clothes to making speeches. Understanding the issues involved requires us to know something about the complex religious and cultural meanings attached to the objects and actions in question, about the histories of legal and social debate on religion's public place, and about the interests and values of the people engaged in these debates. We have only begun to pursue this quest for understanding.

For Further Consideration

*P*eter van der Veer's book *Religious Nationalism* (University of California Press 1994) explores Indian religious nationalism. A very readable comparative study is Mark Juergensmeyer's *The New Cold War?* (University of California Press 1994).

The legal rulings about prayer in the schools are always evolving and would make a good project. A short film called *Keeping the Faith* (1994) explores the topic; another, *For God and Country* (1994), focuses on the issue of religious versus secular laws. (Both from Films for the Humanities and Sciences.) Court cases are usually available online; for example, the Supreme Court decision *Wisconsin v Yoder* is on the Web at USSC+ (*www.usscplus.com;* one of several sources of information on Court decisions). The decision bears careful reading.

Barbara Daly Metcalf's book, *Making Muslim Space in North America and Europe* (University of California Press 1996) is a good resource on that topic. The film *Muslims in France* (Films for the Humanities and Sciences) looks at Muslim immigrants to Lyons, France. Dale Eickelman and James Piscatori's *Muslim Politics* (Princeton University Press 1996) is a good place to learn more about ideas and insitutions of authority in Muslim societies.

References

Ahmed, Leila (1992). *Women and gender in Islam: Historical roots of a modern debate*. New Haven: Yale University Press.

Ainsworth, Mary D. S. (1967). *Infancy in Uganda: Infant care and the growth of love*. Baltimore: Johns Hopkins University Press.

Alexander, Jeffrey C (1982). *The antimonies of classical thought: Marx and Durkheim*. Los Angeles: University of California Press.

Ammerman, Nancy Tatom (1987). *Bible believers: Fundamentalists in the modern world*. New Brunswick, N.J.: Rutgers University Press.

Anderson, Nels (1942). *Desert saints: The Mormon frontier in Utah*. Chicago: University of Chicago Press.

Apter, Andrew (1993). Atinga revisited: Yoruba witchcraft and the cocoa economy, 1950–1951. In Jean Comaroff and John Comaroff (Eds.), *Modernity and its malcontents* (pp. 111–128). Chicago: University of Chicago Press.

Ariès, Philippe (1974). *Western attitudes toward death: From the Middle Ages to the present*. Baltimore: Johns Hopkins University Press.

Atkinson, Jane Monnig (1983). Religions in dialogue: The construction of an Indonesian minority religion. *American Ethnologist, 10*, 684–696.

Atkinson, Jane Monnig (1987). The effectiveness of shamans in an Indonesian ritual. *American Anthropologist, 89*, 342–355.

Atkinson, Jane Monnig (1989). *The art and politics of Wana shamanship*. Los Angeles: University of California Press.

Auslander, Mark (1993). "Open the wombs!": The symbolic politics of modern Ngoni witchfinding. In Jean Comaroff and John Comaroff (Eds.), *Modernity and its malcontents* (pp. 167–192). Chicago: University of Chicago Press.

Babb, Lawrence A. (1983). Destiny and responsibility: Karma in popular Hinduism. In Charles F. Keyes and E. Valentine Daniel (Eds.), *Karma: An anthropological inquiry* (pp. 163–181). Los Angeles: University of California Press.

Babb, Lawrence A. (1986). *Redemptive encounters: Three modern styles in the Hindu tradition*. Los Angeles: University of California Press.

Barker, John (1993). We are Eklesia: Conversion in Uiaku, Papua New Guinea. In Robert W. Hefner (Ed.). *Conversion to Christianity: Historical and anthropological perspectives on a great transformation*, pp. 199–230. Berkeley: University of California Press.

Barth, Fredrik (1987). *Cosmologies in the making: A generative approach to cultural variation in inner New Guinea*. Cambridge: Cambridge University Press.

Bastian, Misty L. (1993). "Bloodhounds who have no friends": Witchcraft and locality in the Nigerian popular press. In Jean Comaroff and John Comaroff (Eds.), *Modernity and its malcontents* (pp. 129–166). Chicago: University of Chicago Press.

Bateson, Gregory (1958). *Naven* (2nd ed.). Stanford, Calif.: Stanford University Press.

Bauman, Richard (1983). *Let your words be few: Symbolism of speaking and silence among seventeenth-century Quakers*. Cambridge: Cambridge University Press.

Bax, Mart (1991). Marian apparitions in Medjugorje: Rivaling religious regimes and state-formation in Yugoslavia. In Eric R. Wolf (Ed.), *Religious regimes and state-formation* (pp. 29–53). Albany: State University of New York Press.

Bell, Diane (1981). Women's business is hard work: Central Australian aboriginal women's love rituals." *Signs 7*(2): 314–337.

Berman, Harold J. (1990). Religious freedom and the challenge of the modern state. In James Davison Hunter and Os Guiness (Eds.), *Articles of faith, articles of peace* (pp. 40–53). Washington, D.C.: The Brookings Institution.

Bloch, Maurice (1982). Death, women and power. In Maurice Bloch and Jonathan Parry (Eds.), *Death and the regeneration of life* (pp. 211–230). Cambridge: Cambridge University Press.

Bloch, Maurice, & Parry, Jonathan (1982). Introduction: Death and the regeneration of life. In Maurice Bloch and Jonathan Parry (Eds.), *Death and the regeneration of life* (pp. 1–44). Cambridge: Cambridge University Press.

Boddy, Janice (1989). *Wombs and alien spirits: Women, men, and the Zár cult in Northern Sudan.* Madison: University of Wisconsin Press.

Bohlen, Celestine (1995). Crying Madonna, Blood and Many, Many Tears. *New York Times,* April 8, 1995, A4.

Bokser, Baruch M. (1984). *The origins of the Seder.* Los Angeles: University of California Press.

Boon, James A. (1990). *Affinities and extremes.* Chicago: University of Chicago Press.

Bossy, John (1983). The mass as a social institution, 1200–1700. *Past and Present, 100,* 29–61.

Bourdieu, Pierre (1972). *Esquisse d'une théorie de la pratique, précédé de trois études d'ethnologie kabyle.* Geneva: Droz.

Bourdieu, Pierre (1990). *The logic of practice.* (Orig. French 1980) Richard Nice, Trans. Stanford: Stanford University Press.

Bourdieu, Pierre (1998). *Practical reason: On the theory of action.* (Orig. French 1994.)

Bowen, John R. (1991). *Sumatran politics and poetics: Gayo history, 1900–1989.* New Haven, Conn.: Yale University Press.

Bowen, John R. (1993). *Muslims through discourse: Religion and ritual in Gayo society.* Princeton, N.J.: Princeton University Press.

Bowlby, John (1980). *Loss: Sadness and depression.* New York: Basic Books.

Boyer, Pascal (2000). Functional origins of religious concepts: Ontological and strategic selection in evolved minds. *Journal of the Royal Anthropological Institute* 6(2): 195–214.

Boyer, Pascal (2000). Cultural inheritance tracks and cognitive predispositions: The example of religious concepts. In H. Whitehouse (Ed.), *Mind, evolution,*

and cultural transmission, pp. 57–89. Oxford: Berg Publishers.

Boyer, Pascal (2001). *Religion Explained.* New York: Basic Books.

Boyer, Paul, & Nissenbaum, Stephen (1974). *Salem possessed: The social origins of witchcraft.* Cambridge, Mass.: Harvard University Press.

Breitowitz, Irving A. (1993). *Between civil and religious law: The plight of the Agunah in American society.* Westport, Conn.: Greenwood Press.

Brison, Karen J. (1992). *Just talk: Gossip, meetings, and power in a Papua New Guinea village.* Los Angeles: University of California Press.

Brown, Diana DeG. (1986). *Umbanda: Religion and politics in urban Brazil.* Ann Arbor, Mich.: UMI Research Press.

Brown, Karen McCarthy (1987). Alourdes; A case study of moral leadership in Haitian vodou. In John Stratton Hawley (Ed.), *Saints and virtues* (pp. 144–167). Los Angeles: University of California Press.

Brown, Michael F. (1997). *The channeling zone: American spirituality in an anxious age.* Cambridge: Harvard University Press.

Brown, Michael F. (2000). The New Age and related forms of contemporary spirituality. In Raymond Scupin (Ed.), *Religion and culture: An anthropological focus,* pp. 421–432. Upper Saddle River, N.J.: Prentice Hall.

Brown, Peter (1987). The saint as exemplar in late antiquity. In John Stratton Hawley (Ed.), *Saints and virtues* (pp. 3–14). Los Angeles: University of California Press.

Brzezinski, Matthew (1994). Pilgrimage to Poland's holiest shrine losing its political role. *New York Times,* August 30, 1994, A12.

Bunzel, Ruth Leah (1992). *Zuni ceremonialism.* Albuquerque: University of New Mexico Press. (Original work published 1932)

Burns, John F. (1997). Gandhi's ashes rest, but not his message. *New York Times,* January 31, 1997, A1, A8.

Burns, J. Patout (1994). The atmosphere of election: Augustinianism as common sense. *Journal of Early Christian Studies, 2*(3), 325–339.

Burridge, Kenelm (1969). *New heaven, new earth: A study of millenarian activities.* New York: Schocken Books.

Bynum, Caroline Walker (1987). *Holy feast and holy fast: The religious significance of food to medieval women.* Los Angeles: University of California Press.

Caldwell, Peter C. (1996). The crucifix and German constitutional culture. *Cultural Anthropology, 11*(2), 259–273.

Campbell, Joseph (1949). *The hero with a thousand faces.* New York: Pantheon Books.

Cannon, Walter B. (1942). "Voodoo" death. *American Anthropologist, 54*, 169–181.

Casanova, José (1994). *Public religions in the modern world.* Chicago: University of Chicago Press.

Chodorow, Nancy (1974). Family structure and feminine personality. In Michelle Z. Rosaldo and Louise Lamphere (Eds.), *Women, culture and society.* Stanford: Stanford University Press.

Christian, William A., Jr. (1984). Religious apparitions and the cold war in southern Europe. In Eric R. Wolf (Ed.), *Religion, power and protest in local communities: The northern shore of the Meditarranean* (pp. 239–266). Berlin: Mouton.

Christian, William A., Jr. (1989). *Person and god in a Spanish valley* (rev. ed.). Princeton, N.J.: Princeton University Press. (Original work published 1972)

Clark, Francis (1967). *Eucharistic sacrifice and the reformation.* Oxford: Basil Blackwell.

Cohn, Norman (1970). *The pursuit of the millennium* (rev. ed.). Oxford: Oxford University Press.

Collier, Jane F., & Michelle Zimbalist Rosaldo (1981). Politics and gender in simple societies. In Sherry B. Ortner and Harriet Whitehead (Eds.), *Sexual meanings* (pp. 275–329). Cambridge: Cambridge University Press.

Comaroff, Jean (1985). *Body of power, spirit of resistance.* Chicago: University of Chicago Press.

Comaroff, Jean, & John Comaroff (1986). "Christianity and colonialism in South Africa." *American Ethnologist 13*:1, pp. 1–22.

Comaroff, Jean, & John Comaroff (1991). *Of Revelation and revolution: Christianity, colonialism, and consciousness in South Africa.* Chicago: University of Chicago Press.

Comaroff, Jean, & John Comaroff (1997). *Of Revelation and revolution: The dialectics of modernity on a South African frontier.* Chicago: University of Chicago Press.

Combs-Schilling, M. E. (1989). *Sacred performances: Islam, sexuality, and sacrifice.* New York: Columbia University Press.

Conkey, Margaret W., & Sarah H. Williams (1991). Original narratives: The political economy of gender in archeology. In Micaela di Leonardo (Ed.), *Gender at the crossroads of knowledge: Feminist anthropology in the postmodern era,* pp. 102–139. Berkeley: University of California Press.

Covington, Dennis (1995). *Salvation on sand mountain: Snake handling and redemption in Southern Appalachia.* Reading, Mass.: Addison-Wesley.

Cragg, Kenneth (1980). *Islam from within: Anthology of a religion.* Belmont, Calif.: Wadsworth.

Danforth, Loring M. (1982). *The death rituals of rural Greece.* Princeton, N.J.: Princeton University Press.

Daniel, Sheryl B. (1983). The tool box approach of the Tamil to the issues of moral responsibility and human destiny. In Charles F. Keyes and E. Valentine Daniel (Eds.), *Karma: An anthropological inquiry* (pp. 27–62). Los Angeles: University of California Press.

Davis, Natalie Zemon (1965). *Society and culture in early modern France.* Stanford, Calif.: Stanford University Press.

Davis, Winston (1980). *Dojo: Magic and exorcism in modern Japan.* Stanford, Calif.: Stanford University Press.

Delaney, Carol (1998). *Abraham on trial: The social legacy of biblical myth.* Princeton: Princeton University Press.

Demos, John Putnam (1982). *Entertaining satan: Witchcraft and the culture of early New England.* Oxford: Oxford University Press.

Doi, L. Takeo (1986). *Amae:* A key concept for understanding Japanese personality structure. In Takie Sugiyama Lebra and William P. Lebra (Eds.), *Japanese culture and behavior* (rev. ed., pp. 121–129). Honolulu: University of Hawaii Press. (Original work published 1962)

Douglas, Mary (1966). The abominations of Leviticus. In Mary Douglas (Ed.), *Purity and danger* (pp. 41–57). London: Routledge & Kegan Paul.

Durkheim, Émile (1995). *The elementary forms of the religious life* (Karen E. Fields, Trans.). New York: The Free Press. (Original work published 1912)

Durkheim, Émile, & Mauss, Marcel (1963). *Primitive classification* (Rodney Needhamn, Trans.). Chicago: University of Chicago Press. (Original work published 1903)

Earhart, H. Byron (1982). *Japanese religion: Unity and diversity* (3rd ed.). Belmont, Calif.: Wadsworth.

Eck, Diana L. (1982). *Banaras: City of light.* Princeton, N.J.: Princeton University Press.

Edelman, Martin (1994). *Courts, politics, and culture in Israel.* Charlottesville: University Press of Virginia.

Eickelman, Dale F. (1976). *Moroccan Islam: Tradition and society in a pilgrimage center.* Austin: University of Texas Press.

Eickelman, Dale F. (1985). *Knowledge and power in Morocco.* Princeton, N.J.: Princeton University Press.

Eickelman, Dale F. (1992). Mass higher education and the religious imagination in contemporary Arab societies. *American Ethnologist 19*(4): 643–655.

Eickelman, Dale F. (1999). Communication and control in the Middle East: Publication and its discontents. In Dale F. Eickelman and Jon Anderson (Eds.), *New media in the Muslim world: The emerging public sphere,* pp. 29–40. Bloomington: Indiana University Press.

Eisenstadt, S. N. (Ed.). (1986). *The origins and diversity of axial age civilizations.* Albany: State University of New York Press.

El Guindi, Fadwa (1999). *Veil: Modesty, privacy and resistance.* Oxford: Berg.

Eliade, Mircea (1954). *The myth of the eternal return.* Princeton, N.J.: Princeton University Press. (Original work published 1949)

Engels, Friedrich (1956). *The peasant war in Germany.* Moscow: Progress. (Original work published 1850)

Evans-Pritchard, E. E. (1937). *Witchcraft, oracles and magic among the Azande.* Oxford: Clarendon Press.

Evans-Pritchard, E. E. (1956). *Nuer religion.* Oxford: Clarendon Press.

Feeley-Harnik, Gillian (1981). *The Lord's table: Eucharist and passover in early Christianity.* Philadelphia: University of Pennsylvania Press.

Fernea, Elizabeth W. (1982). *A veiled revolution* (film).

Firmage, Edwin B. (1991). Religion and the law: The Mormon experience in the nineteenth century. *Cardozo Law Review, 12*(3–4), 765–803.

Fischer, Michael, & Abedi, Mehdi (1990). *Debating Muslims: Cultural dialogues in tradition and postmodernity.* Madison: University of Wisconsin Press.

Foster, Lawrence (1981). *Religion and sexuality: Three American communal experiments of the nineteenth century.* New York: Oxford University Press.

Fox, James J. (1975). On binary categories and primary symbols: Some Rotinese perspectives. In Roy Willis (Ed.), *The interpretation of symbolism* (ASA Studies no. 3), pp. 99–132. London: Malaby Press.

Fox, Richard (1989). *Gandhian utopia: Experiments with culture.* Boston: Beacon Press.

Frankel, Marvin E. (1994). *Faith and freedom: Religious liberty in America.* New York: Hill and Wang.

Fraser, Caroline (1996). Mrs. Eddy builds her empire. *New York Times Book Review,* July 11, 1996, 53–59.

Frazer, James G. (1981). *The golden bough: The roots of religion and folklore.* New York: Avenel Books. (Original work published 1890)

French, Howard W. (1997). The ritual: Disfiguring, hurtful, wildly festive. *New York Times,* January 31, 1997, A4.

Freud, Sigmund (1930). *Civilization and its discontents.* London: Hogarth Press.

Freud, Sigmund (1989). *Totem and taboo.* New York: Norton.

Fuller, C. J. (1992). *The camphor flame: Popular Hinduism and society in India.* Princeton, N.J.: Princeton University Press.

Gargon, Edward A. (1997). Three things matter: Location, location, and feng shui. *New York Times,* January 27, 1997, A4.

Geertz, Clifford (1960). *The religion of Java.* Chicago: University of Chicago Press.

Geertz, Clifford (1966). *Person, time, and conduct in Bali: An essay in cultural analysis.* New Haven, Conn.: Yale University, Southeast Asia Studies, Cultural Report Series No. 14.

Geertz, Clifford (1968). *Islam observed: Religious developments in Morocco and Indonesia.* New Haven, Conn.: Yale University Press.

Gerbrands, Adrian A. (1967). Art and artist in Asmat society. In Michael Rockefeller, *The Asmat of New Guinea.* A. Gerbrands (Ed.) (pp. 11–39). New York: Museum of Primitive Art.

Gill, Sam (1981). *Sacred words: A study of Navajo religion and prayer.* Westport, Conn.: Greenwood Press.

Gill, Sam (1987). *Native American religious action: A performative approach to religion.* Columbia: University of South Carolina Press.

Gluckman, Max (1963). Rituals of rebellion in South East Africa. In Max Gluckman (Ed.), *Order and rebellion in tribal Africa* (pp. 110–137). London: Cohen & West.

Gmelch, George (1978). Baseball magic. *Human Nature, 1*(8).

Gold, Ann Grodzins (1988). *Fruitful journeys: The ways of Rajasthani pilgrims.* Los Angeles: University of California Press.

Golomb, Louis (1993). The relativity of magical malevolence in urban Thailand. In C. W. Watson and Roy

Ellen (Eds.), *Understanding witchcraft and sorcery in Southeast Asia* (pp. 127–145). Honolulu: University of Hawaii Press.

Gombrich, Richard, & Gananath Obeyesekere (1988). *Buddhism transformed: Religious change in Sri Lanka.* Princeton: Princeton University Press.

Goodman, Felicitas D. (1988). *How about demons? Possession and exorcism in the modern world.* Bloomington: Indiana University Press.

Graham, William A. (1987). *Beyond the written word: Oral aspects of scripture in the history of religion.* Cambridge: Cambridge University Press.

Griaule, Marcel (1965). *Conversations with Ogotemmeli: An introduction to Dogon religious ideas.* London: Oxford University Press. (Original work published 1948)

Guillermoprieto, Alma (1990). *Samba.* New York: Knopf.

Gujar, Ram Bhoju, & Gold Ann Grodzins (1992). From the research assistant's point of view. *Anthropology and Humanism Quarterly 17*(3), 72–84.

Haberman, Clyde (1988). Shinto is thrust back onto the nationalist stage. *New York Times,* June 7, 1988, A4.

Hammoudi, Abdellah (1993). *The victim and its masks.* Chicago: University of Chicago Press. (Original work published 1988)

Hardacre, Helen (1989). *Shinto and the state, 1868–1988.* Princeton, N.J.: Princeton University Press.

Harding, Susan Friend (2000). *The Book of Jerry Falwell: Fundamentalist language and politics.* Princeton: Princeton University Press.

Harris, Lis (1985). *Holy days.* New York: Collier Books.

Harris, Marvin (1974). Pig lovers and pig haters. In Marvin Harris, *Cows, pigs, wars and witches* (pp. 35–57). New York: Vintage Books.

Hefner, Robert W. (1993). World building and the rationality of conversion. In Robert W. Hefner (Ed.), *Conversion to Christianity: Historical and anthropological perspectives on a great transformation,* pp. 3–44. Berkeley: University of California Press.

Herdt, Gilbert H. (1981). *Guardians of the flutes: Idioms of masculinity.* New York: McGraw-Hill.

Herdt, Gilbert H. (1982). Fetish and fantasy in Sambia initiation. In Gilbert H. Herdt (Ed.), *Rituals of manhood: Male initiation in Papua New Guinea* (pp.44–98). Los Angeles: University of California Press.

Hertz, Robert (1960). *Death and the right hand* (Rodney and Claudia Needham, Trans.). New York: Free Press. (Original work published 1907)

Hill, Christopher (1961). *The century of revolution, 1603–1714.* New York: W. W. Norton.

Hiltebeitel, Alf (1985). On the handling of the meat, and related matters, in two south Indian buffalo sacrifices. *L'Uomo: Societa Tradizione Sviluppo, 9*(1/2), 171–199.

Hirsch, Susan F. (1994). Kadhi's courts as complex sites of resistance: The state, Islam, and gender in postcolonial Kenya. In Mindie Lazarus-Black and Susan F. Hirsch (Eds.), *Contested states: Law, hegemony and resistance* (pp. 207–230). New York: Routledge.

Hume, David (1993). *Dialogues concerning natural religion* and *The natural history of religion.* Oxford: Oxford University Press. (Original works published 1779 and 1757)

Humphrey, Caroline, & Laidlaw, James (1994). *The archetypal actions of ritual.* Oxford: Oxford University Press.

Hunter, James Davison (1990). Religious freedom and the challenge of modern pluralism. In James Davison Hunter and Os Guiness (Eds.), *Articles of faith, articles of peace* (pp. 54–73). Washington, D.C.: The Brookings Institution.

Imperato, Pascal James (1978). *Dogon cliff dwellers: The art of Mali's mountain people.* New York: Kahan Gallery.

Jaeger, Werner (1961). *Early Christianity and Greek paideia.* Cambridge, Mass.: Harvard University Press.

James, William (1972). *Varieties of religious experience.* London: Fontana. (Original work published 1901–1902)

Johnson, Douglas (1994). *Nuer prophets.* Oxford: Oxford University Press.

Jung, Carl Gustav (1964). *Man and his symbols.* Garden City, N.Y.: Doubleday.

Kammerer, Cornelia Ann (1990). Customs and Christian conversion among Akha highlanders of Burma and Thailand. *American Ethnologist 17*:2, pp. 277–291.

Katz, Richard (1982). *Boiling energy: Community healing among the Kalahari Kung.* Cambridge, Mass.: Harvard University Press.

Keesing, Roger M. (1982). *Kwaio religion: The living and the dead in a Solomon Island society.* New York: Columbia University Press.

Keesing, Roger M. (1992). *Custom and confrontation: The Kwaio struggle for cultural autonomy.* Chicago: University of Chicago Press.

Kenyon, Susan M. (1995). *Zar* as modernization in contemporary Sudan. *Anthropological Quarterly* 68(2): 107–120.

Kipp, Rita Smith, & Rodgers, Susan (1987). Introduction: Indonesian religions in society. In Rita Smith Kipp and Susan Rodgers (Eds.), *Indonesian religions in transition* (pp. 1–31). Tucson: University of Arizona Press.

Kluckhohn, Clyde (1967). *Navaho witchcraft.* Boston: Beacon Press. (Original work published 1944)

Kraybill, Donald B. (1989). *The riddle of Amish culture.* Baltimore: Johns Hopkins University Press.

Kuruwaip, Abraham (1974). The Asmat bis pole: Its background and meaning. *Irian, 3*(2), 32–78.

Kymlicka, Will (1995). *Multicultural citizenship.* Oxford: Oxford University Press.

La Barre, Weston (1964). The snake-handling cult of the American Southeast. In Ward H. Goodenough (Ed.), *Explorations in cultural anthropology* (pp. 309–333). New York: McGraw-Hill.

Laderman, Carol (1983). *Wives and midwives: Childbirth and nutrition in rural Malaysia.* Los Angeles: University of California Press.

Lafaye, Jacques (1976). *Quetzalcoatl and Guadalupe: The formation of Mexican national consciousness 1531–1813* (Benjamin Keen, Trans.). Chicago: University of Chicago Press.

La Fontaine, J. S. (1985). *Initiation.* Harmondsworth, UK: Penguin.

Leibovich, Lori (2000). The online religion with shopping, too. *New York Times,* April 6, 2000, D1, D10.

Leishman, Thomas Linton (1958). *Why I am a Christian Scientist.* New York: Thomas Nelson & Sons.

Leone, Mark (1979). *Roots of modern Mormonism.* Cambridge, Mass.: Harvard University Press.

Lévi-Strauss, Claude (1963a). *Totemism* (Rodney Needham, Trans.). Boston: Beacon Press. (Original work published 1962)

Lévi-Strauss, Claude (1963b). The effectiveness of symbols. In C. Lévi-Strauss, *Structural anthropology* (pp. 180–201). (Claire Jacobson and Brooke Grundfest Schoepf, Trans.). Garden City, N.Y.: Anchor Books. (Original work published 1949)

Lévi-Strauss, Claude (1976). The Story of Asdiwal. In C. Lévi-Strauss, *Structural anthropology* (vol. 2, pp. 146–197). (Monique Layton, Trans.). Chicago: University of Chicago Press. (Original work published 1958)

Lukes, Steven (1973). *Émile Durkheim: His life and work.* Harmondsworth, UK: Penguin.

Lutkehaus, Nancy C. (1995). Gender metaphors: Female rituals as cultural models in Manam. In Nancy C. Lutkehaus and Paul B. Roscoe (Eds.), *Gender rituals: Female initiation in Melanesia* (pp. 183–204). New York: Routledge.

MacCormack, Carol, & Marilyn Strathern (1980). *Nature, culture, and gender.* Cambridge: Cambridge University Press.

Macleod, Arlene Elowe (1991). *Accommodating protest: Working women, the new veiling, and change in Cairo.* New York: Columbia University Press.

Makhlouf, Carla (1979). *Changing veils: Women and modernization in North Yemen.* Austin: University of Texas Press.

Malcolm X (1973). *The autobiography of Malcolm X.* Alex Haley (Ed.), New York: Ballantine Books. (Original work published 1964)

Malinowski, Bronislaw (1954). Magic, science, and religion. In B. Malinowski, *Magic, science, and religion and other essays* (pp. 17–92). Garden City, N.Y.: Anchor Books. (Original work published 1926)

Mankekar, Purnima (1999). *Screening culture, viewing politics: An ethnography of television, womanhood, and nation in post-colonial India.* Durham, N.C.: Duke University Press.

Marx, Karl, & Engels, Friedrich (1965). *The German ideology.* London: Lawrence & Wishart. (Original work published 1846)

Mayer, Ann Elizabeth (1990). The *Shariʻah:* A methodology or a body of substantive rules? In Nicholas Heer (Ed.), *Islamic law and jurisprudence.* Seattle: University of Washington Press.

McPherson, Robert S. (1992). *Sacred land, sacred view: Navajo perceptions of the four corners region.* Salt Lake City: Brigham Young University.

Meigs, Anna (1990). Multiple gender ideologies and statuses. In Peggy Reeves Sanday and Ruth Goodenough (Eds.), *Beyond the second sex.* Philadephia: University of Pennsylvania Press.

Meislin, Bernard J. (1981). Pursuit of the wife's right to a "*Get*" in United States and Canadian courts. *The Jewish Law Annual* (vol. 4). Kinderhook, N.Y.: E. J. Brill.

Metcalf, Peter (1982). *A Borneo journey into death.* Philadelphia: University of Pennsylvania Press.

Miller, Daniel, & Don Slater (2000). *The Internet: An ethnographic approach.* Oxford: Berg.

Miller, Perry (1956). *Errand into the wilderness.* Cambridge, Mass.: Harvard University Press.

Modood, Tariq (1994). Establishment, multiculturalism, and British citizenship. *Political Quarterly, 65*(1), 53–73.

Momen, Moojan (1985). *An introduction to Shi'i Islam.* New Haven, Conn.: Yale University Press.

Morris, Brian (1987). *Anthropological studies of religion.* Cambridge: Cambridge University Press.

Moruzzi, Norma Claire (1994). A problem with headscarves: Contemporary complexities of political and social identity. *Political Theory, 22*(4), 653–672.

Murphy, Joseph S. (1994). *Working the spirit: Ceremonies of the African diaspora.* Boston: Beacon Press.

Nations, Marilyn, & Rebhun, Linda-Anne (1988). Angels with wet wings can't fly: Maternal sentiments in Brazil and the image of neglect. *Culture, Medicine, and Psychiatry, 12,* 141–200.

Nemeroff, Carol, & Rozin, Paul (1992). Sympathetic magical beliefs and kosher dietary practice: The interaction of rules and feelings. *Ethos, 20,* 96–115.

Nolan, Mary Lee, & Nolan, Sidney (1989). *Christian pilgrimage in modern Western Europe.* Chapel Hill: The University of North Carolina Press.

Nuckolls, Charles W. (1998). *Culture: A problem that cannot be solved.* Madison: University of Wisconsin Press.

Obeyesekere, Gananath (1981). *Medusa's hair: An essay on personal symbols and religious experience.* Chicago: University of Chicago Press.

Oe, Kenzaburo (1995). The day the Emperor spoke in human voice. *New York Times Magazine,* May 7, 1995, 103–105.

Ortner, Sherry B. (1996). *Making gender: The politics and erotics of culture.* Boston: Beacon Press.

Ortner, Sherry B., & Harriet Whitehead (1981). *Sexual meanings: The cultural construction of gender and sexuality.* Cambridge: Cambridge University Press.

Palgi, Phyllis, & Abramovitch, Henry (1984). Death: A cross-cultural perspective. *Annual Review of Anthropology, 13,* 385–417.

Parsons, Elsie C. (1939). *Pueblo Indian religion* (2 vols.). Chicago: University of Chicago Press.

Passin, Herbert, & Bennett, John W. (1943). Changing agricultural magic in southern Illinois: A systematic analysis of folk-urban transition. *Social Forces, 22*(1), 98–106.

Peacock, James L., & Tyson, Ruel W., Jr. (1989). *Pilgrims of paradox: Calvinism and experience among the primitive Baptists of the Blue Ridge.* Washington, D.C.: Smithsonian Institution Press.

Peletz, Michael G. (1993). Knowledge, power and personal misfortune in a Malay context. In C. W. Watson and Roy Ellen (Eds.), *Understanding witchcraft and sorcery in Southeast Asia* (pp. 149–177). Honolulu: University of Hawaii Press.

Pernet, Henry (1992). *Ritual masks: Deceptions and revelations* (Laura Grillo, Trans.). Columbia: University of South Carolina Press. (Original work published 1988)

Peters, F. E. (1994). *Muhammad and the origins of Islam.* Albany: State University of New York Press.

Plath, David W. (1964). Where the family of God is the family: The role of the dead in Japanese households. *American Anthropologist, 66,* 300–317.

Pocock, David F. (1973). *Mind, body, and wealth: A study of belief and practice in an Indian village.* Oxford: Blackwell.

Pollack, Andrew (1996). This way to peace of mind: 750 miles and 88 stops. *New York Times,* March 20, 1996, A4.

Pollock, Sheldon (1993). Ramayana and political imagination in India. *Journal of Asian Studies 52*(2): 261–297.

Poole, John Fitz Porter (1982). The ritual forging of identity: Aspects of person and self in Bimin-Kuskusmin male initiation. In Gilbert H. Herdt (Ed.), *Rituals of manhood: Male initiation in Papua New Guinea* (pp. 99–154). Los Angeles: University of California Press.

Povinelli, Elizabeth A. (1993). *Labor's lot: The power, history, and culture of aboriginal action.* Chicago: University of Chicago Press.

Prell, Riv-Ellen (1989). *Prayer and community: The havurah in American Judaism.* Detroit: Wayne State University Press.

Radcliffe-Brown, A. R. (1965). Taboo. In Radcliffe-Brown (Ed.), *Structure and function in primitive society* (pp. 133–152). New York: The Free Press. (Original work published 1939)

Reader, Ian (1991). *Religion in contemporary Japan.* Honolulu: University of Hawaii Press.

Redfield, Robert (1956). *Peasant society and culture.* Chicago: University of Chicago Press.

Remnick, David (1992). Waiting for the apocalypse in Crown Heights. *The New Yorker,* December 21, pp. 52–57.

Richeport, Madeleine (1985). *Macumba, trance and spirit healing.* Film. New York: Filmmaker's Library.

Riding, Alan (1987). In Brazil, Evangelicals are on the rise. *New York Times,* October 25, 1987, A16.

Rogerson, J. W. (1980). Sacrifice in the Old Testament: Problems of method and approach. In M.F.C. Bourdillon and Meyer Fortes (Eds.), *Sacrifice* (pp. 45–59). London: Academic Press.

Rosaldo, Michelle Z. (1974). Woman, culture and society: A theoretical overview. In Michelle Z. Rosaldo and Louise Lamphere (Eds.), *Women, culture and society.* Stanford: Stanford University Press.

Rosaldo, Renato I. (1984). Grief and a headhunter's rage: On the cultural force of emotions. In Edward Bruner (Ed.), *Play, text, and story* (pp. 178–195). Washington, D.C.: American Ethnological Society.

Rosen, Lawrence (1989). *The anthropology of justice.* Cambridge: Cambridge University Press.

Rothstein, Edward (1996). Temple Emanu-El displays High Holidays Services on the Internet. *New York Times,* September 26, 1996, D4.

Rothkrug, Lionel (1980). Religious practice and collective perceptions: Hidden homologies in the Renaissance and Reformation. *Historical Reflections, 7*(1).

Ruthven, Malisa (1984). *Islam in the world.* New York: Oxford University Press.

Sahlins, Marshall (1985). *Islands of history.* Chicago: University of Chicago Press.

Sanders, Todd (2000). Rains gone bad, women gone mad: Rethinking gender rituals of rebellion and patriarchy. *Journal of the Royal Anthropological Institute* (N.S.) 6: 469–486.

Sanger, David E. (1990). For a job well done, Japanese enshrine the chip. *New York Times,* December 11, 1990, A4.

Saunders, E. Dale (1964). *Buddhism in Japan.* Philadelphia: University of Pennsylvania Press.

Sayle, Murray (1996). Nerve gas and the four noble truths. *The New Yorker,* April 1, 1996.

Schauss, Hayyim (1938). *The Jewish festivals: History & observance.* New York: Schocken Books.

Scheper-Hughes, Nancy (1992). *Death without weeping: The violence of everyday life in Brazil.* Los Angeles: University of California Press.

Schimmel, Annemarie (1973). *Mystical dimensions of Islam.* Chapel Hill: University of North Carolina Press.

Shariati, Dr. Ali (1977). *Hajj.* (Somayyah and Yaser, Trans.). Bedford, Ohio: Free Islamic Literatures, Inc.

Sharma, Ursula (1980). *Women, work, and property in Northwest India.* London: Tavistock.

Sharp, Lesley A. (1993). *The Possessed and the dispossessed: Spirits, identity, and power in a Madagascar migrant town.* Berkeley: University of California Press.

Shipps, Jan (1985). *Mormonism: The story of a new religious tradition.* Urbana: University of Illinois Press.

Singer, Milton (1964). The social organization of Indian civilization. *Diogène 45,* 84–119.

Smith, Robert J. (1974). *Ancestor worship in contemporary Japan.* Stanford: Stanford University Press.

Smith, Robert J. (1983). *Japanese society: Tradition, self, and the social order.* Cambridge: Cambridge University Press.

Smith, Wilfred Cantwell (1978). *The meaning and end of religion.* San Francisco: Harper & Row. (Original work published 1962)

Spencer, Jonathan (2000). *A Sinhala village in a time of trouble: Politics and change in rural Sri Lanka.* Oxford: Oxford University Press.

Starhawk (1979). *The spiral dance.* San Francisco: Harper & Row.

Starrett, Gregory (1998). *Putting Islam to work: Education, politics, and religious transformation in Egypt.* Berkeley: University of California Press.

Statler, Oliver (1984). *Japanese pilgrimage.* London: Pan Books.

Steinfels, Peter (1992). The vision that wasn't. Or was it? *New York Times,* September 2, 1992, A14.

Stirrat, R. L. (1992). *Power and religiosity in post-colonial setting: Sinhala Catholics in contemporary Sri Lanka.* Cambridge: Cambridge University Press.

Sudarman, Dea (1984). *Asmat.* Jakarta: Penerbit Sinar Harapan.

Svensson, Frances (1979). Liberal democracy and group rights: The legacy of individualism and its impact on American Indian tribes. *Political Studies, 27,* 421–439.

Swain, Tony (1995). Australia. In Tony Swain and Garry Trompf, *The Religions of Oceania* (pp. 19–118). New York: Routledge.

Swallow, D. A. (1982). Ashes and powers: Myth, rite and miracle in an Indian god-man's cult. *Modern Asian Studies, 16*(1), 123–158.

Tabor, James D. & Gallagher, Eugene V. (1995). *Why Waco?: Cults and the battle for religious freedom in America.* Los Angeles: University of California Press.

Tambiah, S. J. (1970). *Buddhism and spirit cults in northeast Thailand.* Cambridge: Cambridge University Press.

Tambiah, S. J. (1976). *World conqueror and world renouncer.* Cambridge: Harvard University Press.

Tambiah, S. J. (1986). *Sri Lanka: Ethnic fratricide and the dismantling of democracy.* Chicago: University of Chicago Press.

Tambiah, S. J. (1987). The Buddhist arahant: Classical paradigm and modern Thai transformations. In John Stratton Hawley (Ed.), *Saints and Virtues* (pp. 111–126). Los Angeles: University of California Press.

Taylor, Charles (1990). Religion in a free society. In James Davison Hunter and Os Guiness (Eds.), *Articles of faith, articles of peace* (pp. 93–113). Washington, D.C.: The Brookings Institution.

Trillin, Calvin (1994). Drawing the line. *The New Yorker,* December 12, pp. 50–62.

Trompf, Garry (1995). Pacific Islands. In Tony Swain and Garry Trompf, *The religions of Oceania* (pp. 121–222). New York: Routledge.

Turner, Victor (1967). *The forest of symbols: Aspects of Ndembu ritual.* Ithaca: Cornell University Press.

Turner, Victor (1969). *The ritual process: Structure and anti-structure.* Ithaca: Cornell University Press.

Turner, Victor (1974). Pilgrimages as social processes. In *Dramas, fields, and metaphors* (pp. 166–230). Ithaca: Cornell University Press.

Tyler, Patrick E. (1997). Catholics in China: Back to the underground. *New York Times,* January 26, 1997, A1, A8.

Tylor, Edward Burnett (1970). *Primitive culture* (2 vols.). Gloucester, Mass.: Peter Smith. (Original work published 1871)

Urban, Greg (1991). *A discourse-centered approach to culture.* Austin: University of Texas Press.

van Gennep, Arnold (1960). *The rites of passage.* (Monika B. Vizedom and Gabrielle L. Caffee, Trans.). Chicago: University of Chicago Press. (Original work published 1908)

van der Veer, Peter (1994). *Religious nationalisms: Hindus and Muslims in India.* Los Angeles: University of California Press.

Volkman, Toby Alice (1985). *Feasts of honor: Ritual and change in the Toraja highlands.* Urbana: University of Illinois.

Wadley, Susan S., & Derr, Bruce W. (1989). Eating sins in Karimpur. *Contributions to Indian Sociology, 23,* 131–148.

Walker, Sheila S. (1990). Everyday and esoteric reality in the Afro-Brazilian candomblé. *History of Religions, 30,* 103–128.

Wallace, Anthony F. C. (1956). Revitalization movements. *American Anthropologist, 58,* 264–281.

Warner, Marina (1996). Blood and tears. *The New Yorker,* April 8, pp. 63–69.

Watson, James L. (1982). Of flesh and bones: The management of death pollution in Cantonese society. In Maurice Bloch and Jonathan Parry (Eds.), *Death and the regeneration of life* (pp. 155–186). Cambridge: Cambridge University Press.

Waugh, Earle H. (1977). Muharram rites: Community death and rebirth. In Frank E. Reynolds and Earle H. Waugh (Eds.), *Religious encounters with death* (pp. 200–213). University Park: Penn State University Press.

Webb, Malcolm C. (1965). The abolition of the taboo system in Hawaii. *Journal of the Polynesian Society, 74,* 21–39.

Weber, Max (1958). *The protestant ethic and the spirit of capitalism.* (Talcott Parsons, Trans.). New York: Charles Scribner's Sons. (Original work published 1904–1905)

Weber, Max (1978). *Economy and society* (2 vols.). Los Angeles: University of California Press. (Original work published 1956)

Weiner, Annette B. (1976). *Women of value, men of renown: New perspectives in Trobriand exchange.* Austin: University of Texas Press.

Weisman, Steven R. (1990). Akihito performs his solitary rite. *New York Times,* November 23, 1990, A7.

Weller, Robert P. (1987). *Unities and diversities in Chinese religion.* Seattle: University of Washington Press.

Westermarck, Edward Alexander (1968). *Ritual and belief in Morocco* (2 vols.). New Hyde Park, N.Y.: University Books. (Original work published 1926)

Whitehead, Harriet (1987). Fertility and exchange in New Guinea. In Jane Fishburne Collier and Sylvia Junko Yanagisako (Eds.), *Gender and kinship: Essays toward a unified analysis,* pp. 244–267. Stanford: Stanford University Press.

Wikan, Unni (1990). *Managing turbulent hearts: A Balinese formulation for living.* Chicago: University of Chicago Press.

Wilson, Bryan R. (1961). *Sects and society: A sociological study of three religious groups in Britain.* London: William Heinemann,

Witherspoon, Gary (1977). *Language and art in the Navajo universe.* Ann Arbor: University of Michigan Press.

Wolf, Arthur (1974). Gods, ghosts, and ancestors. In Arthur Wolf (Ed.), *Religion and ritual in Chinese society* (pp. 131–182). Stanford: Stanford University Press.

Wolf, Eric (1958). The virgin of Guadalupe: A Mexican national symbol. *Journal of American Folklore, 71,* 34–39.

Woodburn, James (1982). Social dimensions of death in four African hunting and gathering societies. In Maurice Bloch and Jonathan Parry (Eds.), *Death and the regeneration of life* (pp. 187–210). Cambridge: Cambridge University Press.

Worsley, Peter (1968). *The trumpet shall sound* (rev. ed.). New York: Schocken Books.

WuDunn, Sheryl (1996). In Japan, a ritual of mourning for abortions. *New York Times,* January 25, 1996, A1, A8.

Wuthnow, Robert (1988). *The restructuring of American religion: Society and faith since World War II.* Princeton: Princeton University Press.

Wyman, Leland C. (1970). *Blessingway, with three versions of the myth recorded and translated from the Navajo by Father Berard Haile, O.F.M.* Tucson: University of Arizona Press.

Zegwaard, Rev. Gerrad A. (1959). Headhunting practices of the Asmat of Netherlands New Guinea. *American Anthropologist, 61,* 1020–1041.

Zimdars-Schwartz, Sandra L. (1991). *Encountering Mary: From La Salette to Medjugorje.* Princeton, N.J.: Princeton University Press.

Index